ANNUAL EDITIONS

Business Ethics 10/11

Twenty-Second Edition

EDITOR

John E. Richardson
Pepperdine University

Dr. John E. Richardson is a professor of marketing in the George L. Graziadio School of Business and Management at Pepperdine University. He is president of his own consulting firm and has consulted with organizations such as Bell and Howell, Dayton-Hudson, Epson, and the U.S. Navy, as well as with various service, nonprofit, and franchise organizations. Dr. Richardson is a member of the American Management Association, the American Marketing Association, the Society for Business Ethics, and Beta Gamma Sigma honorary business fraternity.

ANNUAL EDITIONS: BUSINESS ETHICS, TWENTY-SECOND EDITION

Published by McGraw-Hill, a business unit of The McGraw-Hill Companies, Inc., 1221 Avenue of the Americas, New York, NY 10020. Copyright © 2011 by The McGraw-Hill Companies, Inc. All rights reserved. Previous edition(s) 2005, 2008, 2009. No part of this publication may be reproduced or distributed in any form or by any means, or stored in a database or retrieval system, without the prior written consent of The McGraw-Hill Companies, Inc., including, but not limited to, in any network or other electronic storage or transmission, or broadcast for distance learning.

Some ancillaries, including electronic and print components, may not be available to customers outside the United States.

Annual Editions® is a registered trademark of The McGraw-Hill Companies, Inc.

Annual Editions is published by the **Contemporary Learning Series** group within The McGraw-Hill Higher Education division.

1 2 3 4 5 6 7 8 9 0 WDQ/WDQ 1 0 9 8 7 6 5 4 3 2 1 0

ISBN 978–0–07–352861–8
MHID 0–07–352861–7
ISSN 1055–5455

Managing Editor: *Larry Loeppke*
Director Specialized Production: *Faye Schilling*
Developmental Editor: *Dave Welsh*
Editorial Coordinator: *Mary Foust*
Editorial Assistant: *Cindy Hedley*
Production Service Assistant: *Rita Hingtgen*
Permissions Coordinator: *Lenny J. Behnke*
Senior Marketing Manager: *Julie Keck*
Marketing Communications Specialist: *Mary Klein*
Marketing Coordinator: *Alice Link*
Senior Project Manager: *Joyce Watters*
Design Specialist: *Margarite Reynolds*
Production Supervisor: *Sue Culbertson*
Cover Graphics: *Kristine Jubeck*

Compositor: Laserwords Private Limited
Cover Images: © Corbis/RF (inset); © PunchStock/RF (background)

Library in Congress Cataloging-in-Publication Data
Main entry under title: Annual Editions: Business Ethics. 2010/2011.
  1. Business Ethics—Periodicals I. Richardson, John E., *comp.* II. Title: Business Ethics.
658'.05

www.mhhe.com

Editors/Academic Advisory Board

Members of the Academic Advisory Board are instrumental in the final selection of articles for each edition of ANNUAL EDITIONS. Their review of articles for content, level, and appropriateness provides critical direction to the editors and staff. We think that you will find their careful consideration well reflected in this volume.

ANNUAL EDITIONS: Business Ethics 10/11
22nd Edition

EDITOR

John E. Richardson
Pepperdine University

ACADEMIC ADVISORY BOARD MEMBERS

Jagdish C. Agrawal
Southwest Florida College

Mary Brown
Bryant & Stratton College

Archie B. Carroll
University of Georgia

Rick Crosser
Metropolitan State College of Denver

Donald A. Drewett
Mount St. Mary College & Marist College

Gerald R. Ferrera
Bentley College

David Gonzales
Oklahoma Wesleyan University

David B. Haddad
Argosy University—San Diego

Kaloayn Hariskov
Savannah College Of Art & Design

Kenneth Harris, Jr.
Concordia University

William J. Kehoe
University of Virginia

Joseph W. Kennedy
Edward Waters College

Mahmoud Khaial
Keiser University

Michael Littman
SUNY College at Buffalo

Tom Mahaffey
St. Francis Xavier University

Tim Mazur
University of Maryland

Kenyetta McCurty
Amridge University

Cheryl Moore
Argosy University

Thomas Mulligan
Brock University

Patrick E. Murphy
University of Notre Dame

Carl Nelson
Polytechnic University

Joseph A. Petrick
Wright State University

John E. Richardson
Pepperdine University

Andrew Sikula
Marshall University Graduate College

Roberta Snow
West Chester University

Eric Teoro
Lincoln Christian College

Barbara Tietsort
University Of Cincinnati

Melodie M. Toby
Kean University

Michael van Breda
Southern Methodist University

Joan Van Hise
Fairfield University

Arturo Vasquez
University of Texas Pan American

Gina Vega
Salem State College—Bertolon School of Business

Harvey J. Weiss
Florida National College

Jonathon West
University of Miami

Caroline Westerhof
California National University

Anita Whitby
Capella University

Don Wicker
Brazosport College

Victor Williams
Argosy University—Atlanta

Preface

In publishing ANNUAL EDITIONS we recognize the enormous role played by the magazines, newspapers, and journals of the public press in providing current, first-rate educational information in a broad spectrum of interest areas. Many of these articles are appropriate for students, researchers, and professionals seeking accurate, current material to help bridge the gap between principles and theories and the real world. These articles, however, become more useful for study when those of lasting value are carefully collected, organized, indexed, and reproduced in a low-cost format, which provides easy and permanent access when the material is needed. That is the role played by ANNUAL EDITIONS.

Recent events have brought ethics to the forefront as a topic of discussion throughout our nation. And, undoubtedly, the area of society that is getting the closest scrutiny regarding its ethical practices is the business sector. Both the print and broadcast media have offered a constant stream of facts and opinions concerning recent unethical goings-on in the business world. Insider trading scandals on Wall Street, the marketing of unsafe products, money laundering, and questionable contracting practices are just a few examples of events that have recently tarnished the image of business.

As corporate America struggles to find its ethical identity in a business environment that grows increasingly complex, managers are confronted with some poignant questions that have definite ethical ramifications. Does a company have any obligation to help solve social problems such a poverty, pollution, and urban decay? What ethical responsibilities should a multinational corporation assume in foreign countries? What obligation does a manufacturer have to the consumer with respect to product defects and safety?

These are just a few of the issues that make the study of business ethics important and challenging. A significant goal of *Annual Editions: Business Ethics 10/11* is to present some different perspectives on understanding basic concepts and concerns of business ethics and to provide ideas on how to incorporate these concepts into the policies and decision-making processes of businesses. The articles reprinted in this publication have been carefully chosen from a variety of public press sources to furnish current information on business ethics.

This volume contains a number of features designed to make it useful for students, researchers, and professionals. These include the *table of contents* with summaries of each article and key concepts in bold italics, a *topic guide* for locating articles on specific subjects related to business ethics, an *Internet References* section and, new to this edition, an *Additional Business Ethics Resources* section, which can be used to further explore article topics.

The articles are organized into five units. Selections that focus on similar issues are concentrated into subsections within the broader units. Each unit is preceded by an overview that provides background for informed reading of the articles, emphasizes critical issues, and presents key points to consider that focus on major themes running through the selections.

Your comments, opinions, and recommendations about *Annual Editions: Business Ethics 10/11* will be greatly appreciated and will help shape future editions. Please take a moment to complete and return the postage-paid *article rating form* on the last page of this book. Any book can be improved, and with your help this one will continue to be.

John E. Richardson
Editor

Contents

Preface	*iv*
Correlation Guide	*xi*
Topic Guide	*xii*
Internet References	*xv*
Additional Business Ethics Resources	*xvii*

UNIT 1
Ethics, Values, and Social Responsibility in Business

Unit Overview   **xxii**

1. **Thinking Ethically: A Framework for Moral Decision Making,** Manuel Velasquez et al., *Issues in Ethics,* Winter 1996
   Outlined here are key steps and five different approaches to dealing with moral issues and helping to resolve **ethical dilemmas.**   **2**

2. **Business Ethics: Back to Basics,** William I. Sauser, *Society for Advancement of Management,* Number 2, 2005
   William Sauser gives an eight-point action list for establishing a strong **ethical culture.** He also provides a decision checklist when **ethical dilemmas** loom.   **5**

3. **Ethics: The Framework for Success,** Steve Hunter, *Strategic Finance,* April 2008
   While some **ethical decisions** are simply a matter of right vs. wrong, Steve Hunter addresses why the tough ethical decisions are right vs. right.   **9**

4. **Authentic Leaders Add Value,** Ken Shelton, *Leadership Excellence,* February 2008
   Ken Shelton points out some of the salient characteristics of **ethical leaders.**   **12**

5. **The Ethical Employee,** Michele Compton, *WIB,* May/June 2007
   The article highlights the importance and ramifications of **management** taking time to make **ethics** a priority with **employees.**   **13**

6. **Truth or Consequences: The Organizational Importance of Honesty,** Erline Belton, *The Nonprofit Quarterly,* Summer 2004
   According to Erline Belton, running an **organization** based on truth requires—and demands—the taking of personal risks and time.   **15**

7. **How to Make Unethical Decisions,** Andrew Sikula, Sr. and John Sikula, *Supervision,* May 2008
   The article explores commonly used but ethically unsound methods of making selections and then presents appropriate standards and benchmarks for determining **ethical actions.**   **19**

8. **Create a Culture of Trust,** Noreen Kelly, *Leadership Excellence,* April 2008
   Noreen Kelly believes that leaders should take the responsibility for creating a culture of shared **values** and meaning, promoting **ethical behavior,** and looking after their **brand** and reputation.   **22**

The concepts in bold italics are developed in the article. For further expansion, please refer to the Topic Guide.

9. **Building an Ethical Framework,** Thomas R. Krause and Paul J. Voss, *CRO,* May/June 2007

    The authors examine 10 questions that should be considered to build an **ethical framework** and to encourage an **ethical corporate culture.**   **24**

10. **Ethical Leadership: Maintain an Ethical Culture,** Ronald E. Berenbeim, *Leadership Excellence,* September 2006

    As an example of **ethical leadership,** Ronald Berenbeim discusses the case of Jawaharlal Nehru.   **26**

UNIT 2
Ethical Issues and Dilemmas in the Workplace

Unit Overview   **28**

Part A. Employee Rights and Duties

11. **Your Privacy for Sale,** *Consumer Reports,* October 2006

    Consumer Reports investigates how our **personal information** is being bought, sold, and sometimes stolen.   **30**

12. **Employers Are Stung with a Hefty Price When Employees Suffer an Identity Theft,** Stephanie Shapson Peet, Esq., *Supervision,* July 1, 2008

    Stephanie Peet examines some of the **legal** background and consequences associated when **identity theft** occurs in the **workplace.**   **35**

13. **Are You Too Family Friendly?,** Susan J. Wells, *HR Magazine,* October 2007

    As the proportion of single and childless workers increases, so do **complaints of unfairness** in **employers' benefits and policies.**   **37**

Part B. Organizational Misconduct and Crime

14. **Employee Theft: Who, How, Why, and What Can Be Done,** William I. Sauser, Jr., *SAM Advanced Management Journal,* Summer 2007

    William Sauser scrutinizes **employee theft** from the perspective of how much employees steal, how they do it, why, and how can it be stopped.   **42**

15. **Businesses Say Theft by Their Workers Is Up,** Sarah E. Needleman, *The Wall Street Journal,* December 11, 2008

    In the wake of the recession, Sarah Needleman relates how more businesses are facing a growing financial threat: **employee theft.**   **52**

Part C. Sexual Treatment of Employees

16. **Gender Issues,** Jennifer Gill, *Inc. Magazine,* April 2005

    Jennifer Gill contends that smaller companies are particularly vulnerable to **sex-discrimination lawsuits** because they tend to have less structured atmospheres and are less likely to have sex-discrimination policies in place.   **54**

Part D. Discriminatory and Prejudicial Practices

17. **Hiring Older Workers,** Stephen Bastien, *The Costo Connection,* July 2007

    Stephen Bastien explains how hiring **older workers** can often contribute unique skills that can contribute to a reliable and dedicated **workforce** that results in significant cost savings in both the short and long term.   **56**

The concepts in bold italics are developed in the article. For further expansion, please refer to the Topic Guide.

18. **Keeping Your Senior Staffers,** Mina Kimes, *Fortune,* July 20, 2009

    Hit by a shortage of engineers, BASF found a way to ***retain older employees.***   **58**

19. **The War over Unconscious Bias,** Roger Parloff, *Fortune,* October 15, 2007

    Roger Parloff describes how Walmart and others are facing ***class-action lawsuits*** for ***job discrimination.***   **59**

Part E. Downsizing of the Work Force

20. **Reflecting on Downsizing: What Have Managers Learned?,** Franco Gandolfi, *SAM Advanced Management Journal,* Spring 2008

    Despite a growing body of evidence that the long- if not short-term consequences of ***downsizing*** are negative, it still remains a respectable and even popular strategy.   **66**

21. **The Factory That Refused to Die,** Nanette Byrnes, *BusinessWeek,* August 3, 2009

    In an Ohio town with rampant ***unemployment,*** the mayor, a worker, and 12 local families fought to save Norwalk Furniture.   **76**

22. **Fear of Firing,** Michael Orey, *BusinessWeek,* April 23, 2007

    Michael Orey analyzes how workers in an expanding list of categories—***women,*** gays, and white men alleging ***bias***—have companies scared to ***lower the ax,*** even if workers' job performances fall seriously short.   **79**

Part F. Whistleblowing in the Organization

23. **Protecting the Whistleblower,** R. Scott Oswald and Jason Zuckerman, *CRO,* January/February 2008

    According to the authors, companies should fine-tune internal probes to make ***whistleblowing*** investigation more of an asset than a liability.   **83**

24. **On Witnessing a Fraud,** Don Soeken, *Business Ethics,* Summer 2004

    A case is presented where saying "no" to the ***scam*** was easy, but deciding whether to report it was considerably harder.   **85**

Part G. Handling Ethical Dilemmas at Work

25. **His Most Trusted Employee Was a Thief,** Shel Horowitz, *Business Ethics,* Winter 2005

    A situation is furnished where a trusted ***employee embezzled*** $20,000 to pay for her child's medical care.   **87**

26. **The Parable of the Sadhu,** Bowen H. McCoy, *Harvard Business Review,* May/June 1997

    The parable presented in this reading has significance for managers as they encounter ***ethical dilemmas*** that involve merging the individual ethic ***(personal values)*** and the corporate ethic ***(organizational values)*** to make the best decisions within the ***corporate culture.*** Bowen McCoy stresses the importance of management agreeing on a process for dealing with dilemmas and ***conflicts of interest.***   **89**

27. **An Ethical Dilemma: How to Build Integrity into Your Sales Environment,** Theodore B. Kinni, *Selling Power,* October 2004

    Contrary to the stereotypical view, ***salesmen*** are not predisposed to face any fewer or more ***ethical dilemmas*** than anyone else. However, according to Theodore Kinni, that doesn't mean that sales organizations can't become ***ethical*** and ***legal*** nightmares.   **94**

The concepts in bold italics are developed in the article. For further expansion, please refer to the Topic Guide.

UNIT 3
Business and Society: Contemporary Ethical, Social, and Environmental Issues

Unit Overview   98

Part A. Changing Perspectives in Business and Society

28. **Trust in the Marketplace,** John E. Richardson and Linnea Bernard McCord, McGraw-Hill/Dushkin, 2000

    The authors scrutinize the significance of companies being cognizant of the precarious nature and powerful advantages of gaining and maintaining trust with their *customers* in the *marketplace*.   100

29. **Businesses Grow More Socially Conscious,** Edward Iwata, *USA Today,* February 14, 2007

    There is growing evidence, according to Edward Iwata, that companies are embracing *CSR* practices because they believe such strategies can be *profitable* and *socially responsible.*   103

Part B. Contemporary Ethical Issues

30. **Women and the Labyrinth of Leadership,** Alice H. Eagly and Linda L. Carli, *Harvard Business Review,* September 2007

    The authors argue that when you put all the pieces together, a new picture emerges for why *women* don't make it into the C-suite.   105

31. **Getting Real about Fakes,** Peggy E. Chaudhry and Stephen A. Stumpf, *The Wall Street Journal,* August 17, 2009

    If companies want to cut into the sales of counterfeit *products,* they need to understand why *consumers* buy them in the first place.   112

32. **The New E-spionage Threat,** Brian Grow, Keith Epstein, and Chi-Chu Tschang, *BusinessWeek,* April 21, 2008

    A *BusinessWeek* probe of rising attacks on America's most sensitive *computer networks* uncovers startling security gaps.   115

Part C. Global Ethics

33. **Sustainable Success,** Lutz Kaufmann et al., *The Wall Street Journal,* June 22, 2009

    For companies operating in *developing countries,* according to the authors, it pays to commit to improving *social and environmental* conditions.   122

34. **Global Diversity: The Next Frontier,** Peter Ortiz, *DiversityInc.,* June 2006

    Peter Ortiz advocates that embracing *diversity globally* requires an appreciation of distinctive *societal, governmental, and cultural values.*   124

35. **Cracks in a Particularly Thick Glass Ceiling,** Moon Ihlwan, *BusinessWeek,* April 21, 2008

    Women in South Korea are slowly changing a corporate culture that lags behind the rest of the country.   127

The concepts in bold italics are developed in the article. For further expansion, please refer to the Topic Guide.

UNIT 4
Ethics and Social Responsibility in the Marketplace

Unit Overview   128

Part A. Marketing Strategy and Ethics

36. **Is Marketing Ethics an Oxymoron?,** Philip Kotler, *Marketing Management,* November/December 2004
    Philip Kotler believes that *marketers* should be proud of their field since they have encouraged and promoted the development of many products and services that have benefited people *worldwide.*   130

37. **The Rise of Trust and Authenticity,** Don Peppers and Martha Rogers, *Sales & Marketing Management,* May/June 2008
    The authors describe the importance of trust and authenticity being key ingredients in *ethical leadership.*   135

38. **Serving Unfair Customers,** Leonard L. Berry and Kathleen Seiders, *Business Horizons,* volume 51, 2008
    Companies commonly adapt "The customer is always right" maxim as a basic premise for delivering *quality service.* A close examination of *customer behavior,* however, reveals that customers can be not only wrong but also blatantly unjust.   136

39. **Dirty Deeds,** Michael Orey, *BusinessWeek,* January 14, 2008
    The *mortgage market meltdown* blighted the landscape with boarded-up houses. Now a few cities are holding lenders accountable for what foreclosure leaves behind.   143

Part B. Ethical Practices in the Marketplace

40. **Searching for the Top,** Stephenie Overman, *HR Magazine,* January 2008
    Executive search consultants, often called headhunters, wrestle with various *ethical issues,* but the question of whether it's OK to raid a company for candidates isn't one of them.   146

UNIT 5
Developing the Future Ethos and Social Responsibility of Business

Unit Overview   150

41. **Creating an Ethical Culture,** David Gebler, *Strategic Finance,* May 2006
    David Gebler examines how *values-based ethics programs* can help *employees* judge right from wrong.   152

42. **Hiring Character,** Dana Telford and Adrian Gostick, *Sales & Marketing Management,* June 2005
    In an excerpt from Dana Telford and Adrian Gostick's new book, *Integrity Works,* they present a look at business leader Warren Buffett's practice of hiring people based on their *integrity.*   156

43. **Outside-the-Box Ethics,** Luis Ramos, *Leadership Excellence,* April 2009
    Luis Ramos discusses five key characteristics of an *ethical culture.*   160

The concepts in bold italics are developed in the article. For further expansion, please refer to the Topic Guide.

44. **The Business Case for Diversity,** Adrienne Selko, *Industry Week,* September 2008

Far from being just another feel-good initiative, **diversity in the workplace** has become a competitive advantage for manufacturers. 162

45. **The True Measure of a CEO,** James O'Toole, *Across the Board,* September/October 2005

James O'Toole elucidates how Aristotle provides us with a set of **ethical** questions to determine the extent to which an organization provides an **environment** conducive to human growth and fulfillment. 164

Test-Your-Knowledge Form 168
Article Rating Form 169

The concepts in bold italics are developed in the article. For further expansion, please refer to the Topic Guide.

Correlation Guide

The *Annual Editions* series provides students with convenient, inexpensive access to current, carefully selected articles from the public press. **Annual Editions: Business Ethics 10/11** is an easy-to-use reader that presents articles on important topics such as *workplace misconduct, social and environmental issues, global ethics, ethics in the marketplace,* and many more. For more information on *Annual Editions* and other *McGraw-Hill Contemporary Learning Series* titles, visit www.mhhe.com/cls.

This convenient guide matches the units in **Annual Editions: Business Ethics 10/11** with the corresponding chapters in two of our best-selling McGraw-Hill Business Ethics textbooks by DesJardins and Ghillyer.

Annual Editions: Business Ethics 10/11	An Introduction to Business Ethics, 4/e by DesJardins	Business Ethics: A Real World Approach, 2/e by Ghillyer
Unit 1: Ethics, Values, and Social Responsibility in Business	**Chapter 1:** Why Study Ethics? **Chapter 2:** Ethical Theory and Business **Chapter 3:** Corporate Social Responsibility **Chapter 4:** Corporate Culture, Governance, and Ethical Leadership	**Chapter 1:** Understanding Ethics **Chapter 2:** Defining Business Ethics **Chapter 4:** Corporate Social Responsibility
Unit 2: Ethical Issues and Dilemmas in the Workplace	**Chapter 4:** Corporate Culture, Governance, and Ethical Leadership **Chapter 5:** The Meaning and Value of Work **Chapter 6:** Moral Rights in the Workplace **Chapter 7:** Employee Responsibilities **Chapter 11:** Diversity and Discrimination	**Chapter 2:** Defining Business Ethics **Chapter 3:** Organizational Ethics **Chapter 7:** Blowing the Whistle
Unit 3: Business and Society: Contemporary Ethical, Social, and Environmental Issues	**Chapter 10:** Business' Environmental Responsibilities **Chapter 12:** International Business and Globalization	**Chapter 2:** Defining Business Ethics **Chapter 9:** Ethics and Globalization
Unit 4: Ethics and Social Responsibility in the Marketplace	**Chapter 8:** Marketing Ethics: Product Safety and Pricing **Chapter 9:** Marketing Ethics: Advertising and Target Marketing	**Chapter 3:** Organizational Ethics **Chapter 8:** Ethics and Technology **Chapter 10:** Making it Stick: Doing What's Right in a Competitive Market
Unit 5: Developing the Future Ethos and Social Responsibility of Business	**Chapter 4:** Corporate Culture, Governance, and Ethical Leadership **Chapter 10:** Business' Environmental Responsibilities	**Chapter 10:** Making it Stick: Doing What's Right in a Competitive Market

Topic Guide

This topic guide suggests how the selections in this book relate to the subjects covered in your course. You may want to use the topics listed on these pages to search the Web more easily.

On the following pages a number of websites have been gathered specifically for this book. They are arranged to reflect the units of this Annual Editions reader. You can link to these sites by going to *http://www.mhhe.com/cls*.

All the articles that relate to each topic are listed below the bold-faced term.

Brands
- 8. Create a Culture of Trust
- 28. Trust in the Marketplace
- 31. Getting Real about Fakes

Business and government
- 34. Global Diversity: The Next Frontier
- 39. Dirty Deeds

Business and law
- 5. The Ethical Employee
- 12. Employers Are Stung with a Hefty Price When Employees Suffer an Identity Theft
- 19. The War over Unconscious Bias
- 22. Fear of Firing
- 23. Protecting the Whistleblower
- 24. On Witnessing a Fraud
- 39. Dirty Deeds

Business environment
- 3. Ethics: The Framework for Success
- 6. Truth or Consequences: The Organizational Importance of Honesty
- 19. The War over Unconscious Bias
- 20. Reflecting on Downsizing: What Have Managers Learned?
- 22. Fear of Firing
- 24. On Witnessing a Fraud
- 34. Global Diversity: The Next Frontier
- 39. Dirty Deeds
- 40. Searching for the Top
- 44. The Business Case for Diversity
- 45. The True Measure of a CEO

Business ethics
- 2. Business Ethics: Back to Basics
- 10. Ethical Leadership: Maintain an Ethical Culture
- 30. Women and the Labyrinth *of* Leadership

Codes of ethics
- 2. Business Ethics: Back to Basics
- 9. Building an Ethical Framework

Conflicts of interest
- 6. Truth or Consequences: The Organizational Importance of Honesty
- 20. Reflecting on Downsizing: What Have Managers Learned?
- 23. Protecting the Whistleblower
- 24. On Witnessing a Fraud
- 26. The Parable of the Sadhu
- 28. Trust in the Marketplace
- 34. Global Diversity: The Next Frontier
- 40. Searching for the Top
- 45. The True Measure of a CEO

Consumer protection
- 11. Your Privacy for Sale
- 36. Is Marketing Ethics an Oxymoron?
- 39. Dirty Deeds

Crime
- 9. Building an Ethical Framework
- 11. Your Privacy for Sale
- 28. Trust in the Marketplace
- 32. The New E-spionage Threat

Discrimination
- 7. How to Make Unethical Decisions
- 13. Are You Too Family Friendly?
- 17. Hiring Older Workers
- 19. The War over Unconscious Bias
- 22. Fear of Firing
- 28. Trust in the Marketplace
- 30. Women and the Labyrinth *of* Leadership
- 35. Cracks in a Particularly Thick Glass Ceiling
- 44. The Business Case for Diversity

Diversity
- 6. Truth or Consequences: The Organizational Importance of Honesty
- 19. The War over Unconscious Bias
- 22. Fear of Firing
- 24. On Witnessing a Fraud
- 44. The Business Case for Diversity
- 45. The True Measure of a CEO

Downsizing
- 20. Reflecting on Downsizing: What Have Managers Learned?

Economic environment
- 13. Are You Too Family Friendly?
- 17. Hiring Older Workers
- 20. Reflecting on Downsizing: What Have Managers Learned?
- 24. On Witnessing a Fraud
- 34. Global Diversity: The Next Frontier
- 39. Dirty Deeds
- 44. The Business Case for Diversity
- 45. The True Measure of a CEO

Employee compensation
- 13. Are You Too Family Friendly?
- 18. Keeping Your Senior Staffers
- 19. The War over Unconscious Bias
- 30. Women and the Labyrinth *of* Leadership
- 45. The True Measure of a CEO

Employee responsibility
- 14. Employee Theft: Who, How, Why, and What Can Be Done
- 15. Businesses Say Theft by Their Workers Is Up
- 24. On Witnessing a Fraud

Employee rights
- 1. Thinking Ethically: A Framework for Moral Decision Making
- 11. Your Privacy for Sale
- 13. Are You Too Family Friendly?
- 19. The War over Unconscious Bias
- 23. Protecting the Whistleblower
- 30. Women and the Labyrinth *of* Leadership
- 38. Serving Unfair Customers

xii

Employee safety
1. Thinking Ethically: A Framework for Moral Decision Making
36. Is Marketing Ethics an Oxymoron?

Environmental concern and disregard
33. Sustainable Success
36. Is Marketing Ethics an Oxymoron?

Equal employment opportunities
19. The War over Unconscious Bias
30. Women and the Labyrinth *of* Leadership
34. Global Diversity: The Next Frontier
35. Cracks in a Particularly Thick Glass Ceiling

Ethical dilemmas
1. Thinking Ethically: A Framework for Moral Decision Making
2. Business Ethics: Back to Basics
9. Building an Ethical Framework
22. Fear of Firing
24. On Witnessing a Fraud
26. The Parable of the Sadhu
28. Trust in the Marketplace
40. Searching for the Top

Ethics
3. Ethics: The Framework for Success
7. How to Make Unethical Decisions
40. Searching for the Top
43. Outside-the-Box Ethics

Ethics training
1. Thinking Ethically: A Framework for Moral Decision Making
2. Business Ethics: Back to Basics
5. The Ethical Employee
9. Building an Ethical Framework
41. Creating an Ethical Culture

Global business ethics
2. Business Ethics: Back to Basics
32. The New E-spionage Threat
33. Sustainable Success
34. Global Diversity: The Next Frontier
35. Cracks in a Particularly Thick Glass Ceiling
36. Is Marketing Ethics an Oxymoron?

Illegal business practices
24. On Witnessing a Fraud
38. Serving Unfair Customers
39. Dirty Deeds

Insider information
22. Fear of Firing

Insider trading
2. Business Ethics: Back to Basics

Leadership
4. Authentic Leaders Add Value

Legal environment
6. Truth or Consequences: The Organizational Importance of Honesty
7. How to Make Unethical Decisions
9. Building an Ethical Framework
11. Your Privacy for Sale
12. Employers Are Stung with a Hefty Price When Employees Suffer an Identity Theft
19. The War over Unconscious Bias

22. Fear of Firing
23. Protecting the Whistleblower
28. Trust in the Marketplace
30. Women and the Labyrinth *of* Leadership
39. Dirty Deeds

Legal environment, business
7. How to Make Unethical Decisions
12. Employers Are Stung with a Hefty Price When Employees Suffer an Identity Theft
19. The War over Unconscious Bias
22. Fear of Firing
23. Protecting the Whistleblower
30. Women and the Labyrinth *of* Leadership

Management practices
9. Building an Ethical Framework
13. Are You Too Family Friendly?
17. Hiring Older Workers
19. The War over Unconscious Bias
20. Reflecting on Downsizing: What Have Managers Learned?
22. Fear of Firing
23. Protecting the Whistleblower
24. On Witnessing a Fraud
26. The Parable of the Sadhu
30. Women and the Labyrinth *of* Leadership
34. Global Diversity: The Next Frontier
35. Cracks in a Particularly Thick Glass Ceiling
38. Serving Unfair Customers
40. Searching for the Top
45. The True Measure of a CEO

Management responsibility
13. Are You Too Family Friendly?
17. Hiring Older Workers
19. The War over Unconscious Bias
20. Reflecting on Downsizing: What Have Managers Learned?
23. Protecting the Whistleblower
38. Serving Unfair Customers
40. Searching for the Top
45. The True Measure of a CEO

Marketing ethics
36. Is Marketing Ethics an Oxymoron?
39. Dirty Deeds
40. Searching for the Top
41. Creating an Ethical Culture

Marketing practices
28. Trust in the Marketplace
36. Is Marketing Ethics an Oxymoron?
38. Serving Unfair Customers
39. Dirty Deeds
40. Searching for the Top

Mergers
20. Reflecting on Downsizing: What Have Managers Learned?

Multinational corporations
19. The War over Unconscious Bias
20. Reflecting on Downsizing: What Have Managers Learned?
26. The Parable of the Sadhu
34. Global Diversity: The Next Frontier
36. Is Marketing Ethics an Oxymoron?

Organizational misconduct
6. Truth or Consequences: The Organizational Importance of Honesty
19. The War over Unconscious Bias
40. Searching for the Top

Product quality
28. Trust in the Marketplace
31. Getting Real about Fakes
36. Is Marketing Ethics an Oxymoron?

Product safety
28. Trust in the Marketplace
36. Is Marketing Ethics an Oxymoron?

Sales ethics
27. An Ethical Dilemma: How to Build Integrity into Your Sales Environment

Sexual harassment
7. How to Make Unethical Decisions

Situation ethics
13. Are You Too Family Friendly?
17. Hiring Older Workers
22. Fear of Firing
24. On Witnessing a Fraud
30. Women and the Labyrinth *of* Leadership
38. Serving Unfair Customers

Social responsibility
13. Are You Too Family Friendly?
17. Hiring Older Workers
20. Reflecting on Downsizing: What Have Managers Learned?
34. Global Diversity: The Next Frontier
36. Is Marketing Ethics an Oxymoron?
39. Dirty Deeds
41. Creating an Ethical Culture
45. The True Measure of a CEO

Technology
32. The New E-spionage Threat

Utilitarianism
20. Reflecting on Downsizing: What Have Managers Learned?
30. Women and the Labyrinth *of* Leadership
36. Is Marketing Ethics an Oxymoron?

Value systems
1. Thinking Ethically: A Framework for Moral Decision Making
7. How to Make Unethical Decisions
9. Building an Ethical Framework

13. Are You Too Family Friendly?
17. Hiring Older Workers
28. Trust in the Marketplace
38. Serving Unfair Customers
41. Creating an Ethical Culture
45. The True Measure of a CEO

Whistleblowing
2. Business Ethics: Back to Basics
22. Fear of Firing
23. Protecting the Whistleblower
24. On Witnessing a Fraud

White-collar crime
39. Dirty Deeds

Women in the workforce
13. Are You Too Family Friendly?
19. The War over Unconscious Bias
30. Women and the Labyrinth *of* Leadership
34. Global Diversity: The Next Frontier
35. Cracks in a Particularly Thick Glass Ceiling

Work environment
2. Business Ethics: Back to Basics
9. Building an Ethical Framework
17. Hiring Older Workers
19. The War over Unconscious Bias
20. Reflecting on Downsizing: What Have Managers Learned?
21. The Factory That Refused to Die
22. Fear of Firing
24. On Witnessing a Fraud
30. Women and the Labyrinth *of* Leadership
35. Cracks in a Particularly Thick Glass Ceiling
38. Serving Unfair Customers
41. Creating an Ethical Culture
45. The True Measure of a CEO

Working conditions
9. Building an Ethical Framework
16. Gender Issues
19. The War over Unconscious Bias
30. Women and the Labyrinth *of* Leadership
35. Cracks in a Particularly Thick Glass Ceiling
38. Serving Unfair Customers
41. Creating an Ethical Culture
45. The True Measure of a CEO

Internet References

The following Internet sites have been selected to support the articles found in this reader. These sites were available at the time of publication. However, because websites often change their structure and content, the information listed may no longer be available. We invite you to visit http://www.mhhe.com/cls for easy access to these sites.

Annual Editions: Business Ethics 10/11

General Sources

Center for the Study of Ethics in the Professions
http://ethics.iit.edu

Sponsored by the Illinois Institute of Technology, this site links to a number of world business ethics centers.

GreenMoney Journal
http://www.greenmoneyjournal.com

The editorial vision of this publication proposes that consumer spending and investment dollars can bring about positive social and environmental change. On this website, they'll tell you how.

U.S. Department of Labor
http://www.dol.gov

Browsing through this site will lead to a vast array of labor-related data and discussions of issues affecting employees and managers, such as the minimum wage.

U.S. Equal Employment Opportunity Commission (EEOC)
http://www.eeoc.gov

The EEOC's mission "is to ensure equality of opportunity by vigorously enforcing federal legislation prohibiting discrimination in employment." Consult this site for facts about employment discrimination, enforcement, and litigation.

Wharton Ethics Program
http://ethics.wharton.upenn.edu/

The Wharton School of the University of Pennsylvania provides an independently managed site that offers links to research, cases, and other business ethics centers.

Ethics Updates/Lawrence Hinman
http://ethics.sandiego.edu/index.html

This site provides both simple concept definitions and complex analysis of ethics, original treatises, and sophisticated search engine capability. Subject matter covers the gamut, from ethical theory to applied ethical venues.

Institute for Business and Professional Ethics
http://commerce.depaul.edu/ethics/

Sponsored by DePaul College of Commerce, this site is interested in research in the field of business and professional ethics. It is still under construction, so check in from time to time.

National Center for Policy Analysis
http://www.ncpa.org

This organization's archive links lead you to interesting materials on a variety of topics that affect managers, from immigration issues, to affirmative action, to regulatory policy.

Open Directory Project
http://dmoz.org/Business/Management/Ethics

As part of the Open Directory Project, this page provides a database of Web sites that address numerous topics on ethics in business.

Working Definitions
http://www.workingdefinitions.co.uk/index.html

This is a British, magazine-style site devoted to discussion and comment on organizations in the wider social context and to supporting and developing people's management skills.

UNIT 1: Ethics, Values, and Social Responsibility in Business

Association for Moral Education (AME)
http://www.amenetwork.org/

AME is dedicated to fostering communication, cooperation, training, and research that links moral theory with educational practices. From here it is possible to connect to several sites of relevance in the study of business ethics.

Business for Social Responsibility (BSR)
http://www.bsr.org

Core topic areas covered by BSR are listed on this page. They include Corporate Social Responsibility; Business Ethics; Community Investment; the Environment; Governance and Accountability; Human Rights; Marketplace; Mission, Vision, Values; and finally Workplace. New information is added on a regular basis. For each topic or subtopic there is an introduction, examples of large and small company leadership practices, sample company policies, links to helping resources, and other information.

Enron Online
http://www.enron.com/corp/

Explore the Enron website to find information about Enron's history, products, and services. Go to the "Press Room" section for Enron's spin on the current investigation.

UNIT 2: Ethical Issues and Dilemmas in the Workplace

American Psychological Association
http://www.apa.org/homepage.html

Search this site to find references and discussion of important ethics issues for the workplace of the 1990s, including the impact of restructuring and revitalization of businesses.

International Labour Organization (ILO)
http://www.ilo.org

ILO's home page leads you to links that describe the goals of the organization and summarizes international labor standards and human rights. Its official UN website locator can point you to many other useful resources.

UNIT 3: Business and Society: Contemporary Ethical, Social, and Environmental Issues

National Immigrant Forum
http://www.immigrationforum.org

The pro-immigrant organization offers this page to examine the effects of immigration on the U.S. economy and society. Click on the links to underground and immigrant economies.

Internet References

Workopolis.com
http://sympatico.workopolis.com

This Canadian site provides an electronic network with a GripeVine for complaining about work and finding solutions to everyday work problems.

United Nations Environment Programme (UNEP)
http://www.unep.ch

Consult this UNEP site for links to topics such as the impact of trade on the environment. It will direct you to useful databases and global resource information.

United States Trade Representative (USTR)
http://www.ustr.gov

This home page of the U.S. Trade Representative provides links to many U.S. government resources for those interested in ethics in international business.

UNIT 4: Ethics and Social Responsibility in the Marketplace

Business for Social Responsibility (BSR)
http://www.bsr.org/

BSR is a global organization that seeks to help companies "achieve success in ways that respect ethical values, people, communities, and the environment." Links to Services, Resources, and Forum are available.

Total Quality Management Sites
http://www.nku.edu/~lindsay/qualhttp.html

This site points to a variety of interesting Internet sources to aid in the study and application of Total Quality Management principles.

U.S. Navy
http://www.navy.mil

Start at this U.S. Navy page for access to a plethora of interesting stories and analyses related to Total Quality Leadership. It addresses such concerns as how TQL can improve customer service and affect utilization of information technology.

UNIT 5: Developing the Future Ethos and Social Responsibility of Business

International Business Ethics Institute (IBEI)
http://www.business-ethics.org/index.asp

The goal of this educational organization is to promote business ethics and corporate responsibility in response to the growing need for transnationalism in the field of business ethics.

UNU/IAS Project on Global Ethos
http://www.ias.unu.edu/research/globalethos.cfm

The United Nations University Institute of Advanced Studies (UNU/IAS) has issued this project abstract, which concerns governance and multilateralism. The main aim of the project is to initiate a process by which to generate jointly, with the involvement of factors from both state- and nonstate institutions in developed and developing countries, a global ethos that could provide or support a set of guiding principles for the emerging global community.

Additional Resources

The following business ethics sites have been selected to support the articles found in this reader. These sites were available at the time of publication. However, because websites often change their structure and content, the information listed may no longer be available. We invite you to visit http://www.mhhe.com/cls for easy access to these sites.

Annual Editions: Business Ethics 10/11

Contents

- Articles/Publications
- Cases/Case Studies
- Corporate Codes of Ethics
- Professional Organizations and Associations
- Resources and Resource Centers

Articles/Publications

Business Corporate Ethics
http://www.washingtonpost.com/ac2/wp-dyn/NewsSearch?st=Business%20Corporate%20Ethics&

Business Corporate Ethics is a special report outlining recent corporate scandals involving ethics violations compiled by the *Washington Post.* Breaking news features, Enron updates, WorldCom activities, accounting probes, as well as timelines and analysis are posted.

Business Ethics Forum
http://www.managementlogs.com/business_ethics.html

The focus of this blog is designed for those "interested in promoting ethical business practices, moral behavior and responsible management in corporations and institutions." Free membership is required to participate in the discussions.

Business Ethics Newsletter
http://www.iese.edu/aplicaciones/news/index.asp?lang=en

Joan Fontrodona and Roberto García Castro edit this newsletter that is affiliated with the IESE Business School at the University of Navarra (Spain). The goal of the Business Ethics Newsletter is to highlight certain stories featuring business ethics that have appeared recently in the media.

Business Ethics: Resources for Educators
An article featured on the SocialFunds.com site discusses the top 100 companies that made the Business Ethics' Best Corporate Citizens List for 2009; can be found at http://www.socialfunds.com/news/article.cgi/2652.html

BusinessWeek Online
http://www.businessweek.com

BusinessWeek Online allows you to search for articles dealing with ethics in business. Use their search feature to retrieve current articles covering a variety of ethical dilemmas affecting the business world including information about the Enron, Tyco, and WorldCom scandals.

Corporate Ethics
http://www.pbs.org/newshour/bb/business/ethics

This online special report featured on the program *NewsHour with Jim Lehrer* covers some of the recent scandals that have been hitting the business world. Links to stories discussing some of the corporations affected by the controversies, online forum resources and background reports dating back to 1995 are included.

Ethics Resource Center (ERC)
http://www.ethics.org

An extensive list of articles dealing with business ethics and related issues can be found in the section, Organizational Ethics Articles: Business at http://www.ethics.org/resources/nr_oearticles.cfm?NavCat=Business.

Financial Scandals
http://www.ex.ac.uk/~RDavies/arian/scandals

Financial Scandals is a site created by Roy Davies that covers some of the "greatest" scandals of all times. The site is divided into 8 sections and is designed for a broad audience, from business executives interested in business ethics issues to financial history enthusiasts.

Fortune.com
http://www.fortune.com

Fortune.com has numerous articles discussing ethics and ethical issues in the corporate world. Type "ethics" in the site's search feature to retrieve the latest articles.

A Question of Ethics
http://www.informationweek.com/825/ethics.htm

As companies move into the e-business arena, new ethical issues arise. This timeless *Informationweek.com* article from February 19, 2001, discusses topics such as compromising customer privacy for advertising gain and trust concerns between employers and employees. Links to other e-business ethics articles can also be found at this site.

Case Studies

Babson Business College: Business Ethics Program
http://roger.babson.edu/ethics/index.htm

The Babson Business Ethics Program is designed to integrate ethics into businesses and business education. Numerous resources are available including the following:

- **Case Studies**
  http://roger.babson.edu/ethics/business.htm

Carnegie Mellon: Ethics Teaching Materials
http://ba.gsia.cmu.edu/ethics/teaching.htm

This site, developed by the Center for International Corporate Responsibility, provides links to the role of ethics instruction in B-school, case studies, tutorials, and business scandal articles. Academic resources, membership organization information, and other ethical materials are also available.

CasePlace.org
http://www.caseplace.org

CasePlace.org is a free service for business faculty and students offered by Aspen Institute's Initiative for Social Innovation through Business (Aspen ISIB). Cases and topics for discussion are posted at this site, and the cases are searchable by topic or discipline.

Additional Resources

Case Studies: Analyses
http://businessmajors.about.com/cs/casestudies/index.htm?once=true&iam=dpile&terms=+IT++case++stud

About.com's collection of case studies is presented at this site. A few are links to sites related to business ethics or related topic areas.

Inc.comGuide: Case Studies in Business Ethics
http://www.inc.com/partners/intel/case-studies.html#content

Editors at Inc.com select the resources found at this site. Case studies covering ethical topics such as environmental challenges, getting involved in the community, and making global connections can be found in this section of their site.

Other Inc.com guides can be found at http://www.inc.com/home/.

Institute for Global Ethics (IGE)
http://www.globalethics.org

IGE is an organization dedicated to promoting "ethical behavior in individuals, institutions, and nations through research, public discourse, and practical action." Numerous resources and articles are provided on the IGE site. The following is an example of a section of this site containing useful materials:

Institute of Business Ethics (IBE)
http://www.ibe.org.uk

The goal of the Institute of Business Ethics (IBE) is to "encourage high standards of corporate and business behavior and the sharing of best practice." Sections of this site to note are Codes of Conduct and News/Resources. The Codes of Conduct section provide links on how to develop a code, what types of information should be included, and links to companies with codes. Latest news dealing with business ethics and links to external sites like the Caux Rountable (http://www.cauxroundtable.org) and the Institute for Global Ethics (http://www.globalethics.org) can be found in the News/Resources section. IBE was established in 1986 and strives to be the "leader in knowledge and practice of corporate business ethics." The development of the IBE site was a joint effort by the Open University and the Institute of Business Ethics and sponsored by the Foundation for Business Responsibilities. It is designed to be an online information center for academics and students interested in business ethics. The case study section is an example of resources found at this site.

Markkula Center for Applied Ethics
http://www.scu.edu/ethics

The Markkula Center for Applied Ethics was founded in 1986 and has grown into one of the most active university applied ethics centers in the U. S. It is based at Santa Clara University and was initially funded by an endowment by Linda and A. C. "Mike" Markkula Jr. Articles, cases, briefings and dialogue in all areas of applied ethics can be found at this online center. Case studies specifically addressing the issue of business ethics can be found at:

- **Business Ethics: Cases**
  http://www.scu.edu/ethics/practicing/focusareas/cases.cfm?fam=BUSI

Corporate Codes of Ethics

Baxter Healthcare: Working with Integrity
http://www.baxter.com/doingbusiness/customers/index.html

Baxter Healthcare works to create an environment that fosters the development of "conscientious ethically-minded people who are committed to integrity, honesty and fairness." The company's "Working with Integrity" document outlines global business practices standards, compliance issues, their bioethics policy, and position statement on bioethics and other ethics resources.

Boeing
http://www.boeing.com

Boeing has a long and diverse history, and ethics is a central component of the company's mission. The Ethics and Business Conduct Committee has been charged with the oversight of the ethics program at Boeing, and the following are some ethics resources available at its site.

- **Code of Conduct**
  http://www.boeing.com/companyoffices/aboutus/ethics/code_of_conduct.pdf
- **Ethics and Business Conduct Program**
  http://www.boeing.com/companyoffices/aboutus/ethics/pro3.pdf
- **Ethics Policies and Procedures**
  http://www.boeing.com/companyoffices/aboutus/ethics/epolicy.htm
- **Values**
  http://www.boeing.com/companyoffices/aboutus/ethics/integst.htm

Cadbury Schweppes: Ethical Business Practices
http://www.cadbury.com/ourresponsibilities/Pages/ourresponsibilities.aspx

A section of the business principles that guide employees at Cadbury Schweppes addresses ethical issues. Areas covered as part of the company's ethical practices include communications, confidentiality, conflict of interest, gifts, and inside information.

Codes of Ethics Online Business
http://ethics.iit.edu/codes/business.html

Illinois Institute of Technology's Center for the Study of Ethics in the Professions developed this online collection of codes on the Web, and it has grown out of the Center's Library of codes that resides in its vertical file. In addition to subject specific codes, like ones for business, resources for authoring a code, case studies, and other information can be found at this site.

Creating a Code of Ethics
http://www.ethicsweb.ca/codes

Chris MacDonald, PhD, Philosophy Department, St. Mary's University (Halifax, Canada) has put together this site with links to resources to assist individuals and groups in writing a code of ethics. He discusses why organizations and institutions should even have a code and provides guidance in writing one. He also provides links to essays on ethics, sample codes and contacts for ethics consultants.

MacDonald has also worked on several other ethics sites including EthicsWeb at http://www.ethicsweb.ca.

Hewlett-Packard (HP)
http://www.hp.com/hpinfo/globalcitizenship/csr/ethics.html

This ethics page outlines the HP values, standards, and guidelines for responsible conduct of business.

IBM: Business Conduct Guidelines
http://www.ibm.com/investor/corpgovernance/cgbcg.phtml

IBM has created a very detailed set of guidelines designed to facilitate ethical conduct within the company. This 5-section document is broken down into several subcategories by topic.

Johnson & Johnson: Our Credo
http://www.jnj.com/our_company/our_credo/index.htm

Johnson & Johnson is not guided by a mission statement that hangs on the wall of the corporation. Instead, a one-page "Credo" guides the actions of the company. A link to the history of the "Credo" is also available.

Additional Resources

Microsoft: Mission & Values
http://www.microsoft.com/mscorp

Microsoft CEO, Steve Ballmer, presented the company's mission, vision, and values in June 2002, and that information is provided on this site.

Occidental Petroleum Corporation: Code of Business Conduct
http://www.oxy.com/SiteCollectionDocuments/code_of_business_conduct.pdf

This document outlines Occidental Petroleum Corporation's guidelines for administering and enforcing the Code of Business Conduct and the company's compliance requirements with applicable laws and ethical standards.

Rite Aid: Code of Ethics and Business Conduct
http://www.riteaid.com/www.riteaid.com/w-content/images/company/governance/code_of_ethics.pdf

The purpose of this 18-page code is to "reinforce and enhance Rite Aid's commitment to an ethical way of doing business." It outlines how Rite Aid puts the company's values and obligations to work. The document also addresses Rite Aid's responsibility to associates, responsibility to the corporation, competing with integrity, interacting with the government, and implementing the code.

Sara Lee: Global Business Practices
http://www.saralee.com/AboutSaraLee/GlobalBusinessPractices.aspx

In September 1997, Sara Lee introduced their Global Business Practices program as a way of conveying the company's values and beliefs to their employees. Over 100 Business Practice Officers currently oversee this ethics program in every unit and department operated by Sara Lee.

ServiceMaster: Code of Conduct
http://corporate.servicemaster.com/overview_conduct.asp

The ServiceMaster Code of Conduct outlines policies, values, and regulations must be followed by every employee at the company. This 33-page document addresses topics such as responsibilities in the workplace, customer relationships, and conflicts of interest.

Weyerhaeuser: Business Conduct
http://www.weyerhaeuser.com/citizenship/businessconduct

Weyerhaeuser is one of the largest owners and producers of softwood and hardwood lumber and lumber products in the world. The company has a "reputation for conducting business honestly and with integrity," and they expect the highest level of ethical and professional conduct from their employees. All employees receive copies of Weyerhaeuser's Code of Ethics and Business Conduct document, plus they must attend ethics training on a regular basis.

Williams-Sonoma, Inc.: Corporate Values
http://www.williams-sonomainc.com/careers/corporate-values.html

This brief overview outlines the values that Williams-Sonoma strives to uphold in order to help the company succeed in "enhancing the quality of life at home." The company's commitment to its people, customers, quality, shareholders and ethical sourcing are addressed.

Professional Organizations and Associations

American Finance Association (AFA)
http://www.afajof.org/default.shtml

Initial planning for the organization that is now AFA began in December 1939 in Philadelphia, PA. AFA is a professional association that deals with financial economic issues and promotes knowledge related to this area.

Better Business Bureau (BBB): Promoting Fairness and Integrity in the Marketplace
http://www.bbb.org

In 1912, the very first BBB was founded, and today, this system is supported by 250,000 local business members throughout the world. The goal of the Better Business Bureau is to "promote and foster the highest ethical relationship between businesses and the public through voluntary self-regulation, consumer and business education, and service excellence."

Business for Social Responsibility (BSR)
http://www.bsr.org

BSR, a global, non-profit organization works to "create a just and sustainable world by working with companies to promote more responsible business practices, innovation and collaboration." It strives to help members be successful and operate successful businesses while upholding the highest ethical standards of professional behavior. Links to free reports on a variety of issues plus other resources are available at this site.

The Caux Roundtable
http://www.cauxroundtable.org

The Caux Roundtable is an organization comprised of senior business leaders from around the world, including Europe, Japan, and North America. These leaders are individuals who "believe that business has a crucial role in developing and promoting equitable solutions to key global issues." One document provided on this site that serves as a guide to all businesses interested in responsible conduct is "The Principles for Business."

The Center for Ethics, Capital Markets and Political Economy
http://www.iath.virginia.edu/cecmpe

This center is a nonprofit organization that was established in 1994. It is designed to be an arena to foster discussion and a resource center for ethics information for "persons who believe that moral concerns should be taken into account in economic and political thinking." Services provided by the Center include sponsoring a working paper series, offering seminars, publishing "Ethics behind the News," and providing other research materials.

The Defense Industry Initiative (DII) Business Ethics and Conduct
http://www.dii.org

DII is a "consortium of U.S. defense industry contractors which subscribes to a set of principles for achieving high standards of business ethics and conduct." Links to ethics training resources plus other resources of interest can be found at this site.

Ethics and Compliance Officer Association (ECOA)
http://www.theecoa.org/AM/Template.cfm?Section=Home&Template=/Templates/TemplateHomepage/EthicsComplianceOfficerAssociation_1510_20070109T133141_LayoutHomePage.cfm

ECOA was founded in 1992 and currently has over 800 members including the ethics officers from over half of the Fortune 100 companies. Resources available on the site include the 2000 EOA Member Survey, educational centers, government-related organizations and links to ethics programs for companies like Honda, Sara Lee, and Lockheed Martin.

European Business Ethics Network (EBEN)
http://www.eben-net.org

The formation of EBEN, a nonprofit organization founded in Brussels in 1987, was considered to be a significant step in recognizing business ethics as an important area of research. Links to ethics organizations, university programs and other research institutions are provided.

Additional Resources

Financial Executives International (FEI)
http://www.financialexecutives.org/eweb/startpage.aspx?site=_fei

FEI was founded in 1931 and is considered to be the "professional association of choice for corporate financial executives." This organization strongly encourages all its members to practice the highest level of professional and ethical conduct.

Financial Planning Association (FPA): Code of Ethics
http://www.fpaforfinancialplanning.org/AboutFPA/CodeofEthics

Seven principles make up the Code of Ethics for FPA, and they are designed to guide members in the practice of professional ethics in the field of financial planning. The formation of FPA came about on January 1, 2000, as the result of the merger of the International Association for Financial Planning (IAFP) and the Institute of Certified Financial Planners (ICFP).

The Kennedy Institute of Ethics
http://kennedyinstitute.georgetown.edu

Georgetown Business Ethics Institute is located at Georgetown University and offers, through its Library and Information Services site, links to aid researchers in their quest for more information concerning business ethics topics.

Institute for Business, Technology & Ethics (IBTE)
http://www.ethix.org

IBTE was founded in 1998 to study the connections and relationships between business, ethics, and technology. The mission of this organization is to "promote good business through appropriate technology and sound ethics." Sections of the IBTE website to note are the Tools for Better Business and the Ethics Forum.

Institute for Global Ethics (IGE)
http://www.globalethics.org

IGE is an organization dedicated to promoting "ethical behavior in individuals, institutions, and nations through research, public discourse, and practical action." Numerous resources and articles are provided on the IGE site.

Institute of Business Ethics (IBE): Code of Ethics
http://www.ibe.org.uk

IBE believes that companies should uphold the highest standards of behavior and professional conduct. This organization "broadcasts" its mission through conferences, consultations, publications, and business ethics training programs. The IBE code of ethics section of the website goes beyond stating its code. It also provides tips on how to make codes effective, information on content included in a code of ethics policy, and links to various company codes of ethics.

The Society for Business Ethics (SBE)
http://www.societyforbusinessethics.org

SBE was founded in 1980 and is an international organization dedicated to the academic study of business ethics. The Ethics Links section of its site provides access to other associations and resource centers.

The Society of Corporate Compliance and Ethics
http://www.corporatecompliance.org/index.htm

The Society of Corporate Compliance and Ethics (SCCE) is a nonprofit organization that "exists to champion compliance standards, corporate governance and ethical practice in the business community and to provide the necessary resources for compliance and ethics professionals and others who share these principles." Membership opportunities and information about SCCE events are listed on this site. Resources, such as newsletters, books, and training kits (some for fee) are also available.

Resources and Centers

BELL: The Business Ethics Links Library
http://libnet.colorado.edu/Bell/frontpage.htm

Gene Hayworth, University of Colorado at Boulder, has created and continues to maintain a site designed to be a starting point for those seeking information regarding corporate ethics and social responsibility. Visitors to the site may select a topic or enter a search term. The following four categories are also available:

1. Academic organizations
2. Ethics organizations
3. Online ethics sources
4. Online ethics publications

Business Ethics
http://bubl.ac.uk/link/b/businessethics.htm

BUBL Link is a mega "catalog" of Internet resources covering various academic subject areas. An extensive section on business ethics has been compiled at this site. Resources include applied business materials, articles about financial scandals, and centers of research for business ethics.

Center for Business Ethics (CBE)
http://www.stthom.edu/Schools_Centers_of_Excellence/Centers_of_Excellence/Center_for_Business_Ethics/About/Index.aqf

The Center for Business Ethics (CBE) is housed on the campus of Bentley University and has been in operation since 1976 under the direction of W. Michael Hoffman. CBE is designed to be a forum for business ethics, and it provides specialized training and educational programs for businesses and their employees. Since CBE's founding, it has sponsored 10 major conferences on the topic of ethical business conduct.

Center for Ethics and Business
http://www.ethicsandbusiness.org/indexlo.htm

Loyola Marymount University (Los Angeles, CA) is the home of the Center for Ethics and Business. The Center acts as a forum for discussing ethical business decisions and dilemmas, including the costs and rewards of operating ethically. Numerous links to ethics programs, centers, and other tools designed to help people deal with ethical dilemmas are presented.

Center for Integrity in Business
http://www.spu.edu/depts/sbe/cib

Business ethics scandals making the news lately have increased the demand for business ethics educational programs and other programs designed to develop ethical business leaders. The Center for Integrity in Business at the School of Business & Economics at Seattle Pacific University has outlined 4 services: **1)** instigating and facilitating an ongoing dialogue; **2)** initiating and supporting a stream of empirical research; **3)** designing and conducting leadership development workshops and executive coaching sessions; **4)** educating and informing a broader audience. Resources available at this site include articles on current issues, instructional resources, and links to other ethics centers.

Complete Guide to Ethics Management
http://www.mapnp.org/library/ethics/ethxgde.htm

Carter McNamara, a business consultant in the Minneapolis/St. Paul region, has developed this free guidebook to help leaders and managers deal with the ethical issues that occur in everyday situations. The resources outlined in this online "book" include 10 myths about business ethics, ethics tools, and guidelines for managing ethics in the workplace.

Additional Resources

E-Ethics Center
http://www.e-businessethics.com

The goal of the E-Ethics Center at Colorado State University is to "create a virtual community of organizations and individuals that share best practices in the improvement of business ethics." Much of the information found at the Center's website has been provided by businesses, nonprofit organizations, government agencies, and other academic institutions. The case studies and ethics links sections listed below are merely two of the resource areas at this site.

- **Business Ethics Case Studies**
  http://www.e-businessethics.com/case.htm
- **Ethics Links**
  http://www.e-businessethics.com/links.htm

Ethical Business: The Search for Research
http://www.eldis.org/go/topics/resource-guides/corporate-responsibility

This ELDIS (Electronic Development and Environmental Information System) guide provides links to case studies, social and environmental standards, resources for informing shareholders and consumers, and more.

The Ethics Classroom
http://www.ethicsclassroom.info

The Ethics Classroom at Kansas State University (KSU) is designed to act as an "interactive forum" for local business leaders and government officials and to be a resource for KSU students taking ethics-related courses. This online classroom provides links to case studies, Internet resources, and ethic poll results.

Ethics on the World Wide Web: Business
http://commfaculty.fullerton.edu/lester/ethics/business.html

Ethics on the World Wide Web is a site designed by the School of Communications at California State University, Fullerton. The annotated list includes links to ethics centers, institutes, and organizations.

Google Directory: Business Ethics
http://directory.google.com/Top/Business/Management/Ethics

Google Directory offers a rather large, annotated compilation of links to sites related to business ethics.

Markkula Center for Applied Ethics
http://www.scu.edu/ethics

The Markkula Center for Applied Ethics was founded in 1986 and has grown into one of the most active university applied ethics centers in the U.S. It is based at Santa Clara University and was initially funded by an endowment by Linda and A. C. "Mike" Markkula Jr. Articles, cases, briefings, and dialogue in all areas of applied ethics can be found at this online center. Resources specifically addressing the issue of business ethics, such as the case study section, can be found at:

- **Business Ethics: Cases**
  http://www.scu.edu/ethics/practicing/focusareas/cases.cfm?fam=BUSI

Online Ethics Center: Ethics in Business
http://temp.onlineethics.org/topics/business.html

The Online Ethics Center was established in the fall of 1995 under a grant from NSF, and its mission is to provide resources "useful for understanding and addressing ethically significant problems that arise" in the work environment. The Ethics in Business section addresses several issues such as ethics in a corporate setting, conflict of interest, intellectual property, and employees who are entrepreneurs on corporate time.

Open Directory: Business Management Ethics
http://dmoz.org/Business/Management/Ethics

Open Directory claims to be the "largest, most comprehensive human-edited directory on the Web." This annotated collection includes links to business ethics publications, resource centers, forums, codes of ethics, and more.

Prudential Business Ethics Center
http://www.pruethics.rutgers.edu

The Prudential Business Ethics Center is housed at Rutgers University, and it is focused on the theory and practice of ethical behavior in business. The mission of the Center is to "help create social capital as well as prosperity for the business and professional communities of New Jersey." Services offered by the Center include providing speakers, supporting ethics courses and publications, conducting case competitions for students, providing consulting services to area businesses, and surveying the ethical attitudes of those in the New Jersey business community.

SOSIG: Professional and Business Ethics
http://www.sosig.ac.uk/roads/subject-listing/World-cat/proethic.html

SOSIG, the Social Science Information Gateway, is part of the UK Resource Discovery Network. The goal of this gateway is to provide high-quality business and other social science resources to students, faculty, and researchers. An extensive array of resources is arranged by type of resources for easier access.

Yahoo! Directory: Business Ethics and Responsibility
http://dir.yahoo.com/Business_and_Economy/Ethics_and_Responsibility

This Yahoo! category has site listings for centers, institutes, and publications. Its Categories section has links to related topics such as corporate accountability, socially responsible investing, sweatshops, and whistleblowing.

The Zicklin Center for Business Ethics Research
http://www.zicklincenter.org

The Carol and Lawrence Zicklin Center at the Wharton School, University of Pennsylvania, was established in 1997 to conduct leading-edge research on business ethics. Research focus areas include global business ethics, corporate governance, social contracts, deception, disclosure, bribery, and corruption. The Research Links section of the site includes information on associations, publications and other ethics-related materials.

UNIT 1
Ethics, Values, and Social Responsibility in Business

Unit Selections

1. **Thinking Ethically: A Framework for Moral Decision Making,** Manuel Velasquez et al.
2. **Business Ethics: Back to Basics,** William I. Sauser, Jr.
3. **Ethics: The Framework for Success,** Steve Hunter
4. **Authentic Leaders Add Value,** Ken Shelton
5. **The Ethical Employee,** Michele Compton
6. **Truth or Consequences: The Organizational Importance of Honesty,** Erline Belton
7. **How to Make Unethical Decisions,** Andrew Sikula, Sr. and John Sikula
8. **Create a Culture of Trust,** Noreen Kelly
9. **Building an Ethical Framework,** Thomas R. Krause and Paul J. Voss
10. **Ethical Leadership: Maintain an Ethical Culture,** Ronald Berenbeim

Key Points to Consider

- Do you believe that corporations are more socially responsible today than they were 10 years ago? Why or why not?
- In what specific ways do you see companies practicing social responsibility? Do you think most companies are overt or covert in their social responsibility activities? Explain your answer.
- What are the economic and social implications of "management accountability" as part of the decision-making process? Does a company have any obligation to help remedy social problems, such as poverty, urban decay, and pollution? Defend your response.
- Using recent examples of stock, financial, and accounting debacles, discuss the flaws in the U.S. financial system that allows companies to disregard ethics, values, and social responsibility in business.

Student Website
www.mhhe.com/cls

Internet References

Association for Moral Education (AME)
http://www.amenetwork.org

Business for Social Responsibility (BSR)
http://www.bsr.org

Enron Online
http://www.enron.com/corp

Ethics Updates/Lawrence Hinman
http://ethics.sandiego.edu/index.html

Institute for Business and Professional Ethics
http://commerce.depaul.edu/ethics

National Center for Policy Analysis
http://www.ncpa.org

Open Directory Project
http://dmoz.org/Business/Management/Ethics

Working Definitions
http://www.workingdefinitions.co.uk/index.html

Ethical decision making in an organization does not occur in a vacuum. As individuals and as managers, we formulate our ethics (that is, the standards of "right" and "wrong" behavior that we set for ourselves) based upon family, peer, and religious influences, our past experiences, and our own unique value systems. When we make ethical decisions within the organizational context, many times there are situational factors and potential conflicts of interest that further complicate the process.

Decisions do not only have personal ramifications—they also have social consequences. Social responsibility is really ethics at the organizational level, since it refers to the obligation that an organization has to make choices and to take actions that will contribute to the good of society as well as the good of the organization. Authentic social responsibility is not initiated because of forced compliance to specific laws and regulations. In contrast to legal responsibility, social responsibility involves a voluntary response from an organization that is above and beyond what is specified by the law.

The eight selections in this unit provide an overview of the interrelationships of ethics, values, and social responsibility in business. The essays in this unit offer practical and insightful principles and suggestions to managers, enabling them to approach the subject of business ethics with more confidence. They also point out the complexity and the significance of making ethical decisions.

© BananaStock/PictureQuest

Thinking Ethically
A Framework for Moral Decision Making

MANUEL VELASQUEZ ET AL.

Moral issues greet us each morning in the newspaper, confront us in the memos on our desks, nag us from our children's soccer fields, and bid us good night on the evening news. We are bombarded daily with questions about the justice of our foreign policy, the morality of medical technologies that can prolong our lives, the rights of the homeless, the fairness of our children's teachers to the diverse students in their classrooms.

Dealing with these moral issues is often perplexing. How, exactly, should we think through an ethical issue? What questions should we ask? What factors should we consider?

The first step in analyzing moral issues is obvious but not always easy: Get the facts.

The first step in analyzing moral issues is obvious but not always easy: Get the facts. Some moral issues create controversies simply because we do not bother to check the facts. This first step, although obvious, is also among the most important and the most frequently overlooked.

But having the facts is not enough. Facts by themselves only tell us what *is*; they do not tell us what *ought* to be. In addition to getting the facts, resolving an ethical issue also requires an appeal to values. Philosophers have developed five different approaches to values to deal with moral issues.

The Utilitarian Approach

Utilitarianism was conceived in the 19th century by Jeremy Bentham and John Stuart Mill to help legislators determine which laws were morally best. Both Bentham and Mill suggested that ethical actions are those that provide the greatest balance of good over evil.

To analyze an issue using the utilitarian approach, we first identify the various courses of action available to us. Second, we ask who will be affected by each action and what benefits or harms will be derived from each. And third, we choose the action that will produce the greatest benefits and the least harm. The ethical action is the one that provides the greatest good for the greatest number.

The Rights Approach

The second important approach to ethics has its roots in the philosophy of the 18th-century thinker Immanuel Kant and others like him, who focused on the individual's right to choose for herself or himself. According to these philosophers, what makes human beings different from mere things is that people have dignity based on their ability to choose freely what they will do with their lives, and they have a fundamental moral right to have these choices respected. People are not objects to be manipulated; it is a violation of human dignity to use people in ways they do not freely choose.

Of course, many different, but related, rights exist besides this basic one. These other rights (an incomplete list below) can be thought of as different aspects of the basic right to be treated as we choose.

- *The right to the truth*: We have a right to be told the truth and to be informed about matters that significantly affect our choices.
- *The right of privacy*: We have the right to do, believe, and say whatever we choose in our personal lives so long as we do not violate the rights of others.
- *The right not to be injured*: We have the right not to be harmed or injured unless we freely and knowingly do something to deserve punishment or we freely and knowingly choose to risk such injuries.
- *The right to what is agreed:* We have a right to what has been promised by those with whom we have freely entered into a contract or agreement.

In deciding whether an action is moral or immoral using this second approach, then, we must ask, Does the action respect the moral rights of everyone? Actions are wrong to the extent

The Case of Maria Elena

Maria Elena has cleaned your house each week for more than a year. You agree with your friend who recommended her that she does an excellent job and is well worth the $30 cash you pay her for three hours' work. You've also come to like her, and you think she likes you, especially as her English has become better and you've been able to have some pleasant conversations.

Over the past three weeks, however, you've noticed Maria Elena becoming more and more distracted. One day, you ask her if something is wrong, and she tells you she really needs to make additional money. She hastens to say she is not asking you for a raise, becomes upset, and begins to cry. When she calms down a little, she tells you her story:

She came to the United States six years ago from Mexico with her child, Miguel, who is now 7 years old. They entered the country on a visitor's visa that has expired, and Maria Elena now uses a Social Security number she made up.

Her common-law husband, Luis, came to the United States first. He entered the country illegally, after paying smugglers $500 to hide him under piles of grass cuttings for a six-hour truck ride across the border. When he had made enough money from low-paying day jobs, he sent for Maria Elena. Using a false green card, Luis now works as a busboy for a restaurant, which withholds part of his salary for taxes. When Maria Elena comes to work at your house, she takes the bus and Luis baby-sits.

In Mexico, Maria Elena and Luis lived in a small village where it was impossible to earn more than $3 a day. Both had sixth-grade educations, common in their village. Life was difficult, but they did not decide to leave until they realized the future would be bleak for their child and for the other children they wanted to have. Luis had a cousin in San Jose who visited and told Luis and Maria Elena how well his life was going. After his visit, Luis and Maria Elena decided to come to the United States.

Luis quickly discovered, as did Maria Elena, that life in San Jose was not the way they had heard. The cousin did not tell them they would be able to afford to live only in a run-down three-room apartment with two other couples and their children. He did not tell them they would always live in fear of INS raids.

After they entered the United States, Maria Elena and Luis had a second child, Jose, who is 5 years old. The birth was difficult because she didn't use the health-care system or welfare for fear of being discovered as undocumented. But, she tells you, she is willing to put up with anything so that her children can have a better life. "All the money we make is for Miguel and Jose," she tells you. "We work hard for their education and their future."

Now, however, her mother in Mexico is dying, and Maria Elena must return home, leaving Luis and the children. She does not want to leave them because she might not be able to get back into the United States, but she is pretty sure she can find a way to return if she has enough money. That is her problem: She doesn't have enough money to make certain she can get back.

After she tells you her story, she becomes too distraught to continue talking. You now know she is an undocumented immigrant, working in your home. What is the ethical thing for you to do?

> This case was developed by Tom Shanks, S.J., director of the Markkula Center for Applied Ethics. Maria Elena is a composite drawn from several real people, and her story represents some of the ethical dilemmas behind the immigration issue.
>
> This case can be accessed through the Ethics Center home page on the World Wide Web: http://www.scu.edu/Ethics/. You can also contact us by e-mail, ethics@scu.edu, or regular mail: Markkula Center for Applied Ethics, Santa Clara University, Santa Clara, CA 95053. Our voice mail number is (408) 554-7898. We have also posted on our homepage a new case involving managed health care.

that they violate the rights of individuals; the more serious the violation, the more wrongful the action.

The Fairness or Justice Approach

The fairness or justice approach to ethics has its roots in the teachings of the ancient Greek philosopher Aristotle, who said that "equals should be treated equally and unequals unequally." The basic moral question in this approach is: How fair is an action? Does it treat everyone in the same way, or does it show favoritism and discrimination?

Favoritism gives benefits to some people without a justifiable reason for singling them out; discrimination imposes burdens on people who are no different from those on whom burdens are not imposed. Both favoritism and discrimination are unjust and wrong.

The Common-Good Approach

This approach to ethics presents a vision of society as a community whose members are joined in the shared pursuit of values and goals they hold in common. This community comprises individuals whose own good is inextricably bound to the good of the whole.

The common good is a notion that originated more than 2,000 years ago in the writings of Plato, Aristotle, and Cicero. More recently, contemporary ethicist John Rawls defined the common good as "certain general conditions that are . . . equally to everyone's advantage."

In this approach, we focus on ensuring that the social policies, social systems, institutions, and environments on which we depend are beneficial to all. Examples of goods common to all include affordable health care, effective public safety, peace among nations, a just legal system, and an unpolluted environment.

Appeals to the common good urge us to view ourselves as members of the same community, reflecting on broad questions concerning the kind of society we want to become and how we are to achieve that society. While respecting and valuing the freedom of individuals to pursue their own goals, the common-good approach challenges us also to recognize and further those goals we share in common.

The Virtue Approach

The virtue approach to ethics assumes that there are certain ideals toward which we should strive, which provide for the full development of our humanity. These ideals are discovered through thoughtful reflection on what kind of people we have the potential to become.

Virtues are attitudes or character traits that enable us to be and to act in ways that develop our highest potential. They enable us to pursue the ideals we have adopted.

Honesty, courage, compassion, generosity, fidelity, integrity, fairness, self-control, and prudence are all examples of virtues.

Virtues are like habits; that is, once acquired, they become characteristic of a person. Moreover, a person who has developed virtues will be naturally disposed to act in ways consistent with moral principles. The virtuous person is the ethical person.

In dealing with an ethical problem using the virtue approach, we might ask, What kind of person should I be? What will promote the development of character within myself and my community?

Ethical Problem Solving

These five approaches suggest that once we have ascertained the facts, we should ask ourselves five questions when trying to resolve a moral issue:

- What benefits and what harms will each course of action produce, and which alternative will lead to the best overall consequences?
- What moral rights do the affected parties have, and which course of action best respects those rights?
- Which course of action treats everyone the same, except where there is a morally justifiable reason not to, and does not show favoritism or discrimination?
- Which course of action advances the common good?
- Which course of action develops moral virtues?

This method, of course, does not provide an automatic solution to moral problems. It is not meant to. The method is merely meant to help identify most of the important ethical considerations. In the end, we must deliberate on moral issues for ourselves, keeping a careful eye on both the facts and on the ethical considerations involved.

This article updates several previous pieces from *Issues in Ethics* by **MANUEL VELASQUEZ**—Dirksen Professor of Business Ethics at SCU and former Center director—and **CLAIRE ANDRE,** associate Center director. "Thinking Ethically" is based on a framework developed by the authors in collaboration with Center Director **THOMAS SHANKS, S. J.,** Presidential Professor of Ethics and the Common Good **MICHAEL J. MEYER,** and others. The framework is used as the basis for many Center programs and presentations.

From *Issues in Ethics*, Vol. 7, No. 1, Winter 1996, pp. 2–5. Copyright © 1996 by Markkula Center for Applied Ethics. Reprinted by permission.

Article 2

Business Ethics
Back to Basics

With business news dominated in recent years by some spectacular examples of ethical malfeasance, confidence in the business world has been shaken. Never mind that the Enrons of the world are actually few and far between. No business or organization can afford even a suspicion of unethical behavior and must take proactive steps to ensure that no suspicions arise. Ethical behavior begins at the top with actions and statements that are beyond reproach and ambiguity. Managements may want to follow an eight-point action list presented here for establishing a strong ethical culture and also a decision checklist when ethical dilemmas loom. Sterling reputations are valuable business assets: they are earned over time but can be lost almost overnight.

WILLIAM I. SAUSER, JR.

Introduction

Enron, Arthur Andersen, Tyco, ImClone, Martha Stewart, WorldCom, Global Crossing, Merrill Lynch, Rite-Aid, Qwest, Adelphia, Kmart, HealthSouth—the list of formerly respected businesses (and business leaders) being charged with breaches of ethical conduct seems to be growing by the day. This is having adverse effects on our economic well-being, on investor confidence, and on the perceived desirability of pursuing business as a respectable calling.

Commenting on the ethical crisis in business leadership, Eileen Kelly (2002) observed, "Recently a new business scandal seems to surface each day. The current volatility of the market reflects the apprehension, the sense of betrayal, and the lack of confidence that investors have in many large corporations and their managements" (p. 4). Marcy Gordon (2002), reporting on a speech by United States Securities and Exchange Commissioner Paul Atkins, noted, "The string of accounting failures at big companies in the last year has cost U.S. households nearly $60,000 on average as some $5 trillion in market value was lost."

Accounting failures are not the only ethical concerns facing modern business organizations. The Southern Institute for Business and Professional Ethics (2002) lists on its website an array of issues that put pressures on business enterprises. These include the globalization of business, work force diversification, employment practices and policies, civil litigation and government regulation, and concerns about environmental stewardship. The institute (on the same website) concluded, "Despite such powerful trends, few managers have been adequately equipped by traditional education to recognize, evaluate, and act upon the ethical dimension of their work."

Columnist Malcolm Cutchins (2002), an emeritus professor of engineering at Auburn University, summed up the problem concisely: "We have seen the effect of not teaching good ethics in business schools. If we continue to neglect the teaching of good principles on a broad scale, we all reap the bad consequences."

Business Ethics

Ethics has to do with behavior—specifically, an individual's moral behavior with respect to society. The extent to which behavior measures up to societal standards is typically used as a gauge of ethicality. Since there are a variety of standards for societal behavior, ethical behavior is often characterized with respect to certain contexts. The Ethics Resource Center says, "*Business Ethics* refers to clear standards and norms that help employees to distinguish right from wrong behavior at work" (Joseph, 2003, p. 2). In the business context, ethics has to do with the extent to which a person's behavior measures up to such standards as the law, organizational policies, professional and trade association codes, popular expectations regarding fairness and rightness, plus an individual's internalized moral standards.

Business ethics, then, is not distinct from ethics in general, but rather a subfield (Desjardins, 2003, p. 8). The subfield refers to the examination and application of moral standards within the context of finance; commerce; production, distribution, and sale of goods and services; and other business activities.

It can be argued that an ethical person behaves appropriately in all societal contexts. This may be so, in which case one might prefer the term "ethics in business" to "business ethics." The distinction is subtle, but serves as a reminder that morality may be generalized from context to context. Adam Smith, for example, saw no need for ethical relativism when it comes to business. "It is impossible to determine just how business became separated from ethics in history. If we go back to Adam Smith, we find no such separation. In addition to his famous book on business and capitalism, *The Wealth of Nations*, Adam Smith also wrote *The Theory of Moral Sentiments*, a book about our ethical obligations to one another. It is clear that Smith believed that business and commerce worked well only if people took seriously their obligations and, in particular, their sense of justice" (Bruner, 1998, p. 46).

May (1995) echoed this important point: "The marketplace breaks down unless it can presuppose the virtue of industry, without which goods will not be produced; and the virtues of "honesty and integrity, without which their free and fair exchange cannot take place."

Standards of Behavior

The law (including statutory, administrative, and case law) is an important and legitimate source of ethical guidance. Federal, state, and local laws establish the parameters (Fieser, 1996), and violation of the law is almost always considered unethical (with the possible exception of civil disobedience as a mechanism for putting the law itself on trial). Pursuing business outside the law is regarded as an obstructionist approach to business ethics (Schermerhorn, 2005, p. 75). Such an individual would almost certainly be labeled unethical.

A second important source of authority is organizational policies, which are standards for behavior established by the employing organization. Typically they are aligned with the law (which takes precedence over them) and spell out in detail how things are done. All employees are expected to adhere to organizational policies. It is very important that managers at the highest level set the example for others by always working within the law and the policies of the organization.

Another important source of ethical guidance is the code of behavior adopted by professional and trade associations. These codes are often aspirational in nature and frequently establish higher standards for behavior than the law requires. Members of a profession or trade association typically aspire to meet these higher standards in order to establish and uphold the reputation of a profession or trade.

These social mores, based on commonly held beliefs about what is right and wrong and fair and unfair, can be powerful determinants of a person's reputation. Behavior that—in the strictest sense—meets legal requirements, organizational policies, and even professional standards may still be viewed by the general public as unfair and wrong (Krech, Crutchfield, and Ballachey, 1962).

A fifth set of standards reflects the individual conscience. Coleman, Butcher and Carson (1980, p. Glossary IV) define "the conscience" as "the functioning of an individual's moral values in the approval or disapproval of his or her own thoughts and actions," and equate it roughly with the Freudian concept of the superego. Highly ethical business leaders typically have moral standards that exceed all four of the lesser standards just listed. These values, learned early in life and reinforced by life's experiences, are internalized standards often based on personal, religious or philosophical understandings of morality (Baelz, 1977, pp. 41–55).

Ethical Dilemmas

An ethical dilemma is a situation where a potential course of action offers potential benefit or gain but is unethical, in that it violates one or more of the standards just described. Behaviors violating laws are, by definition, illegal as well as unethical. The key question for the business leader when presented with an ethical dilemma is: "What to do?" Behavior determines a person's ethical reputation, after all. Ethical leadership is exhibited when ethical dilemmas are resolved in an appropriate manner.

Here is a sampling of some ethical dilemmas that frequently rise in the business setting. Many of these behaviors are illegal as well as unethical.

- Providing a product or service you know is harmful or unsafe
- Misleading someone through false statements or omissions
- Using insider information for personal gain
- Playing favorites
- Manipulating and using people
- Benefiting personally from a position of trust
- Violating confidentiality
- Misusing company property or equipment
- Falsifying documents
- Padding expenses
- Taking bribes or kickbacks
- Participating in a cover-up
- Theft or sabotage
- Committing an act of violence
- Substance abuse
- Negligence or inappropriate behavior in the workplace.

Poor Ethical Choices

Why do people sometimes make poor choices when faced with ethical dilemmas? One set of reasons has to do with flaws of *character*. Such character defects include malice (intentional evil); sociopathy (lack of conscience); personal greed; envy, jealousy, resentment; the will to win or achieve at any cost; and fear of failure. There are also flaws in *corporate culture* that lead even good people to make poor ethical judgments. Weaknesses in corporate culture include indifference, a lack of knowledge or understanding of standards on the part of employees; poor or inappropriate incentive systems; and poor leadership, including the use of mixed signals such as:

- I don't care how you do it, just get it done.
- Don't ever bring me bad news.
- Don't bother me with the details, you know what to do.

- Remember, we always meet our financial goals somehow.
- No one gets injured on this worksite . . . period. Understand?
- Ask me no questions, I'll tell you no lies.

Such statements by managers to their subordinates too often imply that unethical behaviors that obtain the intended results are acceptable to the organization. While it may be difficult—other than through termination or other sanctions—to rid the organization of employees with character flaws, correcting a poor organizational culture is clearly a matter of leadership.

Establishing a Strong Ethical Culture

Business leaders who wish to take proactive measures to establish and maintain a corporate culture that emphasizes strong moral leadership are advised to take the following steps:

1. **Adopt a code of ethics.** The code need not be long and elaborate with flowery words and phrases. In fact, the best ethical codes use language anyone can understand. A good way to produce such a code is to ask all employees of the firm (or a representative group) to participate in its creation (Kuchar, 2003). Identify the commonly-held moral beliefs and values of the members of the firm and codify them into a written document all can understand and support. Post the code of ethics in prominent places around the worksite. Make certain that all employees subscribe to it by asking them to sign it.

2. **Provide ethics training.** From time to time a leader should conduct ethics training sessions. These may be led by experts in business ethics, or they may be informal in nature and led by the manager or employees themselves. A highly effective way to conduct an ethics training session is to provide "what if" cases for discussion and resolution. The leader would present a "real world" scenario in which an ethical dilemma is encountered. Using the organization's code of ethics as a guide, participants would explore options and seek a consensus ethical solution. This kind of training sharpens the written ethical code and brings it to life.

3. **Hire and promote ethical people.** This, in concert with step four, is probably the best defense against putting the business at risk through ethical lapses by employees. When making human resources decisions it is critical to reward ethical behavior and punish unethical behavior. Investigate the character of the people you hire, and do your best to hire people who have exhibited high moral standards in the past. Remember that past behavior is the best predictor of future behavior, so check references carefully. Formal background investigations may be warranted for positions of fiduciary responsibility or significant risk exposure. Base promotional decisions on matters of character in addition to technical competence. Demonstrate to your employees that high ethical standards are a requirement for advancement.

4. **Correct unethical behavior.** This complements step three. When the organization's ethical code is breached, those responsible must be punished. Many businesses use progressive discipline, with an oral warning (intended to advise the employee of what is and is not acceptable behavior) as the first step, followed by a written reprimand, suspension without pay, and termination if unethical behavior persists. Of course, some ethical lapses are so egregious that they require suspension—or even termination—following the first offense. Through consistent and firm application of sanctions to correct unethical behavior, the manager will signal to all employees that substandard moral behavior will not be tolerated.

5. **Be proactive.** Businesses wishing to establish a reputation for ethicality and good corporate citizenship in the community will often organize and support programs intended to give something back to the community. Programs that promote continuing education, wholesome recreation, good health and hygiene, environmental quality, adequate housing, and other community benefits may demonstrate the extent to which the business promotes concern for human welfare. Seeking and adopting best practices from other businesses in the community is also a proactive strategy.

6. **Conduct a social audit.** Most businesses are familiar with financial audits. This concept can be employed in the context of ethics and corporate responsibility as well. From time to time the leader of the business might invite responsible parties to examine the organization's product design, purchasing, production, marketing, distribution, customer relations, and human resources functions with an eye toward identifying and correcting any areas of policy or practice that raise ethical concerns. Similarly, programs of corporate responsibility (such as those mentioned in step five) should be reviewed for effectiveness and improved as needed.

7. **Protect whistle blowers.** A whistle blower is a person within the firm who points out ethically questionable actions taken by other employees—or even by managers—within the organization. Too often corporate whistle blowers are ignored—or even punished—by those who receive the unfortunate news of wrongdoing within the business. All this does is discourage revelation of ethical problems. Instead the whistle blower should be protected and even honored. When unethical actions are uncovered within a firm by one of the employees, managers should step forward and take corrective action (as described in step four). Employees learn from one another. If the owners and managers of a business turn a blind eye toward wrongdoing, a signal is sent to everyone within the firm that ethicality is not characteristic of that organization's culture. A downward spiral of moral behavior is likely to follow.

8. **Empower the guardians of integrity.** The business leader's chief task is to lead by example and to empower every member of the organization to demonstrate the firm's commitment to ethics in its relationships with suppliers, customers, employees, and shareholders. Turn each employee of the firm, no matter what that individual's position, into a guardian of the firm's integrity. When maliciousness and indifference are replaced with a culture of integrity, honesty, and ethicality, the business will reap long-term benefits from all quarters.

A Checklist for Making Good Ethical Decisions

A business leader who takes seriously the challenge of creating a strong ethical culture for the firm must, of course, make good decisions when faced personally with ethical dilemmas. Here is a checklist a manager might wish to follow:

1. Recognize the ethical dilemma.
2. Get the facts.
3. Identify your options.
4. Test each option: Is it legal, right, beneficial? Note: Get some counsel.
5. Decide which option to follow.
6. Double-check your decision.
7. Take action.
8. Follow up and monitor decision implementation.

Number six is key: Double-check your decision. When in doubt consider how each of the following might guide you. Take the action that would allow you to maintain your reputation with those on this list you believe adhere to the highest ethical standards: Your attorney, accountant, boss, co-workers, stakeholders, family, newspaper, television news, religious leader, and Deity.

How would you feel if you had to explain your decision—and your actions—to each of these? If you would not feel good about this, then it is quite likely that you are about to make a poor decision. Double check your decision in this manner before you take any action you may later regret.

Conclusion

A firm's reputation may take years—even decades—to establish, but can be destroyed in an instant through unethical behavior. That is why it is so important for business leaders to be very careful about the things they say and do. Taking the time and effort to establish and maintain a corporate culture of morality, integrity, honesty, and ethicality will pay important dividends throughout the life of the firm. While taking ethical shortcuts may appear to lead to gains in the short term, this type of corporate strategy almost always proves tragic in the longer term.

Every business leader will be faced at one time or another with an ethical dilemma. Many face even daily temptations. How the leader manifests moral integrity when faced with ethical dilemmas sets the tone for everyone else in the organization. This is why it is so important to "walk the talk" by making good ethical decisions every day. Understanding and applying the concepts presented in this article will enable you, as a business leader, to create and maintain an ethical corporate culture in your business. As Carl Skoogland, the former vice president and ethics director for Texas Instruments, recently advised, if you want to create an ethical business, you must *know what's right, value what's right, and do what's right* (Skoogland, 2003).

References

Baelz, P. (1977). *Ethics and belief*. New York: The Seabury Press.

Bruner, R. F., Eaker, M. R., Freeman, E., Spekman, R.E., and Teisberg, E. O. (1998). *The portable MBA, 3rd ed*. New York: Wiley.

Coleman, J. C., Butcher, J. N., and Carson, R. (1980). *Abnormal psychology and modern life, 6th ed,* Glenview, IL: Scott Foresman.

Cutchins, M. (2002, November 20). Business ethics must be taught or we all pay. *Opelika-Auburn News*, p. A4.

Desjardins, J. (2003). *An introduction to business ethics*. Boston: McGraw-Hill.

Fieser, J. (1996). Do businesses have moral obligations beyond what the law requires? *Journal of Business Ethics, 15*, 457–468.

Gordon, M. (2002, November 18). Accounting failures cost $60,000 on average, SEC commissioner says. *Opelika-Auburn News*, p. C4.

Joseph, J. (2003). *National business ethics survey 2003: How employees view ethics in their organizations*. Washington, DC: Ethics Resource Center.

Kelly, E. P. (2002). Business ethics—An oxymoron? *Phi Kappa Phi Forum, 82*(4), 4–5.

Krech, D., Crutchfield, R. S., and Ballachey, E. L. (1962). Culture. Chapter 10 in *Individual in society* (pp. 339–380). New York: McGraw-Hill.

Kuchar, C. (2003). Tips on developing ethics codes for private companies. *GoodBusiness, 2*(3), pages unnumbered.

May, W. F. (1995). The virtues of the business leader. In M. L. Stackhouse, D. P. McCann, S. J. Roels, and P. N. Williams (Eds.), *On moral business* (pp. 692–700). Grand Rapids, MI: Eerdmans.

Schermerhorn, J. R., Jr. (2005). *Management, 8th ed*. New York: Wiley.

Skoogland, C. (2003, October 16). *Establishing an ethical organization*. Plenary address at the Conference on Ethics and Social Responsibility in Engineering and Technology, New Orleans, LA.

The Southern Institute for Business and Professional Ethics. (2002). *The certificate in managerial ethics*. Retrieved August, 14, 2002, from http://www.southerninstitute.org.

DR. SAUSER is Associate Dean for Business and Engineering Outreach and Professor of Management at Auburn University. His interests include organization development, strategic planning, human relations in the workplace, business ethics, and continuing professional education. He is a Fellow of the American Council on Education and the Society for Advancement of Management (SAM). In 2003, he was awarded the Frederick W. Taylor Key by SAM for his career achievements.

Article 3

Ethics
The Framework for Success

While some ethical decisions are simply a matter of right vs. wrong, the tough ethical decisions are right vs. right.

STEVE HUNTER

The widespread attention given to the fall of companies such as Tyco, WorldCom, and Enron has led to an increased focus on ethics in the business world. Because of the enormous pressure to produce higher and better returns, some individuals at corporations have adopted the philosophy, "the ends justify the means." They fall into the trap of setting unrealistic budgets, improbable expectations, and unlikely goals. Not surprisingly, investor confidence has been low due to the many corporate scandals. Despite these results, however, firms continue to allow external sources, such as outside analysts, to define success.

Instead, companies must ask the following question: "Have we replaced our underlying business theme of 'succeeding at all costs' with 'succeeding only the right way'?" An ethical culture can ensure success by establishing appropriate expectations using proper guidelines, thus preventing the need or desire to be involved in any questionable business practices. Ultimately, success is about keeping your word, and companies that live up to their promises are successful.

While it's true that some businesses hold themselves to a higher ethical standard, not all companies operate in an ethical environment. Financial decisions often are made without considering the ethical implications. When companies don't hold themselves to high ethical standards, the impact reverberates throughout the financial markets. Companies are destroyed, jobs are lost, and retirement savings are decimated. One of the government's reactions to corporate wrongdoing was enactment of the Sarbanes-Oxley Act of 2002 (SOX). But as Gary Smith, CEO of CIENA, characterized it in the October 20, 2003, edition of *USA Today*, SOX was "'chemotherapy' to prevent the cancer from recurring after cutting out corporate tumors at Enron, WorldCom, and elsewhere."

Ensuring that an effective ethical culture exists in an organization isn't only a key factor in preventing the kinds of losses brought about by corporate frauds and avoiding the need for costly, burdensome legislation, but it can also enhance a company's reputation, improve morale, and even increase sales. This article examines top management's role in building an ethically minded culture, steps for making sound choices, and examples of ethical issues.

From the Top Down

Establishing ethical standards for a business should be the primary goal of executive management. Companies must design an environment that not only encourages high ethical standards but also produces ethically minded management, employees, suppliers, and customers.

To establish an ethical culture, top management *must* accept responsibility for the ethical climate within their organizations. In reality, the actions of top executives define a company's culture because employees emulate their boss's behavior. Michael Hackworth, author of "Only the Ethical Survive" in the Fall 1999 *Issues in Ethics,* believes top leadership is ultimately responsible for the culture of their organization, including the ethical culture.

To establish an ethical environment, top management needs to use five key elements to build trust: integrity, competence, consistency, loyalty, and openness with employees, vendors, and stakeholders. Stakeholder is a better word than stockholder because it represents the significant effect that business has on the community as a whole. Companies that operate under high ethical values don't have to spend any negative energy hiding wrongdoings if they make all decisions while considering the ethical implications. Most financial analysts agree that no single variable affects the climate of an organization more than the beliefs, practices, and ideas of its top management.

The Good and the Bad

One company that provides a prime example of making good ethical decisions is Johnson & Johnson. In 1982, James Burke, then CEO, faced an ethical dilemma. The company experienced a major crisis when some of its Extra-Strength Tylenol capsules were found laced with cyanide. Faced with a difficult decision, Burke turned to Johnson & Johnson's credo: "We believe our first responsibility is to doctors, nurses, and patients, to mothers and fathers and all others who use our products and services." He ignored the immediate short-term financial implication and adhered to the attitude of "doing the right thing," ordering the recall of more than 31 million bottles at a cost of more than $100 million. This action set a new standard for crisis management. As a result of these events, the company developed the tamper-proof seal and gained even more market share and customer loyalty than it had before the incident.

To make choices like Burke requires individuals to take the steps listed in "A Framework for Thinking Ethically" from the Markkula Center for Applied Ethics at Santa Clara University (www.scu.edu/ethics):

- Be sensitive to ethical issues,
- Explore ethical aspects of a decision,
- Weigh the considerations that impact their course of action, and
- Have the moral courage to make the right ethical choice.

While companies will inevitably face difficult situations, their ability to make ethical decisions must not be compromised for any reason. Consider Exxon, for example. This company refused to accept responsibility for the Valdez accident, and their attempt to blame state and federal officials for delays in containing the spill damaged their reputation. Even today the name Exxon is synonymous with environmental catastrophe. Due to ineffective communication from Exxon, the public questioned their credibility and truthfulness. According to Jennifer Hogue in "What is Crisis Management?" (http://iml.jou.ufl.edu/projects/Spring01/Hogue/crisismanagement.html), a survey conducted by Porter Novelli several years after the accident found that 54% of respondents were still less likely to buy Exxon products.

The Daniel Effect

Everyone within an organization should work together to create the "Daniel Effect." This comes from the Old Testament account of a governing body trying to discredit Daniel in front of the whole kingdom of Babylon. In the *New King James Version,* the Book of Daniel, Chapter 6:3-4, says, "Then this Daniel distinguished himself above the governors and satraps, because an excellent spirit was in him; and the king gave thought to setting him over the whole realm. So the governors and satraps sought to find some charge against Daniel concerning the kingdom; but they could find no charge or fault, because he was faithful; nor was there any error or fault found in him."

Employees would benefit individually from this mindset during their careers by adhering to high ethical standards. Companies must build a strong ethical framework to withstand attacks from the public through frivolous lawsuits, competition's claims of wrongdoing, and any fraud attempted by their employees. Positive public perception is vital to success in the marketplace, which is protected by ethical behavior just as Daniel protected himself from his enemies by remaining faithful to his high moral standards.

Some ethical decisions, such as cheating on taxes, lying under oath, or overstating revenue and understating expenses, are simply a matter of right vs. wrong. The tough ethical decisions are right vs. right. Four such dilemmas include truth vs. loyalty, individual vs. community, short-term vs. long-term, justice vs. mercy. Here are some real-world examples from Rushworth Kidder's *How Good People Make Tough Choices*:

- It is right to find out all you can about your competitor's costs and price structures—and right to obtain information only through proper channels;
- It is right to throw the book at good employees who make dumb decisions that endanger the firm—and right to have enough compassion to mitigate the punishment and give them another chance.
- It is right to protect the endangered spotted owl in the old-growth forests of the American Northwest—and right to provide jobs to loggers.

Unfortunately, no magic formula exists to guide management through these types of decisions. Companies must be willing to equally weigh the ethical repercussions of one decision over the other.

Difficult Choices

In *Moral Courage,* Kidder relates the story of Eric Duckworth. A metallurgist by training, the recently married Duckworth took a position in 1949 with Federal Mogul, a firm that made bearings for internal combustion engines. His job description included examining damaged bearings returned by customers. He would determine the cause of the failure, report to the customers, and recommend changes to correct the problem. Most were due to misuse, improper installation, and lack of lubrication. Sometimes he discovered that the faulty parts were the result of production mistakes. His boss, the chief metallurgist, regularly tried to cover up such faults by refusing to divulge all the facts and by attributing the failure to end users mishandling the bearings, making no effort to compensate customers.

At first, Duckworth rationalized "that he was prepared to commit sins of omission but not of commission." Eventually, a particularly flagrant case drove him to write a completely honest report, which his boss rejected. Summoning his moral courage, he protested that he would resign if they didn't report the true findings to the customer. His boss, as well as the sales department, protested that such findings would cost them customers and perhaps more.

Fortunately, Duckworth previously had made several suggestions that increased the productivity of the manufacturing process and won him the admiration of the CEO, who backed him against his boss. The report went to the customer, who responded with a congratulatory letter that said: "We had always suspected concealment in some of your reports." In the wake of the company's new-found honesty, the customer increased orders. Duckworth later recalled his moral courage, "On one occasion when I was young and idealistic, I succeeded—and have been proud of it ever since."

My own experience illustrates how one benefit of ethical behavior is improved employee morale. The testing lab at a former employer of mine discovered a potential electrical hazard related to a specific motor supplier. Under unique circumstances that required the existence of several conditions, this motor had the potential to deliver an electric shock to the end user. The possible financial impact of rework or possible recall could cost the company millions of dollars. Our management team, aware of the chance for a possible recall, decided to report this issue to the Consumer Product Safety Commission (CPSC). Taking a pro-ethical approach had a positive impact on me and other employees because we all were impressed with the company's commitment to product safety.

Safeguard the Future

Every day, management decisions affect individuals, families, and even nations. Before making a final decision, the goal should be to completely consider the ethical implications, including the immediate financial impact as well as the lasting consequences. If the organization's climate is to not permit wrongdoing of any kind, then employees are more likely to work harder for the company's common good. Ethical decision making safeguards an enterprise's future.

Managing companies in the ever-changing business environment is difficult even without falling into the trap of earnings-only management. But an organization's management can't concentrate on the future if it's worried about any past corrupt business dealings. An ethical culture cultivates realistic expectations with the focus on following sound and unquestionable business principles. Ethics improves goodwill, company perception, employee morale, and even sales. Ethics allows management to be focused on the future, thereby becoming the framework for long-term success.

STEVE HUNTER, is a senior finance manager for equipment at an international company. He has 16 years of experience in accounting and finance. You can reach Steve at (731) 645-4526 or shunter7263@bellsouth.net.

From *Strategic Finance,* April 2008, pp. 51–53. Copyright © 2008 by Institute of Management Accountants—IMA. Reprinted by permission via Copyright Clearance Center.

Authentic Leaders Add Value

Counterfeit leadership comes at a high cost.

KEN SHELTON

Recently on a flight from Phoenix to Salt Lake City, I enjoyed a panoramic view of the Grand Canyon, one of the natural wonders of the world.

Again this month, as I peruse the business press, I'm impressed with the Grand Canyon gap between the results delivered by authentic versus counterfeit leaders (natural wonders of their own worlds). The primary cause of counterfeit? Erosion of vision, purpose, passion, ethics, discipline, and willpower. The primary product of counterfeit leadership? SILT (suboptimal implementation of leadership talent).

Because every other business magazine is caught up in the news and views of celebrity leaders, we try to reinforce the moral "True North" of authentic leadership.

Two decades before Bill George, former CEO of Medtronic, authored *Authentic Leadership* and *True North,* I was writing articles and book chapters on these topics with Stephen Covey. I'm pleased to see these concepts find homes at www.authleadership.com and www.truenorthleaders.com. The Authentic Leadership Institute is identifying many of the best examples (Anne Mulcahy at Xerox, Kevin Sharer at Amgen, GE's Jeff Immelt, Howard Schultz at Starbucks, and Marilyn Carlson Nelson at Carlson Group), and we are featuring their thought leadership.

What Authentic Leaders Do

I like what Robin S. Sharma, president of Sharma Leadership and author of *MegaLiving* (wisdom@robinsharma.com), wrote about 10 things authentic leaders do:

1. *They speak their truth.* We often say things to please others or look good. Authentic leaders consistently talk truth, using words aligned with who they are. Speaking truth is about being clear, honest, and authentic.
2. *They lead from the heart.* Leadership is about people. The best leaders wear their hearts on their sleeves and show their vulnerability. They genuinely care about other people and spend time developing them.
3. *They have rich moral fiber.* Who you are speaks louder than anything you say. Strength of character is true power—and people can feel it. Authentic leaders walk their talk. People trust, respect and listen to them.
4. *They are courageous.* It takes courage to go against the crowd, be a visionary, and do what you think is right. Many people walk the path of least resistance. Authentic leaders take the road less traveled.
5. *They build teams and create communities.* People are looking for a sense of community in their work, a sense of connection. Authentic leaders create workplaces that foster linkages and lasting friendships.
6. *They deepen themselves.* Authentic leaders know themselves, nurture a strong self-relationship, know their weaknesses, play to strengths, and transcend fears.
7. *They are dreamers.* Authentic leaders dare to dream impossible dreams, new possibilities. They create blueprints and fantasies that lead to better products and services.
8. *They care for themselves.* Taking care of your body is a sign of self-respect. Authentic leaders eat well, exercise, care for their bodies, and perform at high levels.
9. *They commit to excellence rather than perfection.* Authentic leaders commit to excellence in all that they do. They raise the standards. What would your life look like if you raised your standards beyond what anyone could ever imagine of you?
10. *They leave a legacy.* To live in the hearts of people is to never die. Success is wonderful; significance is better. You build legacy by adding value to everyone that you deal with and leaving the world better.

"What would your life and leadership look like, how brightly would your light shine, if you stepped out of the limitations that keep you small and stretched yourself into the place that you know you are meant to be?" asks Sharma. "Authentic leadership is all about being the person you know in your heart you are destined to be. It does not come from your title or paycheck—it comes from your being and the person you are."

May you become a more authentic leader this year with *Leadership Excellence.*

Article 5

The Ethical Employee

MICHELE COMPTON

Was it the fall of Enron that started the wave? Or did political malfeasance create the tide? Whatever the instigating event, the issue of ethics in the workplace shows no sign of abating. In fact, the terms "ethics" and "ethical behavior" have quickly become part of mainstream vocabulary.

If you type "ethics" into a Google search, more than 119 million entries are available for your review. In 2002, the Associated Press reported a national scramble on the part of business schools to beef up their ethics programs in business courses.

In the midst of the mad dash to add ethical guidelines to human resource manuals, it's difficult to define exactly what ethics means to the everyday worker.

Top-Down

There are many definitions for ethics: a system of moral principles; the rules of conduct recognized; the rightness and wrongness of certain actions. But there is only one clear, consistent guideline for incorporating ethical practices in the workplace. Ethical conduct starts at the top.

Fraud, stealing, lying and cheating are obvious infringements. However, if a CEO fails to support philanthropic events but expects employees to comply, that's also a mistake.

"Ethics and values are communicated through stories and examples from the top down," says Judy Suiter, member of the McIntosh Chapter in Peachtree City. Ga., and owner of the Competitive Edge, Inc., an organization that provides instructional, assessment and performance-enhancing assistance to companies.

In many cases, a well-versed, memorized and shared mission statement is as far as some employers go toward instituting an ethics policy. But in the case of ethical behavior, the minimum is no longer enough.

According to an article from the publication *Business 2 Business*, ethics begins with the employer. "Ethical employers want to ensure that their employees are above reproach but they must provide them more than lip service to what conduct they will tolerate. Tarnished by shady behavior in the executive suite, many once-solid companies are struggling to regain the confidence of their employees and customers. Management must do more than talk the talk. They must walk the walk."

According to the most recent National Business Ethics Survey by the Ethics Resource Center, companies can add an ethical element to their business with a few, simple additions to their regular best practices, including:

- Make ethics a priority;
- Set a good example of ethical conduct;
- Keep commitments;
- Provide information about culture and compliance;
- Consider ethics in decision-making; and
- Talk about ethics in the workplace.

Businesses that take the time to make ethics a priority will see their good work reflected in their employees.

Businesses that take the time to make ethics a priority will see their good work reflected in their employees.

"Companies that are true to their values have employees that demonstrate those values, through areas such as customer relations and community involvement," says Judy. "We are facing one of the largest labor shortages in U.S. history. How companies treat employees will mean everything."

Don't Swim with the Sharks

They say imitation is the highest form of flattery. So whether you are a business owner, manager or office employee, if you toe the ethical line, others will follow. For the everyday worker, this may be a littler harder to define. You don't cheat, lie on your time sheet or misuse company funds; you've got a great head start. But what about ethics by association?

In the latest trend in ethical evaluation, employers are looking at more than just illegal practices. How you conduct yourself with co-workers in the office also speaks to your ethical views.

One of the quickest ways to put your ethics into question is to participate in the company rumor mill. Family-owned or Fortune 100, every company has one. Usually there are one or two people who have their finger on the pulse of the latest gossip. Co-workers seem to flock to their office to revel in the latest misfortune.

Rumor mills are hard for companies to deter. But corporate giants such as Texas Instruments, which has long been a company known for promoting ethical behavior, establish guidelines for how to quell gossip.

According to TI's website. "Malicious rumors and gossip attack the spirit of the individual and attempt to divide us into groups. The ethical workplace that we strive to build at TI is based on trust, honesty, candor, and teamwork and has no place for the malicious games that people play."

To dispel the urge to rumor, the company issued the following guidelines:

1. "When you pass information, casually or not, do so in a manner that ensures that the message heard by those listening is as accurate as possible. Avoid insinuations, quibbling, and half-truths.
2. If you are not sure of the information's accuracy, don't repeat it.
3. If it is a case of obvious rumor spreading or malicious gossiping, try to stop it in an appropriate manner such as interrupting the speaker and questioning the source of information. Let it be known that you do not approve of such activity.
4. Seek help from co-workers, team members, supervisor, manager or Human Resources—whatever is appropriate to stop the rumor mill."

Knowing how to avoid the water-cooler chat is just one way employees can defend their ethics. However, business cultures are becoming just as popular a skill set. Companies used to hire using skill and personality typing to assess compatibility. In some cases, an ethics assessment has replaced that paradigm.

"Companies are incorporating hiring assessments to reveal behavior styles that could compliment or contrast with the company's cultural and ethical styles," says Judy. "This enhances or even replaces the personality typing that has been used in the past."

Employees have to do more than sign a contract to adhere to company ethics policies: they have to be ready to demonstrate their commitment.

Swimming in the Mainstream

Ethics has taken such a mainstream position that even volunteer organizations are creating a Code of Ethics to which members must adhere.

In fact, the American Business Women's Association was nominated for the 2006 Stanley C. Pace Ethics and Leadership Award from The Ethics Resource Center (ERC) Fellows Program, for its concerted effort to offer more business ethics training to its members through such programs as the "ABWA Extreme Makeover: Ethics and ABWA Groups."

At the end of the day, ethics is really about people—how we treat each other and expect to be treated in return.

At the end of the day, ethics is really about people—how we treat each other and expect to be treated in return.

So while it is important to know and follow company guidelines, how an employee interacts with fellow employees—or how a member supports a fellow member—says more than a single negative behavior.

Tom Peters, author of *In Search of Excellence* (Harpers & Row, 1982), once wrote. "High ethical standards—business or otherwise—are above all, about treating people decently. To me (as a person, business person and business owner) that means respect for a person's privacy, dignity, opinions and natural desire to grow, and people's respect for (and by) co-workers."

From *Women In Business*, May/June 2007, pp. 12–14. Copyright © 2007 by American Business Women's Association. Reprinted by permission.

Truth or Consequences
The Organizational Importance of Honesty

ERLINE BELTON

"We do not err because truth is difficult to see. It is visible at a glance. We err because this is more comfortable."
—Alexander Solzhenitsyn, Nobel Prize Winner, Soviet Writer and U.S. Citizen

We have all experienced the public lie that goes unchallenged. It may be baldly untrue but somehow accepted as the basis for action with life and death consequences. Some of our experience of public lies may be based on differences in values or perceptions, but sometimes what is said just simply violates the facts—this is disheartening and drives people out of public participation.

The same may be said of organizations. A nonprofit may, on the surface, be making every effort to promote teamwork and "the higher good," but if its people continue to perceive a culture that supports a different and less reliable set of operating norms and assumptions than what is written or espoused, they will not bring themselves wholly to our efforts.

Here are some typical reasons for telling lies:

- to avoid pain or unpleasant consequences;
- to promote self-interest and a particular point of view;
- to protect the leaders or the organization;
- to perpetuate myths that hold the organization or a point of view together.

Regardless of why they are told, untruths and lies can cause people to disengage—and they can also diminish the spirit people bring into the workplace. This leads to a sometimes massive loss of applied human intellectual and physical capital assets. A disinvestment of human spirit results in what I refer to as a Gross National People Divestiture (GNPD). The GNPD index in any organization or society can be directly related to the prevalence and magnitude of untruths told and allowed to stand. GNPD occurs when your organization's tolerance of untruth creates a climate of cynical disbelief engendering a lack of trust in information and relationships. This automatically creates management problems that are sometimes difficult to put your finger on but are often very powerfully present nonetheless.

Our challenge is to buck the culture and engage people in building a climate of truth telling that will lead to a newly revived work ethic and heightened individual and collective energy. In order to do this effectively, we must understand the conditions that support the emergence of truth, and understand and eliminate those that routinely undermine its presence in our organizations.

Staying Safe: Are You Avoiding Pain, but Inviting Extinction?

According to psychologist Abraham Maslow, our strongest mutual instinct is to be safe from harm and to protect our sense of well-being. It is this instinct that guides us to avoid risk (or what we perceive to be risk), and to respond cautiously to changes in our environment, relying heavily on familiar patterns of behavior in an effort to promote and sustain a sense of equilibrium. As coworkers or managers, this instinct often propels us to play it safe and go along with the program. Ironically, in a quickly changing environment this is obviously counterproductive.

Thus, too often, we opt for the illusion of stability in order to promote a sense of psychological well-being. This sense is acquired in exchange for at least a fragment of the whole truth; and since we all know "the truth" is relative anyway, we hardly notice the cost. It is true that we all seek solid ground when in doubt. But does that solid ground need to be sameness? Solid ground might be, for instance, a place to stand for something we can believe in and whose integrity we can rely on when all else appears undependable and unpredictable.

Over time illusions dissolve and evaporate. When they do, those who have used them for grounding are left less safe, less secure than ever. And those who have allowed even the smallest of illusions to inform our management decisions, have placed entire organizations, teams and ourselves at risk.

Because of the diversity of perspectives and information available in any group, a collective organizational "truth" has the potential to be stronger and more accurate than any one individual's truth. But it is only when we have the combination of individual as well as collective seeking of truth, that organizational potential is realized. This requires an open atmosphere where people can depend upon one another to engage honestly, respectfully, and with spirit intact. It requires the testing of personal assumptions among people and that requires a level of trust.

More often than not, organizational potential is not realized. Why? Team meetings, team coordination, and team feedback all involve a diversity of people and personalities that have at least one thing in common: they don't want to get hurt; they don't want unpleasant things to happen; they want to feel safe; and they want to contribute. We, as fallible individuals create the environment, and environmental conditions can support either truth or lies.

Conditions That Support Untruths

Groupthink. The tendency to just go along with the crowd, avoid drawing criticism to ourselves, and assume that everyone agrees, is so subtle and unconscious that we are generally unaware of it. As a result, we often all wind up somewhere nobody really wanted to be. For instance, imagine the scenario of an organization trying to decide on whether to apply for a major contract. Most staff members are in favor of going forward while a few are privately concerned that the organization does not have the capacity to handle the work or the money. The push toward acquiring the contract is so strong that the isolated few remain silent for fear of being characterized as pessimists or naysayers. The organization lands the contract and finds itself in terrible straits trying to handle the management challenge. One variation on this is situations in which everyone knows something but there is an undercurrent of pressure not to state it aloud. Colluding in lies can be crippling. In one organization I know, the staff was asked about the biggest lie inhabiting the organization. After much hemming and hawing, one man finally blurted out, "The lie is that we provide good services that the community wants. We don't and we treat any client who complains like a troublemaker." He went on to provide examples. Everyone else around the table nodded agreement immediately. Consider the enormous cost of having kept this silent for years! This was a key organization, serving an isolated immigrant community. Unfortunately the dialogue group did not include the executive director or board members who later did not allow the conversation to progress further. This was seven years ago, and to this day, funders see the organization as "chronically in trouble."

Imaginary conflicts. People often choose their words and edit their facts to protect themselves from anticipated reactions. One person's imaginary conflicts can warp the way information is exchanged. In a team, the distortion is amplified by the processes of repetition and groupthink. Eventually, the distorted facts may culminate in a "self-fulfilling prophecy" where our worst fears materialize precisely because we acted in fear. Think about the executive director that everyone soft pedals around for fear of hitting one of her sacred organizational cows. Rather than gently prodding for potential change or aiming for a more open debate about organizational myths, staff members assume that some topics are "off limits" and live in silence with the uncomfortable consequences. Of course, this only fulfills the idea of the executive director as a leader entrenched in her ways, and prevents her from getting accurate feedback—and so it goes.

Hidden agendas. When individuals have their own interests at heart, or believe that something is true but fail to disclose this fact, seemingly straightforward discussions have a way of going wrong. Unexpected disunity and conflict can undermine team spirit and group confidence, preventing the group from working efficiently and effectively. Self-interest isn't so bad in itself, but when kept underground it acts like a dark matter pulling everything in its direction—down. The most distressing of these situations occur when individuals see themselves as self-righteous warriors using any means necessary in their "struggle for justice."

The Spectrum of Everyday Lies

Exaggerating or underplaying the truth. This is often done for one's own benefit, for that of the team, or for a teammate. These lies usually reflect (or exceed) desired expected outcomes.

Shading the truth. This is usually done to make a point or to protect yourself, your team, or your teammate. Again, such a lie is used to make the impression that things are more like you want or expect them to be than they actually are. These lies are often used in a noble effort to protect others from the truth.

Beating around the bush or throwing up a smoke screen. This is a delay tactic used to enlarge the insulation or cushion of safety between you and somebody who makes you uncomfortable. This category includes situations in which you withhold an opinion or fail to tell a person where he or she really stands with you for fear of creating complications or undesired reactions. It also includes instances when you fail to say no directly, when no is what you mean.

Pretending certainty or expertise. There is a lot of pressure in the work-place to provide answers now, to know the facts, the status, the scoop. These lies are often passed off as bravado, but they create unfounded expectations and dependencies in others, thus setting them up for unpleasant surprises.

Not letting others know your true position. Especially in times of ambiguity or controversy, there is a temptation to cover yourself by either making your stand unclear, or stating it in such a way that it sounds as if you are in agreement with others when, in fact, you are not. This is a common feature of groupthink and often leads to outcomes nobody really wanted, but everybody assumed they did!

Consciously withholding relevant information. This is often used as a kind of power play to leverage the value and impact of information that you have. By not fully disclosing your knowledge, you are in fact manipulating people for your own purposes (whatever they may be).

Perceptions of powerlessness. Especially in teams with strong leaders, people may feel they have no legitimate voice and are vulnerable (by proximity) to the "powers that be." Opting to assume that others know best, some people often let others make choices and decisions for them, and withhold information that might influence the discussion. Once this happens, these people have made themselves powerless to do anything but accept the consequences.

Perceptions of invulnerability. Belonging to a successful team can be exhilarating—so exhilarating that maxims such as "success sows the seeds of its own failure" seem irrelevant and only applicable to somebody else. There is a strong sense of being "in the know" and having a unique advantage over others who are outside the circle of your team. This can lead to carelessness, letting perceptions, communications, and facts slide by without diligent examination and discussion.

Misplaced loyalty or dysfunctional rescuing. Relationships that have longevity often interfere with the ability to be objective about performance, and ultimately one's competence to do the job. Loyalty to these relationships can cause individuals to look the other way and avoid listening to obvious data that suggests that either the person is in the wrong position, or that it is time to move on. Silence on the issues of lack of performance is a major untruth. If unacknowledged it creates disharmony and reduces leadership's credibility. Once acknowledged, and once actions have been taken, an environmental unfreezing occurs that revitalizes human spirit and performance.

Failing to give due credit. A common way of self-promotion in a group setting, this denies or diminishes the value of others' input and contributions. It disempowers people and leads to the inappropriate use of human resources.

Deluding yourself—self-deception. This is perhaps the most common source of everyday lies. You have both conscious and unconscious internal mechanisms that operate to protect you from cold hard facts in the misguided belief that what you don't know won't hurt you. These self-deceptions set you up for hard falls, and introduce faulty information into whatever team dynamic you are part of.

Conditions That Support Truth Telling

Individual examination/accountability. Individual organizations and teams can "build better truths." Since untruths can be intentional, the truth must be intentional. Collective truth for a team is the result of individual encouragement through consent that is informed, uncompelled, and mutual. The leader has a critical and essential role as role model and must understand that his or her behavior is under more scrutiny and will be given more weight than that of the others. If the leader fails at this, the organizational setting will also fail.

Visible commitment to truth telling. Relentlessly stating that truth telling has value is only the first step. Explaining thoughts, acknowledging the power of our words, and being accountable to one another for our actions will demonstrate that concept. In spite of our fear about telling the truth, relationships can be consistently strengthened with truth as the foundation.

Collective truths and collective responsibility. All team members need to collaborate in a dialogue that sets the foundation for an agreed-upon definition and description of "reality." This vision of reality is not complete until each member gives explicit consent and can accept the idea that the view of reality presented, even with qualifications, is one that they can sign on to. Once there is ownership and a feeling of collective responsibility, a future can be created. This kind of dialogue requires personal risk, courage, and time.

The whole truth. Access to reliable, solid, and truthful information is the one commodity every person, regardless of role or position, needs in order to succeed. As people who live or work together, we require information that is communicated openly and freely. Information based on the "whole truth" informs decisions, actions, behavior, and dialogue to support an outcome. Organizations that support truth telling understand that there are four critical components to the whole truth, and to laying the foundation for achieving outcomes that have meaningful results and credibility: information must be complete, timely, accurate, and true.

Information flow. Information creates its leaders' legacies and the values they stand for. Consider an organization's values and beliefs in the context of its history and current reality. All available facts and information (including personal stories, feelings, and visible and invisible reactions) are on the table in an accurate and accessible way; all information is understood and shared.

Free choice, sustained environmental spirit, safety. In organizations that value truth telling, each individual is free to evaluate and decide based solely on the merit of available truthful facts; there isn't even a hint of social, political, or economic coercion. The environment must show evidence that it is "safe" to tell the truth. There must be visible examples of situations where the truth was told, acknowledged, and acted on—and the consequences were *not* punitive. This does not mean that the truth may not bring a fallout; that could very well happen. People will leave organizations in which they don't fit, and that is a positive thing for the organization and the individuals involved.

Laying a Solid Foundation

Running an organization based on truth requires—and demands—the taking of personal risks and time. The perception that time is limited, or the fear that the truth will hurt us, or hurt someone or something we care about, are perhaps the greatest obstacles to organizational truth telling.

Busy men and women are always looking for shortcuts and abbreviations to help speed things along. But truth lies at the very foundation of a successful organization, and you can't lay a solid foundation when you cut corners; doing so places the whole structure in danger of eventual collapse. But if your culture now includes a tolerance for and comfort with lying (as it is described in the aforementioned "spectrum"), you have to be explicit about changing your culture and about what the "whole truth" must include. And then you must patiently and persistently inch your way toward it, in practice. Organizational healing and reconciliation are the natural first steps toward restoring a culture where truth telling is a value. It is through the process of making the change as an organization-wide effort that we reclaim the vital human spirit necessary for renewing our organizations, communities and country. Truth telling leads to freedom. Freedom requires that we challenge the way things are in organizations if we truly want them to accomplish what is in our collective hearts.

ERLINE BELTON is the CEO of the Lyceum Group in Boston. She has been identified by clients as an organization healer, and feels honored to be of service as she practices organization development from her heart and head.

Editors' Note—Recent *NPQ* articles on organizational conflict ("Brave Leadership in Organizational Conflict," by Kenneth Bailey, Winter 2004) and defensive behavior ("Defending Defensiveness," by Sandra Janoff, Spring 2004) have brought a terrific response from readers throughout the country. It is clear that interpersonal skills and behavior, and the organizational systems that either support or undermine a healthy exchange, continue to be of central concern to people in nonprofits. This article by Erline Belton serves as a companion to these other articles, presenting a complementary vision of the group and personal skills that are needed to propel our organizations forward.

From *The Nonprofit Quarterly,* Summer 2004, pp. 57–60. Copyright © 2004 by The Nonprofit Quarterly. Reprinted by permission.

How to Make Unethical Decisions

ANDREW SIKULA, SR. AND JOHN SIKULA

People make decisions and solve problems in a variety of ways. Oftentimes, little if any thought goes into choice selection. Sometimes, even very important decisions are made without serious contemplation of potential alternatives and their consequences. Many different tools/techniques and rationales are utilized in problem solving and decision making with little or no regard to ethical judgment and/or aftermaths. Some ways of making choices are worse than others when using pity parameters. This article discusses commonly used but ethically unsound methods of making selections. Later in the writing, appropriate standards and benchmarks for determining ethical action will be presented.

Unlawful Discrimination

For starters, we can begin by recognizing that all forms of illegal discrimination involve unethical decisions. In general, all unlawful acts are also unethical activities. There are some exceptions to this statement, such as the homeless sleeping in public parks, but such examples and exceptions go beyond the main emphasis of this writing. Later in this article the authors will discuss the fact that legality and morality are not identical. For openers, however, please recognize that personal and personnel employment discrimination in decision making based upon human characteristics of race, color, creed, religion, gender, age, sexual orientation, and/or disability is both unlawful and unethical. More debatable for example, is whether nepotism, that is, giving hiring, promotion and pay preferences to relatives, is legal and/or moral. In most settings, nepotism is legal, although it may violate company policy especially if direct supervision is involved. However, most ethic experts consider nepotism to be immoral because it violates the ethical principles of human fairness, justice, and equal employment opportunity.

Unsophisticated Decision Making Tools & Techniques

Sometimes silly and senseless methods are used to pick among available alternatives. If you want to make unethical decisions, frequently use such popular games as: enee, meenie, minee, mo; pick a number; rock, paper, scissors; and drawing straws. Just as bad ethically but much more frequently used are the ten determination discriminators listed below:

1. Flipping a coin
2. Crystal ball
3. Spinning a wheel
4. Cutting a deck of cards
5. Reading tea leaves, Tarot cards, palms, head bumps, etc.
6. Ouija board
7. Farmer's Almanac
8. Astrology/horoscopes
9. Sorcery/witchcraft
10. Doing nothing and/or relying on past practices

These ten techniques do not need much additional explanation because we all know what they mean and what they involve. As formally trained educators, the authors are amazed as to the frequency with which people admit to relying on such methods, even in very important matters. It should go without saying, but we will nonetheless here state, that ethical excellence and moral management cannot be achieved by utilizing these methods.

Many people are immobilized by difficult decisions. They procrastinate indefinitely, do nothing, and let the chips fall where they may. They may allow others to make decisions for them, or rely on game-like decision making techniques to avoid stress. Such individuals relinquish their free will, which is mankind's most valued asset. Unfortunately, this can then lead to a victim or entitlement mentality where one sees an organization as a villain or enemy causing personal harm or loss to oneself which, they think, preferably can be remedied only by litigation.

Regarding past practices, many people think that it is safe to simply rely on the past and to repeat the same decision(s) made previously. It worked once and might work again. This is a dangerous tactic/strategy because nothing in life is as certain as change. People change, circumstances vary, and timing needs to be adjusted. Making identical decisions and doing things the same way year after year can lead to failure much of the time. It is also boring.

Commonly Used Choice Rationales

Much more complicated and controversial than the previous ten decision techniques are another set of rationalizations used by human beings to justify their choices. These solutions involve cognitions and are much more difficult to recognize as improper preference parameters. It takes serious study and often data-based research findings to convince someone that the following ten rationales are unreliable and anti-intellectual guides for determining or interpreting past, present and/or future ethical behaviors. This is because one's ego and personality are involved, and stating that such directors are not sound ethical indicators is often viewed as a personal attack on one's character and/or integrity. But, after each of the authors having spent over 45 years in higher education, we are convinced, and data-based research supports, that the following rationales are not reliable or sound ethical pointers.

1. First impressions
2. Common sense
3. Feelings
4. Instincts
5. Gut reaction
6. Human nature
7. Groupthink
8. Everyone's doing it
9. Self-interest
10. Conscience

Several items on this list may surprise and/or offend the reader. Additional explanation is needed to clarify these listing inclusions. Abundant research is available proving that first impressions are just as likely to be wrong as right. Common sense is neither common nor sensical. If common sense existed, individuals and institutions would not be having so much difficulty making proper choices. Human feelings, personal instincts, and individual gut reactions are all individually and collectively poor decision determinants. None can withstand the scrutiny of the scientific method when tested empirically. Sometimes, the first five items of this ten-item listing are recognized as being poor ways for others to make decisions. However, to recognize that these five mistakes pertain also to ourselves, is a much more difficult acknowledgement. Seeing faults in others is easy. Recognizing these same deficiencies in ourselves is at least tenfold as challenging.

The next three listed items are collective rather than individual in character. Some people trick themselves into believing that it is human nature to be ethical and to do right and proper things. The opposite is true. Believers accept the concept of original sin where mankind is viewed as sinners in need of repentance. For generations now, schools and colleges, buying into Adam Smith historically and Milton Fiedman et al. presently, have taught that each and every person pursuing their own self-interest will lead to the greater good of corporations, society and the world as a whole. But contrary to popular opinion, greed is not good. And what is best for an individual is not always best for a community. In a free market economy this might be true in theory, but it is a falsehood in actual global practice. Perfect markets assume the free flow of information, goods, services, money and personnel—none of which happens in the real world. Because absolute power corrupts people absolutely, governments have a legitimate role to play in society, and these governments operate ethically best when they are limited and democratic rather than expansive and autocratic in oversight and rule. Self-interest is a justification that needs to be risen above. Higher order decision making requires one to put aside self-interest for the good of a larger group or calling. Needless to say, this is difficult, and it is a very hard lesson to teach and to learn.

Just because a group thinks some way, or everyone seems to be acting in a certain manner, does not constitute ethical behavior. John Gardner has warned us that "the moral majority is neither." The majority of people may not act morally. Laws represent majority opinion, but not always morality reasoning. Laws change over time and geography. Prostitution and gambling are legal in some states but not others. Slavery and polygamy laws have changed over time in different countries and settings. Legality is not morality. Morality is a higher calling and often runs counter to groupthink and community sentiment.

The most difficult truism to buy into from this listing is the fact that your conscience may not always be a proper guide to ethical behavior. A conscience is acquired over time. It is not inherited or part of one's chromosomes or DNA. The conscience is developed over time through education and experience. Some people have learned unethical behavior and they suffer from negative past happenings. A person may have no conscience, or possess one deranged by evil. The conscience is the best ethical guide from the previously listed ten commonly used choice rationales, but it is not a perfect guidance system.

So far we have discussed "How To Make Unethical Decisions" using "Unsophisticated Decision Making Tools and Techniques," and by utilizing "Commonly Used Choice Rationales." If these methodologies do not produce ethical decisions and behaviors, what means can we use to improve and enhance ethical actions?

Appropriate Guides for Determining Ethical Actions

No guidance system is perfect because human misinterpretations of advice can always happen. Given that there may be some human communication problems and limitations, nonetheless, the authors offer the following ten ethical guidance suggestions:

1. Scripture
2. Prayer
3. Learned knowledge
4. Formal education
5. Innate intelligence/wisdom
6. Past experience
7. Correct consultation
8. Meritorious mentoring
9. Positive role modeling
10. Pooled judgment

One of the problems with decision games, tools, and rationales is that they tend to be implemented very quickly or over a very short period of time. Appropriate ethical guidance systems, on the other hand, involve thought, reflection and/or observation often covering months or years of time. Ethical decisions are not made instantaneously. Moral management is a process involving deliberative thought and action. Ethical excellence is achieved by using virtuous values as benchmark standards. These benchmarks provide direction to appropriate behavior.

Although not discussed much in the management and supervision literature, it is an undisputable fact that people use prayer, meditation and/or reflection before making major personal and professional decisions. Scripture, the Bible, and/or the Words of God and Jesus are studied and implemented by Christian decision makers. Other faiths use other sources which they believe provide divine inspiration and guidance.

Human beings also have innate intelligence, learned knowledge, and formal education upon which they rely to help them choose proper alternative actions. Wisdom is developed over time and often comes from the school of hard knocks, past experiences, former failures, and/or selective success stories.

Ethical choices may often result from following the trusted advice of persons with highly developed individual integrity and personal character. The open scrutiny of others, (be it your parents, children, news reporters, et al.), often helps to purify chosen options. This scrutiny, openness, and/or transparency can come from a variety of ethical expert sources including consultants, mentors, and role models. These outsiders must be "correct," "meritorious," and "positive." The authors realize that these are value laden terms, but consensus can be reached on each. Advisors must be righteous, virtuous and exemplar if they are to effectively serve as ethics advocates. Never use advisors with questionable reputations. When utilized properly, ethics experts help to ensure that a person assumes both responsibility for one's behavior, and accountability to others for consequences of individual actions.

Sometimes it is wise to get the counsel of more than one trusted colleague or moral mentor. The best and most ethical decisions can come as a result of the pooled judgment of several monitors. However, it is cautioned here that pooled judgment works best when the consultants number 3-5 in total. Larger groups tend to compromise solutions and average down ethics and decision quality due to groupthink and negotiations. One should not attempt to negotiate between right and wrong. Compromise may be a resolution to a confrontation, but it never results in better ethics and/or a heightened level of integrity.

Conclusion

There are many ways to make unethical decisions. Breaking the law of the land is unethical. Using gamesmanship and quickie tools and techniques also are examples of poor ways to make decisions and to select options. More commonly used are a variety of human rationales which when tested scientifically can prove to be faulty. It is difficult for most people to persistently practice procedural propriety and to exclusively execute ethical excellence. Moral management takes time, tenacity and transparency to implement, but with practice over time, individuals and institutions can learn to replace defective decisions with successful selections.

ANDREW SIKULA, Sr. is the Director of the Graduate School of Management at Marshall University's South Charleston Campus. **JOHN SIKULA** is the Vice President for Regional Centers and Outreach at Ashland University in Ashland, Ohio. Andrew and John Sikula are identical twin brothers and co-authors of the above article.

From *Supervision*, May 2008. Copyright © 2008 by National Research Bureau. Reprinted by permission.

Article 8

Create a Culture of Trust

Take 10 actions to cultivate a spirit of reciprocity.

NOREEN KELLY

Creating a culture of trust starts at the top. Leaders are responsible for creating a culture of shared values and meaning, promoting ethical behavior, and looking after their brand and reputation.

Edgar Schein, an expert on culture, states: "Culture defines leadership. Leaders should be conscious of culture; otherwise, it will manage them."

As guardians of culture, leaders need to live the values. Enron's espoused "values" of respect, integrity, communication and excellence, meant nothing. In a values-based organization, a leader's actions and behaviors align with stated values and beliefs. The leaders at Google, #1 on the list of the *100 Best Companies to Work For,* figured out the formula that works for them: treat people with respect, support their creative endeavors, and adhere to the motto of "Don't be evil."

Another basis for trust is the belief that you, as a leader, are acting in an ethical manner and promoting ethical ideas and practices. Culture plays a greater role than formal ethics and compliance programs when it comes to preventing unethical behaviors. Even after Enron and other scandals and enactment of Sarbanes-Oxley, few leaders have changed their culture to be one where ethical violations are simply not tolerated. This change can only come from the top, and leaders must involve employees at all levels.

Leaders must adopt an enterprise-wide cultural approach to ethics that extends beyond a compliance mentality. By creating a strong ethical culture, shaped by ethical leadership and values, you dramatically reduce misconduct. A well-implemented ethics and compliance program and a strong ethical culture greatly reduce ethics risk.

Reputation is a company's most important asset and a critical factor in earning and creating trust. Based on actions rather than words, reputation is about staying true to who you are. Companies that set high aspirations through their branding and marketing need to live up to that promise. When a gap exists between who a company is and who they say they are, an environment of distrust is created.

In promoting social responsibility, leaders must do right by employees. While protecting the environment, supporting the community, and adopting socially responsible practices are all important, leaders should be first committed to their own employees.

10 Actions Cultivate Trust

To cultivate a culture of trust, follow 10 actions:

1. *Live the values.* Match actions with words. Walk the talk. Live up to the values you espouse. Inspire people through leading by example. Practice and promote alignment with the values daily and send clear signals about what the values are. Make ethics a priority. Model ethical behavior and support those who uphold standards.
2. *Tell the truth.* Be honest. Get rid of hidden agendas. Be simple, straightforward, and consistent. Admit what you don't know when asked a question, and promise to find out. Share what you know, when you know it. If you don't know, say so. If you can't tell, say so.
3. **Communicate, communicate, communicate.** Encourage open communication. Keep employees informed and address issues when you observe them. Create a dialogue. Listen. Engage and involve people at the grassroots of a project or decision when possible. Value people's input and opinions. Communicate the importance of ethics and integrity, along with shared vision and values. Provide clear and consistent communication to key stakeholders.
4. *Be in integrity.* Make good on your promises and commitments. Be realistic. Don't overpromise. Do what you say you're going to do. Take responsibility for your actions and act ethically.
5. *Be authentic.* Engage in honest conversations. Be credible. Be who you say you are. Demonstrate company values through thoughts, words, intentions and actions. Bring words and actions into alignment.
6. *Be accountable.* Admit mistakes. Hold yourself accountable for your actions, words, and decisions to your employees and customers.
7. *Be transparent.* Be visible. Disclose information as needed. Clearly communicate facts to build trust and credibility with stakeholders.
8. *Respect the individual.* Promote mutual trust and respect. Be inclusive. Show empathy. Acknowledge and honor people's feelings and concerns.

9. ***Share information.*** Keep employees informed and address issues when they are observed. Note that decisions may change, and provide timely feedback. Involve people at the grassroots level of a project or decision whenever possible. Involve those who are or could be affected. Sharing of information within and between teams creates dialogue, promotes cooperation, and helps build community over time.

10. ***Do the right thing.*** Much evidence supports the impact of values, ethics and reputation on the bottom line: Values driven companies are the most successful. Companies that fail to look after the reputation aspects of performance ultimately suffer financially. Companies that are great places to work are more financially successful. Organizations with high trust benefit from increased profitability, market value, and lower costs.

Beyond bottom-line implications, leaders should create a culture of trust simply because it's the right thing to do. Adam Smith, author of *The Theory of Moral Sentiments* (1759), believed that virtues like trust, fairness and reciprocity are vital for the functioning of a market economy. Consider the high costs of breaking trust, risking reputation, and sacrificing ethical standards.

Creating a trust culture takes commitment and action. Trust begets trust. Trust sustains trust and repairs lost trust.

Leaders who choose to trust, value, respect, and empower their people are rewarded with motivated and productive people and greater profitability. Leaders who communicate openly and honestly create mutual trust, bolster credibility and engage their people.

Move away from fear-based values toward positive values, and create connections and conversations that maintain trust. In a spirit of reciprocity, participation, dialogue and hope, a culture of trust can be achieved.

NOREEN KELLY is president of Trust Matters. Call 312.988.7562, email noreen@noreenkelly.com. Visit www.noreenkelly.com.

From *Leadership Excellence,* April 2008. Copyright © 2008 by Leadership Excellence. Reprinted by permission.

Article 9

Building an Ethical Framework

10 questions to consider in encouraging an ethical corporate culture.

THOMAS R. KRAUSE AND PAUL J. VOSS

Although we are now several years into the new and landmark regulatory environment that mandates an organizational culture of ethical conduct, there remains little guidance on how to get there. Many companies are engaged in a scramble to create a paper and electronic trail to ward off prosecution, rather than in a well-designed effort to promote or govern the culture of their organizations. While procedure is essential, the lesson we have learned from organizational change efforts is that leadership, rather than rules, finally determines behaviors and their outcomes.

This article suggests 10 primary questions every executive should ask—and expect to have answered thoroughly and well—in order to initiate a culture that encourages and sustains ethical conduct. These questions are meant to be asked and answered among leaders themselves, as well as with employees throughout the organization.

1. What is the relationship between ethics and other performance metrics in the company?
The relative cost of preventing a protracted ethical dilemma or full-fledged scandal is exponentially lower than the costs associated with fixing ethical problems. For example, see "The Cost to Firms of Cooking the Books," by J. Karpoff, D. Lee and G. Martin, forthcoming in *The Journal of Financial and Quantitative Analysis,* for a study of the substantial costs in fines and lost market value to almost 600 firms subject to SEC enforcement before the enactment of the Sarbanes-Oxley Act. Current research demonstrates that ethical companies are more competitive, profitable and sustaining than unethical companies. The challenge for the ethical leader is to find that connection and reveal it to the organization.

2. Have we, as required by the 2004 federal sentencing guidelines, offered ethics training for all of our employees? Does the training provide more than rote introduction of the company's code of conduct?
Ethics training comes in all shapes and sizes, with the most successful moving from theory to practice and from the conceptual to the real. Companies must first settle on an ethical vocabulary, define terms and establish core values. Live case studies can then help leadership and management "solve" relevant ethical dilemmas, both real and hypothetical.

3. What is the relationship between exercising sound ethics and retaining great talent?
Fortune magazine's annual list of the top 100 companies to work for contains a wide variety of companies with no obvious common denominator. Salary, benefits, career opportunities, location and profession all vary. What they do have in common is trust between employee and employer. Ethical behavior with and among employees, then, can lay the groundwork for attracting and retaining the best talent.

4. Have we conducted a "risk assessment" to determine our exposure to major ethical damage? What is our potential Enron?
While each company may have its unique "ethical nightmare," most companies face similar ethical exposures (e.g., to theft and accounting irregularities). Companies must examine the potential hazards of perverse incentives (e.g., compensation based 100 percent on financial goals) and the various "unintended consequences" of policy, procedures and protocols. Companies can reduce or eliminate adverse incentives by never rewarding, intentionally or unintentionally, improper behavior.

Research literature identifies several characteristics predictive of ethical outcomes: management credibility, upward communication, perceived organizational support, procedural justice and teamwork.

5. How can we be proactive in the area of ethics, culture and corporate citizenship?
Leaders need to own and shape the culture as much as they manage, for example, quality initiatives. Research literature identifies several characteristics predictive of ethical outcomes: management credibility, upward communication, perceived

organizational support, procedural justice and teamwork. Well-tested diagnostic tools allow leaders to measure these characteristics and specific behaviors that foster the culture desired.

6. What tone should executive leadership set regarding ethics, integrity and transparency?

Setting an example is just one part of the executive leadership's responsibility. What leaders say, think and feel affects the tone as much as their actions. Mistrust, cynicism or indifference from topmost leaders can erode others' loyalty to the organization, to its mission, to employees and to shareholders. Left unchecked, this tone from the top can also potentially push ethical leaders out the door.

7. What does management need from the board of directors and senior leadership to enhance and buttress corporate ethics?

Employees who see the governing board and executive leadership as unconcerned will discount any directives about ethics that come from them. Consistency and authenticity from the board and executive leadership play a signal role in establishing an ethics initiative. At a minimum this means providing a reasonable budget of time, talent and money.

8. Who is driving ethics and compliance in the company?

The recent American Management Association report *The Ethical Enterprise* (2006) shows that ethical companies do not happen by accident. Companies need to designate internal drivers who move along the discussions, training and initiatives, producing ethical outcomes.

9. Do we have consistency of message between and among the board, the CEO, the senior executive team and the associates in terms of ethics and culture?

We all need to be on the same page, but finding the proper tone and guidance can be tricky. Establishing a common vocabulary can help with this process. For example, what does it mean to act unethically? What is an ethical dilemma? Who were Aristotle, Plato and Machiavelli, and how can they help provide a vocabulary for our company? What ethical model do we want to follow? What can we do to make it stick?

10. What roadblocks now discourage ethical conversations and the implementation of ethical practices, procedures and protocols?

Most people want to act with ethics and integrity, "to do the right thing." Yet our current approach to ethical conversation often does not advance our thinking or practice past our own perspectives. The object of dialogue, as advocated by physicist David Bohm, is "not to analyze things, or to win an argument, or to exchange opinions. Rather, it is to suspend your opinions and . . . to listen to everybody's opinions, to suspend them, and to see what all that means. . . . And if we can see them all, we may then move more creatively in a different direction." (For more information, see "On Dialogue," Ojai, Calif.: David Bohm Seminars, 1990.)

> **Most people want . . . "to do the right thing." Yet our current approach to ethical conversation often does not advance our thinking past our own perspectives.**

Starting the Conversation

Asking these 10 questions at board meetings, in leadership team meetings, and in the course of day-to-day interactions with employees engenders a climate that leads, over time, to zero tolerance for ethical lapses and impropriety. They also help executives assure their own diligence and oversight of ethical risks and threats, and deliver on their promise to employees, shareholders, customers and the community at large.

THOMAS R. KRAUSE, PhD is author of several books and Chairman and Co-founder of Behavioral Science Technology, Inc. (BST), an international performance solutions consulting company. He focuses on executive leadership development and coaching for clients including NASA, BHP Billiton and the FAA. **PAUL J. VOSS**, PhD is Ethics Practice Leader with BST. An author, scholar and lecturer, Dr. Voss' clients include Home Depot, the FBI lab, General Electric and Russell Athletics.

From *CRO*, May/June 2007, pp. 34–35. Copyright © 2007 by CRO Corp., LLC. Reprinted by permission.

Ethical Leadership
Maintain an Ethical Culture

RONALD E. BERENBEIM

In the United States, the consensus regarding the need for ethical business practice has been codified in *The Revised Sentencing Guidelines*, which is widely accepted as an authoritative business conduct guidance document in the United States and elsewhere—a template for sound business practice.

Compliance with the *Guidelines* requires that a high-level person be responsible for the company's ethics program and foster an ethical culture within the company. Such an environment affords assurance that people are free to ask questions and raise concerns. Meeting the demands of the *Guidelines* demands ethical leadership. For example, in Australia, a company can be criminally liable if it fails to maintain a culture that requires compliance with the law—if the culture directs, tolerates, or leads to noncompliance with the criminal provisions proscribing the bribery of foreign public officials. This standard helps companies avoid these problems with descriptions of the necessary structural, operational, and maintenance elements for effective compliance.

Three Lessons from Nehru

As an example of ethical leadership of the highest order, consider the case of Jawaharlal Nehru. In 1937, Nehru had just been elected to a second, consecutive term as President of the Indian National Parliament. Rabindrath Tagore, the Indian poet, philosopher, writer, and Nobel laureate hailed him as "representing the season of youth and triumphant joy." Even a British official wrote of him at the time, "there is no doubt that his manliness, frankness, and reputation for sacrifice attracts a large public."

Though widely held, this favorable view was not unanimous. One anonymous writer vigorously dissented. In a severe attack published in the *Modern Review*, the critic said: "He has all the makings of a dictator in him—vast popularity, a strong will directed to a well-defined purpose, energy, pride, organizational capacity, ability, hardness, and with his love of the crowd, an intolerance of others and a certain contempt for the weak and inefficient. His conceit is formidable. He must be checked. We want no Caesars."

The author of this vitriolic article was none other than Nehru himself. Recalling this episode is not to make a judgment about Nehru but to demonstrate how his behavior in this situation shows an intuitive grasp of the essence of ethical leadership. Nehru understood that a leader is most ethical and effective when his or her power is limited—by institutional arrangements and the criticism that results from harsh public scrutiny. If the Congress Party and the Indian press lacked these resources, he believed that it was necessary for him to supply the discipline that these countervailing forces ordinarily would have imposed.

From this great example of ethical leadership, I draw three lessons:

1. Ethical leaders don't hide from debate. An ethical leader understands that open and contentious debate is essential to making the best possible decisions. And openly debated decisions result in better outcomes. Some years ago, a research study focused on the behavior of members of investment clubs, small and somewhat informal gatherings of private individual investors, in the United States. Those groups in which the members enjoyed one another's company, reached consensus quickly, and were polite and civil, had a much poorer performance record than the clubs whose investment choices were the result of contentious debate.

An ethical leader understands that open and contentious debate is essential to making the best possible decisions. Although encouraging debate is essential, ethical leadership must balance the need for robust discussion with the requirement of commitment to a common purpose. Where such a consensus is lacking there is a danger of polarization, which will cause people to avoid the risk of winding up on the wrong side and in so doing limit their comments to information that everyone already has.

These findings tell us something that most of us already know—and often forget—or at least choose to believe is good advice for other organizations (perhaps even our competitors), but not our own. Leaders who ignore this wisdom put their enterprises at great risk. For confirmation of this view, one need look no further than the U.S. Presidential Commission report released March 30, 2005, on the intelligence failures in Iraq. The report recommended moving "away from the intelligence community's tradition of searching for consensus, in favor of opening up internal debate and including a more diverse spectrum of views."

2. *Ethical leaders are active participants.* Leaders need to be active participants in the debate over alternatives. In some circles, it has become a fashionable corporate model for the CEO to say to the senior executives, "You people thrash it out, reach a consensus, and send me your recommendation." Such a decision-making process has serious flaws. The most robust internal processes are of no avail if the leader is exempt from them. Good leaders don't just subject themselves to the need to test their ideas—they welcome the opportunity and have a zest for intellectual combat. They realize that there is more to leadership than giving orders. Ethical leaders understand that their views and decisions are in large measure determined by their contact with the people they lead.

Among other advantages, these discussions provide a necessary dose of reality. Nehru's self-criticism attacked his own "conceit" and what he believed to be his "intolerance of others and [a certain] contempt for the weak and the inefficient." He seemed to understand that however decisive and effective a leader's decision-making powers may be, the implementation of a decision requires great patience and tolerance. Or to put it another way, as the 19th-century Prussian general Helmuth von Moltke once said, "No plan survives contact with the enemy." And one can only add that untested ideas are likely to be a plan's first casualty.

Another consequence of the arrogance resulting from a leader's isolation and immunity from full disclosure and accountability is a loss of the public esteem that is essential for maintaining power. In the end, Enron was destroyed by the incompetence of its leadership. Had that not been the case, it is still entirely possible that the company would have met a similar fate anyway if and when the public learned of senior management's greed and wanton extravagance.

3. *Institutional sustainability comes first*. This principle entails an understanding of limits—not those that are imposed by institutional arrangements, the need for public approval, or even self discipline—but rather the limits of human mortality. The final task of ethical leadership is to put in place the requirements for institutional sustainability that survives the loss of any one person. Perhaps the best test of leadership is the state of the enterprise 20 years after the leader has left. Are decisions made in an orderly way? Is the leadership accountable? Is the transfer of power completed without serious disruption? Has the founding vision survived but also accommodated itself to changing economic, social, and political realities? The final task of ethical leadership is to put in place the requirements for institutional sustainability that survives the loss of any one person.

Judged by those standards, Nehru gets high marks. He understood that leaders function best when they are subject to limits, understand those constraints, and strive in a human way to function within these boundaries. And as Nehru concluded somberly, the ultimate limit is mortality. At the head of the epilogue to his autobiography, he placed this epigraph from the Talmud: "We are enjoined to labor; but it is not granted to us to complete our labors."

RONALD E. BERENBEIM is a principal researcher and director of The Conference Board's Working Group on Global Business Ethics Principles. This article is based on his presentation at The Conference Board 2005 Global Leadership Development Conference in Mumbai, India, and used with permission.

UNIT 2
Ethical Issues and Dilemmas in the Workplace

Unit Selections

11. **Your Privacy for Sale,** *Consumer Reports*
12. **Employers Are Stung with a Hefty Price When Employees Suffer an Identity Theft,** Stephanie Shapson Peet, Esq.
13. **Are You Too Family Friendly?,** Susan J. Wells
14. **Employee Theft: Who, How, Why, and What Can Be Done,** William I. Sauser, Jr.
15. **Businesses Say Theft by Their Workers Is Up,** Sarah E. Needleman
16. **Gender Issues: Sex Discrimination Lawsuits Are on the Rise. Is Your Company at Risk?,** Jennifer Gill
17. **Hiring Older Workers,** Stephen Bastien
18. **Keeping Your Senior Staffers,** Mina Kimes
19. **The War over Unconscious Bias,** Roger Parloff
20. **Reflecting on Downsizing: What Have Managers Learned?,** Franco Gandolfi
21. **The Factory That Refused to Die,** Nanette Byrnes
22. **Fear of Firing,** Michael Orey
23. **Protecting the Whistleblower,** R. Scott Oswald and Jason Zuckerman
24. **On Witnessing a Fraud,** Don Soeken
25. **His Most Trusted Employee Was a Thief,** Shel Horowitz
26. **The Parable of the Sadhu,** Bowen H. McCoy
27. **An Ethical Dilemma: How to Build Integrity into Your Sales Environment,** Theodore B. Kinni

Key Points to Consider

- What ethical dilemmas do *managers* face most frequently? What ethical dilemmas do *employees* face most often?
- What forms of gender and minority discrimination are most prevalent in today's workplace? In what particular job situations or occupations is discrimination more widespread and conspicuous? Why?
- Whistleblowing occurs when an employee discloses illegal, immoral, or illegitimate organizational practices or activities. Under what circumstances do you believe whistleblowing is appropriate? Why?
- Given the complexities of an organization, where an ethical dilemma often cannot be optimally resolved by one person alone, how can an individual secure the support of the group and help it to reach a consensus as to the appropriate resolution of the dilemma?

Student Website
www.mhhe.com/cls

Internet References

American Psychological Association
http://www.apa.org/homepage.html

International Labour Organization (ILO)
http://www.ilo.org

LaRue Tone Hosmer, in *The Ethics of Management,* lucidly states that ethical problems in business are truly managerial dilemmas because they represent a conflict, or at least the possibility of a conflict, between the *economic performance* of an organization and its *social performance.* Whereas the economic performance is measured by revenues, costs, and profits, the social performance is judged by the fulfillment of obligations to persons both within and outside the organization.

Units 2 through 4 discuss some of the critical ethical dilemmas that management faces in making decisions in the workplace, in the marketplace, and within the global society. This unit focuses on the relationships and obligations of employers and employees to each other as well as to those they serve.

Organizational decision makers are ethical when they act with equity, fairness, and impartiality, treating with respect the rights of their employees. Organizations' hiring and firing practices, treatment of women and minorities, tolerance of employees' privacy, and wages and working conditions are areas in which they have ethical responsibilities.

The employee also has ethical obligations in his or her relationship to the employer. A conflict of interest can occur when an employee allows a gratuity or favor to sway him or her in selecting a contract or purchasing a piece of equipment, making a choice that may not be in the best interests of the organization. Other possible ethical dilemmas for employees include espionage and the betrayal of secrets (especially to competitors), the misuse of confidential data, the theft of equipment, and the abuse of expense accounts.

The articles in this unit are broken down into seven sections representing various types of ethical dilemmas in the workplace. The initial article in the first section, **Employee Rights and Duties,** describes the way our personal information is being bought, sold, and sometimes stolen. The next article examines some of the legal consequences resulting when identity theft occurs in the workplace. The last article in this subsection points out that as the proportion of single and childless employees increases, so do complaints of unfairness in employers' benefits and policies.

In the subsection entitled **Organizational Misconduct and Crime,** articles scrutinize the causes and the costs of employee

© 2007 Getty Images, Inc.

theft and explores how seniors are victimized by some type of financial fraud each year.

The selection under **Sexual Treatment of Employees** takes a close look at how women are treated in the workplace and the expansion of sex-discrimination lawsuits.

The readings in the **Discriminatory and Prejudicial Practices** section considers how hiring older workers can contribute to a reliable and dedicated workforce and why Walmart and others are facing class-action lawsuits for job discrimination.

In the next subsection entitled **Downsizing of the Work Force,** articles reflect on the consequences of downsizing, an example of a factory that was able to survive in the midst of rampant economic pressure to close, and why some companies are fearful of firing certain types of employees.

The selections included under the heading **Whistleblowing in the Organization** disclose why some businesses that once feared whistleblowers are now finding new ways for employees to report wrongdoing and analyzes the ethical dilemma and possible ramifications of whistleblowing.

In the last subsection, **Handling Ethical Dilemmas at Work,** some cases and organizational settings are presented for the reader to wrestle with ethical dilemmas.

Article 11

Your Privacy for Sale

Until Valentine's Day weekend 2005, Elizabeth Rosen had never heard of ChoicePoint. But ChoicePoint, it turns out, knew plenty about her.

That's when Rosen, a nurse, received a letter and found out that the Alpharetta, Ga., company had collected information about her. Among the sensitive items it had: her Social Security number, records of her insurance claims, her current and past addresses, and her employment history. Now ChoicePoint was informing her that it had inadvertently disclosed her information—and that of 165,000 other Americans—to a group of criminals. What galls Rosen more, she says, is that all along, ChoicePoint itself "was profiting by collecting and selling confidential information about me without my knowledge or consent."

ChoicePoint, which has $1 billion in annual revenues, is only one entity in a vast and secretive data industry that feeds on private information about you and millions of other Americans. Its inhabitants include corporate mastodons with access to millions of public records; swarms of private investigators, some of whom lie to obtain confidential information; and hundreds of companies selling background checks, profiles, and address lists, all to meet the surging demand from business, law enforcement, and, increasingly since 9/11, the federal government.

The data collectors say that they're not prying but speeding the retrieval of public records for both consumers and law enforcement, allowing businesses to cut their risks for fraud and helping marketers to zero in on customers who really want their products. "More than two-thirds of what we do is regulated by state and/or federal law," says Chuck Jones, a spokesman for ChoicePoint.

Federal privacy and data-security laws such as the Fair Credit Reporting Act and the Gramm-Leach-Bliley Act do guard some categories of data, including information used to determine eligibility for credit or insurance. But a 2006 investigation by the U.S. Government Accountability Office (GAO) concluded that such protections are limited and that Congress should require information resellers to safeguard all sensitive personal information.

Indeed, CR's three-month investigation found that the practices of the data collectors can rob you of your privacy, threaten you with ID theft, and profile you as, say, a deadbeat or a security risk. Worse, there's no way to find out what they are telling others about you. When our reporters requested their own records, they were told that they could not see everything that was routinely sold to businesses. The meager information they did receive was punctuated with errors.

CR Quick Take

Large data brokers have your numbers—Social Security, phone, and credit cards. They might also know about the drugs you take, what you buy, your political party, and your sexual orientation. When we investigated this secretive industry, we discovered:

- Data brokers are willing to sell even your most sensitive information to paying customers, some of them crooks.
- When CR staffers asked to see their own files, they received scant information. One report contained 31 errors.
- The federal government is a steady customer of the data collectors, but there's no way to know what it collects or exactly how much it pays.
- Pretexters, who lie to get information about you and sell it to anybody, operate largely free of regulation.

The Data Food Chain

Data and list brokers of all stripes and sizes have collected information about individuals for decades. In recent years, however, faster computers and cheaper electronic data storage have fueled the growth of giant information aggregators, such as ChoicePoint. They have put the industry on steroids by feeding on public record databases, acquiring companies with analytic software, and consolidating it all in a centralized online resource where it can be categorized, searched, and sliced into customized slabs for resale.

Among the horde of data brokers, Acxiom, LexisNexis, and ChoicePoint are some of the most prominent. Acxiom, a giant with $1.2 billion in annual revenues, processes a billion records a day. Major clients include American Express, Bank of America, Federated Department Stores—and Consumers Union, the nonprofit publisher of CONSUMER REPORTS. Acxiom officials turned down CR's request for an interview.

LexisNexis, with $2 billion a year in revenues, got its start in Dayton, Ohio, supplying data to the U.S. Air Force. It has long aggregated news, business, and legal documents, but with its acquisition last year of Seisint, which resells public records to law enforcement and private investigators, it is focusing on security. "LexisNexis products and services help to power the consumer economy, fight terrorism, and keep our streets and homes safe," says David Kurt, a company spokesman.

> ### Her Information Sold to Crooks
>
> WHO: Elizabeth Rosen, nurse, California
> WHAT HAPPENED: Rosen learned in February 2005 that she was a victim of a large ChoicePoint data breach. Her credit report revealed no problems initially, but she recently has been hounded by calls from bill collectors who ask for other people. ID theft experts say that those calls may indicate a thief has been using her Social Security number under a different name and address—a growing trend in ID fraud.

> ### A Murder from $150 of Data
>
> WHO: Viola Berkeyheiser, Washington Crossing, Pa.
> WHAT HAPPENED: Berkeyheiser's husband, William, was murdered in 2005 by Stanford Douglas, a mentally ill former co-worker who held a grudge against him for a joke Douglas claimed Berkeyheiser told years earlier. A civil suit filed by Viola Berkeyheiser charges that Douglas located Berkeyheiser through A-Plus Investigations, which bought his address from IRBsearch, another data broker, for a few dollars. Douglas paid A-Plus $150. IRBsearch says, "We have no proof of any of the facts." A-Plus chief executive officer John Ciaccio says that Douglas said he wanted the data for "a legal purpose."

ChoicePoint, which was spun off by Equifax, the credit bureau, in 1997, allows law enforcement to tap its data over the Internet. As the U.S. Marshals Service said in an internal document, "With as little as a first name or a partial address, you can obtain a comprehensive personal profile in minutes." ChoicePoint also keeps claims histories on your auto and homeowners policies and provides access to birth certificates and other vital records, a service it manages for many states.

What They Feed On

The big aggregators (and fleets of smaller ones, including LocatePlus and Intelius) wouldn't exist if there weren't data for them to ingest. Fortunately, for them, the richest resources—public records—are increasingly accessible. Some hire researchers to visit courthouses and county clerks' offices to retrieve information from paper records, but increasingly, state and local governments post records online, making data gathering simpler and less costly for everyone. Open access also increases the potential for misuse of sensitive information. Property deeds, tax liens, and marriage and divorce documents often contain Social Security numbers, dates of birth, and other sensitive information that are golden keys for identity thieves.

A 2004 GAO study found that up to 28 percent of counties in the U.S. posted records with Social Security numbers online. When we checked documents online for Maricopa County, Ariz., an area with the highest per-capita rate of ID theft in 2005, we found individuals' Social Security numbers on deeds, death certificates, federal tax liens, and divorce filings, one of which also included the couple's credit-card account numbers.

Consumers supply tons of data themselves, often unwittingly, because information about purchases, donations, and memberships is now widely shared. "People are surprised that their name even exists on lists," says Greg Branstetter, founder of Hippo Direct, a mailing-list broker in Cleveland. "But most of list creation comes from consumer behavior, whether it is buying from catalogs, ordering magazines, joining associations, or filling out warranty cards." Branstetter recently completed a project that required him to "track down gay-oriented business publications and websites" to provide mailing lists for a client who wanted to market to gay men.

Selling Your Info

Data brokers provide individual background searches for employers and others. They also take in hefty revenues from slicing and dicing your information with data-mining software to create targeted lists to appeal to marketers.

Remember all those colorful bits of detail about your ailments and hobbies that you supplied on warranty cards? In the data industry, they are combined with information drawn from other sources such as public records and credit transactions to provide what Focus USA, a data broker, describes as a "three-dimensional view." Focus's own database covers 105 million U.S. households, with labels such as "Christian Donors," who give twice the portion of their incomes that nonreligious households give to politicians and causes, and a group it calls "Hooked on Plastic," consisting of 4.2 million American families for whom "using credit cards doesn't feel like they're spending money."

Data brokers are not above selling your most sensitive information. InfoUSA, a database marketer with $400 million in sales, promises on its website to "find people who suffer from health conditions such as diabetes" or "search for people taking a certain medication." Clients can order a mailing list of, say, Prozac users or refine the list to include only those with incomes over $100,000 a year. Rakesh Gupta, InfoUSA's database president, says that only "legitimate companies," primarily large pharmaceutical manufacturers, are permitted to buy the lists.

Keeping Your Secrets

Federal law gives you the right to view data that will be used for certain purposes, such as background screening to determine your eligibility for insurance, a job, or an apartment rental. But there's a lot that the law doesn't cover.

Two CONSUMER REPORTS staffers requested copies of their own reports. Acxiom's report for consumers (cost: $5) provided five pages of bare-bones facts such as name, address, phone number, and age. The company included a separate sheet summarizing the range of information that consumers could not view but that the company's business clients could. Among those tidbits: e-mail address, occupation, political party, categories of retail purchases, estimated net worth, and details on their cars. ChoicePoint's free basic report was also skimpy. Only LexisNexis' "Person Report" (cost: $8) provided a little more, listing addresses and birth dates for relatives and neighbors.

The reports also contained several errors, including incorrect addresses, misspellings of names, and an incorrect Social Security number. Data brokers say, however, that they are not in the business of correcting inaccuracies. A letter accompanying the report from LexisNexis, for example, says, "We do not examine or verify our data, nor is it possible for our computers to correct or change data that is incorrect."

"It's easy to see how an ordinary consumer could fail to get a job or an apartment," says Richard Smith, a Boston Internet security consultant, "or even end up on a no-fly list, now that the government is becoming such a big client, too."

Given the sensitivity of the information that brokers distribute, ensuring its security should be a top priority. The three major data brokers have all suffered major breaches in recent years, although only ChoicePoint's thus far has led to censure by the Federal Trade Commission. It slapped the company with a $10 million fine, the largest civil penalty in agency history. It also harshly criticized the company's security and record-handling procedures. Instead of limiting access to legitimate businesses or government agencies, the company released data to crooks whose requests used commercial mail drops as business addresses, "an obvious red flag," the FTC said. As it turned out, a Nigerian fraud ring was behind the breach.

In February 2005 consumers began to learn about the data breach. To date, says Brian Hoffstadt, an assistant U.S. attorney who co-prosecuted the case against the data thieves, $600,000 worth of fraudulent credit-card charges have been documented involving an estimated 100 individual victims. "For the consumers involved, there could be a ripple effect, and we may not know the true impact for quite a while," Hoffstadt says.

Elizabeth Rosen, the nurse whose information was stolen in the ChoicePoint breach, encountered no problems initially. But more than a year later, she began to be hounded by calls from various bill collectors asking for other people. ID theft experts say that's a bad sign, indicating that a thief might have set up accounts using her Social Security number under other names and addresses—a new and growing trend in ID fraud.

In response to the FTC, ChoicePoint has tightened its security procedures, following mandates to verify the identities of businesses seeking to obtain consumer reports, even visiting some and auditing their use of those reports.

A Steady Customer

Since 2002, a rule change at the U.S. Department of Justice has allowed unrelated bits of personal data to be pieced together to target American citizens as potential threats who merit surveillance or investigation, even if no reasonable suspicion of criminal activity exists. The federal government has become a steady buyer of this kind of information. In fiscal 2005, the departments of Justice, Homeland Security, and State, and the Social Security Administration spent $30 million on data-broker contracts, according to a 2006 GAO report, which also suggested that the data-broker business was at odds with widely accepted principles for protecting personal data.

Another example: To help sell military careers to young people, the Pentagon has bought data from brokers. According to the Electronic Privacy Information Center (EPIC), they include American Student List, a company that signed a consent agreement in 2002 with the FTC promising not to distribute student data to brokers for noneducational marketing without disclosing it to students.

The Pentagon's database has accumulated information on the ethnicities, grade-point averages, intended fields of college study, phone numbers, and e-mail addresses of about 30 million Americans between ages 16 and 25. Those in the database can request by letter that the Pentagon not send direct-mail or telemarketing pitches, but they are not permitted to opt out of the database.

Activist groups, such as Leave My Child Alone, based in San Francisco, complain that recruiters repeatedly call students at home or on cell phones. Felicity Crush, the group's spokeswoman, says, "They have the money to farm this out to a private company, but when we asked the Pentagon to establish a toll-free number for opting out, they claim they didn't have money in the budget."

Finding out what the government is buying has proven impossible. When EPIC filed a request under the Freedom of Information Act in 2001 to obtain copies of records relating to federal agencies' use of data brokers, among the documents it received was a Jan. 13, 2000, PowerPoint slide presentation with the ChoicePoint and Federal Bureau of Investigation logos displayed together above the report's title: "A Partnership for the New Millennium." All other text on the slides had been blacked out, and to date, the FBI has failed to deliver 5,000 additional pages of ChoicePoint contracting documents.

"Over the past several years, we've learned about huge databases of information on law-abiding Americans being assembled by the government directly or purchased by the government from private vendors," Sen. Ron Wyden, D-Ore., recently told CR. "These reports raise serious concerns about privacy and consumer rights." In 2003, he introduced legislation to require the FBI and other federal agencies to provide detailed reports to Congress explaining their use of public and private databases. The bill failed to pass, though Wyden hopes to take up the issue again.

On a Pretext

The data industry has a shady element that includes private investigators and others who practice so-called pretexting: impersonating relatives, company officials, or even law-enforcement personnel to obtain confidential consumer information.

The results can be deadly. Case in point: Amy Boyer of Nashua, N.H., was fatally gunned down by Liam Youens, a stalker, as she left work. Youens had obtained, for less than $200, all of the information he needed to track her from Docusearch.com, an online data broker that, court papers say, hired a pretexter to find out where she worked. A civil suit filed against the company charged that Youens maintained a website describing his plans to kill Boyer. The case was settled out of court. Dan Cohn, president of Docusearch, says, "Our policies and the way we do business has changed as a result."

The murder occurred in 1999, but Docusearch and similar "backgrounding" services have only grown. Rob Douglas, founder of PrivacyToday.com, information security consultants, says, "With the advent of the Internet, data brokers learned how much money could be made selling phone and bank records to customers online, and the feeding frenzy was on."

While some websites require that customers complete a "permissible purpose form" stating that they have a legitimate legal reason for requesting someone's confidential information, Douglas says such requirements are usually nothing more than "legal mumbo jumbo" the brokers use to cover themselves in case something goes awry later. He says faxing a fake letterhead identifying you as a member of a law firm or a potential employer usually can get you what you want.

Customers buying covertly obtained information range from large corporations tracking deadbeat customers to snoops checking up on potential mates. According to statements that some data brokers have provided to congressional investigators, their customers also include local and federal law-enforcement personnel who in this way obtain cell-phone records without subpoenas or warrants. "This illicit marriage between law enforcement and black-market information thieves deserves to be fully investigated," Douglas says.

David Gandal, a Loveland, Colo., investigator who has used pretexting to track debtors skipping out on car loans, says, "Just about every major financial institution has paid for this kind of work." He told CR that armed with a few bits of identifying information readily available to most investigators through large commercial databases, a pretexter calls customer service representatives at a phone company or utility. The person then tricks them into revealing account numbers, passwords, and other sensitive information by pretending to be the customer or another company employee, say, someone in tech support. "I'm a man of many voices," Gandal says. "Sometimes I would pretend to be a stroke victim having trouble getting my words out and they'd help by volunteering whatever information I needed."

While pretexting to obtain access to bank records was outlawed in 1999 with the passage of the Gramm-Leach-Bliley Act, no federal law specifically prohibits using such deception to obtain phone, utility, or other customer records.

Fighting Back

A few fledgling efforts to combat the release of personal information have made headway. B. J. Ostergren, a former insurance claims supervisor, launched an effective one-woman campaign to keep her home county in Virginia from posting its

---

What You Can Do

While you have no control over much of the data collection and sharing that occurs, you can limit the amount of information circulating about you. Also, checking the accuracy of those records that you're entitled to see allows you to spot signs of ID theft and fraud.

Opt out of:

Telemarketing. Put your name on the Federal Trade Commission's Do Not Call registry by going to www.donotcall.gov or calling 888-382-1222.

Unwanted solicitations. Ask financial institutions, retailers, and websites not to share your information with other nonaffiliated companies. Contact the Direct Marketing Association at www.dmaconsumers.org/consumerassistance.html; for unsolicited e-mail, www.dmaconsumers.org/consumers/optoutform_emps.shtml.

Sales of your information to others. The Privacy Rights Clearinghouse lists data brokers that offer limited opt-out policies at www.privacyrights.org/ar/infobrokers.htm.

Keep your information private:

Don't fill out surveys on warranty cards. Just provide your name, address, and necessary product information, and your warranty will be honored. Be careful with direct-mail surveys that don't come from companies with which you already do business.

Don't provide sensitive information on the phone, through the mail, or over the Internet unless you've initiated the contact or you're sure that it's from an organization you trust. If in doubt, contact the organization.

Check what's on file about you:

Order your free annual report from each of the major nationwide credit-reporting companies once every 12 months at www.annualcreditreport.com.

Request your files from the major data brokers: ChoicePoint at www.choicetrust.com and LexisNexis at www.lexisnexis.com/terms/privacy/data/obtain.asp. You can call Acxiom at 877-774-2094 or send e-mail to reference report@acxiom.com.

Get medical information. If you've applied for individual health- or life-insurance policies within the past seven years, the MIB Group keeps data that insurers use to help determine your rates. Get a report by calling MIB toll-free at 866-692-6901.

public records on the Internet. To get legislators' attention, she demonstrated the potential for harm in January 2005 by posting on her own website *(www.thevirginiawatchdog.com)* a few Social Security numbers for people whose records she spotted online. Among them: former CIA Director Porter Goss, former Secretary of State Colin Powell, and Florida Gov. Jeb Bush, whose number was blacked out on Dade County online records after she drew attention to it. "I understand why he'd want to black out his number," Ostergren says. "But shouldn't everyone have that right?"

Employers Are Stung with a Hefty Price When Employees Suffer an Identity Theft

STEPHANIE SHAPSON PEET, ESQ.

Worried about having your vital personal information stolen, and anxious to know how to protect yourself against identity thieves?
Well, you'd better be.

According to the Federal Trade Commission, identity theft has been the number one complaint for the past eight consecutive years. Keep in mind one's identity involves much more than credit. A person's identity includes many parts—vital personal information such as Social Security numbers, driver's license numbers, dates of birth, home addresses, email passwords and ATM information—that are exchanged constantly in everyday life, well outside the boundaries of the credit system. Millions of personal data records are traded for profit on the Internet by people who will use these records for suspicious or illegal activities.

If you have not already been a victim of identity theft, chances are at least one of your friends, family members or co-workers has been victimized.

An employer's vulnerability is even greater. An employer could be held liable for any identity theft that occurs within the workplace—even if the employer did not fraudulently use its employees' personal information.

It's the frightening . . . and expensive . . . truth. Happily, you can protect yourself and your employees from becoming a victim; you can minimize your company's risk of liability. If, that is, you know how.

How Does Identity Theft Occur in the Workplace?

Identity theft is the misuse or fraudulent use of an individual's personal information. The bait drawing such crime to the workplace includes personnel files, benefits data, and payroll and tax records—all of which typically reside in the Human Resources department and can be a goldmine for identity thieves. If these files get into the wrong hands, employers can face considerable legal and economic repercussions.

For example, a Michigan jury awarded employees $275,000 after it found that their union neglected to safeguard their Social Security and driver's license numbers. How often does identity theft really happen? A lot. According to a September 2002 report by TransUnion, one of the nation's three credit bureaus, the number one underlying source of identity fraud is theft of employer records.

What Are My Legal Obligations to Protect against ID Theft?

Given the likelihood of liability when employees' files are misused or mishandled, the federal government and some states have created new duties for employers, making them responsible for safeguarding personal information. For example:

- **Federal Government:** As of June 1, 2005, the FTC amended the Fair and Accurate Credit Transactions ("FACT") Act to promulgate a "Disposal Rule" that requires all employers in the U.S., regardless of size, to shred or effectively destroy all documents and electronic files containing personal information derived from a consumer report before discarding them.

    Although the Disposal Rule applies to consumer reports and the information derived from consumer reports, the FTC encourages those who dispose of any records containing a consumer's personal or financial information to take similar protective measures.

- **Arizona:** Beginning January 1, 2009, Arizona Revised Statutes § 44-1373.02 will bar employers and others from using or printing more than five (5) numbers that are reasonably identifiable as being part of a Social Security number.

- **California:** California Civil Code § 1798.81.5 requires businesses that own or license personal information about California residents to implement and maintain reasonable security procedures to protect the information from unauthorized access, use or disclosure. The term "personal information" includes an individual's first name or first initial and last name, in combination with a Social Security number, driver's license number, California identification card number, account number, or credit or debit card number.

Additionally, as of January 1, 2008, California Labor Code § 226(a) requires employers to display no more than the last four (4) digits of the employee's Social Security number on the employee's wage statement.

- **Maryland:** Companion bills H.R. 56 and S.B. 280 bar employers from posting, displaying or printing Social Security numbers and/or requiring people to transmit their Social Security numbers over the Internet. Also, House Bill 388, Laws 2006 prohibits employers from printing an employee's Social Security number on wage payment documents, including attachments to the wage payment check, a notice of direct deposit of an employee's wage or a notice of credit to a debit card or card account.
- **Michigan:** The Social Security Number Privacy Act (Mich. Comp. Laws Ann. § 445.81 et seq.) prohibits employers and others from using more than four digits of a Social Security number and from sending anything through the mail on which a Social Security number is visible from the outside of the envelope. The law also requires any company that obtains Social Security numbers in the course of business to create, and publish in its employee handbook, a privacy policy that ensures their confidentiality, prohibits unlawful disclosure, limits access to that information, mandates procedures for disposal and establishes penalties for violations.
- **Nebraska:** Beginning September 1, 2008, L.B. 674, Laws 2007 will prohibit employers from posting displaying or otherwise making available more than four digits of an employee's Social Security number.
- **Oklahoma:** 40 Oklahoma Statutes Annotated § 173.1(A) prohibits employers from: (1) publicly posting or displaying in any manner an employee's Social Security number; (2) printing the employee's Social Security number on any card required for the employee to access information, products or services provided by the employer; (3) requiring an employee to transmit his or her Social Security number over the internet, unless the connection is secure or the Social Security number is encrypted; (4) requiring an employee to use his or her Social Security number to access an internet website, unless a password or unique personal identification number is also required to access the website; (5) printing the Social Security number on any materials that are mailed to the employee, unless otherwise required by state or federal law. Social Security numbers may be included in applications and forms sent by mail, including documents sent as part of an application or enrollment process, or to establish, amend or terminate an account, contract or policy, or to confirm the accuracy of social security numbers.

What Should I Do?

Thankfully, employers are not helpless in the fight against identity theft. By complying with state and federal statutes and following these simple dos and don'ts, your company can protect its employees and minimize the risk of identity theft and liability.

Do:

- Keep personnel files and all personal data in secure, locked cabinets.
- Make sure only appropriate personnel have access to confidential information.
- Utilize an electronic monitoring system which allows employers to observe who is attempting to access electronically stored confidential information.
- Carefully screen all employees who have access to personal data and conduct background checks when you hire new HR staff.
- Create and publish an identity theft policy which provides instruction on how to handle, secure and destroy appropriate files and encourages employees to report any identity theft crimes to management.
- Provide information to employees about protecting personal items and areas, such as purses, wallets, laptops, desks and lockers.

Don't:

- Never leave original documents or facsimiles in all-access photocopiers.
- Do not include employees' Social Security numbers on paychecks or timecards.
- Do not use Social Security numbers as a reference number of any kind.
- Avoid sending Social Security numbers in the mail.
- Do not transmit Social Security numbers over the internet without the use of encryption technology.
- Do not require employees to access the company website with a Social Security number without password protection or other authentication technology.

STEPHANIE SHAPSON PEET is an attorney with the Philadelphia-based law firm of Obermayer Rebmann Maxwell & Hippel LLP. She is a member of the firm's Labor Relations & Employment Law Department. Ms. Shapson Peet represents management in a wide variety of employment matters, including federal court, state court and administrative proceedings involving Title VII, the Age Discrimination in Employment Act, the Americans With Disabilities Act, the Family and Medical Leave Act, Section 1981, Section 1983 and common law claims involving breach of contract and wrongful discharge. Her phone number is 215-665-3060 and her e-mail address is stephanie.shapsonpeet@obermayer.com.

Article 13

Are You Too Family Friendly?

As the proportion of single and childless workers increases, so do complaints of unfairness in employers' benefits and policies.

SUSAN J. WELLS

Single employees' inner resentment about married peers' family needs can surface innocently enough.

Thomas Harpointner, chief executive officer of AIS Media Inc., recalls the time an employee of his Atlanta-based technology company left work early on Halloween to go trick-or-treating with his children.

"It did raise a few eyebrows," he says, "and some people poked fun about it." Half of AIS Media's employees are unmarried.

Harpointner got the message.

"We realized that this was no joke—it was a real issue," he says. "If someone needs an afternoon off, it shouldn't matter what the reason is. And if one employee gets the privilege, then everyone should—and we should make it a policy," he concluded.

Harpointner did just that, along with attractive enhancements to a set of employee-friendly—not solely family-friendly—benefits that apply to everyone equally and strive to reward everyone fairly by matching employees' individual priorities, "regardless of their lives or career stages, personal situations, whatever," he says.

More employers, and their HR leaders, would be wise to do the same. According to the latest available U.S. Census Bureau data, the nation grows more unmarried with each passing year.

The Shifting Majority

Unmarried and single U.S. residents numbered 92 million in 2006, making up 42 percent of all people 18 and older. That's up from 89 million, or 41 percent, in 2005. Sixty percent of the unmarried and single adult men and women in 2006 had never been married, up from 50 percent in 1970. Another 25 percent were divorced, and 15 percent were widowed.

Slightly more than one in four households, 26 percent, consisted of a person living alone in 2006, up from 17 percent in 1970. And of the nation's 114 million households in 2006, 47.3 percent were headed by unmarried individuals. That figure fluctuates around 50 percent; it hit 50.3 percent in 2005, for instance.

Essentially, more people live together, marry at older ages or not at all, and rear children in cohabiting or solo-parent households, says David Popenoe, professor of sociology emeritus at the New Brunswick, N.J., campus of Rutgers University. Popenoe is founder and co-director of the National Marriage Project, a nonpartisan research organization at the school.

His July 2007 report, *The Future of Marriage in America*, tracks a decline of nearly 50 percent in the annual number of marriages per 1,000 unmarried adult women from 1970 to 2005. It also notes the rise in households without minor children. In 1960, for example, nearly half of all households had children under 18. By 2000, the portion had fallen to less than a third. In a few more years, it's projected to drop to a quarter, according to the report.

These trends contribute to a burgeoning movement to promote singles' rights, with a growing number of advocacy organizations becoming more vocal about what they perceive as unfair treatment by employers, government and society.

The Backlash

Nicky Grist, executive director of the 9,200-member Alternatives to Marriage Project Inc. (AtMP), a nonprofit advocacy organization in Brooklyn, N.Y., insists that the census data should make policy-makers and corporate decision-makers question and address some longtime, commonly held beliefs.

Marital status simply isn't a meaningful or reliable indicator of what's really going on in employees' lives.

"More of the workforce is going to be single, unmarried or childless—or some combination," she says. "Employers—especially now—need to recognize that marital status isn't a defining characteristic of the workplace any longer. It simply isn't a meaningful or reliable indicator of what's really going on in employees' lives."

The trends reignite some of the work/life backlash that first greeted employers' widespread adoption of "family-friendly" benefits decades ago.

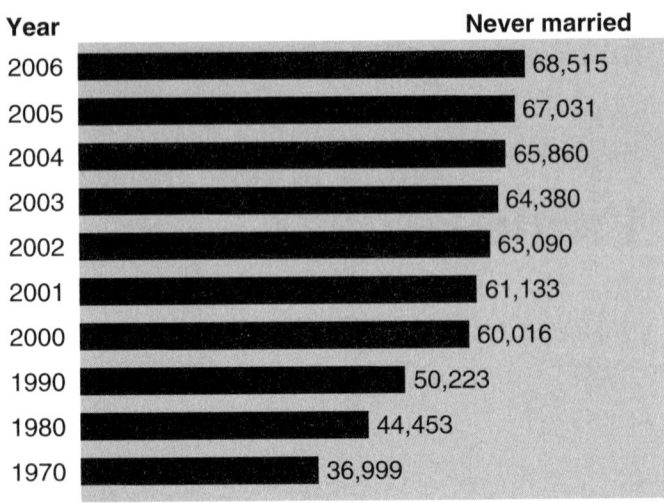

Americans Who Have Never Married, 1970–2006. Total men and women in the U.S. population in thousands.

Source: U.S. Census Bureau, Current Population Survey, 2006 Annual Social and Economic Supplements (released March 2007), and earlier reports.

While 88 percent of 1,909 employees surveyed this spring by staffing and recruitment firm Adecco USA of Melville, N.Y., said they admire working parents' ability to "do it all" when it comes to work and family, 36 percent of men and women said parents' flexibility at work negatively affected team dynamics, and 31 percent said employee morale suffered. Working men ages 35 to 44 reported an even greater negative perception: 59 percent of them said flexibility for working mothers caused resentment among co-workers.

Fueling the Tension

What causes this workplace unease to boil over? Childless singles feel put upon, taken for granted and exploited—whether because of fewer benefits, less compensation, longer hours, mandatory overtime, or less flexible schedules or leaves—by married and child-rearing co-workers.

"The overall assumption tends to be that if you're single, you have nothing better to do—or nothing that qualifies as more important than what your married co-workers have to do—and so you're going to have to pick up what the rest of the workforce can't or won't," explains Bella DePaulo, PhD., a visiting professor of psychology at the University of California-Santa Barbara, and author of *Singled Out: How Singles are Stereotyped, Stigmatized, and Ignored, and Still Live Happily Ever After* (St. Martin's Press, 2006).

On her website, DePaulo collects experiences and complaints from single employees regarding all kinds of perceived work and benefits inequities—and she finds they're frustrated.

"If a single worker complains to a boss or co-worker about such things, they say they often get a hostile response," she says. "No one wants to be unfair—but when the issue's brought out into the open, it's obviously hitting a nerve with both parties."

Even policies dealing with office perks meant to foster employee relations can backfire. For example, DePaulo recalls an annual department picnic at a previous teaching job. Every employee was asked to pay a flat fee—no matter whether they were single or were bringing a spouse and five kids. Although the policy was unfair to singles, effectively causing them to subsidize colleagues' families, confronting the problem without sounding insensitive was a challenge, she says.

Fostering a Singles-Friendly Environment

Wendy Casper, PhD., assistant professor of management in the College of Business Administration, University of Texas at Arlington, has researched single employees' perceptions of how their organizations support their work/life balance in comparison to employees with families.

In a study of 543 singles without children published in the June 2007 issue of the *Journal of Vocational Behavior,* Casper and her colleagues documented that singles viewed more inequity in benefits policies and work/life support from their employers than did employees with families.

"Singles are more in tune with these perceptions than marrieds are," she says. "And company decision-makers, who may have greater access to work/life policies themselves, may not be as intuitive or sensitive to their single employees' views."

As part of the research, Casper identified five measures of a "singles-friendly culture." Social inclusion, equal work opportunities, equal access to benefits, equal respect for nonwork life and equal work expectations are the key, defining characteristics that employers should address, assess and evaluate, the researchers suggest.

They also point to evidence that nonmonetary and more informal elements of employee relations may be as important to equalizing the varied needs of the singles workforce.

"The social inclusion factor had much greater consequences than the other issues did in terms of driving a backlash," says Casper. "Social inclusion plays a big role: When single employees have a sense of attachment and feel more supported at work, it tends to lead to greater retention, productivity and job performance."

Casper speculates that single and childless workers have stronger needs for workplace social inclusion because their relationships and overall sense of community are more likely to be connected to their jobs.

Technology company Texas Instruments Inc. numbers among the employers who have made an effort to increase such inclusive strategies.

To help new employees connect, for example, it started a support group in its IT Services division five years ago. The group sponsors professional development, with "lunch and learn" programs, seminars and mentoring; networking, with happy hours and other events; social events such as WhirlyBall, movies and bowling; and community services such as volunteering and charitable outreach.

Since then, there has been interest among Texas Instruments' other business groups in forming "New Employee Initiative" groups. "It can mean a lot to have a peer group within the company," says Betty Purkey, manager of work/life strategies at the Dallas-based company.

> **Online Resources**
>
> See the online version of this article at www.shrm.org/hrmagazine/07October for links to:
>
> - A U.S. Census Bureau fact sheet on singles' demographics.
> - Census Bureau data on marital status and living arrangements.
> - The Center for Work/Life Law Employer Resource Center.
> - Equal Employment Opportunity Commission guidance on caregiver discrimination and a Q&A for employers.
> - An *HR Magazine* article on caregiver discrimination.
> - A SHRM Online article on ensuring equal treatment for parents and non-parents.
> - A SHRM research paper on work/life balance.
> - A sidebar on benefits preferences among employees.
> - A listing of singles advocacy groups.

Creating a Wider View

To encourage a sense of equality among all demographic groups, more company officials take a wider view of the benefits and work/life programs they provide—with an eye toward diversity, flexibility, neutrality and choice.

"The buzzword shouldn't be 'family-friendly,' " says social psychologist DePaulo. "It should be 'employee-friendly' or 'life-friendly.' "

Indeed, many employers already have renamed their benefits "work/life" or "personal benefits" or have simply gotten rid of the distinction, she notes.

Some employers move to types of benefits that level the playing field by offering something for everyone.

For instance, 70 percent of 326 HR executives surveyed in 2006 by CCH and Harris Interactive said their organizations offer paid-time-off programs bundling vacation, sick and personal leave into one bank of time off that employees can manage more flexibly. In addition, 37 percent of 590 HR professionals polled for the Society for Human Resource Management's 2007 Benefits Survey said their companies offer flexible or cafeteria-benefits plans allowing employees to choose from a variety of benefits and designate a set amount of money to pay for the benefits. These types of plans can allow for different lifestyles without rewarding employees having larger families with more benefits for the same job, for example.

Yet unequal access to employer-sponsored health insurance remains one of the top complaints of many unmarried workers with partners, including AtMP members, says Grist.

According to research by the Human Rights Coalition (HRC), a Washington, D.C., civil rights organization, a majority of *Fortune* 500 companies provided benefits to same-sex domestic partners in 2006. Since then, 17 more companies have added the benefits, bringing the total to 267—or 53 percent of *Fortune* 500 companies, the HRC says.

But while same-sex benefits have been more widely adopted among large organizations, opposite-sex domestic-partner coverage generally has seen slower adoption. In fact, all unmarried couples are still significantly less likely to have health insurance than married people, according to a 2006 study by The Williams Institute on Sexual Orientation Law and Public Policy at the University of California-Los Angeles Law School.

"We found that 20 percent of people in same-sex couples are uninsured, compared with only 10 percent of married people or 15 percent of the overall population," says M.V. Lee Badgett, the institute's research director and co-author of the study. "Unmarried heterosexuals with partners are even worse off, with almost one-third uninsured."

This results in a continuing health-benefits gap for unmarried employees who may be in committed relationships or have other family members they'd like to cover but can't, says Grist. "Access to domestic-partner coverage depends on the definition of your relationship—and whether it's legally recognized," she says. "There's not a clear, legal status that currently describes a lot of these interdependent relationships." Only a few states currently recognize unmarried relationships.

Wayne Wright, PhD., and his partner of eight years, Madeline Holler, fell into that gap two years ago after relocating to Southern California from St. Louis. He had accepted a job as an assistant professor of philosophy at a state university. It was his understanding, he says, that his new job's benefits package included coverage for domestic partners—a perk that he and Holler had enjoyed at his previous employer.

Shortly after their move, however, "our 'unmarriage' began to unravel," Holler says.

It wasn't until orientation for new faculty members, Wright says, that he learned that his employer's domestic-partner coverage applied only to same-sex couples—a distinction that wasn't initially described.

And with the first $400 health insurance premium coming due to continue coverage under COBRA for Holler, Wright felt they had no choice, he says. He booked a hotel room in Las Vegas for the following weekend, and he and Holler were married at the celebrated drive-through on the Strip called The Little White Wedding Chapel.

While they hold no grudges and are secure in their relationship, Wright and Holler also say they felt powerless over what should be a personal life decision. "We absolutely felt forced to do it," Wright says.

Ending Special Deals and Stigma

While companies continue to diversify their benefits, some employers strive to custom tailor the entire employment relationship—including responsibilities, scheduling, workload and benefits—in an effort to end perceived tensions between employee groups and to improve recruitment and retention.

"In the past, an employee who wanted to work in a different way might have made a personal deal with his or her boss," says Ellen Galinsky, president and co-founder of the Families and Work Institute in New York. "Today, employees and employers are working together to find new ways to restructure

ANNUAL EDITIONS

the workplace in unique ways to give people the flexibility they need and to improve bottom-line business measures like productivity and retention."

Take ARUP Laboratories in Salt Lake City, where employees suggested the unusual idea of a seven-days-on, seven-days-off scheme. Workdays are 10 hours each, so employees log 70 hours in all during any given two-week period. They're paid, however, for two 40-hour weeks.

This flexible scheduling, and other forms of flexibility, help the medical-testing company recruit employees in the face of a national health care talent shortage.

Each worker is paired with a counterpart handling the opposite schedule; the two cover for each other if they have conflicts.

"We've created a self-functioning, stable team in which employees essentially get 26 free weeks a year to do with what they choose or need—take time with children, take a class, do volunteer work or go skiing," says Von Madsen, assistant vice president, human resources manager. Along with its menu of equal and neutral employee benefits, the flexible-schedule policy has helped the 2,100-employee company reduce turnover from an industry average of 22 percent to about 14 percent, Madsen says.

The flexibility also has had a positive effect on perceived scheduling and time-off inequities among singles and families.

"It helped eliminate the rift between employees with children and those without, who sometimes felt they had to cover the workload for parents who took additional time off for their children's needs," Madsen says. "It's created a more even footing."

At accounting giant Deloitte & Touche USA LLP, a new approach to career planning will become a corporate mandate in the next year.

Called "mass career customization," the initiative encourages every employee to engage in upfront, open discussion and custom planning about the course of his or her career and life-balance needs, according to Cathleen Benko, vice chairman and managing principal of talent, and co-author of a book about the program, *Mass Career Customization: Aligning the Workforce with Today's Nontraditional Workforce* (Harvard Business School Press, September 2007).

Changing demographics played a part in the design.

"The family structure has fundamentally changed in this country—83 percent of U.S. households are now considered 'nontraditional,' and singles are certainly a part," Benko says. "There's little wonder why many executives are either sensing or already confronting mounting tensions."

Benko suspects these tensions are rooted in the misalignment between the traditional workplace and the largely nontraditional workforce, explaining, "The one-size-fits-all approach no longer works."

Her model divides work into four dimensions—pace, workload, location and schedule, and role—and then builds career objectives in each dimension that match employees' life circumstances along the way, allowing employees to "dial up and down," she says, and then revisiting these choices periodically as circumstances change.

Since 2005, the concept has been pilot tested and is now in the midst of a phased, 12-month rollout companywide, Benko says. Eventually, all 42,000 employees will be enrolled.

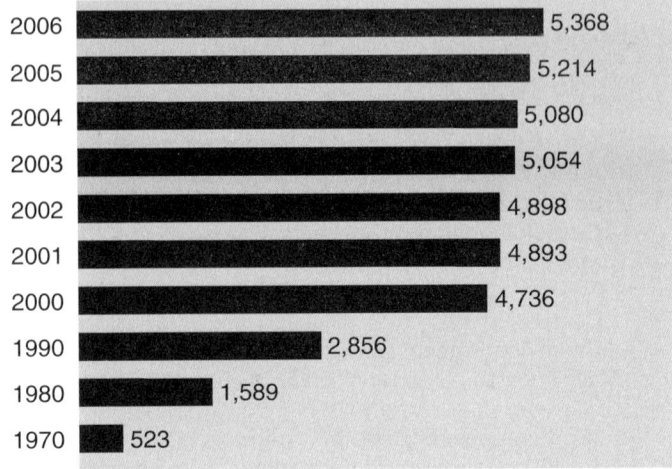

The Number of Unmarried-Couple Households Increases . . . , 1970–2006.

Sources: U.S. Census Bureau, Current Population Survey, 2006 Annual Social and Economic Supplement (released March 2007), and earlier reports.

. . . While the Percentage of Households with One or More Children Decreases, 1970–2006.

Source: U.S. Census Bureau, Statistical Abstract of the U.S., various years.

Interestingly, she notes, the pilots so far have found that "rather than dialing down on their careers, many employees were choosing to dial up," reflecting, in part, the fact that 65 percent of Deloitte's employees are under the age of 35. "Dialing up" refers to increasing one's professional commitment, perhaps by returning to full-time hours or adding hours, seeking the promotion fast-track, or going after opportunities for higher rewards and compensation.

During the pilots, Benko says, employee job satisfaction and retention also rose.

"This approach works because it takes a lattice, rather than ladder, approach to job moves," she says. "Work doesn't have to be an 'up or out' route, and we have a system here that's fluid and adaptable through all life and career stages."

Including All Perspectives

As Deloitte & Touche and other employers test employment customization, one thing is certain: Employment and work/life policies will continue to evolve, as different demographic groups force change and inclusion. And unlike the personal demographic characteristics that workers bring to their jobs, experts say that employers hold the power to create supportive workplace policies.

Demographics change in a clear direction, says DePaulo. Raising awareness and thinking in a broader perspective about the makeup of the workplace become more important. "A singles perspective should be acknowledged right along with the other perspectives. It's not the *only* perspective, but it should be one of them."

SUSAN J. WELLS, a business journalist in the Washington, D.C., area and a contributing editor of *HR Magazine,* has more than 20 years of experience covering business news and workforce issues.

From *HR Magazine*, October 2007, pp. 35–39. Copyright © 2007 by Society for Human Resource Management. Reprinted by permission via the Copyright Clearance Center.

Employee Theft: Who, How, Why, and What Can Be Done

WILLIAM I. SAUSER, JR.

Introduction

The world's major religions, international law, the laws of nations, and most ethical codes around the world proscribe stealing as immoral and illegal. Yet theft by their own employees costs business owners and operators an estimated $100 billion worldwide each year. This article—a summary of literature on employee theft—seeks to answer four questions: (1) How big a problem is employee theft? (2) How do employees steal from their employers? (3) What factors relate to increased employee theft? (4) What steps can be taken to reduce employee theft? In short, how much do employees steal, how do they do it, why, and how can we stop them?

The Nature and Magnitude of Employee Theft

Defining Employee Theft

Hollinger and Clark (1983) define employee theft as "the unauthorized taking, control, or transfer of money and/or property of the formal work organization that is perpetrated by an employee during the course of occupational activity." This definition compares well to Greenberg's (1997) definition of employee theft as "any unauthorized appropriation of company property by employees either for one's own use or for sale to another. It includes, but is not limited to, the removal of products, supplies, materials, funds, data, information, or intellectual property." Greenberg takes pains to note that his definition explicitly and intentionally excludes taking property belonging to one's co-workers, which he characterizes as "professional thievery." Greenberg further distinguishes between *pilferage or petty theft* (misappropriation of items of limited value) and *grand theft* (misappropriation of items of considerable value). These distinctions are among the factors that create wide fluctuations in estimates of the incidence and monetary cost of employee theft. Some estimates include theft from co-workers (or customers, suppliers, and other stakeholders) as a part of employee theft; some include grand theft and even fraud perpetrated against others, while more conservative estimates are limited to pilferage.

Dreyfack (2002) even questions whether it is appropriate to include some incidents of pilferage within estimates of employee theft:

Employee A's paycheck is overstated $1.29; he fails to report it. Employee B forgets that he stuck a pair of pliers he had used on the job in his back pocket, takes it home, and doesn't bother to return the tool. Employee C, paid on piece work, has his output overstated by the checker when he makes the rounds to tally production, and keeps quiet. Are these employees out-and-out crooks or petty thieves?

In a carefully conducted research study of 25 critical care registered nurses working in hospitals, Dabney (1995) found that the majority of his subjects did not perceive petty theft as improper; they saw it as "not really wrong." In fact, theft of general supplies, over-the-counter medicines, and non-narcotic medicines (but not narcotics!) was viewed as a fringe benefit or extra compensation. Other researchers report similar findings; it appears that many work groups have informal norms tolerating or even promoting petty theft (Greenberg, 1990; Greenberg and Tomlinson, 2004; Hollinger and Clark, 1983). Murphy (1993) said, "There is evidence that many individuals engaged in employee theft believe that their acts are not theft at all, that theft is common, in the sense that most employees do the same thing, and that it is socially acceptable."

The fact that there is no universally accepted definition of employee theft makes it difficult to measure with any accuracy the magnitude of the problem. Furthermore, there is no single repository for data about employee theft. Various professional organizations, government agencies, research surveyors, and writers operationally define, measure, and gather statistics about employee theft in different ways. Furthermore, estimates vary in terms of geographical scope, time period considered, type of employee, and a host of other variables. Some writers inflate earlier estimates to reflect today's dollars, others do not. Some report only detected theft, while others adjust their figures to take into account theft that has not been detected—estimated by Davia (2000) to be about 40% of the cases—or theft that has been detected but not exposed due to embarrassment, another 40% of the cases according to Davia. Stating with precision

- A 1974 survey of 100 retail employees found that half of them admitted taking items from their employers. However, 67% of those making this admission did not consider their action to be stealing and 84% admitted to no feelings of guilt in spite of acknowledging that they had taken merchandise (Tatham, 1974).
- A comprehensive research project published in 1983 by the U.S. Department of Justice concluded that roughly one-third of the employees reported some involvement in the taking of company property during the prior year (Clark and Hollinger, 1983).
- 1987 report from the U.S. Department of Justice, based on over 300 interviews and over 200 survey questionnaires from 40 states, found that the organizations reported moderate to very serious problems with both petty theft (37%) and major theft (28%) (Baker and Westin, 1987).
- The Food Marketing Institute (1989) attributed 52.9% of all supermarket theft to employees. A 2004 survey by the same organization found that employee theft accounted for an average loss of $927 per store (Friedrick, 2006).
- In 1993 a pre-employment testing firm rated 52% of 7,443 persons tested as "low desirability for employment" because of admissions related to theft or contemplated theft ("How honest are Americans," 1994).
- In 1994, "employee malpractice" (primarily theft and fraud) accounted for 44% of the losses of Australian retailers, amounting to $955 million (Van Maanenberg, 1995).
- The 17th Annual Retail Theft Survey (2004) found that one in every 27.8 employees was apprehended for theft by his or her employer (based on more than 1.7 million employees) (McTaggart and Tarnowski, 2005).
- According to a 2004 estimate by City of London police, 82% of all fraud in small and medium-sized enterprises was committed by employees (Moody, 2004).
- The British Retail Consortium Retail Crime Survey 2004–2005 indicated that staff theft accounted for 35.1% of retail crime ("Special report," 2006).

Figure 1   Estimates of the magnitude of employee theft.

any overall statistics about the magnitude of employee theft becomes a very tricky matter. With this caveat, here is what the literature revealed.

Frequency of Employee Theft

Figure 1 provides a sampling of some finding in the literature. What can we conclude from it? Is employee theft rampant, as Snyder, Broome, Kehoe, McIntyre, and Blair (1991) claim? Do one-third to one-half of all employees really steal from their employers? "I have employees who look right into our security cameras and still steal," answers the owner of a chain of convenience stores (Buss, 1993). Wimbush and Dalton (1997) were shocked with the high estimates of employee theft, so they conducted their own carefully controlled study of employee theft using three different methods to estimate the percentage of employees who stole from their employer. Their findings: 28.2% using one rather direct method, but 59.2% and 57.9%, respectively, using more subtle methods of detection. "Clearly, our estimates for the base rate for employee theft are potentially disturbing in their magnitude," they concluded.

Hollinger and Clark (1983) provide an excellent summary of research findings with respect to the incidence of employee theft:

> Estimates of the extent of employee-theft involvement abound, ranging widely from 9 percent to 75 percent—all depending on the source of the estimate. . . . Perhaps the most we can say is that theft by employees is a significant and pervasive part of the work experience with between one-half and one-quarter of the typical work force involved in taking company money or property sometime during their employment. (pp. 5–6)

Economic Impact of Employee Theft

Given the findings regarding the incidence of employee theft, it should not be surprising to the reader that estimates of the cost of employee theft also vary widely. This is indeed the case, as figure 2 (another sampling of findings from the literature) indicates.

These findings again illustrate the problems encountered when seeking an estimate of the magnitude of employee theft. Figures are typically reported across economic sectors and nations using calculation methods that vary widely. Wimbush and Dalton (1997), after reviewing a number of findings in the literature, concluded that estimates of losses attributed to employee theft ranged from $6 billion to $200 billion per year, with a best estimate of about $40 billion. They also noted that employee theft accounted for about 70% of business losses and 30% of business failures. Given that their article was published in 1997 and focused primarily on U.S. companies, an estimate that employee theft costs businesses worldwide an estimated $100 billion annually (in today's dollars) is realistically conservative.

Recognition of Employee Theft as an Ethical Problem

No matter what the precise figures, it is apparent that a significant portion of the workforce steals from employers and that the cumulative economic impact of this problem is enormous. Given these assertions, is employee theft widely recognized as an important ethical issue? The answer appears to be a resounding *yes!* The 81 articles in the annotated bibliography supporting this article (Sauser, 2006) came from a variety of research, trade, popular, and governmental organs. Clearly, employee

> - Snyder et al. (1991), citing U.S. Chamber of Commerce statistics, claimed that "Employee theft is a rampant problem throughout American businesses, large and small... An estimated $40 billion is stolen annually from U.S. businesses, ten times the value of street crime... Though the range varies, some loss estimates exceed $200 billion. Even more frightening is the fact that these internal losses are increasing at a 15 percent annual rate."
> - The U.S. Chamber of Commerce estimated in 1994 that internal theft costs American companies more than $60 billion a year, suggesting that the projections cited above are not unrealistic ("How honest are Americans," 1994).
> - Greenberg (1997) concluded from his review of research that employee theft is 10 times more costly than all of the nation's [U.S.] street crime and has been blamed for 30% to 50% of all business failures.
> - Research summarized by Ones and Viswesvaran (1998) led them to estimate that U.S. businesses were losing $40 billion in cash and merchandise to employee theft per year.
> - The National Retail Security Survey conducted by the University of Florida, covering 118 companies in 22 retail markets, estimated that employee theft accounted for an estimated $15 billion in 2001 ("National survey," 2004).
> - An article in the September, 2004, issue of *USBanker* estimated that insider theft (through fraud) costs banks $2.4 billion annually (Krebsbach, 2004).
> - Since 2003, BDO Stoy Hayward (2006) has been releasing an annual survey of fraud research in the United Kingdom. The survey focuses on all types of fraud, including employee theft. They report, "The value of reported fraud continued to rise in 2005, up nearly thirty percent from 2004. The cost of fraud to U.K. businesses now stands close to 1 billion pounds. This is nearly triple the amount of 331 million pounds revealed in 2003."

Figure 2   Monetary loss due to employee theft.

theft is recognized as a problem among retailers, bankers, manufacturers, builders, grocers, small business persons, restauranteurs, hospitals, pharmacies, nursing homes, service providers, law firms, and government agencies. It is even recognized as a problem by librarians. A University of Texas-San Antonio library employee stole more than $200,000 in fines for overdue or lost books and videos from 1997 to 2003 ("Texas staffer," 2004). Oder, St. Lifer, and Rogers (1998) describe the bizarre case of a porter employed at the New York Public Library who stole original Mozart manuscripts and sought to sell them to a used book dealer.

The Southern Institute for Business and Professional Ethics (2005) conducted a survey of 378 chief executive officers of the largest corporations (by revenue) in six southern (U.S.) states. "Stealing/Theft" was listed seventh among the top 10 ethical issues facing the general business community, but second among the top 10 ethical issues facing the respondent's own industry. By industry sector, it was ranked fourth in Health Care and Social Assistance and tied for fourth in Banking, Finance, and Insurance. It was ranked first in Manufacturing and first in Construction.

In a hard-hitting special report, the senior editor of *Professional Builder* provided some insight on why employee theft is regarded as the highest ethical concern in the construction industry. Lurz (2004) claims that job site theft—often perpetrated by insiders—"is endemic to the building industry." He notes:

> Builders have high-value assets delivered every day to remote building sites. Many of these companies are growing fast, more concerned about how to get the next house built than setting up tight internal controls to monitor their employees and others within the expanding production system. The vast majority of builders have fewer than 100 employees, and the production system always includes far more subcontracted workers than employees. This is a recipe for trouble.

Methods Used to Steal from Employers

How do employees steal from their employers? Their methods are myriad. The human mind is innovative and creative, and employees devise new methods to steal every day. In fact, new technologies—such as the Internet, electronic transfer of funds, and electronic banking and securities trading—have opened entirely new ways to steal, including identity theft. Employee theft of personal information is now a leading source of fraud. Says Shreve (2004) "Payroll records, client files and employee applications littered with personal information—including Social Security numbers, residential addresses and birthdates—are becoming increasingly tempting resources for identity theft in the workplace." Daks (2005), for example, reports that insiders at four banks in New Jersey stole and sold information from some 676,000 customer accounts—reportedly the largest ID theft in U.S. history to date.

Every form of business, it seems, features unique ways to steal. Purpura (1984) and Fischer and Janowski (2000) include within their books on security and loss prevention lengthy lists of "tried and true" methods, and figure 3 lists 25 of the common techniques they mention.

Theft schemes common within certain industries are often variations of the "tried and true" methods listed in figure 3. For example, Bogardus (1987) reveals how drug abusers (often nurses) steal drugs from medical facilities. Methods include replacing narcotics with non-narcotic agents, tampering with packaging, altering or falsifying drug sign-out sheets and patient medication records, and theft in the pharmacy and the surgical suite. Gerber (2005) describes common examples of theft in the recreational vehicle (RV) industry:

- A service manager voids a sale on the register and pockets cash paid by a customer.

1. Wearing manufactured items while leaving the workplace. Examples: wearing pairs of pilfered underwear; wearing scrap lead molded to one's body contours.
2. Smuggling out pilfered items by placing them in a lunchbox, pocketbook, bundle of work clothes, radio, umbrella, newspaper, hat, or hair.
3. Hiding merchandise in garbage pails, dumpsters, or trash heaps to be retrieved later.
4. Returning to the workplace after hours, with a pass key, to help themselves to goods.
5. Turning in fictitious bills for fuel and repairs to truck driver employers and then splitting the money with truck stops.
6. Truck drivers colluding with receiving personnel.
7. Padding expense accounts.
8. Receiving kickbacks from vendors for buying high-priced goods.
9. Pocketing money from cash sales and not recording the transaction.
10. Stealing from a cash register then tampering with the tape.
11. Padding payrolls as to hours and rate of pay.
12. Maintaining nonexistent or terminated employees on a payroll and then cashing the paychecks.
13. Pocketing unclaimed wages.
14. Paying fictitious bills to a bogus account and then cashing the checks for their own use (usually accounts payable personnel).
15. "Lapping," which means to steal small amounts from incoming payments and using later payments to cover shortages.
16. Padding overtime reports and kicking back part of the extra pay to the authorizing supervisor.
17. Collusion between maintenance personnel and contract servicemen to steal and sell office equipment.
18. Purchasing agents colluding with vendors to falsify purchase and payment documents. The purchasing agent issues authorization for payment for goods never shipped after forging receipt of shipment.
19. Mailroom and supply personnel packing and mailing merchandise to themselves for resale.
20. Taking income cash without crediting the customer's account.
21. Paying creditors twice and pocketing the second check.
22. Appropriating checks made out to cash.
23. Invoicing goods below regular price and getting a kickback from the purchaser.
24. Manipulating accounting software packages to credit personal accounts with electronic account overages.
25. Issuing (and cashing) checks on returned merchandise not actually returned.

Figure 3   Twenty-five common methods of employee theft.
Sources: Purpura (1984, p. 130), Fischer and Janoski (2000, pp. 65–66).

- A shipping clerk signs for 10 stereos, takes one home and files a shortage report with the carrier.
- An accounts payable clerk generates checks to legitimate vendors. The name on the check is correct, but the address is for her home. Her husband deposits the check into his own business account under the same name.
- A service technician determines the bedroom TV is broken and replaces it, files a warranty claim and takes the "broken" TV home to put in his bedroom.
- A parts clerk gives four friends a 25% discount on their purchases, or scans Model 100 at the register and gives the friend Model 400 instead.

Here are three techniques (all real examples) Knapshaefer (2004) used to illustrate common methods of insider bank fraud: A teller shorts the cash drawer to help pay two months rent to secure a new apartment. A bank vice president sets up a business and agrees to loan his partner some cash by laundering $10,000 from the bank. A bank loan officer, an appraiser, and a real estate broker collude to buy dilapidated property on the cheap and "flip it" by fabricating false records and identities, bilking the bank out of $2.2 million.

Two more instances illustrate the breadth of techniques available for employee theft these days:

- A New Jersey paralegal was sentenced to four years in prison for posing as a lawyer and pocketing more than $100,000 in settlement checks meant to be split between his law firm and its clients. "Most employees who steal hold positions of trust in the firms they bilk," reports Tebo (2003, p. 26).
- Joya Williams was accused of stealing confidential documents and a sample of a Coke product from the Atlanta-based beverage giant while working as an administrative assistant to the company's brand director. Two men were charged along with her with trying to sell the items to PepsiCo Inc. (Weber, 2007). Williams was later sentenced to eight years in prison (Weber, 2007).

Why Employees Steal

Why do employees steal from their employers? Loss prevention experts Fischer and Janowski (2000) proffer "the theft triangle" as a possible answer. They assert:

> Theft occurs when three elements are present: (1) motive, (2) desire, and (3) opportunity. In simple terms, motive is a reason to steal. Motives might be the resentment of an employee who feels underpaid or the vengefulness of an employee who has been passed over for a promotion. Desire builds on motive when the employee imagines the satisfaction or gratification that would come from a potential action. . . . Opportunity is the absence of barriers that prevent someone from taking an item.

From this perspective, employee theft can be deterred by decreasing motive and desire to steal while also reducing opportunities. This idea foreshadows the multi-pronged approaches to deterring employee theft discussed in the following section. First, however, it is important to delve deeper into the question of motivation for theft. We will first review some thoughts shared in the popular literature about why employees steal, then turn our attention to some of the findings of the major research studies undertaken in recent years to answer this question.

Motives Discussed by Various Experts

Wells (2005), an accountant, says, "Employees who like their jobs are less likely to engage in deviant behavior, including fraud and theft. They see that acting against the interests of their employers is a way of 'getting back' at inequities such as inadequate compensation, unlikable bosses, and undesirable working conditions." In a similar vein, Speizer (2004) describes the typical employee-thief found in grocery retailing: "What you have is a pool of people who are generally pretty honest when they start, but slowly they become disenchanted, disenfranchised, and they begin to seek equity in the only way they know: work less or steal." Skarlicki and Folger (1997) state, "If organizational decisions and managerial actions are deemed unfair or unjust, the affected employees experience feelings of anger, outrage, and resentment," and these feelings may result in counterproductive employee behavior like theft. Bassett (1993) suggests that "most thefts in nursing homes are committed by employees who feel underpaid, overworked, and underappreciated." Gray (1997) also weighs in on possible motives for employee theft: "Fraud perpetrators come from all walks of life, all economic circumstances, and all social classes. . . . Some common instigators are a crisis in personal finances, a drug or gambling habit, revenge against an employer, a non-financial personal crisis, and acceptance of employment with intention to steal."

Greenberg (1990) lists six traditional plausible explanations for employee theft: attempts to ease financial pressure, moral laxity, available opportunities, expressions of job dissatisfaction, norms tolerating theft, and feelings of exploitation by the company on the part of the employees. He contrasts these traditional explanations with his own theoretical construct, which he calls the STEAL motive (Greenberg, 1997). This social motivational construct has four components: approval—adherence to supervisory norms condoning theft; support—adherence to work group norms condoning theft; even the score—desire to harm, strike back at the employer; and thwart—violating work group norms regulating theft. Greenberg presents considerable research evidence to support his belief that employee theft "is a behavior that is carefully regulated by organizational norms and work group norms, and that stealing is an effective way of supporting these norms."

The experts thus present a variety of reasons for employee theft, ranging from character flaws and personal crises through disenchantment, disenfranchisement, job dissatisfaction, feelings of inequity, and desire for revenge to work group norms condoning theft combined with opportunity. Interestingly, the major research studies conducted over the past 20 years seem to support—at least in part—*all* of these reasons. Let us now examine some of these key research studies.

Clark and Hollinger, 1983

This comprehensive research project, published by the U.S. Department of Justice in 1983, represented the state of the art in employee theft research some two decades ago. Data were collected over three years, commencing in 1978. A total of 47 business corporations from three industry sectors participated: 16 retail department chains, 21 general hospitals, and 10 electronic manufacturing firms located in Minneapolis-St. Paul, Cleveland, and Dallas-Fort Worth. A total of 9,175 employees were surveyed, and an additional 247 executives were interviewed. Here are the key findings of this research:

- In each of the industry sectors surveyed, roughly one-third of the employees reported some involvement in the taking of company property during the prior year.
- The highest levels of property theft were reported by the younger (16 to mid-twenties), unmarried, and male employees. In each type of industry, employees with the greatest unrestricted access to and knowledge about the property stolen were the occupational groups reporting the highest levels of theft.
- Theft was more likely with employees expressing dissatisfaction with their employment—especially dissatisfaction with their immediate supervisors and the company's attitude toward the workers.
- The single factor most predictive of theft involvement was the employee's perception of getting caught—the greater the perceived risks, the less the theft. The higher the proportion of the workforce apprehended for theft, the lower the overall theft rate.

Reflecting on these findings, Hollinger and Clark (1983) provided these conclusions about motives for employee theft:

- Employees who feel exploited by the company or by their supervisors (who represent the company in the eyes of the employees) are more involved in theft and acts against the organization to correct perceptions of inequity or injustice.
- Many younger employees express no remorse or guilt for their deviance because they perceive their work situation as a mutually exploitive one.
- Informal social controls initiated by fellow co-workers, such as gossip, ridicule, and ostracism, are much more effective in reducing theft than formal actions of management.
- Actions taken unilaterally by management will be substantially less effective unless they are correspondingly accepted and integrated into the normative consensus of the various work groups within the organization.
- If the employees conclude that their contributions to the work place are not appreciated or that the organization does not seem to care about the theft of its property, expect to find greater levels of theft.

Baumer and Rosenbaum, 1984

Baumer and Rosenbaum (1984) summarize five sets of variables found to correlate with employee theft in a survey of over 1,400 employees from nine retail companies. See figure 4 for their findings about personal characteristics, occupational characteristics, job satisfaction, deterrent effects, and organizational controls that influence the prevalence of employee theft.

1. *Personal characteristics:* Employee theft was significantly higher among employees who were young, male, Caucasian, never married, living in higher-income households but contributing less than 20% of the total income, and concerned about their financial, educational, or career situation.
2. *Occupational characteristics:* Employee theft was significantly higher among employees with lower-paying jobs, lower-status jobs, jobs providing easiest access to merchandise and money (e.g., sales clerks, cashiers, and managers), and more numerous and frequent social interactions with co-employees.
3. *Job satisfaction:* Employee theft was significantly higher among employees who were dissatisfied with their immediate supervisors, with the organization for which they worked, with opportunities for promotion, and with the day-to-day workload.
4. *Deterrent effects:* Employee theft was significantly higher among employees who believed they would not get caught, assumed their employers were unaware of employee theft, concluded that employees were infrequently checked for violations of company policies, and thought that no one would care if certain things were stolen and that management and co-workers would not react to theft as a serious problem.
5. *Organizational controls:* Theft rates were higher in organizations that did not actively promote anti-theft policies and conducted less careful and less extensive pre-employment screening.

Figure 4 Baumer and Rosenbaum's correlates of employee theft.
Source: Baumer and Rosenbaum (1984, pp. 47–48).

Recent Behavioral Research

More recent research, while less comprehensive than the two major studies just discussed, has added to our knowledge about reasons for employee theft and some of the variables that affect the incidence of it. Much of Greenberg's recent research has its theoretical basis in *equity theory,* a motivational theory proposed by Adams in 1965. The gist of equity theory is that workers experiencing underpayment inequity will seek to redress that inequity by such actions as theft. Unjust treatment leads to efforts to gain retribution, either through passive withholding of services or through overt actions such as sabotage, theft, or other counterproductive behaviors. Greenberg published two papers (1990, 1993) that confirmed the importance of equity theory for understanding employee motivations for theft. Another of Greenberg's studies (2002) found that theft was greater (a) among employees with lower moral development than among those with higher moral development, (b) within an office that had no ethics program as opposed to one that did, and (c) when the company, as opposed to coworkers, stood to be victimized. Weber, Burke, and Pentico (2003) also found that employee theft was lower in an organization where an ethical work climate prevailed, as opposed to a matched organization where ethics was not stressed.

Research on Employee Screening Devices

Paralleling the behavioral studies has been a rise in research focused on efforts to predict employee theft (and other deviant workplace behaviors) using employee screening devices called *integrity tests.* Jones and Terris (1983) found that a screening test administered to 86 home improvement center employees reliably predicted future theft and counter productivity. Employee-thieves generally reported more rumination over theft behavior, toleration of theft acts, projection of theft in others, rationalization of theft, and inter-thief loyalty than honest employees. "A typical employee-thief believes he is an 'average' person in a basically dishonest world," report Jones and Terris.

Over the past two decades research on employee screening devices has burgeoned, with integrity tests being devised and sold by a number of test publishers. Bernardin and Cooke (1993) examined two of these proprietary tests and found them to be good predictors of detected theft in an empirical study of 111 retail convenience store employees; these results were consistent across race and gender. Jones, Slora, and Boye (1990) reported similar results in their study of pre-employment screening in the supermarket industry. In a massive and highly sophisticated meta-analytic study using data from 183 independent studies of 25 different integrity tests—and a total of 576,460 test-takers—Ones, Viswesvaran, and Schmidt (1993) found that the employee screening devices were valid predictors of such counterproductive behaviors as theft, illegal activities, absenteeism, tardiness, drug abuse, dismissal for theft, and violence on the job. Conscientiousness (dependability, carefulness, responsibility) appears to be the psychological construct being measured by these various integrity tests (Ones et al., 1993).

In a 1998 review of research on integrity testing, Ones and Viswesvaran noted that evidence continues to mount that integrity tests are valid predictors of employee theft and a host of other counterproductive behaviors at work. They claim, based on recent research, that: (1) U.S. businesses still lose in excess of $40 billion in cash and merchandise to employee theft per year, (2) as many as 5,000 companies may use pre-employment tests, assessing about 5,000,000 applicants yearly, and (3) 45 commercial integrity tests are available in the United States.

Two Major Summaries

Murphy (1993), in a major work summarizing most of the research on employee theft (and other manifestations of employee dishonesty in the workplace) conducted prior to 1993, provided these conclusions:

- On the whole, research on employee theft does not support the most widely cited explanation for theft—the theory that people steal because they need or want the money. . . . The most promising explanations for employee theft and other counterproductive behaviors appear to be couched in terms of three variables: (1) attitudes toward the job and the organization, (2) attitudes toward theft and counterproductive behavior, and (3) informal workplace norms regarding theft and counter-productive behavior.

- Individuals who are dissatisfied with their jobs or who feel no real loyalty to or connection with the organization are more likely to steal than satisfied employees with close ties to the organization. . . . Individuals who feel that they have been unfairly treated may steal or engage in other acts of deviance to "even the score."
- The worst-case scenario from the perspective of a manager trying to control employee theft may be a work group that is highly cohesive, with the ability and willingness to apply strong sanctions to deviant members, but with norms that tolerate or encourage particular types of employee theft.

Greenberg and Tomlinson (2004) drew similar conclusions from their review of the literature on motives for employee theft. They noted five major perspectives on reasons for employee theft. Why do employees steal from their employers? The answer you get depends on the expert you ask: (1) clinical psychologists—deviant personality; (2) industrial psychologists—ineffective selection procedures; (3) criminologists—vices, such as gambling and substance abuse; (4) specialists in workplace security—the inevitable result of inadequate auditing, monitoring, and control procedures; (5) organizational scientists—a form of social behavior. Accepting the idea that all five perspectives may contain truth, it becomes important to consider all five when assembling an effective procedure to combat employee theft.

Methods Used to Deter Employee Theft

The majority of the articles identified during the present literature review included one or more suggestions for deterring employee theft. Most of them recommended a multi-pronged deterrence program that included several techniques such as pre-employment screening, removal of temptation, use of financial and operational controls, organizational culture change, and identification and prosecution of offenders. For example, BDO Stoy Hayward (2006) outlined a four-point program that includes pre-employment screening, background checks, and reference checks; employee training on company policy and procedures, especially codes of conduct and whistle-blowing policies; periodic assessment, updating, and communication of company policies; and adequate fraud insurance coverage. Buss's (1993) recommendations included applicant screening, honesty testing, use of stealth surveillance and investigative techniques, fair treatment of employees (including profit sharing), insurance, fidelity bonds, and aggressive prosecution. Sternberg (2001) recommended closely reviewing monthly financial statements, accounting for all inventory, denying opportunity, screening all new employees, and stating clearly that theft will not be tolerated and perpetrators will be arrested. With respect to curbing theft in retail stores, Amato-McCoy (2003) indicated that retailers using a multi-pronged loss prevention program consisting of training, policies, and technology reported less shrinkage than those without a formal program.

Several of the experts provided specific suggestions for modifying organizational culture to reduce the incidence of employee theft. For example, Boye and Jones (1997) recommended a comprehensive approach outlined as follows: Set the example; treat employees with trust, respect, and dignity; attempt to enrich employees' jobs; provide fair and adequate compensation; adopt and communicate a policy concerning counterproductive behavior; consistently punish unacceptable counterproductive acts; and reduce job stress. Schinnerer's (2003) comprehensive ethics program to reduce employee theft and other counterproductive behaviors includes these components: Clearly communicated company values; a strategy to implement and maintain an ethical culture; goals and objectives to guide program implementation; a way to measure the efficacy of ethical programs; incentives for ethical behaviors; engaging and ongoing training; executives who model ethical behavior; resources for ethics programs; and overlap between employee and company values.

A pamphlet prepared by the U.S. Small Business Administration (undated) provides a number of practical suggestions for deterring theft in small businesses. A key passage provides this piece of advice:

> The best profit safeguard you can have in a store is the employee whose integrity is beyond question. . . . The store with the greatest proportion of honest employees suffers the least from theft loss. The trick is to take every precaution to ensure that the people you hire are honest to begin with. Then, take pains to maintain the kind of store climate that will encourage them to stay honest.

Ways to create an organizational climate or culture that encourages honesty are discussed in detail by Sauser (2005), Sauser and Sims (2007), and Trevino and Nelson (2004). Creating a culture of integrity is important in every organization, whether large or small.

Biddick (2004) argues that small businesses are particularly vulnerable to employee theft because they typically lack the sophisticated controls and systems larger companies use, they tend to function more informally, and they frequently deal in cash. He recommends that small business owners or operators assess risk, set a personal ethical example, run a background check on the bookkeeper, never cede all responsibilities for fiscal operations to any one person, become knowledgeable about financial basics, check bills and credit card and bank statements, be on the lookout for employee kickbacks from vendors, and take responsibility for the company's finances. Fenn (1995) and Davies (2003) provide similar practical advice. Monahan (2005) notes, "Well trained employees familiar with the telltale signs of theft [detect] more fraud than any other security method. A [firm] that emphasizes integrity, honesty and open lines of communication reduces its risk for fraud."

Security and loss prevention experts provide a number of detailed suggestions for reducing temptation and opportunity for theft by employees. Kimiecik (1995) describes a dizzying array of possible controls, and Clark (1984) identifies a number of methods department stores and specialty stores use to deter theft, including employee education in loss prevention, improved paperwork and accounting methods, increasing the security force, improving employee screening, increasing control at the cash register, increasing control over purchasing, prosecuting offenders, increasing control by the district manager, using electronic or magnetic tags, stationing guards, using locks and chains, limiting access areas, using mirrors and observation booths, employing an outside shopping service, planting undercover security personnel, displaying both visible and concealed TV monitors, conducting background and reference checks and credit checks, using personality and psychological tests, and conducting security and loss prevention interviews.

From an accounting control perspective, Mamis (1994) suggests conducting a semiannual audit of procedures, ensuring that bank statements are opened and examined by someone other than the bookkeeper, requiring annual vacations, accounting for voided checks, changing computer passwords frequently, and conducting occasional surprise audits. Miracle's (2005) practical suggestions include reviewing the everyday procedures for managing inventory and bill paying, limiting check-signing authority, avoiding use of credit cards issued in the company's name, considering pre-employment screening, watching the small stuff, and putting a clear anti-theft policy in place. Connick (2005) reinforces this last suggestion: "In addition to appropriate reporting and supervision practices, employers should consider a clear policy statement that theft will not be tolerated and identify the possible consequences. In addition, when faced with an allegation of theft, the employer must react, but not overreact."

How might we summarize these various perspectives—and this wealth of advice—regarding methods to deter employee theft? Since employee theft appears to be a complex behavior with multiple determinants, most experts recommend a multi-pronged approach to deterrence. Components of an effective comprehensive program would include changing organizational culture, implementing controls, clarifying policies, using sanctions (including prosecution), screening employees, and working to improve employee job satisfaction. This author's recommended strategy is summarized in figure 5.

Conclusions and Recommendations

Considerable research has been conducted over the years on employee theft, and some key trends have emerged. Here are 10 conclusions drawn from this body of research:

1. Estimates of the extent of employee theft vary widely, but virtually every writer estimates that worldwide financial loss from employee theft ranges in the tens (or even hundreds) of billions of dollars annually. An estimate of $100 billion worldwide per year appears to be realistically conservative.

To Reduce Employee Theft:

- Screen Out Potential Employee-Thieves
  - Check references
  - Conduct background investigations
  - Use integrity tests

- Create an Organizational Culture of Character
  - Establish a code of conduct
  - Set a personal example of integrity
  - Show respect for all employees

- Remove Temptations to Steal
  - Employ accounting controls
  - Use security devices
  - Audit operations and procedures

- Punish Theft and Reward Honesty
  - Discipline or dismiss employees who steal
  - Prosecute criminal theft and fraud
  - Share the rewards of honest work

Figure 5 Recommended multi-pronged strategy for reducing employee theft.

2. Employee theft is identified as an ethical problem in virtually every sector of business, and seems to be particularly problematic in banking, finance, and insurance; retailing; health care and social assistance; and manufacturing and construction.

3. There is support for the belief that one-third to one-half of all employees steal at least once from their employer. Employee theft ranges in magnitude from pilferage and petty theft to fraud and grand theft. Many employee-thieves do not see petty theft as "really wrong." Instead, pilferage is often viewed as a perquisite of employment.

4. There are many ways employees steal from their employers. The human mind is innovative, and every employment situation can be viewed as an interesting challenge to those bent on stealing. New technologies—such as the internet, electronic transfer of funds, and electronic banking and securities trading—have opened new avenues for employee theft, including theft of customer identities.

5. Five perspectives are evident in the literature on employee theft, those of clinical psychologists (deviant behavior), industrial psychologists (employee selection issues), criminologists (vices like gambling and substance abuse), security experts (inadequate controls), and organizational scientists (work group norms, sanctions, and organizational culture). Recommendations for combating employee theft depend on professional perspective.

6. Numerous controls are available to discourage employee theft, and there is clear evidence that many are effective. Neglecting to implement operational and financial controls is a poor practice that will likely tempt employees to steal.

7. Pre-employment screening (through reference checks and background investigation) seems to be an effective tool for reducing employee theft and other forms of counterproductive employee behavior. Commercially available integrity tests are useful in combating employee theft.
8. Management's fairness and respect toward employees appear to be major determinants of the extent of employee theft, as do work group norms, organizational culture, and employee job satisfaction. These behavioral constructs deserve considerable attention from anyone seeking to reduce employee theft.
9. A multi-pronged approach to deterring employee theft is recommended by most experts. Components of an effective program include changing organizational culture, implementing operational and financial controls, clarifying policies, using sanctions (including prosecution), screening employees, and working to improve employee job satisfaction.
10. Conclusions and recommendations from the popular and scientific literature tend to converge. Experts and general writers generally agree that employee theft is a major ethical problem with multiple causes, and that many effective tools are available as deterrents.

Organizational scientists are encouraged to conduct additional research directed toward the four questions examined in this article: How much do employees steal, how do they do it, why do they do it, and how can we stop them? Likewise, employers are encouraged to take the steps discussed here and diagrammed in figure 5 in an effort to reduce the costly ethical problem of employee theft.

References

Adams, J.S. (1965). Inequity in social exchange. In L. Berkowitz (Ed.), *Advances in experimental social psychology: 2* (pp. 267–299). San Diego, CA: Academic Press.

Amato-McCoy, D.M. (2003). Employee training defends against employee shrink. *Stores, 85*(5), LP20.

Baker, M.A., and Westin, A.F. (1987). *Employer perceptions of workplace crime.* Washington, DC: U.S. Department of Justice Bureau of Justice Statistics, NCJ-101851.

Bassett, J.W. (1993). Internal theft. *Nursing Homes: Long Term Care Management, 42*(4), 34–37.

Baumer, T.L., and Rosenbaum, D.P. (1984). *Combating retail theft: Programs and strategies.* Boston: Butterworth.

BDO Stoy Hayward. (2006). *FraudTrack 3: Rising fraud in the spotlight.* (Annual Survey 2006, "Inside Job"). London: BDO Stoy Hayward LLP.

Bernardin, H.J., and Cooke, D.K. (1993). Validity of an honesty test in predicting theft among convenience store employees. *Academy of Management Journal, 36,* 1097–1108.

Biddick, K. (2004). Think big when protecting small business from employee theft. *Nation's Restaurant News, 38*(36), 26.

Bogardus, D.E. (1987). *Missing drugs.* Salt Lake City, UT: Medical Management Systems.

Boye, M.W., and Jones, J.W. (1997). Organizational culture and employee counterproductivity. In R. A. Giacalone and J. Greenberg (Eds.), *Antisocial behavior in organizations* (pp. 172–184). Thousand Oaks, CA: Sage Publications.

Buss, D. (1993). Ways to curtail employee theft. *Nation's Business, 81*(4), 36–37.

Clark, A.A.M. (1984). *Employee theft and methods of deterrence.* Unpublished doctoral dissertation, Texas Woman's University.

Clark, J.P., and Hollinger, R.C. (1983). *Theft by employees in work organizations: Executive summary.* Washington, DC: U.S. Department of Justice National Institute of Justice.

Connick, E. (2005, May). Theft in the workplace. *Saskbusiness, 26*(3), 13.

Dabney, D. (1995). Neutralization and deviance in the workplace: Theft of supplies and medicines by hospital nurses. *Deviant Behavior: An Interdisciplinary Journal, 16,* 313–331.

Daks, M.C. (2005). Banks need to bolt the door twice. *NJBIZ, 18*(24), 3–4.

Davia, H.R. (2000). *Fraud 101: Techniques and strategies for detection.* New York: Wiley.

Davies, K.R. (2003). Broken trust: Employee stealing. *Dealernews, 39*(12), 22.

Dreyfack, R. (2002). Are stealing and petty theft synonymous? *Plant Engineering, 56*(6), pages unnumbered.

Fenn, D. (1995). Preventing employee pilferage. *Inc. 17*(2), 112.

Fischer, R. J., and Janoski, R. (2000). *Loss prevention and security procedures: Practical applications for contemporary problems.* Boston: Butterworth-Heinemann.

Food Marketing Institute. (1989). *The food marketing industry speaks, 1989: Loss prevention issues study highlights.* Washington, DC: Institute Report.

Friedrick, J. (2006). Combating theft requires vigilance. *Gourmet News, 71*(2), 15–16.

Gerber, G. (2005). A crime of opportunity. *RV Trade Digest, 25*(3), 14–15.

Gray, R.T. (1997). Clamping down on worker crime. *Nation's Business, 85*(4), 44–45.

Greenberg, J. (1990). Employee theft as a reaction to under-payment inequity: The hidden cost of pay cuts. *Journal of Applied Psychology, 75,* 561–568.

Greenberg, J. (1993). Stealing in the name of justice: Informational and interpersonal moderators of theft reactions to underpayment equity. *Organizational Behavior and Human Decision Processes, 54,* 81–103.

Greenberg, J. (1997). The STEAL motive: Managing the social determinants of employee theft. In R.A. Giacalone and J. Greenberg (Eds.), *Antisocial behavior in organizations* (pp. 85–108). Thousand Oaks, CA: SAGE Publications.

Greenberg, J. (2002). Who stole the money, and when? Individual and situational determinants of employee theft. *Organizational Behavior and Human Decision Processes, 89,* 985–1003.

Greenberg, J., and Tomlinson, E.C. (2004). The methodological evolution of employee theft research: The DATA cycle. In R.W. Griffin and A.M.O'Leary-Kelly (Eds.), *The dark side of organizational behavior* (pp. 426–461). San Francisco: Jossey-Bass.

Hollinger, R.C., and Clark, J.P. (1983). *Theft by employees.* Lexington, MA: Lexington Books.

How honest are Americans? (1994, December). *USA Today Magazine, 123*(2595), 6.

Jones, J.W., and Terris, W. (1983). Predicting employees' theft in home improvement centers. *Psychological Reports, 52,* 197–201.

Jones, J.W., Slora, K.B., and Boye, M.W. (1990). Theft reduction through personnel selection: A control group design in the supermarket industry. *Journal of Business and Psychology, 5,* 275–279.

Kimiecik, R.C. (1995). *Loss prevention guide for retail businesses.* New York: Wiley.

Knapshaefer, J. (2004). Deterring fraud when it's an 'inside job.' *Community Banker, 13*(6), 42–46.

Krebsbach, K. (2004). The inside job. *USBanker, 114*(9), 24–25.

Lurz, B. (2004). Stop, thief! *Professional Builder, 69*(9), 112–117.

Mamis, R.A. (1994). Discouraging the inside job. *Inc. 16*(4), 122.

McTaggart, J., and Tarnowski, J. (2005). Employee theft, shop-lifting prevail at retail. *Progressive Grocer, 84*(16), 12.

Miracle, B. (2005). Who's minding the store? *Florida Trend, 48*(2), 38.

Monahan, J. (2005). Raiding the cookie jar. *Independent Banker, 55*(6), 19.

Moody, A. (2004). Fraud hits small firms. *Director, 57*(7), 32.

Murphy, K.R. (1993). *Honesty in the workplace.* Pacific Grove, CA: Brooks/Cole.

National survey shows employee theft at record high. (2004). *Home Channel News, 30*(2), 4–5.

Oder, N., St. Lifer, E., and Rogers, M. (1998). $100K manuscript theft at NYPL. *Library Journal, 123*(4), pages unnumbered.

Ones, D.S., and Viswesvaran, C. (1998). Integrity testing in organizations. In R.W. Griffin, A. O'Leary-Kelly, and J. Collins (Eds.), *Dysfunctional behavior in organizations* (pp. 243–276). Stamford, CT: JAI Press.

Ones, D.S., Viswesvaran, C., and Schmidt, F.L. (1993). Comprehensive meta-analysis of integrity test validities: Findings and implications for personnel selection and theories of job performance. *Journal of Applied Psychology, 78,* 679–703.

Purpura, P.P. (1984). *Security and loss prevention.* Boston: Butterworth.

Sauser, W.I., Jr. (2005). Ethics in business: Answering the call. *Journal of Business Ethics, 58,* 345–357.

Sauser, W.I., Jr. (2006). *Review of literature related to employee theft.* Unpublished manuscript, Auburn University, Auburn, AL.

Sauser, W.I., Jr. (2007). Fostering an ethical culture for business: The role of HR managers. In R. R. Sims (Ed.), *Human resources management: Contemporary issues, challenges and opportunities* (pp. 253–285). Greenwich, CT: Information Age Publishing.

Schinnerer, J. (2003). The ROI of an effective ethics program. *Workspan, 46*(10), 52.

Shreve, M. (2004). Employers slow to recognize identity theft. *Business Insurance, 38*(36), 4–5.

Skarlicki, D.P., and Folger, R. (1997). Retaliation in the workplace: The roles of distributive, procedural, and interactional justice. *Journal of Applied Psychology, 82,* 434–443.

Snyder, N.H., Broome, O.W., Jr., Kehoe, W.J., McIntyre, J.T., Jr., and Blair, K.E. (1991). *Reducing employee theft: A guide to financial and organizational controls.* New York: Quorum.

Southern Institute for Business and Professional Ethics (2005). *The Southeast Survey of CEOs on Business Ethics.* Retrieved from http://www.southerninstitute.org/Surveyfr.htm

Special report: Combination therapy, (2006, January 10). *Instore: The Magazine for Retail Marketing and Design,* p. 27.

Speizer, I. (2004). An anti-shrinkage strategy. *Workforce Management, 83*(9), 52–53.

Sternberg, J. (2001, June 1). To eliminate employee theft, remove the opportunity. *TWICE: This Week in Consumer Electronics, 16*(1), pages unnumbered.

Tatham, R.L. (1974). Employee views on theft in retailing. *Journal of Retailing, 50*(3), 49–55.

Tebo, M. G. (2003). Thwarting thieves. *ABA Journal, 89*(12), 26.

Texas staffer charged with felony theft. (2004). *American Libraries, 35*(6), 34.

Trevino, L.K., and Nelson, K.A. (2004). *Managing business ethics: Straight talk about how to do it right* (3rd ed.). New York: Wiley.

U.S. Small Business Administration. (undated). *Curtailing crime—Inside and out.* Undated government publication deposited in the Auburn University Library's depository on 22 July 1987. Management Aids Number 5.005.

Van Maanenberg, D. (1995). *Effective retail security: Protecting the bottom line.* Port Melbourne, Victoria, Australia: Butterworth-Heinemann.

Weber, H.R. (2006, July 9). Cola caper points to need for tough employee screening. *Opelika-Auburn News* (Alabama), 2D.

Weber, H.R. (2007, May 24). Woman gets 8 years in Coke secrets case. *USA Today,* 5B.

Weber, J., Burke, L. B., and Pentico, D. W. (2003). Why do employees steal? *Business and Society, 42,* 359–380.

Wells, J. (2005). Internal controls can give you ulcers. *The Practical Accountant, 38*(8), 48.

Wimbush, J.C., and Dalton, D.R. (1997). Base rate for employee theft. *Journal of Applied Psychology, 82,* 756–763.

Dr. William I. Sauser is Associate Dean for Business and Engineering Outreach and Professor of Management at Auburn University. His interests include organizational development, strategic planning, human relations in the workplace, business ethics, and continuing professional education. He is a Fellow of the American Council on Education and the Society for Advancement of Management (SAM). In 2003, he was awarded the Frederick W. Taylor Key by SAM for his career achievements.

Businesses Say Theft by Their Workers Is up

Companies find that trusted employees often commit the crimes, and they believe the recession is to blame.

SARAH E. NEEDLEMAN

In October, an accountant at **321 Takeoff** Inc. in New York became suspicious after an employee who normally filed weekly expense reports for around $80 began requesting $120.

When Alona Fromberg-Elkayam, the branding agency's president, approached the employee, she says she was met with flimsy excuses. She fired the employee, a midlevel designer.

In the wake of the recession, more businesses are facing a growing financial threat: employee theft. New research shows that employers are seeing an increase in internal crimes, ranging from fictitious sales transactions and illegal kickbacks to the theft of office equipment and retail products meant for sale to customers.

Employers suspect that workers are pilfering from them to cope with financial difficulties at home or in anticipation of being laid off.

What's more, it's often the most trusted workers who are committing the thefts.

"In leaner financial times, people have a tendency to give in to temptation to commit criminal behavior," says Brian J. Mich, head of anticorruption compliance and investigations at BDO Consulting in New York.

At the same time, he says, "employers give additional attention to the bottom line, which results in more fraud being discovered. It's a little hard to tell which is the chicken or the egg."

About 20% of employers polled last month said workplace theft has become a moderate to very big problem recently, according to a survey from the Institute for Corporate Productivity Inc., in conjunction with HR.com.

The survey, to be released Thursday, polled managers and executives at 392 U.S. companies representing a range of sizes and industries. When asked if they had noticed a recent rise in monetary theft among employees, such as fraudulent transactions or missing cash, 18% said yes, 41% were unsure and the rest said they hadn't.

Further, 24% of respondents said they had detected an increase in stolen nonmonetary items, such as retail products and office supplies, while 43% were unsure and 33% hadn't.

In 2007, companies lost an average of $2.4 million to fraud, the majority of it by employees, up from $1.7 million in 2005, according to PricewaterhouseCoopers LLP, which conducts biannual surveys of around 5,400 companies of all sizes world-wide.

Employers are hot targets for theft because workers "know their systems, controls and weaknesses, and they can bide their time waiting for the right opportunity," says Mark R. Doyle, president of Jack L. Haynes International Inc., a provider of workplace crime-prevention services based in Fruitland Park, Fla.

The elimination of perks such as employee discounts and holiday parties can aggravate the problem, adds Mr. Mich, who, prior to joining BDO, worked for 12 years as a white-collar prosecutor in New York.

"They're thinking, 'I'm not being treated fairly by my employer anyway so I'm going to take this indulgence here,'" he explains.

It's not that theft doesn't happen when times are good, says Bob Zierk, vice president of human resources for Black & Decker Corp.'s hardware and home improvement division, but these issues "come up with increasing frequency in a difficult economy."

Though he hasn't noticed a rise in employee theft lately at the manufacturer, he says, he saw the problem intensify in past downturns when he worked at other companies during his 32-year career in human resources.

To many employers' chagrin, the workers guilty of the most grandiose theft frequently turn out to be those they'd deemed highly trustworthy, says Mr. Mich.

"They are people being given access to systems and information that allow them to commit fraud," he says. Their crimes—typically theft of small amounts of money over long periods of time—often go unnoticed until economic downturns, he adds, because that's when companies generally become more vigilant about counting pennies.

A 2007 study from Pricewaterhouse shows that senior-level employees with an average tenure of 7½ years are responsible for 25% of all reported internal frauds. Overall, 85% of fraudsters are male, 44% are between the ages of 31 and 40, 38% possess at least a bachelor's degree, and 12% typically hold a postgraduate degree or higher.

Since workplace pilfering sometimes goes undetected, it's unclear how much more severe the problem is now than in healthier times. According to Jack L. Haynes International, employee theft in the retail sector has been on the rise every year since 2003.

A survey the firm conducted earlier this year of 24 large retailers with more than 2.3 million employees found that roughly one out of every 28 workers was apprehended for stealing in 2007, a nearly 18% increase from 2006.

Retail employers typically track their inventories closely, which is why they're able to provide such detailed data, says Mr. Doyle.

Workers who steal even small amounts of money or goods from an employer risk big repercussions. In addition to sacking internal thieves, many employers file civil lawsuits against them, says Bob Riordan, partner and leader of the labor-and-employment practice group at **Alston & Bird** LLP in Atlanta. Some even press criminal charges, which can result in jail time.

An employer's best defense against worker theft is prevention, asserts Mr. Riordan. "You want to maintain an environment where your employees have some sense of a code of conduct or integrity," he says.

The installation of video cameras, tracking devices and other monitoring tools can also help deter workers from pilfering, but employers should first review local laws on the practice.

"There is an increasing trend at the state level to prohibit invasive monitoring," warns Mr. Riordan.

Also consider how the strategy might affect employee morale. "You need to be aware of the culture of the workplace you're dealing with," he says. "Video monitoring in a warehouse might be fine, but in an office environment it might be viewed as crossing the line."

The survey from the Institute for Corporate Productivity shows that about 17% of respondents recently added extra security measures and 20% are conducting audits more frequently in the wake of increased employee theft or because of suspicions of theft.

And 28% say they're communicating with employees more about internal theft.

Still, no matter what preventive methods employers take, breaches are likely to occur on occasion, even in good economic times, says Black & Decker's Mr. Zierk.

"You're bound to run into periodic issues," he says. "In every company I've ever worked for, part of my time has been spent dealing with people who use poor judgment."

From *The Wall Street Journal,* December 11, 2008, p. B8. Copyright © 2008 by Dow Jones & Company, Inc. Reprinted by permission via the Copyright Clearance Center.

Gender Issues

Sex-discrimination lawsuits are on the rise. Is your company at risk?

JENNIFER GILL

For large corporations, the news has been grim: Last July, Boeing agreed to pay as much as $72.5 million to settle a class-action lawsuit by female employees. That same month, Morgan Stanley paid $54 million to settle a similar suit.

Sex-discrimination suits against small companies don't make headlines but they are just as common. In fact, nearly half of all sex-discrimination charges—running the gamut from sexual harassment to gender-related firing—filed with the Equal Employment Opportunity Commission last year were aimed at firms with 200 or fewer employees. And claims could surge in the years ahead as more women gain confidence from high-profile cases in the news, according to Cari Dominguez, chairperson of the EEOC. Many female baby boomers are entering their 50s and are "looking to leave a legacy," Dominguez says. "Women are taking on the role of whistleblower."

Smaller companies are particularly vulnerable because they tend to have less structured atmospheres and are less likely to have formal sex-discrimination policies in place, Dominguez adds. "A lack of infrastructure and awareness of the issues can lead a small business to run afoul of the law," she warns.

Donna Salyers, founder and president of Donna Salyers's Fabulous Furs, a faux-fur retailer based in Covington, Ky., learned that lesson three years ago. Back then, the retailer—which has 35 full-time employees, an online store, a retail shop in Covington, and celebrity clients such as longtime *Cosmopolitan* editor Helen Gurley Brown—was struggling to recover from the economic impact of the 9/11 terrorist attacks. Then Salyers received more shocking news: The EEOC was suing Fabulous Furs for sexual harassment on behalf of four temporary employees in the company's distribution center who claimed that their supervisor made offensive remarks to them. The women, who had been let go after the company's busy season, also claimed that they were fired in retaliation for their complaints. Salyers soon found herself consumed with the lawsuit, watching as her legal bills skyrocketed to $100,000. Finally, last fall, she decided to settle. Her company, which admitted no wrongdoing in the case, paid $45,000 in damages to the plaintiffs and agreed to implement a new sexual-harassment policy. "Small businesses like ours aren't equipped to handle these claims," says Guy van Rooyen, CEO of Fabulous Furs. "It's like a smack in the face."

Salyers, who founded Fabulous Furs in 1989, is determined that this never happen again. Before the lawsuit, her company's sex-discrimination policy consisted of little more than the standard guidelines in an employee handbook. After the suit was filed, however, she hired a full-time human resources director to develop and review her company's employee policies. As part of the settlement, she also created a complaint hot line for workers and began holding annual sex-discrimination seminars for managers. By being up-front about what is and is not permissible, Salyers hopes to limit her company's exposure to any future claims.

The EEOC's Dominguez wishes more privately owned companies would follow suit. Until recently, the commission's efforts have been focused on large corporations. But now, smaller companies are the top priority, says Dominguez, who has launched an aggressive outreach program to educate small and midsize businesses. "They're the brave new world for us," she says. "That's where the growth opportunities are for the country's economy, but I see liability potential, as well."

Federal antidiscrimination laws apply to businesses with 15 or more employees, and state or local statutes often cover even smaller ones. In Chicago, for instance, companies with just a single employee can be sued for discrimination. To find out where your company stands, call the small-business liaison at your local EEOC field office (see www.eeoc.gov for a list of offices). The liaison will explain the law, provide educational materials for your staff, and even make free presentations at your workplace.

Next, spell out your firm's antiharassment and equal-opportunity policies in an employee handbook. Most companies follow a standard template, which can be found on the website of the Employment Law Information Network (www.elinfonet.com). In the handbook, tell employees whom to contact in the event of a complaint. Be sure to name someone besides the employee's direct manager, in case the issue involves that person. Merely providing the information in a handbook may not be enough, so follow Salyers's lead by posting your policy in areas frequented by employees, such as the kitchen or the restroom.

Many female baby boomers are entering their 50s and are looking to leave a legacy. They're taking on the role of whistleblower.

Bear in mind that guidelines written in legalese can be difficult to understand. For instance, an employee may realize that telling a dirty joke is a no-no. But he may not be aware that asking a female subordinate about her childcare arrangements is a bad idea. One comment isn't an actionable offense, and federal law does not prohibit simple teasing, offhand comments, or isolated incidents that aren't extremely serious. But there could be trouble if the conduct is frequent and severe enough to create a hostile work environment or results in a tangible employment action, such as firing or demotion. To help clarify the law for your staff, hire an employment lawyer to hold annual sex-discrimination seminars. Some trade associations and chambers of commerce also offer workshops for members.

Finally, be sure to keep a written record of your employees' shortcomings, advises Susan Stahlfeld, a partner at law firm Miller Nash's Seattle office. In a surprising number of cases, managers criticize employees verbally during reviews but give them high marks on written evaluations. Such evaluations can be critical to your company's defense if, say, an employee claims she was fired based solely on her sex. "It comes down to what you have in that person's file," Stahlfeld says.

Of course, even if you take every precaution, sex-discrimination complaints may arise. To prevent them from snowballing into lawsuits, investigate each one immediately. "Putting your head in the sand is never a good idea," says Jill

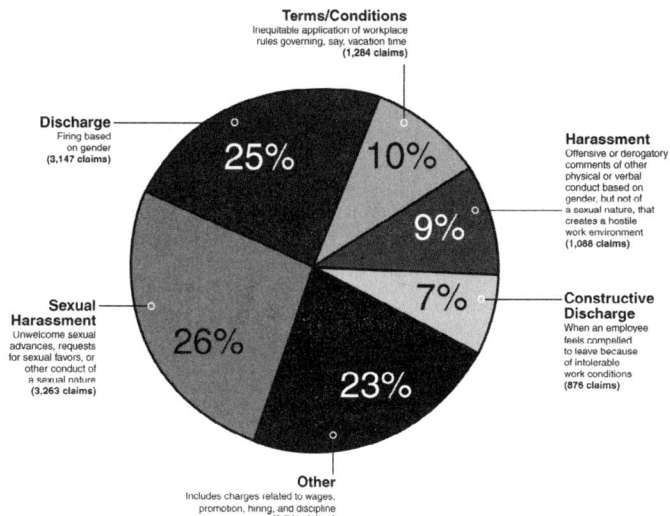

Figure 1 Discrimination Decoded. Last year, 12,399 sex-discrimination claims were filed against U.S. companies with between 15 and 100 workers. Here is a breakdown of the types of claims filed.

Schwartz, of Jill S. Schwartz & Associates, an employment law firm in Winter Park, Fla. For instance, if a female worker questions why she's being paid $10,000 less than her male counterpart, go over performance reviews and take her tenure into consideration. If there's a reason other than gender for the pay difference, explain it to her. If not, fix the discrepancy. As the recent spate of high-profile lawsuits has proved, granting a raise will cost much less than going to court.

From *Inc., Magazine,* April 2005, pp. 38, 40. Copyright © 2005 by Mansueto Ventures LLC. Reprinted by permission.

Hiring Older Workers

Unique skills, values come through the experience of age.

STEPHEN BASTIEN

Wanted: Employees who are honest, responsible, dependable, loyal, focused, organized and mature. Is this too much to ask?

American employers spend millions of hours each year placing ads, prescreening, interviewing, hiring and training workers, only to find that many of the new hires work for only a few months and then decide they don't want to be "just a clerk" anymore or feel something better has come along as they work their way up the corporate ladder.

Where can American employers find dependable, steady employees who have no plans to move up and out? Employees who are dedicated to the job at hand and take pride in their work? Employees who cost less to hire, train and maintain?

The answer, I have found in many of my own business ventures, is senior citizens, or, for the purposes of this article, older workers.

Here are 10 advantages of hiring older workers that may solve managers' difficulties with maintaining a reliable, dedicated work-force and result in significant cost savings in both the short and long term.

1. Dedicated workers produce better quality work, which can result in significant savings. Stories abound of highly committed older workers finding others' potentially costly mistakes in everything from incorrect zip codes and misspelling of client names to pricing errors and accounting mistakes.
2. Punctuality seems to be a given for older workers. They look forward to going to work each day, so they arrive on time and ready to work.
3. Honesty is common among many older workers, whose values include personal integrity and a devotion to the truth.
4. Detail-oriented, focused and attentive workers add an intangible value that rubs off on all employees and can save thousands of dollars. One business owner described a case in which one of his older workers saved the company more than $50,000 on one large mailing job. His 75-year-old clerical worker recognized that all of the zip codes were off by one digit. Neither his mailing house nor his degreed and highly paid marketing manager had noticed it.
5. Pride in a job well done has become increasingly scarce among employees. Younger workers want to put in their time at work and leave, while older employees willingly stay later to get a job done because of their sense of pride in the final product.
6. Organizational skills among older workers mean employers who hire them are less likely to be a part of this startling statistic: More than a million staff hours are lost each year due to workplace disorganization.
7. Efficiency and the confidence to share their recommendations and ideas make older workers ideal employees. Their years of experience in the workplace give them superior understanding of how jobs can be done more efficiently, which saves companies money. Their confidence, built up over their years in the workforce, means they'll not hesitate to share their ideas with management.
8. Maturity comes from years of life and work experience and makes for workers who get less "rattled" when problems occur.
9. Setting an example for other employees is an intangible value many employers appreciate. Older workers make excellent mentors and role models, so training other employees is less difficult.
10. Reduced labor costs may be a benefit when hiring older workers. Most already have insurance plans from prior employers or have an additional source of income. They understand that working for a company can be about much more than just collecting a paycheck.

Employers who are hesitant to hire older workers should consider these benefits. Older workers' unique skills and values make hiring them a simple matter of rethinking the costs of high turnover in a more youthful workforce versus the benefits of experience and mature standards that older workers bring to the mix. So the next time you need to make a hiring decision, seriously consider older workers. Their contribution could positively impact the bottom line for years to come.

STEPHEN BASTIEN is an author and authority on entrepreneurship. His current venture, Bastien Financial Publications (www.usbj.biz), offers businesses the latest developments through daily newsletters. To contact him, call 1-800-407-9044 or send an e-mail to steve@creditnews.com.

From *The Costco Connection,* July 2007, p. 19. Copyright © 2007 by Stephen Bastien. Reprinted by permission.

Article 18

Keeping Your Senior Staffers

Hit by a shortage of engineers, BASF found a way to retain older workers.

MINA KIMES

With layoffs rampant, holding on to workers ought to be the least of a company's worries—unless those employees are scientists and engineers. According to the National Science Foundation, nearly 40% of these skilled workers in the U.S. are more than 50 years old, and the pipeline of talent to replace them is shrinking. IHS Cambridge Energy Research Associates predicts a 7% to 11% shortage of experienced engineers in 2011. America is not alone; industrial powerhouses Germany and Japan face similar demographic challenges.

BASF, the German chemical giant, which makes, among other products, ammonia, fertilizer, and plastics, says it has found a way to beat the crunch. The $91-billion-a-year company has been around for more than a century, and its skilled workforce of production managers, scientists, and engineers, while not quite that old, have decades of experience under their belts. By 2020 the majority of BASF's German employees will be 50 to 65 years old. "It's become apparent that we're going to hit a wall," says CFO Kurt Bock, himself a sprightly 50. BASF's demographic problem is bigger than most because it mainly operates in Germany, Japan, and the U.S., where the elderly make up an increasingly large chunk of the population.

While the company is trying to replenish its workforce from the bottom up, even sending its scientists to teach classes in elementary schools, that may only address the problem of 2050. A more pressing concern is the next decade. "If we don't deal with aging," says Hartmut Lang, BASF's HR chief, "we'll face a serious challenge." Three years ago BASF decided to create a series of programs aimed at boosting workers' longevity and productivity.

One initiative focuses simply on maintaining health. Doctors visit laboratories and plants, where they assess the physical condition of individuals who volunteer and offer them advice. Another targets the facilities themselves. In office settings, notes Lang, the company has instituted "ergonomics checks" for furniture. At the plants, managers divvy up labor among different generations to reduce stress on older employees. Peter Gleich, a plant manager in Ludwigshafen, Germany, says, "We're also looking at organization to boost productivity"—which means putting younger and older people together in teams to take advantage of both generations' skill sets.

Yet even if senior employees work longer and better, they'll have to leave eventually—and they'll take much of their experience with them. "For the engineers, transferring knowledge to their successors is easier said than done," says Bock. BASF encourages older staffers to take on a mentee. To ensure expertise gets passed on, BASF created teaching sessions called *Wissensstafette,* or knowledge relay, where older workers share their knowledge with newcomers. It also changed its compensation scheme to reward mentoring. Now 360-degree evaluations are conducted to get feedback from those being mentored—a rare approach in Germany, where most bonuses are based solely on seniority.

If BASF can unlock the potential of its older workers, its golden years may still be ahead.

From *Fortune*, July 20, 2009, p. 146. Copyright © 2009 by Fortune Magazine. Reprinted by permission.

Article 19

The War over Unconscious Bias

Wal-Mart and others are facing class actions for job discrimination. But the biggest problem isn't their policies, it's their managers' *unwitting* **preferences. Can any company be immune?**

ROGER PARLOFF

Last February a federal appeals court panel in San Francisco decided, 2–1, to allow the largest class action employment discrimination case ever convened to go forward against Wal-Mart Stores. The class includes the more than two million women who have worked at any of the company's more than 4,000 retail stores nationwide since Dec. 26, 1998.

The case, known as *Dukes v. Wal-Mart,* accuses the retailer of discouraging the promotion of women store employees to managerial positions and of paying them less than men across all job positions. The suit seeks changes in the company's internal procedures, more than $1 billion in back pay, and punitive damages.

Wal-Mart denies any wrongdoing and asserts that it has put "enormous resources in seeking to have a diverse workplace and to make sure that women and minorities are having the best possible opportunities to succeed," as its lead lawyer, Theodore Boutrous Jr. of Gibson Dunn & Crutcher, puts it. (Boutrous has represented Time Inc., which publishes FORTUNE.) Wal-Mart has asked the full appeals court to reconsider the panel's approval of the class. ("Class certification" means the court believes that the claims by various employees share enough common elements to proceed as one combined suit rather than endless individual suits.) If Wal-Mart fails to win that, it will probably seek U.S. Supreme Court review.

Gender discrimination is always an incendiary accusation, and this case carries added emotional freight because Wal-Mart is Wal-Mart. It's not just the world's biggest private employer and the most admired company in this magazine's 2003 and 2004 surveys but also the most abhorred in other circles, particularly for its anti-union, penny-pinching labor practices.

But while the *Dukes* case does make some charges of intentional wrongdoing, it focuses mainly on three generic, almost abstract accusations that have become fixtures of nearly every contemporary employment discrimination dispute. These one-size-fits-all charges are less criticisms of Wal-Mart than of our society as a whole. It will be the rare large company that feels confident it could repel any of them.

Whether the defendant is Wal-Mart, Costco, Home Depot, FedEx, General Electric, MetLife, Merrill Lynch, Smith Barney, Morgan Stanley, Deloitte & Touche, or American Express—to name just a few that have been hit with such suits—the cases all stem from statistical evidence showing that the percentage of women or minority employees in portions of the workforce is markedly lower than in the available labor pool. The percentage of women or minorities in lower-level positions often far exceeds the percentage of those who are ever promoted to managerial positions, and their share keeps shrinking the higher up the corporate hierarchy one goes. (Sound like any companies you know?) Experts will often also present statistical analyses purporting to show that women or minorities are, on average, paid less than men or whites.

Once the statistical disparities have been established, the plaintiffs go on to make a second generic accusation: that "unconscious" bias is rife at the company. Supported by expert psychological testimony, the plaintiffs argue that managers in charge of promotion and pay decisions are unwittingly engaging in "spontaneous" and "automatic" stereotyping and "in-group favoritism" that results in the most desirable jobs at the company being filled by people who look like the incumbents, who are usually white males. (The companies' only defense is to challenge the admissibility of the expert testimony, which almost never works.)

Finally, the plaintiffs present the testimony of an expert organizational sociologist who explains that the company's promotion and pay procedures provide too much discretion to managers, allowing their unconscious biases to run rampant. (Know any companies where pay and promotion decisions have significant discretionary components?)

In case after case, these themes are debated by a regular cast of experts. Each side relies on a handful of statisticians, economists, psychologists, and sociologists, and the two teams go to battle in courtrooms around the country, much as the New England Patriots and Miami Dolphins play their scheduled rematches at least twice a year, sometimes at home and sometimes away. Usually the contests end with the class being certified and the defendant then settling for an eight-digit sum rather than risk facing a jury and the enormous exposure that a class action carries.

No scam is being perpetrated. What we are seeing is the clash of two sharply opposed philosophies of how active a company must become in the face of a phenomenon that is endemic and appropriately controversial in our country: workforce numbers that, when analyzed in certain plausible ways—though not in others—show discrepancies between how men and women, or blacks and whites, or the disabled and abled, are paid and promoted.

Such statistical disparities are not illegal per se, according to the Supreme Court, nor do they create any duty on the employer's part to ensure the numbers improve. But as we'll see, in practice employers are under precisely such pressure.

As maybe they should be. Whether you think forcing employers to monitor and increase their diversity is good or bad probably depends on your intuition as to whether existing statistical disparities generally reveal discrimination or whether they instead reflect a complex stew of social, historical, and cultural legacies that no company can or should be expected to correct. It also depends on how you feel about racial or gender quotas and preferences. Though such mechanisms are illegal, they will obviously be tempting to employers who want to avoid being hit with class-action employment discrimination lawsuits. For there is only one sure-fire way to inoculate oneself against such suits, and that is to have workforce numbers that look good even when analyzed by a plaintiffs' expert. And the cheapest and fastest way to get those is to use quotas or preferences.

> "The rulings in the Wal-Mart case virtually guarantee that employers will be subjected to employment discrimination class actions with billions of dollars in potential damages."
>
> —U.S. Chamber of Commerce

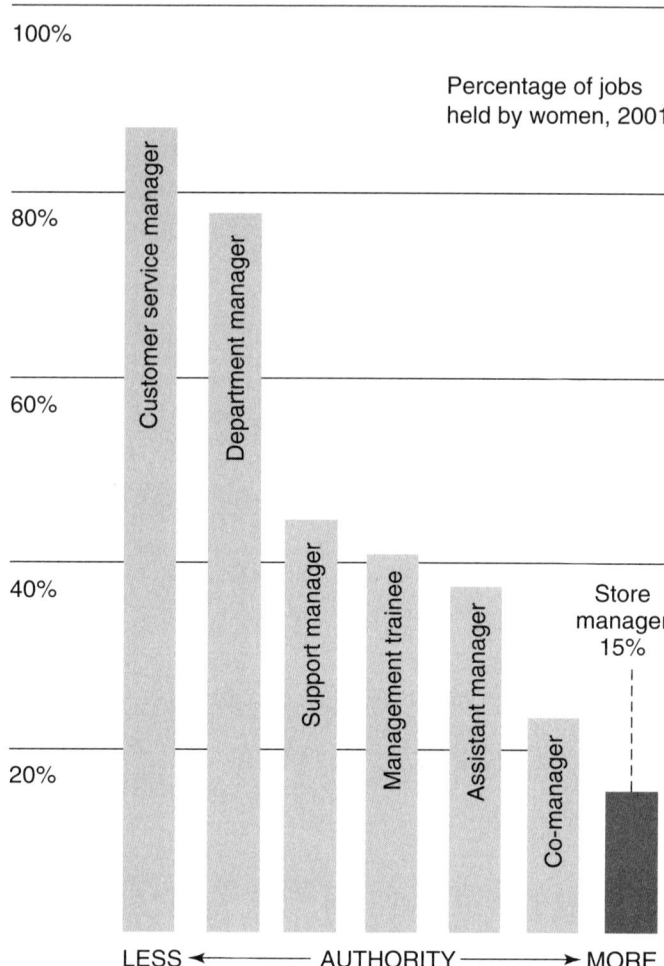

The plaintiffs' view. Discrimination in promotions at Wal-Mart is demonstrated by the numbers: As job authority increases, the percentage of women in those positions decreases.

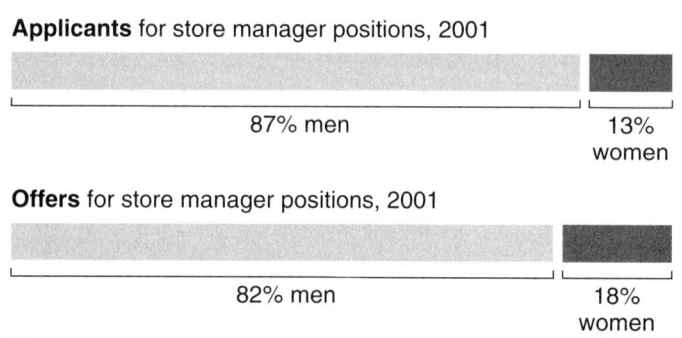

The defense's view. There's no gender discrimination at Wal-Mart: In fact, women were offered store manager positions at a higher rate than their rate of application.

Sources: Report of plaintiffs' expert Richard Drogin (plaintiff); report of Wal-Mart expert Joan G. Haworth (defendant).

The Wal-Mart class action is no aberration; it's an epitome. It shares a common skeletal structure with almost every employment discrimination class action today and thus opens a telling window on a looming litigation threat to corporate America. The rulings in the Wal-Mart case "virtually guarantee that employers will be subjected to large-scale employment discrimination class actions with billions of dollars in potential damages, even . . . where only a few individuals complain of discrete instances of disparate treatment," the U.S. Chamber of Commerce asserted in an amicus brief.

The Wal-Mart rulings could end up representing a high-water mark, however. The underlying legal battles seem destined for the Supreme Court. The urgent question is whether the current Court—with its staunchly conservative five-justice majority, sharp aversion to race-conscious remedies, and weak respect for prior precedent—will allow this situation to persist. The Wal-Mart suit may be the case that gives us the answer.

The federal employment discrimination laws, first enacted in 1964, prohibit two types of discrimination. The most easily understood variety is called disparate treatment: The plaintiff alleges that the employer treated him worse than some other employee because of race, color, religion, sex, or national origin.

Then there is "disparate impact." Here the plaintiff need not allege discriminatory intent. Instead he charges only that the defendant company is using some employment practice that, while possibly well intentioned, isn't essential to the job and acts in a way that systematically disadvantages a protected group. Employees have successfully challenged practices like requiring a high school diploma for certain blue-collar jobs (which put African Americans at a disadvantage in particular times and places); written tests (which put minorities at a disadvantage because of poor schools, language barriers, or cultural bias); and height requirements (which put Asian women seeking to become flight attendants at a disadvantage).

Though disparate treatment and disparate impact cases are both aimed at eradicating the same thing, there is potential tension between them. The goal of disparate treatment cases is to guarantee every worker equal opportunity, but not equal outcomes. The focus of disparate impact cases is on equal outcomes. If one pursues equal outcomes too single-mindedly, one can compromise the principle of equal opportunity by inducing the use of quotas.

In 1988 the Supreme Court faced what it recognized to be a momentous crossroads. A black bank teller who had been turned down for a promotion four times in favor of white applicants asked the Court to let her sue on a disparate impact theory, even though the only "employment practice" she challenged was the bank's policy of giving unbridled discretion to managers about whom to promote. It had long been recognized that unfettered discretion was vulnerable to *intentional* discrimination, and this bank employee was now arguing that it was also vulnerable to *subconscious* discrimination.

On the one hand, the Court's failure to allow such a suit might have permitted employment procedures that resulted in the functional equivalent of intentional discrimination. On the other, to permit it would come close to allowing plaintiffs to sue on the basis of statistical disparities alone. That in turn might force employers to adopt surreptitious quotas, even though courts have said they are illegal.

In the end, the Court let the case, known as *Watson v. Fort Worth Bank & Trust,* go forward, even while asserting that "an employer's policy of leaving promotion decisions to the unchecked discretion of lower-level supervisors should itself raise no inference of discriminatory conduct." Four of the eight justices participating, led by Justice Sandra Day O'Connor, stressed that statistical disparities alone were not suspect. She wrote, "It is completely unrealistic . . . to suppose that employers can eliminate, or discover and explain, the myriad of innocent causes that may lead to statistical imbalances in the composition of their workforces."

One of the first class actions to make use of the *Watson* precedent was *Stender v. Lucky Stores.* That case, brought in the late 1980s against a supermarket chain in Northern California, was handled by two men who would play key roles in employment discrimination litigation, including the Wal-Mart case. The first was a young but already accomplished employment lawyer, Brad Seligman. And the second was an organizational sociologist, William Bielby, who was an expert witness in the case. Bielby (pronounced BILL-by) had been studying gender segregation in the workplace since the 1960s and was then testifying in his first litigation. (Now 60, he is a professor at the University of Illinois in Chicago.)

Lucky Stores was a family-owned business, where store managers chose whom to place in which jobs without any job postings, written guidelines, or oversight. At Lucky Stores there was near total gender segregation: Almost all the cashiers were women, for instance, while almost all the managerial-track jobs were held by men. "So the issue there became, How do you get this extreme outcome when everything seems so fluid?" recalls Bielby.

The innocent possibility was that women sought out different jobs because of the responsibilities of raising children: They wanted lighter, more regular hours; no night shifts or weekends; and no geographic relocations. The illegal possibility was that male managers were, at least to some degree, *assuming* that these would be women's preferences, inadvertently blocking those who *did* want more responsibility from ever getting it. (Intentional discrimination was also possible, of course, but if that could be proved, one would not need a disparate impact theory.)

"There are studies that show that the strongest predictor of whether an opening is filled by a man or woman is whether the previous incumbent was man or woman."

—Plaintiffs expert William Bielby

In the *Lucky Stores* case Bielby testified both about the psychological literature concerning unconscious stereotypes and about the way the unfettered discretion given to managers at Lucky Stores allowed such stereotypes to run unchecked. "There are studies that show," Bielby says today, "that the strongest predictor of whether an opening is filled by a man or woman is whether the previous incumbent was a man or woman.... It's built into our understandings of what the work is about and who does the work, and it becomes the air you breathe."

In 1992, U.S. District Judge Marilyn Hall Patel ruled for the plaintiffs at trial, emphasizing Bielby's testimony in her opinion. (The case was settled for $107 million.) Judge Patel's ruling alerted other plaintiffs employment lawyers to the power of such testimony. Soon they were calling Bielby or a handful of other psychologists and sociologists to provide similar testimony in their cases.

In December 1999, Brad Seligman got a call from a New Mexico lawyer who had won several sex discrimination suits against Wal-Mart on behalf of individual women employees. The lawyer said he thought there was a much bigger problem and wanted Seligman's advice about bringing a class action.

Seligman, now 56, heads a nonprofit group called the Impact Fund. It operates from modest offices in the Berkeley marina. He founded the group in 1992—endowing it with $1.25 million of his own money—to mount, as its name suggests, high-impact employment discrimination cases. From his earlier days in private practice Seligman knew that while it was rewarding to win a nice recovery for an individual, a class action victory could "change a company." Given his political views, he says, that was much more gratifying.

Seligman, who dresses casually in a sweater, khakis, and sandals with white socks, is a child of the '60s. He started college at the University of California at Santa Cruz in 1969, became active in left-wing politics, dropped out, moved to Berkeley, and then moved again to a secluded cabin in Sonoma County. In late 1974, when he found himself unable to meet his $10-a-month rent, he applied to law school. "But my image of being a lawyer was strictly the white hat," he recalls. "I wanted it to have some meaning."

In 1980 he joined a private employment discrimination firm in San Francisco, excelled, became managing partner, and became rich. "Given my political background," he says, being wealthy "was fairly embarrassing at some level." In addition, he was becoming frustrated by "the imperatives of being in private practice"—i.e., staying profitable. "The market dynamics of these cases [puts an] emphasis on producing a large damages pot as quickly as possible," he explains, "and not so much on what I was interested in, which was systemic change."

In 1991, at age 40, he resigned his partnership, and the next year he started the Impact Fund. By the late 1990s, Seligman was looking to use the fund to broker partnerships between nonprofits and private class-action firms to launch significant cases. For-profit firms like 67-lawyer Cohen Milstein Hausfeld & Toll—which Seligman ultimately brought into the *Dukes* case as one of the Fund's five co-counsels—could provide the financial muscle and staff, while nonprofit partners lent the case credibility with the press and grass-roots groups, and made sure that the for-profits didn't grab a "cheap, early settlement," Seligman explains.

Upon getting the inquiry about Wal-Mart, Seligman called Marc Bendick, an economist who had then served as an expert in more than 75 employment cases. Bendick had a database of information compiled from forms, called EEO-1s, that large companies are required to file with the Equal Employment Opportunity Commission, breaking down their workforces by gender and race.

Bendick told Seligman that Wal-Mart's profile was skewed and that "compared to its major competitors, it stuck out like a sore thumb," as Seligman recalls. Bendick eventually computed that women composed 63.4% of Wal-Mart's hourly (nonmanagerial) workers yet just 33.6% of the store's salaried managers. More damning, the company's numbers were far below those of its 20 top competitors, which averaged 56.5% women at the store manager level.

Though these numbers are powerful, some caution is in order. Such "benchmark" or "comparator" studies—in which a company's EEO-1 data is compared to that of a group of purportedly similar companies—are a staple of class-action employment litigation, and the outcomes depend on how one defines the comparison group. Wal-Mart disputes Bendick's list of comparison companies and claims that when a broader group is used—reflecting Wal-Mart's wide geographic footprint and the variety of products and services it sells—it falls within the norm. It also claims that if Wal-Mart had counted its highest-level hourly-wage supervisors as "managers" on its EEO-1 forms, the way it believes several of Bendick's comparator firms do, the entire purported disparity vanishes.

Seligman filed the *Dukes* case in San Francisco federal court in June 2001. The mammoth discovery process then began, which, by mid-2003, had led to the taking of 200 depositions and the collection of millions of documents.

> **"This case represents Wal-Mart's worst nightmare, their policies are going to be judged by a San Francisco jury and a San Francisco judge."**
>
> —Plaintiffs lawyer Brad Seligman

Through that process, Seligman maintains that he unearthed evidence that "biased attitudes were at the very top of the company." Such evidence would support a disparate treatment claim—i.e., the charge that Wal-Mart intentionally discriminated—as well as a disparate impact claim. Seligman will produce proof, for instance, that at Monday morning meetings of high-level Sam's Club executives, female store employees were often referred to as "Janie Q's." A woman executive who found the term (of unknown origin) demeaning complained about it, but others continued to use it. While some in Bentonville, Ark., might have considered "Janie Q." endearing, it will likely sound condescending and offensive to a jury in San Francisco. (Wal-Mart tried to move the case to Arkansas, but U.S. District Judge Martin Jenkins denied the motion. "This case represents Wal-Mart's worst nightmare," Seligman says. "Their policies are going to be judged by a San Francisco jury and a San Francisco judge." San Francisco is in the Ninth Circuit, whose federal appeals court is regarded as the nation's most liberal.)

Through the discovery process Seligman also harvested more statistical data, in which his experts detected more gender disparities. The most important related to pay. According to computations performed by Richard Drogin, a statistician who by 2003 had served as a plaintiffs expert in about 30 cases, women store employees were paid less than men across all job positions (both hourly and managerial), even though women, on average, had more seniority and better performance evaluations. He calculated that women hourly workers were paid, on average, $1,100 less per year than men, while women managerial workers received $14,500 less. The compensation disparity claims became the most potent in the case, because they could potentially require back-pay reimbursements to every class member, not just the fraction who might have become managers.

The primary mechanism that was allegedly producing all these gaps was, once again, the granting of too much discretion to store managers, which predictably gave their unconscious bias free rein. To provide testimony on the literature relating to unconscious stereotyping and an analysis of why Wal-Mart's procedures failed to channel managerial discretion adequately, Seligman retained Bielby.

How can a court treat 4,000 Wal-Mart store managers as acting in exactly the same way when the plaintiffs' theory is that those store managers are granted too much autonomy?

Bielby would provide testimony on one additional critical issue. Seligman needed to finesse what defendants claim is an internal contradiction in all class actions that challenge a company's granting of "unfettered discretion" to managers. If each store's local manager is being granted unbridled discretion, one might expect to see significant differences in how each store treats men and women. Stores run by female store managers, for instance, might show less gender discrimination than those run by men.

Some male managers might also be better able to resist subconscious stereotyping than others. How can a court treat 4,000 store managers as acting identically for purposes of a class action when the plaintiffs' whole theory of the case is that those store managers are being granted too much autonomy?

In a rebuttal to that sort of argument, Bielby opined in his report that "a strong and widely shared organizational culture promotes uniformity of practices throughout an organization," and that Wal-Mart had such a culture. That could be inferred from such factors as Wal-Mart's "emphasis on the company's founder and its history, a mission statement defined by core values, frequent communication about the culture to employees," and so on. (None of those traits is unusual among big corporations, and Bielby has provided similar testimony in cases against, for instance, Home Depot, Brookshire Grocery Co., US Bancorp Piper Jaffray, and FedEx Express.)

To mount its statistical defense, Wal-Mart retained Joan Haworth, an economist who had, by then, served as an expert in more than 65 employment cases. As for the purported promotional disparities the plaintiffs experts had found—that women's presence in salaried managerial positions was far lower than their presence in the hourly workforce from which they were drawn—she found that the plaintiffs were simply failing to take into account employees' interest in such promotions. Her data showed that women were actually being offered store manager jobs in numbers that exceeded their percentage in the applicant pool. During the years 1999 to 2002, for instance, 12% of the applicants were women, while 17% of the offers went to women.

As for the plaintiffs' claims of pay disparity, defense expert Haworth likewise reached very different conclusions from plaintiffs' expert Drogin. She claimed that Drogin's analyses did not adequately take into account crucial factors, like the number of hours worked and whether they included night-shift work, which pays more. But her overarching criticism was that his approach amounted to pretending that a single person was making all promotion and pay decisions throughout Wal-Mart nationwide, when, according to depositions, most pay determinations were made at the store manager level or, in the case of certain specialty department employees, at the district manager level. When she performed statistical analyses at the store and district levels, reflecting Wal-Mart's claims about the way that decisions are made, she found that 92.8% of all the standard Wal-Mart and Supercenter stores showed no statistically significant pay disparities. Of the remainder, 5.2% showed disparities favoring men, while 2.0% showed disparities favoring women. In other words, more than 90% of class members worked at stores where women were statistically no worse off than men. Wal-Mart's argument, then, was that if a class action must be filed, it should be brought against the specific stores with disparities favoring men.

By September 2003, the case was ready for the all-important arguments on class certification, at which a judge considers whether to let the case proceed as a class action. This is often the decisive event in such a case, since disapproval of the class renders litigation impractical for most class members, while certification creates such large exposure for the defendant as to force settlement. In the Wal-Mart case an important part of the class certification proceeding was a challenge by Wal-Mart to the admissibility of psychological and sociological testimony on unconscious bias, which it challenged as junk science.

Such challenges have been routine features of class action employment cases since at least 1997, when one was brought by lawyers for Home Depot. (Home Depot lost its bid to exclude the testimony and eventually settled for $87.5 million.) The crux of the defense argument is always that the effects of unconscious stereotyping in the workplace are still too unproven to be the subject of helpful courtroom testimony. Defense experts argue that the plaintiffs' experts ignore or gloss over studies that cut against the plaintiffs' thesis, and that they overgeneralize from lab experiments that may have little bearing on real-world work settings. A typical stereotyping study, for instance, might involve college students who are asked to choose the more qualified applicant from among two fictional candidates—one male and one female, say—on the basis of résumés alone. Such experiments might not predict how real managers behave in work settings when choosing among employees that they've worked with closely for months. There's no question that a large body of scientific literature on unconscious stereotyping exists; the dispute is over what, if any, inferences can safely be drawn from it to particular workplace situations.

Wal-Mart lost its attempt to exclude the stereotyping testimony. Judge Jenkins ruled—as have most judges—that the defense experts' critiques went to the weight to be given the evidence, not its admissibility, and weight could be assessed by the jury.

Similarly, Judge Jenkins declined to resolve the numerous statistical disputes that had been presented to him. He ruled that at a class certification hearing he was not supposed to resolve such issues, which were to be deferred to a later stage of the litigation. The plaintiffs only had to present a theory that was plausible, which they had done. That's the ruling that was upheld by an appeals panel this past February, and which Wal-Mart is still appealing.

Meanwhile, the suits keep coming. In the 15 years since the *Lucky Stores* case, sociologist Bielby estimates that he has served as an expert witness for plaintiffs in "50 or 60" employment discrimination cases. (One of the cases is against a group of Hollywood film and TV studios, including entities owned by Time Warner, which also owns FORTUNE's publisher.) During that period he has obviously encountered many companies that were vastly more sophisticated than the family-run grocery chain he first critiqued. These have included FORTUNE 500 companies, many of which have written antidiscrimination policies, substantial human resources operations, and in-house legal departments counseling them on how to behave. Nevertheless, Bielby keeps finding failings in the companies' procedures. "The issues in the more sophisticated companies," he explains, "often have to do with, Are there specific vulnerabilities you can point to?"

In a race discrimination class action against FedEx, Bielby critiqued a performance review system that was based in part on objective factors spelled out in employee manuals. Bielby nevertheless found the process to be inadequate for a litany of reasons: "Judgments about the weights to be assigned to individual components of a performance dimension in order to obtain an overall rating . . . are left to the discretion of individual managers"; FedEx did no auditing to ensure that managers were adhering to the written guidelines; it didn't monitor whether there were racial disparities in the outcomes of these reviews; its training of the people performing the reviews lacked "hands-on rating exercises with instructor feedback" and was not "repeated at regular intervals"; and FedEx was not holding the raters accountable for how they performed the rating task, "with real consequences for inadequate performance." The class was certified in September 2005, and the parties announced a $53.5 million tentative settlement in April.

Just what sort of procedures would win Bielby's blessing? He concedes that no neutral procedural mechanism in itself will ever be sufficient; it must also be accompanied by auditing of the decision-making process, monitoring of the racial and gender outcomes, and holding decision-makers "accountable" for their "contributions" to diversity.

And therein lies the rub. To a pragmatic businessman, it may sound like Bielby is saying that companies should dock the pay of managers if they don't meet numerical diversity goals—creating a powerful incentive for managers to adopt surreptitious quotas and preferences. Bielby maintains that he's not recommending any such thing. The monitoring of outcomes that he's advocating is merely diagnostic testing, he insists. As for the "accountability" piece of it, he says, "make it part of the manager's job to contribute to the company's EEO goals. And by that I don't mean quotas or the number of men vs. women promoted. [Make clear] what the company's vision is of EEO and how that translates into specific responsibilities and duties for someone that has authority to make decisions about hiring, promotion, pay, and so on. And do that in a meaningful way—that's part of their performance evaluation—so they know that it's not just feel-good talk."

Since Wal-Mart filed its reconsideration motion in late February, both the appellate courts and the Supreme Court have issued a series of rulings that make Judge Jenkins's certification of the Wal-Mart class action appear ever more precarious. In its past term, for instance, the Court rendered two highly controversial, quite conservative 5–4 rulings in the area of antidiscrimination law.

"Neither case directly applies to our case," says Seligman, "but both cases say something deeply troubling about the direction of the U.S. Supreme Court." In the second of them, the Court struck down voluntary, race-conscious school-assignment programs adopted to achieve racial balance.

"Racial balancing is not permitted," Chief Justice John Roberts wrote.

If *Dukes v. Wal-Mart* does reach the Supreme Court, the suit will present a blockbuster test case, with potential to change the face of contemporary employment discrimination class actions. Given their near-universal exposure to such suits, FORTUNE 500 companies should be praying that it does.

From *Fortune*, October 15, 2007. Copyright © 2007 by Fortune Magazine. Reprinted by permission.

Article 20

Reflecting on Downsizing: What Have Managers Learned?

FRANCO GANDOLFI

Introduction

Organizational downsizing as a change management strategy has been adopted for more than two decades (Gandolfi, 2007). In the 1980s and early 1990s, it was implemented primarily by firms experiencing difficult economic times (Gandolfi, 2006). However, since the mid-1990s, downsizing has become a leading strategy of choice for a multitude of firms around the world (Mirabal and DeYoung, 2005). The prime impetus of most downsizing efforts is the desire for an immediate reduction of costs and increased levels of efficiency, productivity, profitability, and competitiveness (Farrell and Mavondo, 2004). Over the years, this strategy has generated a great deal of interest among scholars, managers, and the popular press. Some authors suggest that the research-based body of knowledge is still relatively underdeveloped (Macky, 2004), while others stress the confusion surrounding downsizing (Williams, 2004; Gandolfi, 2008). The adoption of strategic downsizing has remained popular (Maurer, 2005), yet significant empirical and anecdotal evidence suggests that the overall consequences are negative (Zyglidopoulos, 2003).

The primary objective of this article is to review the consequences of downsizing, focusing on the following questions: Does downsizing work? Have firms reaped the much anticipated benefits? In other words, what do we know about the effects and after-effects of downsizing? This paper draws out implications for executives and showcases five downsizing lessons that managers should consider. Finally, the paper suggests future research for this topic.

Downsizing: Background

Back in the mid-1970s, Charles Handy first predicted that the technological revolution would transform the lives of millions of individuals through a process he aptly termed 'down-sizing' (Appelbaum, Everard, and Hung, 1999). While few understood his prediction at the time, we now know that downsizing has been adopted as a management technique on a global scale (Macky, 2004). Firms have implemented downsizing as a "reactive response to organizational bankruptcy or recession" (Ryan and Macky, 1998) and proactively as a human resource (HR) strategy (Chadwick, Hunter, and Walston, 2004). Reflecting upon its pervasiveness, it is evident that downsizing has attained the status of a fully-fledged restructuring strategy (Cameron, 1994) with the intent of attaining a new level of competitiveness (Littler, 1998).

Admittedly, downsizing is not new. It came into prominence as a topic of both academic and practical concern in the 1980s and became a management mantra (Lecky, 1998) in the 1990s. The latter period subsequently became the "downsizing decade" (Dolan, Belout, and Balkin, 2000). Downsizing has transformed hundreds of thousands of firms and governmental agencies and the lives of tens of millions of employees around the world (Amundson, Borgen, Jordan, and Erlebach, 2004). The notion of downsizing has emerged from a number of disciplines and draws upon a wide range of management and organizational theories. The body of literature is extensive reflecting its prevalence in the U.S., the U.K., Canada, Western Europe, Australia, New Zealand, and Japan (Littler, 1998; Gandolfi and Neck, 2003; Farrell and Mavondo, 2004; Macky, 2004).

A single definition of downsizing does not exist across studies and disciplines. Still, it is clear that it means a contraction in the size of a firm's workforce. Cascio (1993) posits that downsizing is the planned elimination of positions or jobs whose primary purpose is to reduce the workforce, while Gandolfi (2006) adds that a myriad of terms have been used euphemistically in reference to downsizing, including "brightsizing" and "rightsizing."

Downsizing is ubiquitous. While manufacturing, retail, and service have accounted for the highest levels, downsizing has occurred in both the private and public sectors (Macky, 2004). Downsizing statistics show a sobering picture. The U.S. Bureau of Labor Statistics (BLS) reported that more than 4.3 million jobs were cut between 1985 and 1989 (Lee, 1992). The *New York Times* stated that more than 43 million jobs had been eliminated between 1979 and 1996 (Cascio, 2003). Cameron (1994) reported that 85% of the *Fortune 500* firms downsized between 1989 and 1994, and 100% had downsizing-related plans in the ensuing five years. Substantial evidence suggests that downsizing remains a popular restructuring strategy (Mirabal and DeYoung, 2005; Gandolfi, 2008).

Why do firms resort to downsizing? What are the driving forces? While downsizing is viewed as complicated and multifaceted (Gandolfi, 2006), it has generally been adopted either reactively or proactively (Macky, 2004). To put a single downsizing cause forward is problematic and underrates its inherent complexity. Each downsizing decision reflects a combination of company-specific, industry-specific, and macroeconomic factors (Drew, 1994). Downsizing firms frequently point to deregulation, globalization, mergers and acquisitions (M&A) activities, global competition, technological innovation, and a shift in business strategies to obtain and retain competitive advantages (Dolan, Belout, and Balkin, 2000; Sahdev, 2003; Gandolfi, 2008).

Downsizing Consequences

Downsizing has deep financial, organizational, and social consequences, covered extensively in the change management literature. A closer analysis of the overall effects presents a complex picture with the following questions emerging:

- Is downsizing an effective strategy?
- Does downsizing engender improved financial performance?
- Have firms reaped financial and organizational improvements?

The overall picture of the financial effects of downsizing is negative. While a few firms have reported financial improvements, the majority have failed to report increased levels of efficiency, effectiveness, productivity, and profitability (Cascio, 1993; Macky, 2004; Gandolfi, 2008). Table 1 presents a non-exhaustive overview of some of the findings.

In light of the available cross-sectional and longitudinal data, the following conclusions can be made:

- Most firms adopting downsizing strategies do not reap economic and organizational benefits;
- Non-downsized firms financially outperform downsized forms in the short-, medium-, and long-run;
- While some firms have shown positive financial outcomes, there is no empirical evidence to suggest a correlation between downsizing and improved financial performance;
- Some firms have reported positive financial indicators in the short term, yet the long-term financial consequences of downsizing have been shown to be consistently negative.

Downsizing also transcends financial consequences. A significant body of literature reports that downsizing has profound consequences on the workforce, the so-called "after," "side," or "secondary" downsizing effects (Littler, Dunford, Bramble, and Hede, 1997; Macky, 2004). At least three categories of people are directly affected by downsizing: survivors, victims, and executioners. A survivor remains with the firm, a victim is downsized out of a job involuntarily, while an executioner is entrusted with the downsizing implementation (Gandolfi, 2006). Table 2 presents the three categories of affected individuals with some of the major research findings.

While it could be presumed that it is better to be a downsizing survivor rather than a victim, does evidence support this? Determining and comparing the symptoms exhibited by victims and survivors, Devine and colleagues (2003) assert that surviving downsizing is difficult given the high levels of stress experienced by survivors compared to the victims (Devine, Reay, Stainton, and Collins-Nakai, 2003). The argument rests partly on the disparity in resources available to victims compared with those available to survivors. Victims commonly receive transition packages and outplacement services, while survivors receive very little, if any, resources and support. Devine et al. (2003) compared the outcomes for displaced and continuing employees, finding that the victims who found employment post-downsizing reported considerably more positive outcomes than did those who remained in the downsized environment. The victims felt lower levels of stress on the job, reported higher levels of perceived job control, and experienced fewer negative effects than the survivors. In light of that, the following conclusions can be made:

- Downsizing produces considerable human consequences;
- Downsizing affects the entire workforce, survivors, victims, and executioners, in a most profound manner;
- Survivors generally find themselves with increased workloads and job responsibilities while frequently receiving few or no resources, training, and support;

Table 1 Financial Effects of Downsizing

Researcher	Findings	Bottom-line
Zemke (1990)	A study conducted in 1989 and repeated in 1990 by the Philadelphia outplacement firm Right Associates. HR executives from 500 downsized firms said that the implementation of downsizing did not generate financial gains, but had in fact negative economic effects on the firm—25% in 1989 and 28% in 1990. Managers also reported significant "aftershocks" following downsizing.	• No financial gains reported • Negative economic effects • Significant "aftershocks"
Worrell, Davidson, and Sharma (1991)	Examined the impact of downsizing announcements on stock returns for a sample of 194 firms that announced layoffs during 1979–1987. They examined the stock returns of companies from 90 days prior to the announcement of the downsizing in the Wall Street Journal to 90 days after the announcement. There was a significantly negative market reaction to the announcements with the cumulative loss in stock value being about 2% of the value of the equity of the firms. For firms that provided restructuring and consolidation as the reason for the layoffs, there was a 3.6% increase in stock value over the 180-day test period, while stocks of firms citing financial distress as the reason for downsizing declined an average of 5.6% over the same period.	• Negative market reaction following downsizing announcements • Declining stock values post-downsizing
De Meuse, Vanderheiden, and Bergmann (1994).	Conducted a large downsizing study of Fortune 100 companies measuring their financial performance over a five-year period, that is, two years prior to the announcement, the year of the announcement, and two years after the announcement. Statistical tests revealed no significant positive relationships for any of the financial variables. De Meuse et al. (1994) concluded that empirical evidence did not support the contention that downsizing leads to improved financial performance.	• No improved financial performance
Clark and Koonce (1995)	Carried out a U.S. study revealing that approximately 68% of all surveyed downsizing, restructuring, and reengineering efforts did not generate financial gains and benefits.	• 68% of firms failed to improve financial performance
Downs (1995)	Studied the financial implications following downsizing and reported that the severance pay expenses from downsizing, in particular, can be enormous. Downs (1995) cites Dow Chemical's experience with manager layoffs in the 1990s as "horribly expensive" and "destructive to shareholders' value" (Appelbaum et al., 1999).	• Severe negative financial implications following downsizing
Estok (1996)	Watson Wyatt Worldwide carried out a study of 148 major Canadian firms showing that 40% of downsizing efforts did not result in decreased expenses, and that more than 60% of firms did not experience an increase in profitability.	• 40% of firms failed to decrease expenses • 60% failed to increase profitability
Cascio, Young, and Morris (1997)	Studied data from the Standard and Poor (S&P) 500 between 1980 and 1994 examining 5,479 occurrences of changes in employment in terms of two dependent financial variables. They reported that firms engaging in downsizing did not show significantly higher returns than the average companies in their own industries.	• No higher financial returns after downsizing
Clark and Koonce (1995)	Reported that 68% of all downsizing activities were financially unsuccessful. Those that downsized and restructured specifically to become more profitable and efficient realized neither outcome. They concluded that downsizing outcomes were "tremendous disappointments" that fell well short of expectations (Williams, 2004).	• 68% of firms reported unsuccessful financial results after downsizing • Downsizing seen as disappointments
Cascio (1998)	Examined 311 S&P 500 firms that had downsized between 1981 and 1990 and concluded that downsizing per se did not lead to improved financial performance.	• Downsizing failed to produce positive financial results
Lecky (1998)	A major Australian study conducted by the Queensland University of Technology disclosed that a mere 40% of firms achieved an increase in productivity and only half accomplished a decrease in overall costs following downsizing.	• 60% of firms failed to improve productivity • 50% failed to decrease costs
Kirby (1999)	Reported that several longitudinal studies in Australia showed a consistently negative financial picture in that six out of ten downsized firms failed to cut overall costs or increase productivity.	• 60% of firms failed to cut costs • 60% of firms failed to increase productivity

(continued)

Table 1 Financial Effects of Downsizing (continued)

Researcher	Findings	Bottom-line
Appelbaum, Everard, and Hung (1999)	Cited a Mitchell & Co. study of 16 North American firms that had cut more than 10% of their respective workforces between 1982 and 1988. It was shown that two years after the initial stock price increase, 10 of the 16 stocks were quoting below market by 17–48% and 12 were below the comparable companies in their industries by 5–45%. Appelbaum et al. (1999) concluded that such results depicted the true financial impact of downsizing on firms.	• Firms cutting more than 10% of workforce underperformed non-cutters in terms of stock price
Morris, Cascio, and Young (1999)	Studied the financial performance of the S&P 500 Index subsequent to changes in employment from 1981 to 1992. The key indicators constituted overall profitability and the stock market performance. The tabulation showed that firms with stable employment consistently outperformed companies with employment downsizing. Also, firms that "upsized" (i.e., employment increases exceeded 5%) generated stock returns that were 50% higher than those of stable and downsized firms in the year that they upsized, and cumulative stock returns that were 20% higher over three years. Morris et al. (1999) concluded that a consistently positive correlation between downsizing and improved financial performance could not be established. Rather, empirical evidence suggested that downsizing was unlikely to lead to improvements in a firm's financial performance.	• Firms with stable employment outperformed firms with downsizing • Firms that upsized outperformed firms with stable and downsizing workforces • No correlation between downsizing and improved financial performance
Gandolfi (2001)	Conducted an extensive analysis of financial performance of large downsized banks in Australia. Empirical evidence suggested that the majority of downsized firms were unable to cut overall costs and to improve profitability. Only few study cases reported satisfactory financial improvements.	• Majority of firms failed to cut costs • Majority of firms failed to increase profitability
Griggs and Hyland (2003)	Watson Wyatt Worldwide conducted a study of 1,005 firms in 1991 and reported that widely anticipated economic and organizational benefits for downsized companies failed to materialize. Empirical evidence suggested that a mere 46% of downsized firms cut overall costs, fewer than 33% increased profitability, and only 21% reported satisfactory improvements in ROI.	• 54% of firms failed to cut costs • 66% failed to increase profitability • 9% failed to show satisfactory ROI
De Meuse, Bergmann, Vanderheiden, and Roraff (2004)	Conducted one of the most systematic longitudinal analyses of financial performance of downsized firms. The study examined the long-term relationships of downsizing on five measures of financial performance from 1987 until 1998. It was found that downsized firms performed significantly poorer up to two years following the announcement. Beginning with the third year, none of the differences reached statistical significance. When analyzing the magnitude of downsizing, the data revealed that firms that had downsized a small number of employees (i.e., up to 3%) performed significantly better in the announcement year, while firms that downsized more than 10% of the workforce significantly underperformed firms laying off less.	• Downsized firms underperformed others up to two years after announcement • Firms cutting more than 10% of workforce underperformed firms with less downsizing
Macky (2004)	Reported that a New Zealand study comprising 45 firms listed on the stock exchange and 110 nonlisted companies employing 50 or more people showed that firms that had downsized between 1997 and 1999 financially underperformed firms that had not engaged in downsizing. Macky (2004) concluded that despite the widespread use of downsizing, there was still little convincing research to show that downsizing produces the financial benefits expected by managers.	• Non-downsizers outperformed downsized firms financially • No correlation between downsizing and improved financial performance
Gandolfi (2008)	Conducted an extensive longitudinal study of financial performance of downsized firms in Australia and Switzerland. Empirical evidence suggested that the majority of downsized firms were unable to cut overall costs. Gandolfi (2008) concluded that downsizing *per se* did not lead to improved financial performance.	• Majority of firms failed to cut costs • Majority of firms failed to increase profitability

Source: Developed for this research.

Table 2   Downsizing Categories of Affected Individuals

Category	Findings	Bottom-line
Survivors	Display a number of symptoms during and after downsizing. The *first* sickness, the survivor syndrome, is a set of emotions, behaviors, and attitudes exhibited by surviving employees (Littler et al., 1997). Brockner (1988) asserts that downsizing engenders a variety of psychological states in survivors: guilt, positive inequity, anger, relief, and job insecurity. These mental states influence the survivors' work behaviors and attitudes, such as motivation, commitment, satisfaction, and job performance. Kinnie, Hutchinson, and Purcell (1998) identified survivor symptoms, including increased levels of stress, absenteeism, and distrust, as well as decreased levels of work quality, morale, and productivity. Cascio (1993) argues that the survivor syndrome is characterized by decreased levels of morale, employee involvement, work productivity, and trust towards management. Lecky (1998) reports that the survivor syndrome manifests itself in negative morale, decreased employee commitment, and increased concern about job security. Gettler (1998) observed similar symptoms among survivors in New Zealand, Australia, and South Africa suggesting a drop in productivity in line with data from the U.S. and Europe. The *second* sickness, survivor guilt, is a feeling of responsibility or remorse for some offence and is often expressed in terms of depression, fear, and anger (Noer, 1993). The reality of survivor guilt is comparable to the concept of combat syndrome, which refers to the feelings experienced by a soldier in combat upon the death of a fellow soldier. Feelings of relief for his own survival are often followed by feelings of immense guilt for his own survival (Allen, 1997). Cameron, Freeman, and Mishra (1993) assert that survivor guilt may occur when survivors work overtime or receive paychecks. Additionally, survivors may perceive that traditional attributes, such as loyalty, individual competence, and diligence are no longer valued since their co-workers, who had displayed such traits, were victims of downsizing. Littler et al. (1997) point out that survivor guilt arises when survivors perceive that their own performance merited no better treatment than that accorded the downsized victims. Schweiger, Ivancevich, and Power (1987) contend that it is not the terminations *per se* that create hostility, anger, bitterness, and survivor guilt but the manner in which the terminations were handled. Survivors expressed feelings of anger and disgust that their peers were downsized and felt guilt that they were not directly involved in the downsizing. The survivors also believed that their co-workers performed at least as well or even better than the survivors. Thus, the survivors' perceived feelings of bitterness, anger and disgust regarding the layoffs of co-workers may potentially result in survivor guilt (Appelbaum et al., 1999). The *third* sickness, survivor envy, reflects a survivor's feelings of envy towards the victims (Kinnie et al., 1998). Survivors presume that victims obtain special retirement packages and new jobs with more attractive compensation.	Sickness 1: Survivor syndrome • guilt • positive inequity • anger • relief • job insecurity Mental states influence • motivation • commitment • satisfaction • work performance Symptoms include • higher levels of stress • higher levels of absenteeism • higher levels of distrust • higher levels of job insecurity • decreased work quality • decreased morale • decreased productivity • decreased employee involvement • decreased trust toward management Sickness 2: Survivor guilt • depression • fear • anger Sickness 3: Survivor envy • feelings of envy toward victims
Victims	Strong evidence of adverse psychological effects resulting from job loss, including psychological stress, ill health, family problems, marital problems, reduced self-esteem, depression, psychiatric morbidity, helplessness, anxiety, and feelings of social isolation (Greenglass and Burke, 2001). There is some evidence suggesting that job loss caused by downsizing may generate permanent damage to the victims' careers (Dolan et al., 2000). Victims have reported a loss of earning power upon, reemployment (Konovsky and Brockner, 1993). Studies suggest that victims have encountered feelings of cynicism, uncertainty, and decreased levels of commitment and loyalty that carry over to the next job (Macky, 2004). The focus in most downsized firms is on the victimized employees (Amundson et al., 2004) who are considered the primary victims of a downsizing and who need counseling, support, help, and re-training. Victims often receive generous outplacement services and financially attractive incentive packages (Gandolfi, 2006). These benefits generally include outplacement support, personal and family counseling, relocation expenses, retraining, and a variety of lucrative incentive packages, such as severance pay and benefits packages (Allen, 1997).	Psychological effects • psychological stress • ill health • family and problems • reduced self-esteem • psychiatric morbidity • depression • helplessness and anxiety • feelings of social isolation Other effects • damage to career • loss of earning power • feelings of cynicism, uncertainty, decreased levels of commitment and loyalty in future employment
Executioners	Likely to be an employee, manager, or consultant entrusted with the planning, execution, and evaluation of a downsizing activity (Downs, 1995). Little research has been documented on the emotional responses and reactions of the subjects implementing downsizing. Some evidence suggests that the implementers of downsizing suffer from similar psychological and emotional effects as the victims and survivors (Gandolfi, 2007) in that carrying downsizing responsibilities is emotionally taxing and professionally challenging (Clair and Dufresne, 2004).	Psychological effects • Similar effects as victims and survivors Emotional effects • Similar effects as victims and survivors

Source: Developed for this research.

- Victims commonly obtain outplacement services and financial packages when exiting the downsized firms;
- Survivors suffer from a range of downsizing-related sicknesses;
- Executioners suffer similar effects to those of victims and survivors.

Learning from the Past: What Have Executives Learned?

It is not presumptuous to state that organizations have failed to reap widely anticipated downsizing gains. Additionally, firms have been forced to contend with considerable human consequences. Still, there is sporadic evidence that a few firms have engaged in practices that generated positive effects. Considering the current findings, what have executives learned? What downsizing lessons can be deduced? Is it possible to determine best downsizing practice?

It must be understood that the reduction of workforces *per se* is not new. Workforces have always fluctuated, particularly in response to economic crises. This was the prevailing paradigm prior to the mid-1980s. However, the tide turned half way through the 1980s in that downsizing became decoupled from the business cycle (Gandolfi, 2005) and manifested itself as a fully-fledged, proactive HR strategy (Chadwick et al., 2004). As a result, downsizing attained the status of a restructuring strategy (Cameron, 1994). In the following decade, downsizing became a way of life (Filipowski, 1993) and a corporate panacea (Nelson, 1997). Paradoxically, this unprecedented development took place despite downsizing successes. The following are five downsizing lessons for executives contemplating a downsizing strategy:

Lesson 1: Downsizing Preparation

Research shows that organizations conduct downsizing without adequate HR plans, policies, and programs (Appelbaum, 1997; Gandolfi, 2001). Firms are also inadequately prepared for downsizing and severely neglect the survivors (Doherty and Horsted, 1995; Allen, 1997; Gandolfi and Neck, 2003). To some degree, this unpreparedness explains why firms have not been able to implement downsizing successfully. Why and how should managers prepare their firms for downsizing? Cameron (1994) draws attention to a U.S. firm that introduced a new HR system for all employees one year *prior to* the downsizing announcement. As a result of this proactive measure, the firm reported positive financial and organizational outcomes with minimal disruption and pain among the surviving and departing workforces. Similar findings were reported in a cross-sectional study in the Australian banking industry (Gandolfi, 2001). These examples demonstrate that proactive preparation for downsizing can positively contribute to a firm's preparedness for any major change. Therefore, the first implication for managers is to plan strategically and prepare proactively for downsizing. Executives will need to ensure that the firm's culture can and will embrace major change successfully. This will contribute to an organization's attaining change readiness (Gandolfi, 2006), which is a key requirement for successful downsizing and an indispensable factor of most change endeavors.

Lesson 2: Specific Downsizing Training

Firms are frequently ill-prepared for downsizing and fail to provide adequate training, support, and assistance to survivors. Gandolfi (2006) contends that while the workforce generally receives job-specific professional training and development, attention to personal development and growth during downsizing is confined to managers. Gandolfi (2006b) found that enhancing an employee's physical lifestyle, mental capacity, and emotional growth had the potential to proactively prepare the workforce for change and help individuals cope successfully with downsizing. Table 3 showcases the three categories of personal growth and development.

There is an increased awareness and understanding that survivors lack training, support, and assistance during and after the implementation of downsizing (Appelbaum et al., 1997; Macky, 2004; Gandolfi, 2006). This is remarkable given that survivors commonly face new job responsibilities (Mitchell, 1998), experience increased workloads (Dolan et al., 2000), and are driven to work harder after downsizing (Makawatsakul and Kleiner, 2003). Would it not make sense for the survivors to receive much needed training, support, and assistance in the wake of this new-found reality? Executives should ensure that firms invest in their workforces proactively and provide training, support, and assistance throughout the downsizing process. Without a doubt, a thoroughly prepared and adequately equipped workforce is more likely to be able to cope with and thrive in the wake of downsizing.

Lesson 3: Downsizing and the Survivor Syndrome

Downsizing survivor sicknesses have been referred to as "aftershocks" (Zemke, 1990) and the "aftermath" (Clark and Koonce, 1995) of downsizing. Clearly, the remaining

Table 3 Categories of Personal Development and Growth

Physical Lifestyle	Mental Capacity	Emotional Growth
Sports	Change management skills	Emotional reactions to change
Sauna	Stress management skills	The nature of change
Aerobics	Communication skills	The purpose of change
Massages	Interpersonal skills	The stages of change
Yoga classes	Presentation skills	Preparation for change
Fitness classes	Leadership skills	Self-awareness
Weightlifting classes	Teamwork skills	Counseling
Rock climbing	Mentoring and coaching skills	On-line emotional support
Table tennis	Conflict resolution skills	Emotional intelligence

Source: Adapted from Gandolfi (2006b).

employees play a significant role during downsizing in the sense that they either facilitate or impede the outcomes (Mishra and Spreitzer, 1998). This is a profound insight. Studies have shown that the lack of financial success following downsizing is frequently accompanied by the emergence of survivor illnesses. Scholars remain puzzled as to why firms ignore the survivors. Are those individuals not supposed to be the *cream of the crop* and, ultimately, the linchpins of future profitability? Did the survivors not endure because they are part of the solution rather than part of the problem? Downsizing experts have studied the survivor syndrome and the exhibited behaviors at the workplace extensively. To sum up the findings, many survivors exhibit work behaviors and attitudes that are dysfunctional to the firm and their own work performance (Beylerian and Kleiner, 2003). As a result, the impact of downsizing on the survivors is believed to be one of the major reasons for the failure of downsizing efforts and resulting long-term problems (Devine et al., 2003). Without a doubt, executives must pay considerable attention to survivors if they are serious about executing downsizing successfully. This includes a clear strategy on how to take care of the survivors during all downsizing phases (Gandolfi, 2001). Therefore, managers need to make sure that the survivors receive full access to counseling, support, help, and retraining (Allen, 1997) as well as timely, honest, and unbiased information (Dolan et al., 2000).

Lesson 4: Counting the Downsizing Costs

Downsizing entails considerable financial cost. Research conducted by the University of Colorado reveals that the direct and indirect, or hidden, costs of downsizing are frequently underestimated (Gandolfi, 2001). There is even evidence suggesting that downsizing costs can minimize or negate any productivity gains (Littler et al., 1997). Longitudinal data from Australian, South African, and New Zealand firms show that no gain would result if the extra costs associated with downsizing were factored in (Gettler, 1998). Table 4 presents the direct and indirect costs.

In 2006, the H. J. Heinz Company, one of the world's largest food producers, reported that earnings had slumped due to high costs related to downsizing (The Associated Press, 2007). A European firm reported an increase of 40% in recruitment and a 30% increase in training and development costs for new employees following its controversial downsizing. These unexpected expenses more than off-set the minimal productivity savings achieved through downsizing (Gandolfi, 2001).

Lesson 5: Downsizing as a Last Resort

A firm must carefully consider its options and assess the feasibility and applicability of cost reduction alternatives before deciding to downsize. Downsizing must be a last resort. While a substantial number of articles discussing the alternatives to downsizing have emerged, there is a lack of understanding of downsizing-related layoffs as they pertain to the actual cost-reduction stages. It is vital for an organization to recognize the cost-reduction stage that characterizes the firm's current business position and environment. Thus, a firm needs to determine the expected duration of the business downturn. Several HR practices are available as alternatives to downsizing to reduce costs. Some popular approaches include natural attrition, hiring freezes, mandatory vacations, reduced workweeks, limited overtime pay, salary reductions, facility shutdowns, and employee sabbaticals. Each technique has its own applicability, advantages, and disadvantages.

Table 4 Costs of Downsizing

Direct Costs
- Severance pay, in lieu of notice
- Accrued holiday and sick pay
- Administrative processing costs

Indirect (hidden) Costs
- Recruiting and employment costs of new hires
- Training and retraining
- Potential charges of discrimination
- Survivor syndromes

Source: Adapted from Littler et al. (1997), Gettler (1998), Gandolfi (2001).

Future Research and Concluding Comments

Downsizing remains complex. While the body of literature is extensive and many valuable lessons have been learned over the past 30 years, the reactive and proactive practice of downsizing has continued unabated despite its dubious track record. In the 1990s, downsizing was declared the most understudied business phenomenon (Cameron, 1994; Freeman, 1994; Luthans and Sommer, 1999). The author of this paper would like to add that downsizing is probably also one of the most misunderstood and misinterpreted contemporary business phenomena. More research and, more important, a greater depth of understanding is required to establish and continue a meaningful dialogue between the business and academic communities. Some of the more pressing issues that need to be addressed and empirically examined include the following:

- What is the significance of the survivor syndrome?
- Is there a correlation between the survivor syndrome and the outcome of downsizing?
- What is the specific role of executioners during downsizing?
- What are the medium- and long-term personal and professional consequences for downsizing victims, survivors, and executioners?
- How and why should firms be prepared for downsizing? What is the best practice?
- What are the long-term financial consequences of downsizing?
- How do the frequency and magnitude of downsizing affect financial performance?
- How do alternatives to downsizing fare compared with downsizing-related layoffs?

This article reviewed the consequences of downsizing. While ample evidence suggests that downsizing produces negative outcomes, it is clear that downsizing-related permanent layoffs must be avoided at all costs. The paper presented five downsizing lessons that managers should consider before deciding to downsize.

References

Allen, R.K. (1997). Lean and mean: Workforce 2000 in America. *Journal of Workplace Learning, 9*(1). Retrieved from http://www.emerald-library.com/brev/08609ae1.html

Amundson, N., Borgen, W., Jordan, S., and Erlebach, A. (2004). Survivors of downsizing: Helpful and hindering experiences, *The Career Development Quarterly, 52,* 256–271.

Appelbaum, S.H., Delage, C., Labibb, N., and Gault, G. (1997). The survivor syndrome: Aftermath of downsizing. *Career Development International, 2*(6). Retrieved from http://www.emerald-library.com/brev/13702fd1.html

Appelbaum, S.H., Everard, A., and Hung, L. (1999). Strategic downsizing: Critical success factors. *Management Decision, 37*(7), 535–559.

Beylerian, M., and Kleiner, B. H. (2003). The downsized workplace. *Management Research News, 26,* 97–108.

Brockner, J. (1988). The effects of work layoffs in survivors: Research, theory and practice. *Research in Organizational Behavior, 10,* 213–255.

Cameron, K.S. (1994). Strategies for successful organizational downsizing, *Human Resource Management, 33*(2), 189–211.

Cameron, K.S., Freeman, S.J., and Mishra, A.K. (1993). Downsizing and redesigning organizations, In G. Huber and W. Glick (eds), *Organizational Change and Redesign* (pp 19–63) Oxford University Press, New York.

Cascio, W.F. (1993). Downsizing: What do we know? What have we learned? *Academy of Management Executive, 7*(1), 95–104.

Cascio, W.F., Young, C., and Morris, J. (1997). Financial consequences of employment change decisions in major U.S. corporations. *Academy of Management Journal, 40*(5), 1175–1189.

Cascio, W.F. (1998). *Applied psychology in human resource management,* 5th edition. Prentice Hall, Upper Saddle River, NJ.

Cascio, W.F. (2003, November). Responsible restructuring: Seeing employees as assets, not costs, *Ivey Business Journal Online.*

Chadwick, C., Hunter, L., and Walston, S. (2004). Effects of downsizing practices on the performance of hospitals. *Strategic Management Journal, 25*(5), 405–420.

Clair, J.A., and Dufresne, R.L. (2004). Playing the grim reaper: How employees experience carrying out a downsizing. *Human Relations, 57*(12), 1597–1625.

Clark, J., and Koonce, R. (1995). Engaging organizational survivors. *Training & Development, 49,* 8, 22–30.

Crainer, S., and Obleng, E. (1995). Re-engineering: Overview. *The Financial Times Handbook of Management,* edited by Stuart Crainger, FT Pitman Publishing, 231–241.

De Meuse, K.P., Vanderheiden, P.A., and Bergmann, T.J. (1994). Announced layoffs: Their effect on corporate financial performance. *Human Resource Management, 33*(4), 509–530.

De Meuse, K.P., Bergmann, T.J., Vanderheiden, P.A., and Roraff, C.E. (2004). New evidence regarding organizational downsizing and a firm's financial performance: A long-term analysis. *Journal of Managerial Issues, 16,* 155–177.

Devine, K., Reay, T., Stainton, L., and Collins-Nakai, R. (2003). The stress of downsizing: Comparing survivors and victims. *Human Resource Management, 42,* 109–124.

Doherty, N., and Horsted, J. (1995, January 12). *Helping survivors to stay on board.* People Management, Personnel Publications Limited, London.

Dolan, S., Belout, A., and Balkin, D.B. (2000). Downsizing without downgrading: Learning how firms manage their survivors. *International Journal of Manpower, 21*(1), 34–46.

Downs, A. (1995). *Corporate executions.* Amacom, New York, NY.

Drew, S.A.W. (1994). Downsizing to improve strategic position. *MCB Management Decision, 32,* 1.

Estok, D. (1996). The high cost of dumbsizing. *Macleans's, 109*(23), 28–29.

Farrell, M., and Mavondo, F. (2004). The effect of downsizing strategy and reorientation strategy on a learning orientation. *Personnel Review, 33*(4), 383–402.

Filipowski, D. (1993, November). Don't rush downsizing: Plan, plan, plan. *Personnel Journal, 72*(11), 64–76.

Freeman, S.J. (1994). Organizational downsizing as convergence or reorientation: Implications for human resource management. *Human Resource Management, 33*(2), 213–238.

Gandolfi, F. (2001). *How and why should training and development be implemented during the process of organizational downsizing?* Unpublished thesis for the award of Doctor of Business Administration (DBA), Southern Cross University, Australia.

Gandolfi, F., and Neck, P. (2003). Organizational downsizing: A review of the background, its development, and current status, *The Australasian Journal of Business and Social Inquiry, 1,* 1.

Gandolfi, F. (2005). How do organizations implement downsizing? An Australian and New Zealand study. *Contemporary Management Research, 1*(1), 57–68.

Gandolfi, F. (2006). *Corporate downsizing demystified: A scholarly analysis of a business phenomenon.* The ICFAI University Press, Hyderabad, India.

Gandolfi, F. (2006b). Personal development and growth in a downsized banking organization: Summary of methodology and findings. *Journal of Human Resource Development International (HRDI), 9*(2), 207–226.

Gandolfi, F. (2007). How do large Australian and Swiss banks implement downsizing? *Journal of Management & Organization, 13*(2), 145–159.

Gandolfi, F. (2008). Learning from the past—Downsizing lessons for managers. *The Journal of Management Research, 8*(1), 1–14.

Gettler, L. (1998, June 16). Survey: Downsizing doesn't cut costs, *Sydney Morning Herald,* 27.

Greenglass, E.R., and Burke, R.J. (2001). Downsizing and restructuring, implications for stress and anxiety. *Anxiety, Stress, and Coping, 14,* 1–13.

Griggs, H.E., and Hyland, P. (2003). Strategic downsizing and learning organizations. *Journal of European Industrial Training, 24*(2–4), 177–187.

Kinnie, N., Hutchinson, S., and Purcell, J. (1998). Downsizing: Is it always lean and mean? *Personnel Review, 27*(4), 296–311.

Kirby, J. (1999, March 22). Downsizing gets the push. *Business Review Weekly.*

Konovsky, M.A., and Brockner, J. (1993). Managing victim and survivor layoff reactions: A procedural justice perspective, in R. Cropanzano (ed.), *Justice in the workplace: Approaching fairness in human resource management* (133–153), Lawrence Erlbaum, New Jersey.

Lecky, S. (1998, July 4). The failure of slash and earn. *Sydney Morning Herald,* 83–87.

Lee, C. (1992, July). After the cuts. *Training,* 17–23.

Littler, C.R. (1998). Downsizing organizations: The dilemmas of change. *Human Resources Management Bulletin,* CCH Australia Limited, Sydney.

Littler, C.R., Dunford, R., Bramble, T., and Hede, A. (1997). The dynamics of downsizing in Australia and New Zealand. *Asia Pacific Journal of Human Resources, 35*(1), 65–79.

Luthans, B.C., and Sommer, S.M. (1999). The impact of downsizing on workplace attitudes, *Group and Organization Management, 24*(1), 46–70.

Macky, K. (2004). Organisational downsizing and redundancies: The New Zealand workers' experience. *New Zealand Journal of Employment Relations, 29*(1), 63–87.

Makawatsakul, N., and Kleiner, B.H. (2003). The effect of downsizing on morale and attrition. *Management Research News, 26,* 2–4.

Maurer, H. (2005, December 5). Downsizing in Detroit. *The Business Week.*

Mirabal, N., and DeYoung, R. (2005). Downsizing as a strategic intervention. *Journal of American Academy of Business, 6*(1), 39–45.

Mishra, A.K., and Spreitzer, G.M. (1998). Explaining how survivors respond to downsizing: The role of trust, empowerment, justice, and work redesign. *Academy of Management Review, 23*(3), 567–588

Mitchell, G. (1998). *The Trainer's Handbook: The AMA Guide to Effective Training,* 3rd edition, AMACOM American Management Association, New York.

Morris, J.R., Cascio W.F., and Young, C.E. (1999, Winter). Downsizing after all these years: Questions and answers about who did it, how many did it, and who benefited from it. *Organizational Dynamics,* 78–87.

Nelson, B. (1997). The care of the un-downsized. *Training & Development, 51*(4), 40–43.

Noer, D. (1993). *Healing the wounds: Overcoming the trauma of layoffs and revitalizing downsized organizations.* Jossey-Bass, San Francisco, CA.

Ryan, L., and Macky K.A. (1998). Downsizing organizations: Uses, outcomes and strategies. *Asia Pacific Journal of Human Resources, 36*(2), 29–45.

Sahdev, K. (2003). Survivors' reactions to downsizing: The importance of contextual factors. *Human Resource Management Journal, 13*(4), 56–74.

Schweiger, D.M., Ivancevich, J.M., and Power, F.R. (1987). Executive actions for managing human resources before and after acquisition. *Academy of Management Executive, 1*(2), 127–138.

Smeltzer, L.R., and Zener, M.F. (1994). Minimizing the negative effect of employee layoffs through effective announcements. *Employee Counseling Today, 6*(4).

The Associated Press. (2007). *Heinz earnings fall on costs of downsizings.* Retrieved March 1, 2006 from http://www.nytimes.com/2006/03/01/business/01heinz.html?_r=1&oref=slogin

Williams, S.M. (2004). Downsizing—intellectual capital performance anorexia or enhancement? *The Learning Organization, 11*(4/5), 368–379.

Worrell, D.L., Davidson, W.N., and Sharma, V.M. (1991). Layoff announcements and stockholder wealth. *Academy of Management Journal, 34,* 662–678.

Zeffane, R., and Mayo, G. (1994). Rightsizing: The strategic human resources management challenge of the 1990s, *Management Decision, 32*(9).

Zemke, R. (1990, November). The ups and downs of downsizing. *Training,* 27–34.

Zyglidopoulos, S.C. (2003). The impact of downsizing on the corporate reputation for social performance. *Journal of Public Affairs, 4*(1), 11–25.

Dr. Franco Gandolfi, currently director of the MBA/EMBA programs at Regent University, specializes in human resource management and change management and regularly advises corporations in Australia and Switzerland. His published books include *Corporate Downsizing Demystified: A Scholarly Analysis of a Business Phenomenon.*

From *SAM Advanced Management Journal,* Spring 2008. Copyright © 2008 by Society for Advancement of Management. Reprinted by permission.

Article 21

The Factory That Refused to Die

In an Ohio town with rampant unemployment, the mayor, a worker, and 12 local families fought to save Norwalk Furniture.

NANETTE BYRNES

The Norwalk Custom Order Furniture factory in Norwalk, Ohio, is 430,000 square feet, enough to encompass four football fields. On a rainy June afternoon, though, the facility is quiet—except for the sounds of a radio playing 1970s rock classics and the occasional hum of a sewing machine or pop of a staple gun. This time last year more than 300 people worked on the floor, producing hundreds of pieces of furniture a day. Now the headcount is 59.

That Norwalk is still producing furniture at all, however, is a business miracle. The 107-year-old manufacturer has been buffeted by the housing bust, Chinese competition, its own poor judgment, and the credit crunch—a toxic brew if there ever was one. Last year Norwalk's owners, the fourth generation of the founding Gerken family, gave up the fight and closed the factory's doors, unable to meet the demands of lenders. Dozens of retailers who relied on the company stood to go out of business themselves.

But instead of becoming one more piece of bad news floating on a sea of economic disasters, Norwalk has emerged as a survivor of sorts. An unlikely coalition of investors, factory workers, and politicians have joined together to reopen the factory. Now the business is above water, if just barely.

These people and thousands of fighters like them are the difference between 9.5% national unemployment and something even worse. Companies big and small are struggling to deal with the double whammy of slowing sales and restricted credit. U.S. bankruptcy filings surged to 7,874 in May, a 55% rise from a year earlier, according to bankruptcy tracker AACER. With loan delinquencies soaring too, banks—along with CIT Group and other other commercial lenders—are raising their credit standards: Federal Reserve figures show that banks have tightened up on small business lending for 10 consecutive quarters. "It's very difficult for banks to embrace lending to smaller businesses," says Robert Coleman, editor of the La Canada (Calif.)-based *Coleman Report,* which tracks small business loans.

Against that grim backdrop Norwalk has somehow managed to survive. The company was founded in 1902, when upholsterer Charles Edward Gerken first crafted a chair for his son, Raymond. Over the decades, Norwalk came to own all or part of 13 different companies, from wood exporters to low-end furniture makers. None, however, was as profitable as the core custom-order furniture business, which produced its upscale wares in the Norwalk factory in Ohio and sold them through 57 franchises around the country and through independent dealers that carried multiple brands.

Earlier this decade foreign competition in the furniture industry intensified, particularly at the low end. Imports from China rose 154% from 2001 to 2005, to more than $12 billion. But because the strong housing market was fueling demand for high-end furniture, Norwalk kept production steady.

When the real estate market crashed, the company's fortunes quickly changed. Sales plunged from $163 million at the peak in 2005 to $137 million in 2007, according to investment bank Beacon Associates. In the first four months of 2008, the company had revenues of just $40 million and was on track to lose $4.9 million for the year.

Making matters worse, Jim and Bill Gerken, the fourth-generation cousins running the company, were slow to cut costs and pare the losses. Instead they tapped their $13 million credit line to keep the business afloat. "Most of what happened to Norwalk was our own mismanagement," admits Bill Gerken. "I'd love to blame someone else, but we screwed up."

In early 2008 the Gerkens grew concerned about Norwalk's performance. They persuaded factory workers to take a cut in benefits, hired restructuring firm Morris Anderson, and in April submitted a turnaround plan to their bank of 12 years, Dallas-based Comerica. But the bankers were reluctant to give the Gerkens all the money they asked for and demanded a personal guarantee as collateral, says Bill Gerken. The cousins balked. "Why would we sign those personal guarantees?" asks Gerken. "That would have been insane."

Banks, of course, were dealing with their own nightmare in 2008: the credit crunch. Comerica, which was headquartered in Detroit for 158 years before moving to Texas in 2007, held a worrisome number of loans made to hard-hit manufacturers in the upper Midwest and was heavily exposed to the California real estate meltdown. In July 2008, Comerica announced that its quarterly net income had dropped 71% from a year earlier (though its capital position remained strong). One day later it pulled Norwalk's credit line. "They were doing what other banks were doing at the time," says Norwalk's controller, Peg Whitehurst. A spokesman for Comerica says the bank was trying to find a solution for Norwalk outside of bankruptcy, even though the company was in default on its loan, and says Norwalk management's decisions led to its problems.

Without the credit line, the Gerkens could no longer meet payroll, and on July 18, 2008, they shut the factory doors, seemingly for good.

That's when Norwalk's mayor, Sue Lesch, sprang into action. Lesch grew up on a farm in nearby Peru, Ohio, and was the owner of a construction company and served as a fund-raiser for the Catholic Church before taking office in 2004. Since then she has spent much of her time on economic matters. With a population of 16,000, Norwalk is the biggest town in a county whose unemployment rate sits at 15.4%, among the worst in the country. "We've just been hit and hit and hit," says Lesch. Although she attends a prayer group and tries to walk every day to relieve stress, "I don't sleep well," she says.

Lesch focused much of her attention last summer on trying to save Norwalk Furniture. "This company not only was the largest factory in town—theirs were the best jobs in town," she says. Lesch repeatedly called the bank to badger it into reconsidering its credit decision. She drove to Columbus to lobby state officials for an emergency loan and to hunt up potential buyers. She assigned her business development team to canvass local investors as well. The team found several groups of potential investors, but Comerica wasn't negotiating.

When factory worker Kim Gross heard that Comerica was refusing to talk with potential buyers, she decided to organize a protest. The mother of three has deep connections to Norwalk Furniture. She has been sewing cushion backs and pillows there for 20 years. Her grandmother worked there before her. And Norwalk is where she met her husband, Jeff, a plant manager. Gross persuaded 40 fellow employees to take three pickup trucks filled with armchairs and sofas to Comerica's Detroit offices, two hours away. When they got there they put the furniture on the sidewalk, carrying signs and marching in hopes of attracting media coverage. "We thought, 'This is crazy. Why not let these investors make an offer?'" TV stations and newspapers sent reporters, and by that afternoon the bank had agreed to talk to potential investors.

More than 1,000 miles away, near Denver, retailer Jodi Zippo's once-thriving business was crashing. Zippo, a former telecom executive, and her husband, Rob, a sales manager for an electronics manufacturer, had put their life's savings into a Norwalk furniture store in an upscale Colorado mall. Jodi had left the telecom field in 2001 to spend more time with her two young daughters. But she'd always wanted to build a business of her own, and she had a knack for interior design. In March 2007 she bought the Norwalk store—and quickly tripled the average sale amount, pushing the outlet from the 46th most productive of Norwalk's 57 franchise stores to No. 3. Business was so good that Zippo paid down $125,000 of her $415,000 small business loan, also held by Comerica, in just 12 months. But when Norwalk lost its credit line and closed, her business ground to a halt.

Zippo thought of shutting the store but was distraught at the idea of running into people who'd given her money for furniture and then gotten stiffed. Her husband told her it was O.K. to fail, but that only panicked her more. "I said back to him, 'Don't talk to me that way. It's not going to fail. I don't fail,'" Zippo recalls. "Deep down I thought, 'Oh my god. We're going to fail.'"

The agitating in Ohio was paying off, though. On July 28, Comerica agreed to meet with potential buyers. Over the course of a day, in a conference room at Cleveland's airport, the bankers talked with a series of private equity firms and individual investors. Comerica was there at the request of Ohio Lieutenant Governor Lee Fisher, who on Lesch's urging had put a $1.8 million loan offer on the table. Eventually one group of private equity investors made an acceptable bid, and while they did due diligence through the month of August, Norwalk reopened its doors and resumed operations.

But by Labor Day the deal was in trouble. The investors have since filed suit in Huron County Common Pleas Court accusing Comerica of demanding they complete their due diligence faster than was possible, among other things. On Sept. 16, after the two sides couldn't come to terms, Norwalk closed its doors for the second time, almost certainly for good.

Then something extraordinary happened. A group of 12 local families called the company and said they were interested in making a bid for just the Ohio factory. Both Comerica and the Gerkens liked the idea. After just a few days of due diligence, the investors bought the plant for $4 million. The next week the investors started taking applications to rehire workers.

The new company is called Norwalk Custom Order Furniture and is run by Daniel J. White, one of the 12 investors. White has long ties to the town of Norwalk—his family has lived there for more than 100 years—and he says concern for the community is what drove him to step in. Before taking the reins at Norwalk, White, a retiree, had founded Geotrac of America, a company specializing in the flood zone research required by mortgage lenders, which he sold in 2004.

For the 12 families that invested in Norwalk, reviving the factory meant a stronger local economy and higher property values.

For most of the other 11 Norwalk investors, the desire to save well-paying jobs wasn't purely humanitarian. Doing so would mean a stronger local economy, higher property values, and better business in general, says Tom Bleile, one of the investors and co-owner of the Saw Mill Creek Resort on the shore of Lake Erie, a half hour to the north. "If our community benefits, then we benefit," says Bleile.

In his first two weeks as CEO, White visited 28 of Norwalk's retailers. They had been without product for 30 to 60 days, and many were on the verge of bankruptcy. They'd been caught off guard by Norwalk's problems and "felt betrayed," White says. He quickly took steps to win them back. First he started work on the $4.5 million in orders that had gone unfulfilled. Next he changed the company's production cycle to make sure retailers wouldn't have to wait months before they could start selling Norwalk's newest line.

White insists the new Norwalk is built to last. The company has no significant debt aside from the $1.8 million loan from the state of Ohio and a $225,000 equipment loan from the town of Norwalk. White expects the Norwalk plant to generate more than $25 million in sales by 2011, less than half the level it once enjoyed but far more sustainable.

Jodi Zippo's outlook is brighter these days, too. When Norwalk closed last year, she was on the hook for $280,000 worth of orders. Sitting at her husband's desk in their Littleton (Colo.) home one night, she called one customer after another to beg them for a chance to find another vendor. By the end of the night all but four agreed, and she had to refund only $25,000. Still, she's out some $150,000 worth of floor models and samples she sold for a fraction of their value last fall because she thought Norwalk would no longer be making them. All 31 lenders she has approached to refinance her Comerica loan have declined.

But now that Norwalk is back producing furniture, Zippo is selling it again, along with several other lines. Sales are improving, and she's current on her loan payments. The panic attacks she suffered last summer have eased. "We're past the scary part," she says.

For Kim Gross, survivor guilt may be creeping in. She and her husband, Jeff, were among the 94 workers who successfully reapplied for their jobs at the factory. Most of the 800 who applied were turned away, including many with decades' worth of experience. Gross has run into some of them at the grocery store, and the encounters have been awkward. Now Gross shops at odd hours to avoid her former factory mates.

Rightly or wrongly, much of the anger around town is directed toward the former owners. Bill and Jim Gerken may have mismanaged Norwalk, but they also fought desperately to save it. Now they're financially devastated. Bill says 90% of his net worth was tied up in the company, and all of it is gone. "No one lost more than I did," he says. Mayor Lesch says the Gerkens "were wonderful" through the process, talking to her every day. "It's so easy to point fingers from the outside," she says. "It's always more complicated than that."

While the Norwalk saga created rifts in this small Ohio town, it will be remembered more for bringing people together. Whenever a prominent company is about to close, "the temptation for too many people is to throw up their hands and say it's inevitable," says Lesch. "We said, 'Wait a minute, this is really, really important. We're going to stand up and fight.'"

From *BusinessWeek*, August 3, 2009, pp. 38–42. Copyright © 2009 by BusinessWeek. Reprinted by permission of the McGraw-Hill Companies.

Article 22

Fear of Firing

How the threat of litigation is making companies skittish about axing problem workers.

MICHAEL OREY

Would you have dared fire Hemant K. Mody? In February, 2003, the longtime engineer had returned to work at a General Electric Co. (GE) facility in Plainville, Conn., after a two-month medical leave. He was a very unhappy man. For much of the prior year, he and his superiors had been sparring over his performance and promotion prospects. According to court documents, Mody's bosses claimed he spoke disparagingly of his co-workers, refused an assignment as being beneath him, and was abruptly taking days off and coming to work late.

But Mody was also 49, Indian born, and even after returning from leave continued to suffer a major disability: chronic kidney failure that required him to receive daily dialysis. The run-ins resumed with his managers, whom he had accused flat out of discriminating against him because of his race and age. It doesn't take an advanced degree in human resources to recognize that the situation was a ticking time bomb. But Mody's bosses were fed up. They axed him in April, 2003.

The bomb exploded last July. Following a six-day trial, a federal court jury in Bridgeport, Conn., found GE's termination of Mody to be improper and awarded him $11.1 million, including $10 million in punitive damages. But the award wasn't for discrimination. The judge found those claims so weak that Mody wasn't allowed to present them. Instead, jurors concluded that Mody had been fired in retaliation for complaining about bias. GE is seeking to have the award overturned, and a spokesman said, "We feel strongly there is no basis for this claim." Through his attorney, Mody declined to discuss the case with *BusinessWeek*.

If this can happen to GE, a company famed for its rigorous performance reviews, with an HR operation that is studied worldwide, it can happen anywhere. It has never been easier for U.S. workers to go to court and allege that they've been sacked unfairly. Over the past 40 years federal, state, and local lawmakers have steadily expanded the categories of workers who enjoy special legal protection—a sprawling group that now includes women, minorities, gays, whistleblowers, the disabled, people over 40, employees who have filed workers' compensation claims, and workers who have been called away for jury duty or military service, among others. Factor in white men who believe that they are bias victims—so-called reverse-discrimination lawsuits—and "it's difficult to find someone who doesn't have some capacity to claim protected status," observes Lisa H. Cassilly, an employment defense attorney at Alston & Bird in Atlanta.

These workers wield a potent weapon. They can force companies to prove in court that there was a legitimate business reason for their termination. And once a case is in court, it's expensive. A company can easily spend $100,000 to get a meritless lawsuit tossed out before trial. And if a case goes to a jury, the fees skyrocket to $300,000, and often much higher. The result: Many companies today are gripped by a fear of firing. Terrified of lawsuits, they let unproductive employees linger, lay off coveted workers while retaining less valuable ones, and pay severance to screwups and even crooks in exchange for promises that they won't sue. "I've seen us make decisions [about terminations] that in the absence of this litigious risk environment, you'd have a different result," acknowledges Johnny C. Taylor, Jr., head of HR at IAC/InterActiveCorp (IACI), the conglomerate that runs businesses such as Match.com and Ticketmaster.

Managers often fail to build a case for firing by shying away from regular and candid evaluations.

The fear of firing is particularly acute in the HR and legal departments. They don't directly suffer when an underperformer lingers in the corporate hierarchy, but they may endure unpleasant indirect consequences if that person files a lawsuit. Says Dick Grote, an Addison (Tex.) talent management consultant: "They don't get their bonuses based on the number of lawsuits they win. They get their bonuses based on the number of lawsuits they don't get involved in."

This set of divergent incentives puts line managers in a tough position. When they finally decide to get rid of the underperforming slob who plays PC solitaire all day in her cubicle, it can be surprisingly tough to do. And that, in turn, affects productive workers. "Few things demotivate an organization faster than tolerating and retaining low performers," says Grant Freeland, a regional leader in Boston Consulting Group's organization practice.

But it's often the supervisors themselves who bear much of the blame when HR says someone can't be shown the door. That's because most fail to give the kind of regular and candid evaluations that will allow a company to prove poor performance if a fired employee hauls them into court. Honest, if harsh, reviews not only offer legal cover, but they're also critical for organizations intent on developing top talent. "There were definitely a lot of situations where a supervisor got fed up with somebody and wanted to terminate them, but there's no paperwork," says Sara Anderson, who worked in HR at Perry Ellis International (PERY) and Kenneth Cole Productions Inc. (KCP) in New York. Frequently, the work that the manager suddenly claims is intolerable is accompanied by years of performance evaluations that say "meets expectations." Says Anderson: "You look in the file, and there's nothing there to prove [poor performance], so it's like it didn't happen."

Untouchable Nation

Fired workers who fall into a protected category have special legal status. These days, it's harder than you might imagine to find an American worker who wouldn't fall into one—or sometimes several—of these categories.

Total Labor Force: 151.4 million
- Minorities (31%)
- 40 and over (52%)
- Female (46%)
- Unprotected*: White males under 40 (16%)

*But not if the employee is: Disabled, gay, a whistle-blower, a veteran, foreign-born, called for jury duty, a workers' compensation claimant.

Data: U.S Bureau of Labor Statistics, 2006.

When Mody Signed GE's Job application in 1998, the form said his employment was "at will" and "the Company may terminate my employment at any time for any reason."

Well, not exactly.

The notion that American workers are employed "at will"—meaning, as one lawyer put it, you can be fired if your manager doesn't like the color of your socks—took root in the laissez-faire atmosphere of the late 19th century, and as an official matter is still the law of the land in every state, save Montana. The popular conception of at-will employment is exemplified by the television show *The Apprentice,* which features Donald Trump pointing a finger at an underling and ousting him or her on the spot. That dramatic gesture makes great television, but it isn't something that happens very frequently anymore in the American workplace.

The rise of unions was the first development to put a check on summary dismissal. Collective-bargaining agreements outlined the specific kinds of infractions that could lead to termination, and set up procedures for discipline and review that a company must follow before a worker can be fired. But unions generally didn't deal with the problem of discrimination, and in some cases perpetuated it.

For most American workers now, their status as at-will employees has been transformed by a succession of laws growing out of the civil rights movement in the 1960s that bar employers from making decisions based on such things as race, religion, sex, age, and national origin. This is hardly controversial. Even the legal system's harshest critics find little fault with rules aimed at assuring that personnel decisions are based on merit. And most freely acknowledge that it is much easier to fire people in the U.S. than it is in, say, most of Western Europe. Mass layoffs, in fact, are a recurring event on the American corporate scene. On Apr. 17, for example, Citigroup Inc. (C) announced it will shed some 17,000 workers.

Yet even in these situations, RIFs (for "reduction in force") are carefully vetted by attorneys to assess the impact on employees who are in a legally protected category. And these days the majority of American workers fall into one or more such groups. Mody, for example, belonged to three because of who he was (age, race, and national origin) and two more because of things he had done (complained of discrimination and taken medical leave). That doesn't mean such people are immune from firing. But it does mean a company will have to show a legitimate, non-discriminatory business reason for the termination, should the matter ever land in court.

As it happens, the judge in Mody's case tossed out his discrimination claims. But the retaliation allegation did go to the jury—a development that is increasingly blindsiding businesses. Plaintiffs are winning large sums not because a company discriminated against them, but because the company retaliated when they complained about the unproven mistreatment.

The rules surrounding retaliation may sound crazy, but they are one of the big reasons why the fear of firing is so prevalent. Retaliation suits are a hot growth area in employment law. In 2005 and 2006, retaliation claims represented 30% of all charges individuals filed with the Equal Employment Opportunity Commission, a required first step before most discrimination cases can go to federal court. That's up from about 20% just 10 years ago. "Even if there isn't a good discrimination claim, the employee has a second bite at the apple," notes Martin W. Aron of defense firm Edwards Angell Palmer & Dodge in Short Hills, N.J. Last year the U.S. Supreme Court increased the legal risk to business by ruling that improper retaliation can involve acts far short of firing or demoting someone. So even excluding an employee from meetings, relocating his or her office, or other intangible slights could lead to liability.

Of course, prohibitions against retaliation exist for a good reason. Without them, many workers would find it too risky to come forward with even legitimate complaints. Yet defense attorneys are deeply suspicious that some workers abuse the protection. Fearing their jobs may be in jeopardy, they may quickly contact HR with an allegation of discrimination or call a corporate hotline to report misconduct, thereby cloaking themselves in the protection of anti-retaliation law. "That's a fairly common fact scenario," says Mike Delikat of Orrick Herrington & Sutcliffe in New York, a law firm that represents businesses. "The best defense is a good offense."

After 1991, when Congress allowed punitive damages and jury trials in job discrimination cases, litigation in the area exploded. In 2006, 14,353 employment cases were filed in federal court, up from 8,273 in 1990, though down from a peak of 20,955 in 2002. It should be noted that these statistics, which include both unlawful termination cases and other types of claims, dramatically understate the frequency with which companies deal with these issues. For every case that's filed in court, several more are quietly settled well beforehand.

Many of the lawsuits may seem ridiculous. IBM (IBM) is currently defending a case filed by James C. Pacenza, a plant worker it dismissed for visiting an adult Internet chat room while on the job. In his lawsuit, Pacenza claims that his propensity to such behavior stems from post-traumatic stress disorder, which he suffers as a result of military service in Vietnam, and that IBM violated the Americans with Disabilities Act. He also alleges that two other employees who had sex on an IBM desk were "merely transferred," so he was treated with undue harshness. Pacenza's attorney, Michael D. Diederich Jr., says his client "didn't violate any of IBM's policies regarding computer usage."

Even when employers beat back silly suits, it often doesn't feel like much of a victory. That's because meritless cases can still tie up companies in burdensome and expensive proceedings for years. In October, 2002, Southview Hospital in Dayton fired Karen Stephens, a nurse who worked in a unit for premature babies and other at-risk newborns. Six other nurses had reported that Stephens was abusive to infants, according to court filings, spanking them when they were fussy, wagging their noses until they screamed in pain, pinching their noses shut to force-feed them, and calling them "son of a bitch." Stephens, who was 60 at the time, sued Kettering Adventist Healthcare Network, which operates Southview, denying "inappropriate" conduct and alleging that the real reason she was let go was age discrimination.

Only after a year and a half of legal dueling did a federal district judge in Dayton toss out Stephens' claims in April, 2005. But then she appealed, and it took another year—and an additional round of legal briefing—before the U.S. Court of Appeals for the Sixth Circuit upheld the dismissal, noting that "Stephens has offered no evidence to indicate that she did not mistreat the infants," or that Kettering did not have a "legitimate, nondiscriminatory reason for discharging her." Kettering declined to comment on the case. "I never lost a baby in 25 years," Stephens said in an interview.

The cost and distraction of lawsuits lead many employers to engage in contortional, and at times perverse, litigation avoidance. Defense attorney Cassilly offers the story of one of her clients, a hospital in the Southeast forced to reduce its ranks because of budget cuts. The head of one department elected to let go a female employee in favor of keeping a more junior male, whom he had spent a great deal of effort to recruit and whom he felt was more valuable. But the hospital overrode that choice and laid off the man out of concern that it would be more exposed in a lawsuit by the woman.

Another of Cassilly's clients, a manufacturer, acquired a new facility and quickly identified one worker as having "a variety of performance problems." But the woman, an African American, had nothing in her personnel file indicating prior trouble, which made firing her a risky bet. So the company put her on a six-month "performance improvement program" to document her deficiencies—and to find out if she could mend her ways. She couldn't, and, Cassilly notes, her client "had to suffer through her poor performance during the whole period."

Early this year, Cassilly got a call from the client. They had just discovered that the woman, an office administrator, had stolen thousands of dollars from the company, and they promptly dismissed her. "It was almost a case where the company was delighted to find out they were the victim of theft," Cassilly says, as opposed to having to defend far more subjective performance evaluations.

Even in the face of theft, Revolution Partners, a small investment banking advisory firm in Boston, balked before showing one of its employees the door. The woman had used her company credit card for a personal shopping spree and plane ticket, but Revolution retained an employment attorney, got the woman to sign a form waiving her right to sue for wrongful dismissal, and after she was fired took no legal action to recover the amounts improperly charged. "We're a little firm, and the last thing I need is to spend a lot of time on a lawsuit, whether it's warranted or not," says Peter Falvey, one of Revolution's co-founders.

Falvey isn't alone. A number of defense attorneys and HR managers said companies they work for prefer to buy themselves peace of mind over facing the prospect of being sued. "They don't want the publicity or the expense," says Robert J. Nobile, an attorney at Seyfarth Shaw in New York. "Some of them say, Hey, we'll swallow our pride and pay 10 grand now rather than 100 grand later." That's an approach that makes IAC's Taylor shudder. "If that becomes your norm, then you train the plaintiffs' bar and your departing employees that they should expect something on the way out, no matter how poorly they perform," he says.

Many observers put much of the blame for fear of firing on HR. "The problem is much more with HR managers being nervous Nellies than it is a problem in actual legal exposure," says consultant Grote. The bigger risk is retaining poor performers, not terminating them, he says, provided the firing is done properly.

Indeed, at most companies HR is essentially a support function that gets called in only when a personnel problem has reached the crisis stage. At that point, the best they may be able to do is suggest the kind of risk-avoidance measures that drive managers crazy—such as requiring that an employee's deficiencies actually be documented in writing for an extended period before he or she is fired. This can be avoided, says Amy Rasner, a former HR manager in the fashion industry, if human resources personnel are teamed with line managers, working with them on an ongoing basis to develop and communicate specific, measurable performance objectives to employees.

In interview after interview, attorneys and HR execs say the biggest problem they confront in terminations is the failure of managers to have these kinds of conversations. In a 2005 Hewitt

For Every 10,000 Lawsuits, Few Losses, but High Cost

The maneuvering companies engage in to avoid wrongful-termination lawsuits is out of proportion to the risk of actually losing in court. One big reason: the high cost of litigating claims, even the ones that end up with the company winning.

Out of 10,000 Employment Suits	Stage of Lawsuit	Cumulative Cost for a Company to Defend a Single Lawsuit
	Filing	
7,000	Settle (most settlements are for nuisance value)	$10,000
	Summary Judgment	
2,400	Get resolved by summary judgment and other pretrial rulings	$100,000
	Start of Trial	
600	Go to trial	$175,000
	End of Trial	
186	Trials are won by plaintiffs	$250,000*
	Appeal	
13**	Plaintiffs victories survive appeal	$300,000

Sources: Cornell Law School; Hofstra Labor & Employment Law Journal; BW reporting.
*Assumes a five-day trial.
**Out of 22 trial losses typically appealed by companies.

Associates (HEW) survey of 129 major U.S. corporations, 72% said managers' ability to carry out performance management discussions and decisions effectively was the part of their personnel evaluation process most in need of improvement.

The reasons for this, of course, are varied. Some managers simply see the whole review process as a bureaucratic waste of time. It's also not easy to do. Many supervisors have been promoted into their jobs because they excelled in operations, not because they are skilled as managers. What's more, they've often spent a lot of time working alongside the very people they now oversee, so giving candid feedback to friends and former peers may be awkward. Managers in this position are "the biggest chickens on earth," says Fred Kiel, an executive-development consultant at KRW International Inc. in Minneapolis.

Ironically, when it came to handling personnel issues involving Mody, GE managers appear to have done most things right, offering regular and candid performance appraisals and involving HR and legal personnel at an early stage when matters began to sour. In trial exhibits and testimony, Mody's GE supervisors described him as a talented but prickly worker. Performance reviews and other documents faulted both his people and leadership skills.

But in the trial against GE, Mody's attorney, Scott R. Lucas of Stamford, Conn., laid out the details of what he labeled a campaign of retaliation against his client. Following a July, 2002, memo in which Mody accused the company of discrimination, Lucas told jurors, Mody's boss began complaining that he was absent and tardy too often. In a court filing, Lucas called this "a contrived performance issue," and says Mody was also "falsely criticized for lack of output."

What's more, just six weeks after having given Mody a "very favorable review," his boss gave Mody a "very poor and critical evaluation," according to the filing. Mody was excluded from various conferences and removed from "meaningful contribution" to projects. At one point, Mody's boss allegedly told him: "There are things I can ask you to do that if I asked you to do them, you would just quit." The last straw for Mody came when he returned from medical leave and was asked to do an assignment that he alleged was low-level and intentionally demeaning.

On July 18, jurors awarded Mody about $1.1 million in back pay and compensatory damages and—in one of several aspects of the case being challenged by GE—a tidy $10 million in punitive damages. Even for a company as big as GE, an $11.1 million verdict is plenty of cause to justify a fear of firing. But Mark S. Dichter, head of the employment practice at Morgan Lewis & Bockius in Philadelphia, thinks that's the wrong lesson to draw from the Mody case and other similar lawsuits. "I can design HR policies that can virtually eliminate your risk of facing employment claims, but you'll have a pretty lousy workforce," says Dichter. "At the end of the day, you have to run your business."

OREY is a senior writer for *BusinessWeek* in New York.

Protecting the Whistleblower

Companies should fine-tune internal probes to make investigation more asset than liability.

R. SCOTT OSWALD AND JASON ZUCKERMAN

In litigating whistleblower retaliation claims, we have found that poorly conducted internal investigations can be extraordinarily helpful to plaintiffs and harmful to employers. In particular, investigations that are intended to discredit the concerned employee or cover up wrongdoing to protect the accused will, at a minimum, deprive the employer of an affirmative defense and can also provide circumstantial evidence of retaliatory intent.

Employers, however, can take fairly simple measures to prevent an investigation from becoming more of a liability than an asset. Following are five tips for conducting an effective internal investigation.

- **Keep the Concerned Employee Apprised of the Investigation.** For any employees, disclosing wrongdoing is a daunting experience. Therefore, a concerned employee likely will be anxious about potential retaliation and focused on achieving a prompt resolution to the problem or wrongdoing that the employee disclosed.

If the concerned employee believes that the company is not taking the employee's concerns seriously or is failing to take necessary corrective actions, the employee likely will pursue other avenues to remedy the problem, such as contacting the media or a regulatory agency. Accordingly, it is essential for the investigator to keep the concerned employee apprised of the status of the investigation. The investigator should periodically update the concerned employee regarding the investigator's findings and give the concerned employee a chance to respond and provide additional information, documents or corroborating witnesses.

At the conclusion of the investigation, the concerned employee should be informed of corrective actions, such as strengthened internal controls to prevent the type of accounting fraud that the concerned employee brought to light.

- **Focus on the Concerned Employee's Allegation Rather than the Employee's Motive.** The surest sign that an investigation is pretextual is when the investigation focuses on the concerned employee's motive for disclosing wrongdoing. As a matter of law, a whistleblower's motive is irrelevant. Accordingly, the investigation should focus on uncovering the veracity of the concerned employee's allegations, not on discrediting the source of the allegations.

- **Protect the Concerned Employee and Witnesses from Retaliation.** Not surprisingly, an employee accused of misconduct can be prone to resent the accuser and employees who assisted in an investigation. Accordingly, the employer should stay attuned to any retaliation resulting from an investigation, and should promptly respond to any retaliation.

If the concerned employee is harassed or subjected to pretextual discipline, co-workers would be chilled from disclosing wrongdoing. A chilled work environment is harmful to any organization because it will undermine management's ability to learn early on of future wrongdoing or misconduct. Moreover, a retaliatory investigation can result in liability for the employer.

For example, retaliating against a whistleblower by conducting a sham investigation and intentionally spreading false allegations of misconduct by the whistleblower gives rise to a claim of intentional infliction of emotional distress and other tort and employment actions.

Moreover, the Supreme Court recently clarified that a retaliation claim does not require proof of a tangible adverse job detriment, such as a termination or a demotion. Instead, the standard for retaliation is whether the conduct in question would dissuade an objective, reasonable person from making or supporting a charge of discrimination, or engaging in other forms of protected conduct.

Therefore, investigations must be conducted in a manner that will not discourage employees from reporting additional misconduct or wrongdoing.

- **Pay Heed to the Rights of the Accused.** Investigative findings based on uncorroborated allegations or dubious evidence can expose an employer to liability for a negligent investigation claim. Before taking any corrective actions based on the investigation's finding, such as terminating a manager accused of harassment, the investigative findings should be carefully scrutinized by at least one company official who was not involved in the investigation and has no stake in the outcome.

Factors to assess include whether the investigator failed to pursue leads, such as failing to interview a key witness; whether the investigator gave undue weight to hearsay; and whether the documentary evidence is consistent with the investigator's conclusions. Moreover, it is critical throughout an investigation to avoid defaming the accused.

- **Steer Clear of Unlawful Investigation Techniques and Preserve the Authenticity of Electronic Documents.** The Hewlett-Packard "pretexting" scandal, which resulted in a $14.5 million settlement and other sanctions, is a stark reminder of the importance of complying with state and federal privacy laws.

Throughout the investigation, consider whether any particular technique might run afoul of state wiretapping laws, the Electronic Communications Privacy Act, the Fair Credit Reporting Act or the Health Insurance Portability and Accountability Act.

Investigators should also take steps to avoid inadvertent corruption of electronic documents. As most documents are now created and transmitted electronically, an investigation will likely entail the gathering and review of various types of electronic documents. Merely opening or reading an electronic file, such as an email or a spreadsheet, alters the metadata of the file.

The metadata itself could contain critical evidence that might resolve conflicting accounts, such as when a document was transmitted, received or opened. To ensure that evidence uncovered in an investigation will retain its authenticity and be deemed reliable in potential litigation, create a "mirror image" or bit-by-bit copy of the source drive or database.

R. SCOTT OSWALD and **JASON ZUCKERMAN** are Principals at The Employment Law Group. They represent employees in whistleblower retaliation claims brought under the Sarbanes-Oxley Act and other protection provisions.

From *CRO*, January/February 2008. Copyright © 2008 by FosteReprints. Reprinted by permission.

On Witnessing a Fraud

Saying no to the scam was easy, but deciding whether to report it was harder.

DON SOEKEN

Skiers in bright parkas swooshed by on the slopes as Joe pushed open the gleaming silver doors of the Highland Ski Club, ready to begin another day as computer technician. It was expensive living in the tourist town of Bastcliff, Colo., but Joe loved it. Little did he know, on this fine November morning, of the emotional storm that approached just inside the doors.

The nightmare began innocently enough, when a supervisor tapped Joe on the shoulder and murmured, "We've had an energy surge in the computer system. Will you check out the damage and report to the club manager?"

"Sure thing," said Joe. "I'll get right on it."

He found a relatively minor problem. The surge had fried a few underground wires and computer circuits, which would have to be replaced at a cost of about $15,000. When Joe reported this to the supervisor and the club manager, their response surprised him. They asked him to dig up nearly all the underground wire and cable, then dispose of it before the insurance adjuster arrived. If that were done, the cost of the repair job paid by the insurance company would come to $600,000.

"Wow, I don't think that's something I want to do," Joe told them. But his superiors assured him that if the scam were discovered, the company would be liable rather than him personally. They also noted the plan would allow the club to install a new computer system, which Joe had been asking for.

"I'm sorry," Joe said. "It's fraud, and I refuse to be part of it."

The club manager scowled angrily, and then shrugged as Joe left the room. Minutes later Joe was dismayed to learn that his fellow employee Todd was on his way to dig up the good wiring and stash it in a dumpster far removed from the clubhouse.

To clear his head, Joe stepped out into the cold bright air. Should he report the scam, he asked himself, or let it go? What should he do?

C. Fred Alford, Professor of Government and Politics, University of Maryland, College Park

Ever since my book on whistleblowing (Whistleblowers: Broken Lives and Organizational Power) was published, I've been contacted once a month from would-be whistleblowers asking what they should do. Usually the cases are complex, both factually and ethically. The first part of this case isn't. Joe is being asked to go along with felony fraud, and he has no choice but to say no. The second part is harder: Should he inform the insurance company and possibly get his friend Todd in trouble?

My advice is yes, he should make that phone call. You can't let something like this go—it's like seeing a traffic accident and not reporting it.

Joe will no doubt be fired, and will have to find new work. But he's in a field with a lot of jobs, unlike the field of nuclear engineering, for example, where whistleblowers have little chance to start over. I assume Joe has not been working at the ski club for years and years, since most of these jobs are staffed by young people looking for adventure.

If some or all of this is true, I recommend Joe move to another state, come up with a convincing explanation for the gap in his employment record, and get on with his life. Most whistleblowers want vindication—they want to fight a lawsuit for reinstatement. But it's enough to have done the right thing and move on.

Here my advice is practical rather than moral. Rather than explaining why he was fired, I'm suggesting Joe leave that job out of his resume and make something up to fill the gap. I recommend he lie. Not about having done something bad, but about having done something moral.

Don Soeken's Comments

Even at the risk of losing his job, Joe behaved with the ethical integrity he had been taught to value during childhood: he refused to be part of a fraud. Joe did what too many of us are afraid to do, in standing up for what's right.

As for reporting the fraud, I agree that Joe must call the insurance company. Prof. Alford introduces a surprising twist, in suggesting that when Joe loses his job, he should lie to smooth out his employment record. This is a question on which I think good people will disagree. I recommend that Joe keep the resume correct and list someone at the ski club who could help him get another job.

What Actually Happened

Joe reported the $600,000 attempted fraud to the insurance company, and admitted to his bosses he was the whistleblower. He was fired. The ski club received money from the insurance company, which was slow to investigate, and the outcome of that investigation is unknown. No negative consequences happened to Joe's coworker who dug up the cable. Joe later discovered the ski club had defrauded insurance companies on several occasions.

Joe found it hard to get another job, since his personnel file held a negative assessment of his job performance. Several evaluations said he had "problems with authority." Before the whistleblowing, similar evaluations had described Joe's work as superior. Soon, Joe was struggling with clinical depression.

He filed a lawsuit to seek various kinds of compensation—including lost wages. After years of legal wrangling, the judge ordered both mediation and settlement talks. Joe settled for an undisclosed payment. The company did not admit wrongdoing.

DON SOEKEN (helpline@tidal wave.net) is director of Integrity International, which provides counseling support and expert witness testimony for whistleblowers. See www.whistleblowing.us.

All cases in What Would You Do? are real, though disguised.

His Most Trusted Employee Was a Thief

Jane had taken $20,000 to pay for a child's medical care.

SHEL HOROWITZ

Jane had worked for Edward faithfully for four years, and he trusted her with all the intimate details of his business. She was the one he relied on to solve any problem, to handle his paper-work, to be his personal confidante. She didn't have an accounting background, but she exercised day-to-day oversight over his company's finances, including depositing all the checks and cash that came in. Edward considered Jane a close personal friend. And while she was well-compensated, he paid out-of-pocket for special medical treatment for one of her children, when it fell outside the employee health plan that covered her, but not her family.

Jane had earned Edward's complete trust—until the day he discovered that, over the course of years, she had embezzled $20,000. When Edward confronted her, Jane immediately admitted the theft. She apologized and explained it was to pay for her child's high medical expenses. She agreed to begin a repayment plan, but Edward knew she didn't have the financial resources to pay back the entire $20,000.

Logic would dictate that Edward immediately terminate Jane and begin the process of criminal prosecution—but this was a close friend. Cold logic wasn't the only thing working here; there was a history of so many years working side by side. If only Jane had asked him, Edward would have contributed further toward the child's treatment. Now, what would sending Jane to jail accomplish? It wouldn't repair his trust, and it would not bring back the lost dollars. And how could he leave those children with no parent to take care of them, to say nothing of the medical problems? At the same time, if he allowed Jane to escape responsibility for her actions, who is to say she wouldn't do it again?

Archie Carroll
Robert W. Scherer Chair of Management Terry College of Business, University of Georgia

Carroll presented this case to the Social Issues in Management on-line faculty discussion group, asking for advice on behalf of the business owner, who is a friend of his (names have been changed). Comments below reflect both Carroll's own thoughts, as well as input from 15 of his colleagues.

When I asked my faculty colleagues about this, their advice ranged the gamut. Some said keep Jane as an employee, since she'd feel enough guilt and shame that she would not repeat the bad behavior (and thus Edward could avoid the high cost of training a replacement). At the other extreme, some said Edward should consider criminal prosecution.

As much as a consensus existed, it was that criminal prosecution would not help the situation, especially as the business owner wanted to put the episode behind him. There was recognition that the employee had worked "above and beyond," and that it would not help her family to put them through the trial and possible imprisonment. There was, of course, strong agreement that the embezzlement was wrong and that the business should institute accounting controls to prevent a similar theft in the future.

Some of the more innovative suggestions included:

- Fire Jane, but have her demonstrate how she was able to circumvent his fraud controls so that a future employee couldn't repeat the theft.
- Show generosity and forgive the money, out of respect for Jane's difficult financial situation.
- Hire Jane back on a probationary basis, and either forgive the debt or have her pay it back in small increments.
- Have her sign a promissory note, treating the theft as a loan.

ANNUAL EDITIONS

What Actually Happened

Edward fired Jane. He forgave half of the $20,000 taken, in recognition of the extra effort she had gone to on his behalf for four years. For the other $10,000, he had her execute a promissory note to repay $100 per month (eight years and four months to repay in full). He felt, however, that this money was tainted. Instead of keeping it, he plans to donate it to charity. Edward will also upgrade his accounting controls (which already involve five people), but also take a much more active role in monitoring his company's financial situation.

SHEL HOROWITZ, (shel@principledprofits.com) author of *Principled Profit: Marketing That Puts People First,* initiated the Business Ethics Pledge movement at www.principledprofits.com/25000influencers.html.

From *Business Ethics,* Winter 2005. Copyright © 2005 by New Mountain Media, LLC. Reprinted by permission.

Article 26

The Parable of the Sadhu

After encountering a dying pilgrim on a climbing trip in the Himalayas, a businessman ponders the differences between individual and corporate ethics.

BOWEN H. MCCOY

Last year, as the first participant in the new six-month sabbatical program that Morgan Stanley has adopted, I enjoyed a rare opportunity to collect my thoughts as well as do some traveling. I spent the first three months in Nepal, walking 600 miles through 200 villages in the Himalayas and climbing some 120,000 vertical feet. My sole Western companion on the trip was an anthropologist who shed light on the cultural patterns of the villages that we passed through.

During the Nepal hike, something occurred that has had a powerful impact on my thinking about corporate ethics. Although some might argue that the experience has no relevance to business, it was a situation in which a basic ethical dilemma suddenly intruded into the lives of a group of individuals. How the group responded holds a lesson for all organizations, no matter how defined.

The Sadhu

The Nepal experience was more rugged than I had anticipated. Most commercial treks last two or three weeks and cover a quarter of the distance we traveled.

My friend Stephen, the anthropologist, and I were halfway through the 60-day Himalayan part of the trip when we reached the high point, an 18,000-foot pass over a crest that we'd have to traverse to reach the village of Muklinath, an ancient holy place for pilgrims.

Six years earlier, I had suffered pulmonary edema, an acute form of altitude sickness, at 16,500 feet in the vicinity of Everest base camp—so we were understandably concerned about what would happen at 18,000 feet. Moreover, the Himalayas were having their wettest spring in 20 years; hip-deep powder and ice had already driven us off one ridge. If we failed to cross the pass, I feared that the last half of our once-in-a-lifetime trip would be ruined.

The night before we would try the pass, we camped in a hut at 14,500 feet. In the photos taken at that camp, my face appears wan. The last village we'd passed through was a sturdy two-day walk below us, and I was tired.

During the late afternoon, four backpackers from New Zealand joined us, and we spent most of the night awake, anticipating the climb. Below, we could see the fires of two other parties, which turned out to be two Swiss couples and a Japanese hiking club.

To get over the steep part of the climb before the sun melted the steps cut in the ice, we departed at 3:30 A.M. The New Zealanders left first, followed by Stephen and myself, our porters and Sherpas, and then the Swiss. The Japanese lingered in their camp. The sky was clear, and we were confident that no spring storm would erupt that day to close the pass.

At 15,500 feet, it looked to me as if Stephen were shuffling and staggering a bit, which are symptoms of altitude sickness. (The initial stage of altitude sickness brings a headache and nausea. As the condition worsens, a climber may encounter difficult breathing, disorientation, aphasia, and paralysis.) I felt strong—my adrenaline was flowing—but I was very concerned about my ultimate ability to get across. A couple of our porters were also suffering from the height, and Pasang, our Sherpa sirdar (leader), was worried.

Just after daybreak, while we rested at 15,500 feet, one of the New Zealanders, who had gone ahead, came staggering down toward us with a body slung across his shoulders. He dumped the almost naked, barefoot body of an Indian holy man—a sadhu—at my feet. He had found the pilgrim lying on the ice, shivering and suffering from hypothermia. I cradled the sadhu's head and laid him out on the rocks. The New Zealander was angry. He wanted to get across the pass before the bright sun melted the snow. He said, "Look, I've done what I can. You have porters and Sherpa guides. You care for him. We're going on!" He turned and went back up the mountain to join his friends.

I took a carotid pulse and found that the sadhu was still alive. We figured he had probably visited the holy shrines at Muklinath and was on his way home. It was fruitless to question why he had chosen this desperately high route instead of the safe, heavily traveled caravan route through the Kali Gandaki gorge. Or why he was shoeless and almost naked, or how long he had been lying in the pass. The answers weren't going to solve our problem.

Stephen and the four Swiss began stripping off their outer clothing and opening their packs. The sadhu was soon clothed from head to foot. He was not able to walk, but he was very much alive. I looked down the mountain and spotted the Japanese climbers, marching up with a horse.

When I reached them, Stephen glared at me and said, "How do you feel about contributing to the death of a fellow man?"

Without a great deal of thought, I told Stephen and Pasang that I was concerned about withstanding the heights to come and wanted to get over the pass. I took off after several of our porters who had gone ahead.

On the steep part of the ascent where, if the ice steps had given way, I would have slid down about 3,000 feet, I felt vertigo. I stopped for a breather, allowing the Swiss to catch up with me. I inquired about the sadhu and Stephen. They said that the sadhu was fine and that Stephen was just behind them. I set off again for the summit.

Stephen arrived at the summit an hour after I did. Still exhilarated by victory, I ran down the slope to congratulate him. He was suffering from altitude sickness—walking 15 steps, then stopping, walking 15 steps, then stopping. Pasang accompanied him all the way up. When I reached them, Stephen glared at me and said: "How do you feel about contributing to the death of a fellow man?"

I did not completely comprehend what he meant. "Is the sadhu dead?" I inquired.

"No," replied Stephen, "but he surely will be!"

After I had gone, followed not long after by the Swiss, Stephen had remained with the sadhu. When the Japanese had arrived, Stephen had asked to use their horse to transport the sadhu down to the hut. They had refused. He had then asked Pasang to have a group of our porters carry the sadhu. Pasang had resisted the idea, saying that the porters would have to exert all their energy to get themselves over the pass. He believed they could not carry a man down 1,000 feet to the hut, reclimb the slope, and get across safely before the snow melted. Pasang had pressed Stephen not to delay any longer.

The Sherpas had carried the sadhu down to a rock in the sun at about 15,000 feet and pointed out the hut another 500 feet below. The Japanese had given him food and drink. When they had last seen him, he was listlessly throwing rocks at the Japanese party's dog, which had frightened him.

We do not know if the sadhu lived or died.

For many of the following days and evenings, Stephen and I discussed and debated our behavior toward the sadhu. Stephen is a committed Quaker with deep moral vision. He said, "I feel that what happened with the sadhu is a good example of the breakdown between the individual ethic and the corporate ethic. No one person was willing to assume ultimate responsibility for the sadhu. Each was willing to do his bit just so long as it was not too inconvenient. When it got to be a bother, everyone just passed the buck to someone else and took off. Jesus was relevant to a more individualistic stage of society, but how do we interpret his teaching today in a world filled with large, impersonal organizations and groups?"

I defended the larger group, saying, "Look, we all cared. We all gave aid and comfort. Everyone did his bit. The New Zealander carried him down below the snow line. I took his pulse and suggested we treat him for hypothermia. You and the Swiss gave him clothing and got him warmed up. The Japanese gave him food and water. The Sherpas carried him down to the sun and pointed out the easy trail toward the hut. He was well enough to throw rocks at a dog. What more could we do?"

"You have just described the typical affluent Westerner's response to a problem. Throwing money—in this case, food and sweaters—at it, but not solving the fundamentals!" Stephen retorted.

I asked, "Where is the limit of our responsibility in a situation like this?"

"What would satisfy you?" I said. "Here we are, a group of New Zealanders, Swiss, Americans, and Japanese who have never met before and who are at the apex of one of the most powerful experiences of our lives. Some years the pass is so bad no one gets over it. What right does an almost naked pilgrim who chooses the wrong trail have to disrupt our lives? Even the Sherpas had no interest in risking the trip to help him beyond a certain point."

Stephen calmly rebutted, "I wonder what the Sherpas would have done if the sadhu had been a well-dressed Nepali, or what the Japanese would have done if the sadhu had been a well-dressed Asian, or what you would have done, Buzz, if the sadhu had been a well-dressed Western woman?"

"Where, in your opinion," I asked, "is the limit of our responsibility in a situation like this? We had our own well-being to worry about. Our Sherpa guides were unwilling to jeopardize us or the porters for the sadhu. No one else on the mountain was willing to commit himself beyond certain self-imposed limits."

Stephen said, "As individual Christians or people with a Western ethical tradition, we can fulfill our obligations in such a situation only if one, the sadhu dies in our care; two, the sadhu demonstrates to us that he can undertake the two-day walk down to the village; or three, we carry the sadhu for two days down to the village and persuade someone there to care for him."

"Leaving the sadhu in the sun with food and clothing—where he demonstrated hand-eye coordination by throwing a rock at a dog—comes close to fulfilling items one and two," I answered. "And it wouldn't have made sense to take him to the village where the people appeared to be far less caring than the Sherpas, so the third condition is impractical. Are you really saying that, no matter what the implications, we should, at the drop of a hat, have changed our entire plan?"

The Individual versus the Group Ethic

Despite my arguments, I felt and continue to feel guilt about the sadhu. I had literally walked through a classic moral dilemma without fully thinking through the consequences. My excuses for my actions include a high adrenaline flow, a superordinate goal, and a once-in-a-lifetime opportunity—common factors in corporate situations, especially stressful ones.

Real moral dilemmas are ambiguous, and many of us hike right through them, unaware that they exist. When, usually after the fact, someone makes an issue of one, we tend to resent his or her bringing it up. Often, when the full import of what we have done (or not done) hits us, we dig into a defensive position from which it is very difficult to emerge. In rare circumstances, we may contemplate what we have done from inside a prison.

Had we mountaineers been free of stress caused by the effort and the high altitude, we might have treated the sadhu differently. Yet isn't stress the real test of personal and corporate values? The instant decisions that executives make under pressure reveal the most about personal and corporate character.

As a group, we had no process for developing a consensus. We had no sense of purpose or plan.

Among the many questions that occur to me when I ponder my experience with the sadhu are: What are the practical limits of moral imagination and vision? Is there a collective or institutional ethic that differs from the ethics of the individual? At what level of effort or commitment can one discharge one's ethical responsibilities?

Not every ethical dilemma has a right solution. Reasonable people often disagree; otherwise there would be no dilemma. In a business context, however, it is essential that managers agree on a process for dealing with dilemmas.

Our experience with the sadhu offers an interesting parallel to business situations. An immediate response was mandatory. Failure to act was a decision in itself. Up on the mountain we could not resign and submit our résumés to a headhunter. In contrast to philosophy, business involves action and implementation—getting things done. Managers must come up with answers based on what they see and what they allow to influence their decision-making processes. On the mountain, none of us but Stephen realized the true dimensions of the situation we were facing.

One of our problems was that as a group we had no process for developing a consensus. We had no sense of purpose or plan. The difficulties of dealing with the sadhu were so complex that no one person could handle them. Because the group did not have a set of preconditions that could guide its action to an acceptable resolution, we reacted instinctively as individuals. The cross-cultural nature of the group added a further layer of complexity. We had no leader with whom we could all identify and in whose purpose we believed. Only Stephen was willing to take charge, but he could not gain adequate support from the group to care for the sadhu.

Some organizations do have values that transcend the personal values of their managers. Such values, which go beyond profitability, are usually revealed when the organization is under stress. People throughout the organization generally accept its values, which, because they are not presented as a rigid list of commandments, may be somewhat ambiguous. The stories people tell, rather than printed materials, transmit the organization's conceptions of what is proper behavior.

For 20 years, I have been exposed at senior levels to a variety of corporations and organizations. It is amazing how quickly an outsider can sense the tone and style of an organization and, with that, the degree of tolerated openness and freedom to challenge management.

Organizations that do not have a heritage of mutually accepted, shared values tend to become unhinged during stress, with each individual bailing out for himself or herself. In the great takeover battles we have witnessed during past years, companies that had strong cultures drew the wagons around them and fought it out, while other companies saw executives—supported by golden parachutes—bail out of the struggles.

Because corporations and their members are interdependent, for the corporation to be strong the members need to share a preconceived notion of correct behavior, a "business ethic," and think of it as a positive force, not a constraint.

As an investment banker, I am continually warned by well-meaning lawyers, clients, and associates to be wary of conflicts of interest. Yet if I were to run away from every difficult situation, I wouldn't be an effective investment banker. I have to feel my way through conflicts. An effective manager can't run from risk either; he or she has to confront risk. To feel "safe" in doing that, managers need the guidelines of an agreed-upon process and set of values within the organization.

After my three months in Nepal, I spent three months as an executive-in-residence at both the Stanford Business School and the University of California at Berkeley's Center for Ethics and Social Policy of the Graduate Theological Union. Those six months away from my job gave me time to assimilate 20 years of business experience. My thoughts turned often to the meaning of the leadership role in any large organization. Students at the seminary thought of themselves as antibusiness. But when I questioned them, they agreed that they distrusted all large organizations, including the church. They perceived all large organizations as impersonal and opposed to individual values and needs. Yet we all know of organizations in which people's values and beliefs are respected and their expressions encouraged. What makes the difference? Can we identify the difference and, as a result, manage more effectively?

The word *ethics* turns off many and confuses more. Yet the notions of shared values and an agreed-upon process for dealing with adversity and change—what many people mean when they talk about corporate culture—seem to be at the heart of the ethical issue. People who are in touch with their own core beliefs and the beliefs of others and who are sustained by them can be more comfortable living on the cutting edge. At times, taking a tough line or a decisive stand in a muddle of ambiguity

When Do We Take a Stand?

I wrote about my experiences purposely to present an ambiguous situation. I never found out if the sadhu lived or died. I can attest, though, that the sadhu lives on in his story. He lives in the ethics classes I teach each year at business schools and churches. He lives in the classrooms of numerous business schools, where professors have taught the case to tens of thousands of students. He lives in several casebooks on ethics and on an educational video. And he lives in organizations such as the American Red Cross and AT&T, which use his story in their ethics training.

As I reflect on the sadhu now, 15 years after the fact, I first have to wonder, What actually happened on that Himalayan slope? When I first wrote about the event, I reported the experience in as much detail as I could remember, but I shaped it to the needs of a good classroom discussion. After years of reading my story, viewing it on video, and hearing others discuss it, I'm not sure I myself know what actually occurred on the mountainside that day!

I've also heard a wide variety of responses to the story. The sadhu, for example, may not have wanted our help at all—he may have been intentionally bringing on his own death as a way to holiness. Why had he taken the dangerous way over the pass instead of the caravan route through the gorge? Hindu businesspeople have told me that in trying to assist the sadhu, we were being typically arrogant Westerners imposing our cultural values on the world.

I've learned that each year along the pass, a few Nepali porters are left to freeze to death outside the tents of the unthinking tourists who hired them. A few years ago, a French group even left one of their own, a young French woman, to die there. The difficult pass seems to demonstrate a perverse version of Gresham's law of currency: The bad practices of previous travelers have driven out the values that new travelers might have followed if they were at home. Perhaps that helps to explain why our porters behaved as they did and why it was so difficult for Stephen or anyone else to establish a different approach on the spot.

Our Sherpa sirdar, Pasang, was focused on his responsibility for bringing us up the mountain safe and sound. (His livelihood and status in the Sherpa ethnic group depended on our safe return.) We were weak, our party was split, the porters were well on their way to the top with all our gear and food, and a storm would have separated us irrevocably from our logistical base.

The fact was, we had no plan for dealing with the contingency of the sadhu. There was nothing we could do to unite our multicultural group in the little time we had. An ethical dilemma had come upon us unexpectedly, an element of drama that may explain why the sadhu's story has continued to attract students.

I am often asked for help in teaching the story. I usually advise keeping the details as ambiguous as possible. A true ethical dilemma requires a decision between two hard choices. In the case of the sadhu, we had to decide how much to sacrifice ourselves to take care of a stranger. And given the constraints of our trek, we had to make a group decision, not an individual one. If a large majority of students in a class ends up thinking I'm a bad person because of my decision on the mountain, the instructor may not have given the case its due. The same is true if the majority sees no problem with the choices we made.

Any class's response depends on its setting, whether it's a business school, a church, or a corporation. I've found that younger students are more likely to see the issue as black-and-white, whereas older ones tend to see shades of gray. Some have seen a conflict between the different ethical approaches that we followed at the time. Stephen felt he had to do everything he could to save the sadhu's life, in accordance with his Christian ethic of compassion. I had a utilitarian response: do the greatest good for the greatest number. Give a burst of aid to minimize the sadhu's exposure, then continue on our way.

The basic question of the case remains, When do we take a stand? When do we allow a "sadhu" to intrude into our daily lives? Few of us can afford the time or effort to take care of every needy person we encounter. How much must we give of ourselves? And how do we prepare our organizations and institutions so they will respond appropriately in a crisis? How do we influence them if we do not agree with their points of view?

We cannot quit our jobs over every ethical dilemma, but if we continually ignore our sense of values, who do we become? As a journalist asked at a recent conference on ethics, "Which ditch are we willing to die in?" For each of us, the answer is a bit different. How we act in response to that question defines better than anything else who we are, just as, in a collective sense, our acts define our institutions. In effect, the sadhu is always there, ready to remind us of the tensions between our own goals and the claims of strangers.

---

is the only ethical thing to do. If a manager is indecisive about a problem and spends time trying to figure out the "good" thing to do, the enterprise may be lost.

Business ethics, then, has to do with the authenticity and integrity of the enterprise. To be ethical is to follow the business as well as the cultural goals of the corporation, its owners, its employees, and its customers. Those who cannot serve the corporate vision are not authentic businesspeople and, therefore, are not ethical in the business sense.

At this stage of my own business experience, I have a strong interest in organizational behavior. Sociologists are keenly studying what they call corporate stories, legends, and heroes as a way organizations have of transmitting value systems. Corporations such as Arco have even hired consultants to perform an audit of their corporate culture. In a company, a leader is a person who understands, interprets, and manages the corporate value system. Effective managers, therefore, are action-oriented people who resolve conflict, are tolerant of ambiguity, stress, and change, and have a strong sense of purpose for themselves and their organizations.

If all this is true, I wonder about the role of the professional manager who moves from company to company. How can he or she quickly absorb the values and culture of different organizations? Or is there, indeed, an art of management that is totally transportable? Assuming that such fungible managers do exist, is it proper for them to manipulate the values of others?

What would have happened had Stephen and I carried the sadhu for two days back to the village and become involved with the villagers in his care? In four trips to Nepal, my most interesting experience occurred in 1975 when I lived in a Sherpa home in the Khumbu for five days while recovering from altitude sickness. The high point of Stephen's trip was an invitation to participate in a family funeral ceremony in Manang. Neither experience had to do with climbing the high passes of the Himalayas. Why were we so reluctant to try the lower path, the ambiguous trail? Perhaps because we did not have a leader who could reveal the greater purpose of the trip to us.

Why didn't Stephen, with his moral vision, opt to take the sadhu under his personal care? The answer is partly because Stephen was hard-stressed physically himself and partly because, without some support system that encompassed our involuntary and episodic community on the mountain, it was beyond his individual capacity to do so.

I see the current interest in corporate culture and corporate value systems as a positive response to pessimism such as Stephen's about the decline of the role of the individual in large organizations. Individuals who operate from a thoughtful set of personal values provide the foundation for a corporate culture. A corporate tradition that encourages freedom of inquiry, supports personal values, and reinforces a focused sense of direction can fulfill the need to combine individuality with the prosperity and success of the group. Without such corporate support, the individual is lost.

That is the lesson of the sadhu. In a complex corporate situation, the individual requires and deserves the support of the group. When people cannot find such support in their organizations, they don't know how to act. If such support is forthcoming, a person has a stake in the success of the group and can add much to the process of establishing and maintaining a corporate culture. Management's challenge is to be sensitive to individual needs, to shape them, and to direct and focus them for the benefit of the group as a whole.

For each of us the sadhu lives. Should we stop what we are doing and comfort him; or should we keep trudging up toward the high pass? Should I pause to help the derelict I pass on the street each night as I walk by the Yale Club en route to Grand Central Station? Am I his brother? What is the nature of our responsibility if we consider ourselves to be ethical persons? Perhaps it is to change the values of the group so that it can, with all its resources, take the other road.

BOWEN H. MCCOY retired from Morgan Stanley in 1990 after 28 years of service. He is now a real estate and business counselor, a teacher and a philanthropist.

Editor's Note—This article was originally published in the September/October 1983 issue of *HBR*. For its republication as an HBR Classic, Bowen H. McCoy has written the commentary "When Do We Take a Stand?" to update his observations.

Article 27

An Ethical Dilemma
How to Build Integrity into Your Sales Environment

THEODORE B. KINNI

Contrary to the stereotypical view, salespeople are not predisposed to face any fewer, or any more, ethical dilemmas than anyone else. But that doesn't mean that sales organizations can't become ethical—and legal—nightmares. Just ask Lake Forest, Illinois-based TAP Pharmaceutical Products Inc.

According to a story in *Business Week,* (June 24, 2002—"A Whistle-Blower Rocks an Industry" by Charles Haddad), in 1995, when TAP hired Douglas Durand as vice president of sales, the company owned the best-selling prostate cancer drug, Lupron, which was generating $800 million in annual revenues. The only problem, as Durand quickly discovered, was that TAP was building and maintaining Lupron's market share illegally.

Durand found that TAP's sales force was busy sowing a minefield of explosive ethical and legal problems. With management's knowledge and approval, the company's salespeople were offering doctors a 2 percent kickback, in the guise of an administrative fee, to prescribe Lupron. They were also distributing undocumented samples of the drug and encouraging doctors to sell them—in addition to offering every one of the nation's urologists a game show's wealth of televisions, vacations and high-tech gadgets in return for treating their patients with Lupron.

The new sales exec tried to clean up the mess, but found himself ignored and shut out in TAP's numbers-driven business culture. Frustrated, Durand began documenting the abuses and, within a year, brought suit under the federal whistle-blower law. In October 2001, TAP paid an $875 million fine to the government. Durand, who had left the company in early 1996, received $77 million for his evidence and testimony in the successful prosecution.

Admittedly, most sales organizations are not dealing with problems as extreme as TAP's—if you are, go straight to legal counsel. But every day, salespeople and their managers are faced with a variety of ethical dilemmas that have the potential to negatively impact their lives and their companies. The key question: How do you equip your sales force to deal with ethical dilemmas?

Ethics Flow Downhill

A formal code of sales ethics is probably not the right place to start. "You can't just slap an ethics code on a sales force like a barnacle on the side of a whale," says Marjorie Kelly, publisher of *Business Ethics* and author of *The Divine Right of Capital: Dethroning the Corporate Aristocracy* (Berrett-Koehler Pub., 2001).

Instead, sales ethics should be an extension of the organization's ethics, which in turn are an extension of organizational values. At privately held Seventh Generation Inc., the nation's leading brand of nontoxic, environmentally safe household products, there is no code dedicated to sales ethics. "We don't look at sales ethics differently than we look at ethics in general," explains Jeffrey Hollender, president of the Burlington, Vermont-based company. "Sales ethics emanate from organizational values. And there is a lot of work that we do in developing organizational values that obviously then impacts everything we do. Quite honestly, we have never found it necessary to define sales ethics any differently than we look at our general ethics."

San Francisco, California-based Charles Schwab & Company Inc., a company noted for having avoided the ethical meltdown among the stock brokerages, is another firm that has not found the need for a formal statement of sales ethics. "It's a values-driven company," says Parke Boneysteele, senior vice president of sales and service effectiveness. "So, our values are to be fair, empathetic and responsive in serving clients; to respect and reinforce fellow employees and respect the value of teamwork; to strive relentlessly to innovate in how we provide value; and then, to always earn and be worthy of our clients' trust. And that is what we are all about."

The fact that sales ethics do not require a dedicated code is not, however, to be construed as a free pass to ignore them. At both Schwab and Seventh Generation, sales ethics are always on the radar. Even when strong organizational values are in place, the application of broad-based ethics to the sales process remains a critical issue.

Salespeople need special training that says, 'Here are some boundaries,' some things that you can and cannot do that will allow you to adhere to the code of ethics and still be . . . effective.

Creating Ethical Specificity

"Salespeople need special training that says, 'Here are some boundaries,'" says Jeff Salters, programs director of Washington, D.C.-based Ethics Resource Center—"some things that you can and cannot do that will allow you to adhere to the code of ethics and still be an effective salesperson."

Salespeople need dedicated attention when it comes to ethics, not because they are less ethical than other employees, but because they face greater ethical exposures than most other employees. Patrick Murphy, professor at Notre Dame's Mendoza College of Business and director of the Institute for Ethical Business Worldwide, says, "One thing that makes selling ethics a bit different than other organizational ethics is that most salespeople are on the road. So, when they get hit with an ethical dilemma, often they have to deal with it on their own as opposed to in a meeting or checking with a boss down the hall. Organizations need to be sensitive to the fact that salespeople are often on their own and need to have a support structure."

The ethical support you create for your sales force should address two categories of ethical issues. There are issues that are generic to the sales discipline—that arise from the act of selling itself, such as overpromising—and those that are specific to your company and industry, such as the FDA's regulations for pharmaceuticals.

First and foremost, of course, are the legal issues, which Murphy identifies in the forthcoming textbook *Ethical Marketing* (Prentice Hall, August 2004), such as federal regulations and applicable state and local regulations, including the Uniform Commercial Code, cooling-off laws, and Green River ordinances. Aside from notable exceptions such as the Lupron debacle, most salespeople don't stray into this territory and most companies are active about ensuring that they never do.

Less well covered, however, is ethics support that addresses what Murphy calls, "the gray areas of selling." These represent issues that, while not necessarily illegal, can cause great damage to sales careers and companies. They are:

1. The use of company assets, including abuses of equipment such as cars and computers, and expense reports;
2. Customer relationships, which includes such abuses as overstocking, overselling, overpromising, overtelling, and underinforming;
3. Competitor relationships, including disparagement, tampering and spying;
4. Relationships with peers and supervisors, including such abuses as territory poaching and false reporting;
5. Conflicts of interest, including improper disclosure;
6. Gifts and entertainment in excess of corporate and customer policies; and
7. Bribery and facilitation, specifically in countries in which they are accepted practices and not illegal.

"If companies have a formal policy regarding gray areas, then the salesperson can tell the customer that they are not allowed to offer tickets to more than one game once a season or once a month or things of that nature," says Murphy. "That is where I think specificity, if you will, helps the salespeople when they get put in a tough spot."

Translating Ethics into Reality

Ensuring the linkage between sales ethics and organizational values and creating policies that specify behavior is all well and good, but doesn't guarantee ethical compliance. After all, Enron had a value statement and a 65-page *Code of Ethics,* a copy of which now resides in the Smithsonian. So, how do you ensure that your sales force lives up to the highest ethical standards?

First, build ethics into your hiring process. "Alignment from a values perspective is about 50 percent of the equation on a new hire," says Hollender of Seventh Generation's employment process. "We would not want to hire someone who is 100 percent focused on the result and 0 percent focused on the process. What you have to find is people who are very committed to the result, but understand that the process through which they achieve that result is of equal importance. It's a very different mind-set."

"Forward-thinking companies are even going as far as doing initial testing to check for ethical values. They test salespeople prior to hire," says Anthony Zuanich, a veteran sales manager who worked at IBM and ADP before becoming senior vice president of sales at the HR Outsourcing division of Aon Consulting Worldwide, an arm of Chicago, Illinois-based AON Corp.

Second, provide new hires with written policies and ask them to sign them to indicate both comprehension and compliance. "Salespeople should get new-hire packets that document ethics issues and policies, including the ethical dilemmas that are unique to that company," explains Zuanich. "New salespeople should be educated and sign off that they agree to the policies and will not harm the company's reputation as well as their own by not following these ethical guidelines."

Third, build ethics and values into the training curriculum. "Then its about reinforcement," says Schwab's Boneysteele. "We have it in our new-hire training, in our manager training, in our sales training, we always have conversations and discussions about values . . . we talk about it as vision and values as opposed to ethics."

Schwab's training is designed to help employees distinguish between appropriate and inappropriate behavior. "We have a segment where we ask people to come up with things that would be contra to the values and discuss them as part of our new-hire training," says Boneysteele.

The reinforcement of ethics extends into the training provided by sales managers. "As we ask for results, as every good sales manager should," explains Tony Zuanich, "we need to be aware of where there are areas where the salesperson could cross the line. You have to document those areas as a manager and point them out to the salespeople."

Build Ethics into the Process

There are two adages that companies that are serious about creating a highly ethical sales forces would do well to keep in mind. "You get what you pay for" and "What gets measured, gets done."

A Primer for Handling Ethical Dilemmas

At one time or another, virtually every sales professional will face an ethical dilemma. SP asked ethics consultant and speaker Frank Bucaro how salespeople should deal with customers or employers who ask them to do something they consider unethical.

First, understand that unethical behavior is driven by emotions, such as greed, stress and fear. "You cannot deal with ethics on an emotional level, says Bucaro. "When emotions take control, ethics take a hit. So I encourage people when confronted with an unethical situation to take a break, step back."

Next, rationally analyze the situation. "There is a four-step process for considering an ethical decision. It takes some reflection," says Bucaro. "Number 1, you need to identify the action or behavior that is causing the problem. Number 2, what are the circumstances in which this is happening? By that I mean, what do we know about the situation; what you don't know can lead you to the wrong decision. Number 3, what are the criteria by which you are making this decision? Is it Sarbanes-Oxley? Is it the law? Is it the code of ethics? Is it because you think it is right or wrong? Identify the criteria. Number 4 is always, always, get communal wisdom. Find someone who is in your corner and bounce this off that person. We sometimes get too close to a situation and don't always see what we need to see."

Finally, act. "Once you know what is acceptable and what is not acceptable, what is negotiable and what is not; then that is the line in the sand," says Bucaro of customer-initiated dilemmas. "You say, 'I really can't do that because it would jeopardize my credibility, our ethics, and the way this company is set up. I hope you can appreciate that, but this is why we can't do it.'"

And if your employer is the initiator? "Take the high road," says Bucaro. "That might mean saying, 'I am not quite sure I understand all of the reasons why you are asking me to do this, but let me share with you why I am concerned. And I would like your wisdom here in helping me understand why you are asking me to do this.'"

What if the boss says, just do it? "If they ask you to do that once and you do it, do you think they'll ask you to do it again? Sure," says Bucaro. "There is what I call the PTP Factor, that is the 'price to pay.' If the price is too high, you have to refuse. That's where the rubber hits the road. Either you believe in those values or you don't. Because if you make one exception, you will have to make many more."

"Sales ethics need to be designed into the process," says Marjorie Kelly. "This arises out of a recognition that incentive shapes behavior much more than codes. So companies need to look at how they have structured incentives and what kind of behavior that drives. Is your commission structure sending an opposite message from your ethics code?"

Seventh Generation, for instance, created an employee review system that uses 360-degree appraisals to evaluate behavior relative to the corporate values (community, growth, leadership, responsibility, service and trust) as well as performance. "Half of that evaluation is about their traditional business responsibilities, and half of it is about their behavior relative to the values of the company," says Hollender. "Salespeople are evaluated not just on meeting sales objectives and managing expenses, but also in terms of the progress they make in growing from a personal perspective in ways that are in alignment with our values. And they cannot earn 100 percent of their bonus, even if they necessarily double the sales in their budget, if they aren't also making progress in this personal-development area, as well as some kind of community involvement and community service."

At Schwab, some of the gray areas of selling, such as conflicts of interest, have been effectively eliminated by the structure of the company and its compensation programs. "We've kept investment banking conflicts out of our business model," says Boneysteele. "Our customer-facing people are not compensated on whether or not a client picks a particular stock. We don't pay our front-line reps based on revenue that is generated by trading activity. So there are an awful lot of what might be industry gray zones that we just don't get into."

Here are a few more ideas for building sales ethics into the structure and process of sales:

1. Deliver ethics support to the field. "With technology, in particular cell phones and even instantaneous computer communication, your salespeople could literally step out of a meeting and call the office and get support and information," says Notre Dame's Murphy. "I think that companies need to use technology for their ethical benefit and encourage their salespeople to do the same."

2. Create a process for considering ethical issues. "Is there a hotline that I can call if I see something that is unethical or illegal happening?" asks ethics consultant Frank Bucaro. "Is there a number that I can call anonymously and report it?"

3. Use ethics violations as teaching tools. "In your weekly sales meeting," says Tony Zuanich, "take those dilemmas and use them to educate people. Explain what happened and discuss it."

4. Make ethics and values part of your sales presentation. "Even though it often takes time directly away from the sales presentation," says Seventh Generation's Hollender, "we try to make the presentation of our values and operating principles part of what is presented to our customers, so that they understand our commitment, understand what to expect from us."

5. Make your policies public. Schwab maintains a "business practices disclosure" section on its public website that explains exactly how representatives in 10 sales-related functions are compensated.

Ensuring the linkage between sales ethics and organizational values and creating policies that specify behavior is all well and good, but doesn't guarantee ethical compliance.

Sales Ethics Compliance

Ultimately, the ethical level of a sales force is dependent on management's willingness to comply. If compliance and enforcement are ignored and/or applied inconsistently, salespeople will quickly learn that ethical behavior is not a priority.

The first issue in enforcement is consistency in compliance. "Very often organizations put policies and procedures into place that they'd like all of their employees to adhere to. However, many of them make exceptions when it comes to the sales force because the sales force is typically what helps to drive their profits," says Jeff Salters of the Ethics Resource Center. "The way we approach ethics here is, we like to talk about a consistency of message, a congruency of policies and procedures. So you can't state these principles and say, 'We want to adhere to the law, we want to adhere to our code,' and then make exceptions. Actual behavior trumps your stated policy."

Salters points to the pharmaceutical industry as an example: "Doctors might prescribe drugs that were approved for one purpose for other purposes. There are some firms that would discourage a doctor from doing that, even though it might limit the amount of sales they could make of that drug. There are regulations that say you should not sell a drug other than for its intended or approved purpose. When those lines become blurred, some firms try to adhere to a higher standard; some other firms wouldn't care."

The second issue is consistency in enforcement. "I think that in the selling function there is always that inclination or potential proclivity of the people in the higher sales management or up the marketing ladder to look the other way and not ask too many questions about how some salespeople get the sales they do," says Patrick Murphy. "And I think that in this day and age that really comes back to haunt people."

The only ethical answer is what Tony Zuanich calls a "no-excuse response." He says, "The severity of the ethics violation depends on what the issue was, but I think you always need to send a clear message with violators. That sends the message to the rest of the sales force that that kind of behavior will not be tolerated. And in the end, that kind of management will help the results of companies."

"I have and I will terminate employment," says Zuanich. "I will give you a very real one—a difficult case from a past employer. We had a person who was a top producer who gained a reputation for just having an incredible work ethic. We're talking about a salesperson who had a big ego. That person felt like a top gun—indispensable to the company—and the rules didn't necessarily apply. There was a policy about poaching in other salespeople's territories. The person was caught once and given a warning. It happened again and we sent a message. It's a tough thing to do for a results-oriented company, but we had to terminate our very top producer."

From *Selling Power*, October 2004, pp. 109–112. Copyright © 2004 by Selling Power. Reprinted by permission.

UNIT 3

Business and Society: Ethical, Social, and Environmental Issues

Unit Selections

28. **Trust in the Marketplace,** John E. Richardson and Linnea Bernard McCord
29. **Businesses Grow More Socially Conscious,** Edward Iwata
30. **Women and the Labyrinth of Leadership,** Alice H. Eagly and Linda L. Carli
31. **Getting Real about Fakes,** Peggy E. Chaudhry and Stephen A. Stumpf
32. **The New E-spionage Threat,** Brian Grow, Keith Epstein, and Chi-Chu Tschang
33. **Sustainable Success,** Lutz Kaufmann et al.
34. **Global Diversity: The Next Frontier,** Peter Ortiz
35. **Cracks in a Particularly Thick Glass Ceiling,** Moon Ihlwan

Key Points to Consider

- How well are organizations responding to issues of work and family schedules, day care, and telecommuting?
- Should corporations and executives face criminal charges for unsafe products, dangerous working conditions, or industrial pollution? Why or why not?
- What ethical dilemmas is management likely to face when conducting business in foreign environments?

Student Website
www.mhhe.com/cls

Internet References

National Immigrant Forum
http://www.immigrationforum.org

Workopolis.com
http://sympatico.workopolis.com

United Nations Environment Programme (UNEP)
http://www.unep.ch

United States Trade Representative (USTR)
http://www.ustr.

Both at home and abroad, there are social and environmental issues that have potential ethical consequences for management. Incidents of insider trading, deaths resulting from unsafe products or work environments, AIDS in the workplace, and the adoption of policies for involvement in the global market are a few of the issues that need to be seriously addressed by management.

This unit investigates the nature and ramifications of prominent ethical, social, and environmental issues facing management today. The unit articles are grouped into three sections. The first article scrutinizes the importance of companies gaining and maintaining trust in the marketplace. The last two articles in this subsection, **Changing Perspectives in Business and Society,** provide some thoughtful insight on ways companies are embracing CSR practices and why in the near future the product-safety landscape is likely to see some significant change.

The first article in the second subsection, **Contemporary Ethical Issues,** reflects a new picture of why women aren't making it to the C-suite. The second article investigates the reasons for consumers buying counterfeit products. The last article in this subsection probes deeply into rising attacks on the most sensitive U.S. computer networks.

The subsection **Global Ethics** concludes this unit with readings that provide helpful insight on ethical issues and dilemmas inherent in multinational operations. They describe adapting ethical decisions to a global marketplace and offer guidelines for helping management deal with product quality and ethical issues in international markets as well as examining the complex social issues faced by professional women in South Korea.

© Phillip Spears/Getty Images

Trust in the Marketplace

JOHN E. RICHARDSON AND LINNEA BERNARD MCCORD

Traditionally, ethics is defined as a set of moral values or principles or a code of conduct.

... Ethics, as an expression of reality, is predicated upon the assumption that there are right and wrong motives, attitudes, traits of character, and actions that are exhibited in interpersonal relationships. Respectful social interaction is considered a norm by almost everyone.

... the overwhelming majority of people perceive others to be ethical when they observe what is considered to be their genuine kindness, consideration, politeness, empathy, and fairness in their interpersonal relationships. When these are absent, and unkindness, inconsideration, rudeness, hardness, and injustice are present, the people exhibiting such conduct are considered unethical. A genuine consideration of others is essential to an ethical life. (Chewning, pp. 175–176).

An essential concomitant of ethics is of trust. Webster's Dictionary defines trust as "assured reliance on the character, ability, strength or truth of someone or something." Businesses are built on a foundation of trust in our free-enterprise system. When there are violations of this trust between competitors, between employer and employees, or between businesses and consumers, our economic system ceases to run smoothly. From a moral viewpoint, ethical behavior should not exist because of economic pragmatism, governmental edict, or contemporary fashionability—it should exist because it is morally appropriate and right. From an economic point of view, ethical behavior should exist because it just makes good business sense to be ethical and operate in a manner that demonstrates trustworthiness.

Robert Bruce Shaw, in *Trust in the Balance*, makes some thoughtful observations about trust within an organization. Paraphrasing his observations and applying his ideas to the marketplace as a whole:

1. Trust requires consumers have confidence in organizational promises or claims made to them. This means that a consumer should be able to believe that a commitment made will be met.
2. Trust requires integrity and consistency in following a known set of values, beliefs, and practices.
3. Trust requires concern for the well-being of others. This does not mean that organizational needs are not given appropriate emphasis—but it suggests the importance of understanding the impact of decisions and actions on others—i.e. consumers. (Shaw, pp. 39–40)

Companies can lose the trust of their customers by portraying their products in a deceptive or inaccurate manner. In one recent example, a Nike advertisement exhorted golfers to buy the same golf balls used by Tiger Woods. However, since Tiger Woods was using custom-made Nike golf balls not yet available to the general golfing public, the ad was, in fact, deceptive. In one of its ads, Volvo represented that Volvo cars could withstand a physical impact that, in fact, was not possible. Once a company is "caught" giving inaccurate information, even if done innocently, trust in that company is eroded.

Companies can also lose the trust of their customers when they fail to act promptly and notify their customers of problems that the company has discovered, especially where deaths may be involved. This occurred when Chrysler dragged its feet in replacing a safety latch on its Minivan (Geyelin, pp. A1, A10). More recently, Firestone and Ford had been publicly brought to task for failing to expeditiously notify American consumers of tire defects in SUVs even though the problem had occurred years earlier in other countries. In cases like these, trust might not just be eroded, it might be destroyed. It could take years of painstaking effort to rebuild trust under these circumstances, and some companies might not have the economic ability to withstand such a rebuilding process with their consumers.

A *20/20* and *New York Times* investigation on a recent ABC *20/20* program, entitled "The Car Dealer's Secret" revealed a sad example of the violation of trust in the marketplace. The investigation divulged that many unsuspecting consumers have had hidden charges tacked on by some car dealers when purchasing a new car. According to consumer attorney Gary Klein, "It's a dirty little secret that the auto lending industry has not owned up to." (*ABC News 20/20*)

The scheme worked in the following manner. Car dealers would send a prospective buyer's application to a number of lenders, who would report to the car dealer what interest rate the lender would give to the buyer for his or her car loan. This interest rate is referred to as the "buy rate." Legally a car dealer is not required to tell the buyer what the "buy rate" is or how much the dealer is marking up the loan. If dealers did most of the loans at the buy rate, they only get a small fee. However, if they were able to convince the buyer to pay a higher rate, they made considerably more money. Lenders encouraged car dealers to charge the buyer a higher rate than the "buy rate" by agreeing to split the extra income with the dealer.

David Robertson, head of the Association of Finance and Insurance Professionals—a trade group representing finance managers—defended the practice, reflecting that it was akin to a retail markup on loans. "The dealership provides a valuable service on behalf of the customer in negotiating these loans," he said. "Because of that, the dealership should be compensated for that work." (*ABC News 20/20*)

Careful examination of the entire report, however, makes one seriously question this apologetic. Even if this practice is deemed to be legal, the critical issue is what happens to trust when the buyers discover that they have been charged an additional 1–3% of the loan without their knowledge? In some cases, consumers were led to believe that they were getting the dealer's bank rate, and in other cases, they were told that the dealer had shopped around at several banks to secure the best loan rate they could get for the buyer. While this practice may be questionable from a legal standpoint, it is clearly in ethical breach of trust with the consumer. Once discovered, the companies doing this will have the same credibility and trustworthiness problems as the other examples mentioned above.

The untrustworthiness problems of the car companies was compounded by the fact that the investigation appeared to reveal statistics showing that black customers were twice as likely as whites to have their rate marked up—and at a higher level. That evidence—included in thousands of pages of confidential documents which *20/20* and *The New York Times* obtained from a Tennessee court—revealed that some Nissan and GM dealers in Tennessee routinely marked up rates for blacks, forcing them to pay between $300 and $400 more than whites. (*ABC News 20/20*)

This is a tragic example for everyone who was affected by this markup and was the victim of this secret policy. Not only is trust destroyed, there is a huge economic cost to the general public. It is estimated that in the last four years or so, Texas car dealers have received approximately $9 billion of kickbacks from lenders, affecting 5.2 million consumers. (*ABC News 20/20*)

Let's compare these unfortunate examples of untrustworthy corporate behavior with the landmark example of Johnson & Johnson which ultimately increased its trustworthiness with consumers by the way it handled the Tylenol incident. After seven individuals, who had consumed Tylenol capsules contaminated by a third party died, Johnson & Johnson instituted a total product recall within a week costing an estimated $50 million after taxes. The company did this, not because it was responsible for causing the problem, but because it was the right thing to do. In addition, Johnson & Johnson spearheaded the development of more effective tamper-proof containers for their industry. Because of the company's swift response, consumers once again were able to trust in the Johnson & Johnson name. Although Johnson & Johnson suffered a decrease in market share at the time because of the scare, over the long term it has maintained its profitability in a highly competitive market. Certainly part of this profit success is attributable to consumers believing that Johnson & Johnson is a trustworthy company. (Robin and Reidenbach)

The e-commerce arena presents another example of the importance of marketers building a mutually valuable relationship with customers through a trust-based collaboration process. Recent research with 50 e-businesses reflects that companies which create and nurture trust find customers return to their sites repeatedly. (Dayal . . . . p. 64)

In the e-commerce world, six components of trust were found to be critical in developing trusting, satisfied customers:

- State-of-art reliable security measures on one's site
- Merchant legitimacy (e.g., ally one's product or service with an established brand)
- Order fulfillment (i.e. placing orders and getting merchandise efficiently and with minimal hassles)
- Tone and ambiance—handling consumers' personal information with sensitivity and iron-clad confidentiality
- Customers feeling that they are in control of the buying process
- Consumer collaboration—e.g., having chat groups to let consumers query each other about their purchases and experiences (Dayal . . . , pp. 64–67)

Additionally, one author noted recently that in the e-commerce world we've moved beyond brands and trademarks to "trustmarks." This author defined a trustmark as a

> . . . (D)istinctive name or symbol that emotionally binds a company with the desires and aspirations of its customers. It's an emotional connection—and it's much bigger and more powerful than the uses that we traditionally associate with a trademark. . . . (Webber, p. 214)

Certainly if this is the case, trust—being an emotional link—is of supreme importance for a company that wants to succeed in doing business on the Internet.

It's unfortunate that while a plethora of examples of violation of trust easily come to mind, a paucity of examples "pop up" as noteworthy paradigms of organizational courage and trust in their relationship with consumers.

In conclusion, some key areas for companies to scrutinize and practice with regard to decisions that may affect trustworthiness in the marketplace might include:

- Does a company practice the Golden Rule with its customers? As a company insider, knowing what you know about the product, how willing would you be to purchase it for yourself or for a family member?
- How proud would you be if your marketing practices were made public . . . shared with your friends . . . or family? (Blanchard and Peale, p. 27)
- Are bottom-line concerns the sole component of your organizational decision-making process? What about human rights, the ecological/environmental impact, and other areas of social responsibility?
- Can a firm which engages in unethical business practices with customers be trusted to deal with its

employees any differently? Unfortunately, frequently a willingness to violate standards of ethics is not an isolated phenomenon but permeates the culture. The result is erosion of integrity throughout a company. In such cases, trust is elusive at best. (Shaw, p. 75)

- Is your organization not only market driven, but also value-oriented? (Peters and Levering, Moskowitz, and Katz)
- Is there a strong commitment to a positive corporate culture and a clearly defined mission which is frequently and unambiguously voiced by upper-management?
- Does your organization exemplify trust by practicing a genuine relationship partnership with your customers—*before, during, and after* the initial purchase? (Strout, p. 69)

Companies which exemplify treating customers ethically are founded on a covenant of trust. There is a shared belief, confidence, and faith that the company and its people will be fair, reliable, and ethical in all its dealings. ***Total trust is the belief that a company and its people will never take opportunistic advantage of customer vulnerabilities***. (Hart and Johnson, pp. 11–13)

References

ABC News 20/20, "The Car Dealer's Secret," October 27, 2000.

Blanchard, Kenneth, and Norman Vincent Peale, *The Power of Ethical Management*, New York: William Morrow and Company, Inc., 1988.

Chewning, Richard C., *Business Ethics in a Changing Culture* (Reston, Virginia: Reston Publishing, 1984).

Dayal, Sandeep, Landesberg, Helen, and Michael Zeissner, "How to Build Trust Online," *Marketing Management*, Fall 1999, pp. 64–69.

Geyelin, Milo, "Why One Jury Dealt a Big Blow to Chrysler in Minivan-Latch Case," *Wall Street Journal*, November 19, 1997, pp. A1, A10.

Hart, Christopher W. and Michael D. Johnson, "Growing the Trust Relationship," *Marketing Management*, Spring 1999, pp. 9–19.

Hosmer, La Rue Tone, *The Ethics of Management*, second edition (Homewood, Illinois: Irwin, 1991).

Kaydo, Chad, "A Position of Power," *Sales & Marketing Management*, June 2000, pp. 104–106, 108ff.

Levering, Robert; Moskowitz, Milton; and Michael Katz, *The 100 Best Companies to Work for in America* (Reading, Mass.: Addison-Wesley, 1984).

Magnet, Myron, "Meet the New Revolutionaries," *Fortune*, February 24, 1992, pp. 94–101.

Muoio, Anna, "The Experienced Customer," *Net Company*, Fall 1999, pp. 25–27.

Peters, Thomas J. and Robert H. Waterman Jr., *In Search of Excellence* (New York: Harper & Row, 1982).

Richardson, John (ed.), *Annual Editions: Business Ethics 00/01* (Guilford, CT: McGraw-Hill/Dushkin, 2000).

_____, *Annual Editions: Marketing 00/01* (Guilford, CT: McGraw-Hill/Dushkin, 2000).

Robin, Donald P., and Erich Reidenbach, "Social Responsibility, Ethics, and Marketing Strategy: Closing the Gap Between Concept and Application," *Journal of Marketing*, vol. 51 (January 1987), pp. 44–58.

Shaw, Robert Bruce, *Trust in the Balance*, (San Francisco: Jossey-Bass Publishers, 1997).

Strout, Erin, "Tough Customers," *Sales Marketing Management*, January 2000, pp. 63–69.

Webber, Alan M., "Trust in the Future," *Fast Company*, September 2000, pp. 209–212ff.

Dr. John E. Richardson is Professor of Marketing in the Graziadio School of Business and Management at Pepperdine University, Malibu, California. **Dr. Linnea Bernard McCord** is Associate Professor of Business Law in the Graziadio School of Business and Management at Pepperdine University, Malibu, California.

An original essay written for this volume. Copyright © 2000 by John E. Richardson. Reprinted by permission.

Businesses Grow More Socially Conscious

EDWARD IWATA

Activists have argued for decades that companies, as good corporate citizens, are morally obligated to adopt socially responsible business practices. On their end, companies say they exist to sell products, make money and please shareholders—not to save the world.

But those clashing views may be finding common ground, say business experts on the movement known as "corporate social responsibility," or CSR.

There's growing evidence that companies are embracing CSR practices—whether it's reducing factory and transportation pollution, using natural materials for packaging or treating workers fairly—because they believe such strategies can be profitable and socially responsible.

"All of a sudden, corporate responsibility is an idea whose time has arrived," says Julie Fox Gorte, chief social investment strategist at the Calvert Group, which manages socially responsible mutual funds. "We're seeing more companies who think it's not just a philosophy, but good for business, too."

Study Shows Value

Christine Arena, a San Francisco business consultant and author of *The High-Purpose Company*, says more corporations are using CSR not for feel-good philanthropy or to polish their public image, but as long-term corporate strategy.

Arena and 10 MBA students at McGill University studied 75 U.S. corporations, including Wal-Mart, McDonald's, Volvo, JetBlue, outdoor retailer Patagonia, clothing designer Eileen Fisher and agricultural products company John Deere.

They found that many are visionary, risk-taking companies that Arena calls "the early adopters, the alphas of the modern business world." The companies are staking their business growth and future on environmental and social goals. For instance:

- **General Electric (GE).** CEO Jeffrey Immelt announced GE's "Ecoimagination" initiative two years ago, and the conglomerate hopes to double its revenue from environmentally clean technology to $20 billion by 2010. Among the products and services: fuel-efficient jet and train engines, wind turbine power, energy-saving fluorescent light bulbs and water purification projects.

- **Toyota (TM).** Critics scoffed when it launched the Prius hybrid car in the USA in 2000 and in Japan a decade ago. Today, the Prius is so popular that Toyota expects to sell millions of hybrid cars and SUVs worldwide by 2010 in the Prius, Highlander, Lexus and Camry models. Now, Ford Motor, Nissan, General Motors and others are going the hybrid route.

- **Wegmans Food Markets.** While many businesses suffer from poor staff morale, this $4 billion retailer boasts a worker-friendly culture and cost savings from low turnover of employees. Workers enjoy generous salaries and benefits, vacation time and training. Each year, 130,000 job hunters apply to Wegmans—ranked No.1 in *Fortune*'s "Best Large Companies to Work For" list in 2005.

"It's not a fleeting fad," Arena says. "These companies are investing money in a way that creates social, environmental and financial value. They can't afford to stop investing in this higher purpose."

But many companies still ignore CSR issues, she says. In her study, 14 of 75 failed the litmus test. They preached social values, but made fewer investments in CSR practices than "high-purpose" companies did.

Companies such as ExxonMobil (XOM), she says, face lawsuits and a public backlash when they fall short on environmental and social issues. A federal judge recently ruled that ExxonMobil must pay $2.5 billion in damages from the Exxon Valdez oil tanker spill in 1989.

Economists and executives have debated for decades whether CSR practices help the bottom line. The late economist Milton Friedman panned social values in the boardroom, saying the No.1 goal of businesses is to boost shareholder value. Leading scholars such as David Vogel, author of *The Market for Virtue,* believe the positive impact of CSR on businesses is overblown.

But CSR gained momentum in the 1980s, when the anti-apartheid movement forced firms to withdraw investments from South Africa, and in the 1990s, when garment and retail companies were blasted for their suppliers' sweatshop labor conditions. More companies realized they could not ignore the link between their businesses and social issues.

In the most sweeping research on the topic, the University of Redlands' Marc Orlitzky and the University of Iowa's Sara Rynes and Frank Schmidt looked at 52 studies—covering 34,000 companies worldwide—on corporate social responsibility over a 30-year period.

'A Virtuous Cycle'

Their 2004 study found that well-run, profitable businesses also boasted strong social and environmental records, and vise versa. Overwhelmingly, firms that rewarded employees with good work climates and higher pay and benefits ultimately saw stronger sales and stock prices, plus less employee turnover.

"It's a virtuous cycle," Rynes says. "As a company becomes more socially responsible, its reputation and financial performance go up, which causes them to become even more socially responsible."

Clearly, CSR isn't going away.

"Some still think CSR is a distraction," Orlitzky says. "But more business strategists now believe that social responsibility has economic value."

Hundreds of corporations churn out annual "CSR reports" that tout their social consciences and business practices. Investors poured $179 billion in 2005—up from only $12 billion a decade earlier—into socially responsible mutual funds, reports the Social Investment Forum. Businesses and environmental groups are even joining forces.

Last month, the U.S. Climate Action Partnership—a new alliance that includes GE, DuPont (DD), Alcoa (AA), Caterpillar (CAT), Duke Energy (DUK), Environmental Defense and the Natural Resources Defense Council—urged lawmakers and the White House to reduce greenhouse gas emissions and hasten technology research.

DuPont's Transition

Many CSR experts point to DuPont, the $27 billion chemical manufacturer in Wilmington, Del., as a company evolving successfully from the old smokestack industry era into the environmentally aware 21st century.

DuPont used to rely heavily on fossil fuels to make paint, plastics and polymers. But in the 1990s, DuPont—renowned for its R&D that created products such as the synthetic fiber nylon—decided to pour billions of dollars into safe, environmentally friendly products.

For instance, DuPont and British food refiner Tate & Lyle make Bio-PDO—a corn-based chemical used in cosmetics, detergents and material in carpeting and clothing—at a $100 million plant in Loudon, Tenn.

Since 1990, DuPont has cut greenhouse gas emissions by 72% and air carcinogen emissions by 92% at its facilities worldwide, says Dawn Rittenhouse, DuPont's director of sustainable development.

But DuPont, like other companies that claim to be socially responsible, still faces some issues.

DuPont faces lawsuits alleging that perfluorooctanoic acid (PFOA), a chemical compound used in the making of Teflon, poses public health risks and contaminates drinking water—charges denied by DuPont.

Two years ago, DuPont agreed to a $16 million settlement with the Environmental Protection Agency after it was accused of failing to report data on PFOA, a likely carcinogen. DuPont later volunteered to halt by 2015 all PFOA emissions from its plants.

Beyond the legal fights, DuPont keeps plowing new ground. The company vows to make $2 billion a year in revenue by 2015 from 1,000 products that save energy and reduce pollutants.

"What's good for business," Rittenhouse says, "must also be good for the environment and for people worldwide."

From *USA Today Newspaper*, February 14, 2007, p. 3B. Copyright © 2007 by USA Today, a division of Gannet Co., Inc. Reprinted by permission via Rightslink.

Women and the Labyrinth *of* Leadership

When you put all the pieces together, a new picture emerges for why women don't make it into the C-suite. It's not the glass ceiling, but the sum of many obstacles along the way.

ALICE H. EAGLY AND LINDA L. CARLI

If one has misdiagnosed a problem, then one is unlikely to prescribe an effective cure. This is the situation regarding the scarcity of women in top leadership. Because people with the best of intentions have misread the symptoms, the solutions that managers are investing in are not making enough of a difference.

That there is a problem is not in doubt. Despite years of progress by women in the workforce (they now occupy more than 40% of all managerial positions in the United States), within the C-suite they remain as rare as hens' teeth. Consider the most highly paid executives of *Fortune 500* companies—those with titles such as chairman, president, chief executive officer, and chief operating officer. Of this group, only 6% are women. Most notably, only 2% of the CEOs are women, and only 15% of the seats on the boards of directors are held by women. The situation is not much different in other industrialized countries. In the 50 largest publicly traded corporations in each nation of the European Union, women make up, on average, 11% of the top executives and 4% of the CEOs and heads of boards. Just seven companies, or 1%, of *Fortune* magazine's Global 500 have female CEOs. What is to blame for the pronounced lack of women in positions of power and authority?

In 1986 the *Wall Street Journal's* Carol Hymowitz and Timothy Schellhardt gave the world an answer: "Even those few women who rose steadily through the ranks eventually crashed into an invisible barrier. The executive suite seemed within their grasp, but they just couldn't break through the glass ceiling." The metaphor, driven home by the article's accompanying illustration, resonated; it captured the frustration of a goal within sight but somehow unattainable. To be sure, there was a time when the barriers were absolute. Even within the career spans of 1980s-era executives, access to top posts had been explicitly denied. Consider comments made by President Richard Nixon, recorded on White House audiotapes and made public through the Freedom of Information Act. When explaining why he would not appoint a woman to the U.S. Supreme Court, Nixon said, "I don't think a woman should be in any government job whatsoever . . . mainly because they are erratic. And emotional. Men are erratic and emotional, too, but the point is a woman is more likely to be." In a culture where such opinions were widely held, women had virtually no chance of attaining influential leadership roles.

Times have changed, however, and the glass ceiling metaphor is now more wrong than right. For one thing, it describes an absolute barrier at a specific high level in organizations. The fact that there have been female chief executives, university presidents, state governors, and presidents of nations gives the lie to that charge. At the same time, the metaphor implies that women and men have equal access to entry- and mid-level positions. They do not. The image of a transparent obstruction also suggests that women are being misled about their opportunities, because the impediment is not easy for them to see from a distance. But some impediments are not subtle. Worst of all, by depicting a single, unvarying obstacle, the glass ceiling fails to incorporate the complexity and variety of challenges that women can face in their leadership journeys. In truth, women are not turned away only as they reach the penultimate stage of a distinguished career. They disappear in various numbers at many points leading up to that stage.

Metaphors matter because they are part of the storytelling that can compel change. Believing in the existence of a glass ceiling, people emphasize certain kinds of interventions: top-to-top networking, mentoring to increase board memberships, requirements for diverse candidates in high-profile succession horse races, litigation aimed at punishing discrimination in the C-suite. None of these is counterproductive; all have a role to play. The danger arises when they draw attention and resources away from other kinds of interventions that might attack the problem more potently. If we want to make better progress, it's time to rename the challenge.

Walls All Around

A better metaphor for what confronts women in their professional endeavors is the labyrinth. It's an image with a long and varied history in ancient Greece, India, Nepal, native North and South America, medieval Europe, and elsewhere. As a contemporary symbol, it conveys the idea of a complex journey toward a goal worth striving for. Passage through a labyrinth is not simple or direct, but requires persistence, awareness of one's progress, and a careful analysis of the puzzles that lie ahead. It is this meaning that we intend to convey. For women who aspire to top leadership, routes exist but are full of twists and turns, both unexpected and expected. Because all labyrinths have a viable route to the center, it is understood that goals are attainable. The metaphor acknowledges obstacles but is not ultimately discouraging.

If we can understand the various barriers that make up this labyrinth, and how some women find their way around them, we can work more effectively to improve the situation. What are the obstructions that women run up against? Let's explore them in turn.

Vestiges of prejudice. It is a well-established fact that men as a group still have the benefit of higher wages and faster promotions. In the United States in 2005, for example, women employed full-time earned 81 cents for every dollar that men earned. Is this true because of discrimination or simply because, with fewer family demands placed on them and longer careers on average, men are able to gain superior qualifications? Literally hundreds of correlational studies by economists and sociologists have attempted to find the answer.

One of the most comprehensive of these studies was conducted by the U.S. Government Accountability Office. The study was based on survey data from 1983 through 2000 from a representative sample of Americans. Because the same people responded to the survey repeatedly over the years, the study provided accurate estimates of past work experience, which is important for explaining later wages.

The GAO researchers tested whether individuals' total wages could be predicted by sex and other characteristics. They included part-time and full-time employees in the surveys and took into account all the factors that they could estimate and that might affect earnings, such as education and work experience. Without controls for these variables, the data showed that women earned about 44% less than men, averaged over the entire period from 1983 to 2000. With these controls in place, the gap was only about half as large, but still substantial. The control factors that reduced the wage gap most were the different employment patterns of men and women: Men undertook more hours of paid labor per year than women and had more years of job experience.

Marriage and parenthood are associated with higher wages for men but not for women.

Although most variables affected the wages of men and women similarly, there were exceptions. Marriage and parenthood, for instance, were associated with higher wages for men but not for women. In contrast, other characteristics, especially years of education, had a more positive effect on women's wages than on men's. Even after adjusting wages for all of the ways men and women differ, the GAO study, like similar studies, showed that women's wages remained lower than men's. The unexplained gender gap is consistent with the presence of wage discrimination.

Similar methods have been applied to the question of whether discrimination affects promotions. Evidently it does. Promotions come more slowly for women than for men with equivalent qualifications. One illustrative national study followed workers from 1980 to 1992 and found that white men were more likely to attain managerial positions than white women, black men, and black women. Controlling for other characteristics, such as education and hours worked per year, the study showed that white men were ahead of the other groups when entering the labor market and that their advantage in attaining managerial positions grew throughout their careers. Other research has underscored these findings. Even in culturally feminine settings such as nursing, librarianship, elementary education, and social work (all specifically studied by sociologist Christine Williams), men ascend to supervisory and administrative positions more quickly than women.

The findings of correlational studies are supported by experimental research, in which subjects are asked to evaluate hypothetical individuals as managers or job candidates, and all characteristics of these individuals are held constant except for their sex. Such efforts continue the tradition of the Goldberg paradigm, named for a 1968 experiment by Philip Goldberg. His simple, elegant study had student participants evaluate written essays that were identical except for the attached male or female name. The students were unaware that other students had received identical material ascribed to a writer of the other sex. This initial experiment demonstrated an overall gender bias: Women received lower evaluations unless the essay was on a feminine topic. Some 40 years later, unfortunately, experiments continue to reveal the same kind of bias in work settings. Men are advantaged over equivalent women as candidates for jobs traditionally held by men as well as for more gender-integrated jobs. Similarly, male leaders receive somewhat more favorable evaluations than equivalent female leaders, especially in roles usually occupied by men.

Interestingly, however, there is little evidence from either the correlational or the experimental studies that the odds are stacked higher against women with each step up the ladder—that is, that women's promotions become progressively less likely than men's at higher levels within organizations. Instead, a general bias against women appears to operate with approximately equal strength at all levels. The scarcity of female corporate officers is the sum of discrimination that has operated at all ranks, not evidence of a particular obstacle to advancement as women approach the top. The problem, in other words, is not a glass ceiling.

Resistance to women's leadership. What's behind the discrimination we've been describing? Essentially, a set of widely shared conscious and unconscious mental associations about women, men, and leaders. Study after study has affirmed that people associate women and men with different traits and link men with more of the traits that connote leadership. Kim Campbell, who briefly served as the prime minister of Canada in 1993, described the tension that results:

> I don't have a traditionally female way of speaking.... I'm quite assertive. If I didn't speak the way I do, I wouldn't have been seen as a leader. But my way of speaking may have grated on people who were not used to hearing it from a woman. It was the right way for a leader to speak, but it wasn't the right way for a woman to speak. It goes against type.

In the language of psychologists, the clash is between two sets of associations: communal and agentic. Women are associated with communal qualities, which convey a concern for the compassionate treatment of others. They include being especially affectionate, helpful, friendly, kind, and sympathetic, as well as interpersonally sensitive, gentle, and soft-spoken. In contrast, men are associated with agentic qualities, which convey assertion and control. They include being especially aggressive, ambitious, dominant, self-confident, and forceful, as well as self-reliant and individualistic. The agentic traits are also associated in most people's minds with effective leadership—perhaps because a long history of male domination of leadership roles has made it difficult to separate the leader associations from the male associations.

As a result, women leaders find themselves in a double bind. If they are highly communal, they may be criticized for not being agentic enough. But if they are highly agentic, they may be criticized for lacking communion. Either way, they may leave the impression that they don't have "the right stuff" for powerful jobs.

Given this double bind, it is hardly surprising that people are more resistant to women's influence than to men's. For example, in meetings at a global retail company, people responded more favorably to men's overt attempts at influence than to women's. In the words of one of this company's female executives, "People often had to speak up to defend their turf, but when women did so, they were vilified. They were labeled 'control freaks'; men acting the same way were called 'passionate.'"

Verbally intimidating others can undermine a woman's influence, and assertive behavior can reduce her chances of getting a job or advancing in her career.

Studies have gauged reactions to men and women engaging in various types of dominant behavior. The findings are quite consistent. Nonverbal dominance, such as staring at others while speaking to them or pointing at people, is a more damaging behavior for women than for men. Verbally intimidating others can undermine a woman's influence, and assertive behavior can reduce her chances of getting a job or advancing in her career. Simply disagreeing can sometimes get women into trouble. Men who disagree or otherwise act dominant get away with it more often than women do.

Self-promotion is similarly risky for women. Although it can convey status and competence, it is not at all communal. So while men can use bluster to get themselves noticed, modesty is expected even of highly accomplished women. Linguistics professor Deborah Tannen tells a story from her experience: "This [need for modesty] was evident, for example, at a faculty meeting devoted to promotions, at which a woman professor's success was described: She was extremely well published and well known in the field. A man commented with approval, 'She wears it well.' In other words, she was praised for not acting as successful as she was."

Another way the double bind penalizes women is by denying them the full benefits of being warm and considerate. Because people expect it of women, nice behavior that seems noteworthy in men seems unimpressive in women. For example, in one study, helpful men reaped a lot of approval, but helpful women did not. Likewise, men got away with being unhelpful, but women did not. A different study found that male employees received more promotions when they reported higher levels of helpfulness to coworkers. But female employees' promotions were not related to such altruism.

While one might suppose that men would have a double bind of their own, they in fact have more freedom. Several experiments and organizational studies have assessed reactions to behavior that is warm and friendly versus dominant and assertive. The findings show that men can communicate in a warm or a dominant manner, with no penalty either way. People like men equally well and are equally influenced by them regardless of their warmth.

It all amounts to a clash of assumptions when the average person confronts a woman in management. Perhaps this is why respondents in one study characterized the group "successful female managers" as more deceitful, pushy, selfish, and abrasive than "successful male managers." In the absence of any evidence to the contrary, people suspect that such highly effective women must not be very likable or nice.

Issues of leadership style. In response to the challenges presented by the double bind, female leaders often struggle to cultivate an appropriate and effective leadership style—one that reconciles the communal qualities people prefer in women with the agentic qualities people think leaders need to succeed. Here, for instance, is how Marietta Nien-hwa Cheng described her transition to the role of symphony conductor:

> I used to speak more softly, with a higher pitch. Sometimes my vocal cadences went up instead of down. I realized that these mannerisms lack the sense of authority. I strengthened my voice. The pitch has dropped.... I have stopped trying to be everyone's friend. Leadership is not synonymous with socializing.

It's difficult to pull off such a transformation while maintaining a sense of authenticity as a leader. Sometimes the whole

effort can [...]
think that [...]
a man. Th[...]
Women le[...]
labyrinth [...]
Fortune 1[...]
critical or [...]
male man[...]

Does a [...]
to be a p[...]
journalist [...]
head coa[...]
basketbal[...]
to Krzyz[...]
a woman would. Really." Sokolove proceeded to describe Krzyzewski's mentoring, interpersonally sensitive, and highly effective coaching style.

More scientifically, a recent meta-analysis integrated the results of 45 studies addressing the question. To compare leadership skills, the researchers adopted a framework introduced by leadership scholar James MacGregor Burns that distinguishes between transformational leadership and transactional leadership. Transformational leaders establish themselves as role models by gaining followers' trust and confidence. They state future goals, develop plans to achieve those goals, and innovate, even when their organizations are generally successful. Such leaders mentor and empower followers, encouraging them to develop their full potential and thus to contribute more effectively to their organizations. By contrast, transactional leaders establish give-and-take relationships that appeal to subordinates' self-interest. Such leaders manage in the conventional manner of clarifying subordinates' responsibilities, rewarding them for meeting objectives, and correcting them for failing to meet objectives. Although transformational and transactional leadership styles are different, most leaders adopt at least some behaviors of both types. The researchers also allowed for a third category, called the laissez-faire style—a sort of non-leadership that concerns itself with none of the above, despite rank authority.

The meta-analysis found that, in general, female leaders were somewhat more transformational than male leaders, especially when it came to giving support and encouragement to subordinates. They also engaged in more of the rewarding behaviors that are one aspect of transactional leadership. Meanwhile, men exceeded women on the aspects of transactional leadership involving corrective and disciplinary actions that are either active (timely) or passive (belated). Men were also more likely than women to be laissez-faire leaders, who take little responsibility for managing. These findings add up to a startling conclusion, given that most leadership research has found the transformational style (along with the rewards and positive incentives associated with the transactional style) to be more suited to leading the modern organization. The research tells us not only that men and women do have somewhat different leadership styles, but also that women's approaches are the more generally effective—while men's often are only somewhat effective or actually hinder effectiveness.

Is It Only a Question of Time?

It is a common perception that women will steadily gain greater access to leadership roles, including elite positions. For example, university students who are queried about the future power of men and women say that women's power will increase. Polls have shown that most Americans expect a woman to be elected president or vice president within their lifetimes. Both groups are extrapolating women's recent gains into the future, as if our society were on a continuous march toward gender equality.

But social change does not proceed without struggle and conflict. As women gain greater equality, a portion of people react against it. They long for traditional roles. In fact, signs of a pause in progress toward gender equality have appeared on many fronts. A review of longitudinal studies reveals several areas in which a sharp upward trend in the 1970s and 1980s has been followed by a slowing and flattening in recent years (for instance, in the percentage of managers who are women). The pause is also evident in some attitudinal data—like the percentage of people who approve of female bosses and who believe that women are at least as well suited as men for politics.

Social scientists have proposed various theories to explain this pause. Some, such as social psychologist Cecilia Ridgeway, believe that social change is activating "people's deep seated interests in maintaining clear cultural understandings of gender difference." Others believe progress has reached its limit given the continuing organization of family life by gender, coupled with employer policies that favor those who are not hampered by primary responsibility for child rearing.

It may simply be that women are collectively catching their breath before pressing for more change. In the past century, feminist activism arose when women came to view themselves as collectively subjected to illegitimate and unfair treatment. But recent polls show less conviction about the presence of discrimination, and feminism does not have the cultural relevance it once had. The lessening of activism on behalf of all women puts pressure on each woman to find her own way.

Another part of this picture, based on a separate meta-analysis, is that women adopt a more participative and collaborative style than men typically favor. The reason for this difference is unlikely to be genetic. Rather, it may be that collaboration can get results without seeming particularly masculine. As women navigate their way through the double bind, they seek ways to project authority without relying on the autocratic behaviors that people find so jarring in women. A viable path is to bring others into decision making and to lead as an encouraging teacher and positive role model. (However, if there is not a critical mass of other women to affirm the legitimacy of a participative style, female leaders usually conform to whatever style is typical of the men—and that is sometimes autocratic.)

Demands of family life. For many women, the most fateful turns in the labyrinth are the ones taken under pressure of family responsibilities. Women continue to be the ones who interrupt their careers, take more days off, and work part time. As a result, they have fewer years of job experience and fewer hours of employment per year, which slows their career progress and reduces their earnings.

In one study of Chicago lawyers, researchers sought to understand why women were much less likely than men to hold the leadership positions in large law firms—the positions that are most highly paid and that confer (arguably) the highest prestige. They found that women were no less likely than men to begin their careers at such firms but were more likely to leave them for positions in the public sector or corporate positions. The reasons for their departures were concentrated in work/family trade-offs. Among the relatively few women who did become partners in a firm, 60% had no children, and the minority who had children generally had delayed childbearing until attaining partner status.

There is no question that, while men increasingly share housework and child rearing, the bulk of domestic work still falls on women's shoulders. We know this from time-diary studies, in which people record what they are doing during each hour of a 24-hour day. So, for example, in the United States married women devoted 19 hours per week on average to housework in 2005, while married men contributed 11 hours. That's a huge improvement over 1965 numbers, when women spent a whopping 34 hours per week to men's five, but it is still a major inequity. And the situation looks worse when child care hours are added.

Mothers provide more child care hours than they did in earlier generations—despite the fact that fathers are putting in a lot more time than in the past.

Although it is common knowledge that mothers provide more child care than fathers, few people realize that mothers provide more than they did in earlier generations—despite the fact that fathers are putting in a lot more time than in the past. National studies have compared mothers and fathers on the amount of their primary child care, which consists of close interaction not combined with housekeeping or other activities. Married mothers increased their hours per week from 10.6 in 1965 to 12.9 in 2000, and married fathers increased theirs from 2.6 to 6.5. Thus, though husbands have taken on more domestic work, the work/family conflict has not eased for women; the gain has been offset by escalating pressures for intensive parenting and the increasing time demands of most high-level careers.

Even women who have found a way to relieve pressures from the home front by sharing child care with husbands, other family members, or paid workers may not enjoy the full workplace benefit of having done so. Decision makers often assume that mothers have domestic responsibilities that make it inappropriate to promote them to demanding positions. As one participant in a study of the federal workforce explained, "I mean, there were 2 or 3 names [of women] in the hat, and they said, 'I don't want to talk about her because she has children who are still home in these [evening] hours.' Now they don't pose that thing about men on the list, many of whom also have children in that age group."

One study suggests that social capital is even more necessary to managers' advancement than skillful performance of traditional managerial tasks.

Underinvestment in social capital. Perhaps the most destructive result of the work/family balancing act so many women must perform is that it leaves very little time for socializing with colleagues and building professional networks. The social capital that accrues from such "nonessential" parts of work turns out to be quite essential indeed. One study yielded the following description of managers who advanced rapidly in hierarchies: Fast-track managers "spent relatively more time and effort socializing, politicking, and interacting with outsiders than did their less successful counterparts . . . [and] did not give much time or attention to the traditional management activities of planning, decision making, and controlling or to the human resource management activities of motivating/ reinforcing, staffing, training/developing, and managing conflict." This suggests that social capital is even more necessary to managers' advancement than skillful performance of traditional managerial tasks.

Even given sufficient time, women can find it difficult to engage in and benefit from informal networking if they are a small minority. In such settings, the influential networks are composed entirely or almost entirely of men. Breaking into those male networks can be hard, especially when men center their networks on masculine activities. The recent gender discrimination lawsuit against Wal-Mart provides examples of this. For instance, an executive retreat took the form of a quail-hunting expedition at Sam Walton's ranch in Texas. Middle managers' meetings included visits to strip clubs and Hooters restaurants, and a sales conference attended by thousands of store managers featured a football theme. One executive received feedback that she probably would not advance in the company because she didn't hunt or fish.

Management Interventions That Work

Taking the measure of the labyrinth that confronts women leaders, we see that it begins with prejudices that benefit men and penalize women, continues with particular resistance to women's leadership, includes questions of leadership style and authenticity, and—most dramatically for many women—features the challenge of balancing work and family responsibilities. It becomes clear that a woman's situation as she reaches her peak career years is the result of many turns at many challenging junctures. Only a few individual women have made the right combination of moves to land at the center of power—but as for the rest, there is usually no single turning point where their progress was diverted and the prize was lost.

What's to be done in the face of such a multifaceted problem? A solution that is often proposed is for governments to implement and enforce antidiscrimination legislation and thereby require organizations to eliminate inequitable practices. However, analysis of discrimination cases that have gone to court has shown that legal remedies can be elusive when gender inequality results from norms embedded in organizational structure and culture. The more effective approach is for organizations to appreciate the subtlety and complexity of the problem and to attack its many roots simultaneously. More specifically, if a company wants to see more women arrive in its executive suite, it should do the following:

Increase people's awareness of the psychological drivers of prejudice toward female leaders, and work to dispel those perceptions. Raising awareness of ingrained bias has been the aim of many diversity-training initiatives, and no doubt they have been more helpful than harmful. There is the danger they will be undermined, however, if their lessons are not underscored by what managers say and do in the course of day-to-day work.

Change the long-hours norm. Especially in the context of knowledge work, it can be hard to assess individuals' relative contributions, and managers may resort to "hours spent at work" as the prime indicator of someone's worth to the organization. To the extent an organization can shift the focus to objective measures of productivity, women with family demands on their time but highly productive work habits will receive the rewards and encouragement they deserve.

Reduce the subjectivity of performance evaluation. Greater objectivity in evaluations also combats the effects of lingering prejudice in both hiring and promotion. To ensure fairness, criteria should be explicit and evaluation processes designed to limit the influence of decision makers' conscious and unconscious biases.

Use open-recruitment tools, such as advertising and employment agencies, rather than relying on informal social networks and referrals to fill positions. Recruitment from within organizations also should be transparent, with postings of open positions in appropriate venues. Research has shown that such personnel practices increase the numbers of women in managerial roles.

Ensure a critical mass of women in executive positions—not just one or two women—to head off the problems that come with tokenism. Token women tend to be pegged into narrow stereotypical roles such as "seductress," "mother," "pet," or "iron maiden." (Or more colorfully, as one woman banker put it, "When you start out in banking, you are a slut or a geisha.") Pigeonholing like this limits women's options and makes it difficult for them to rise to positions of responsibility. When women are not a small minority, their identities as women become less salient, and colleagues are more likely to react to them in terms of their individual competencies.

Avoid having a sole female member of any team. Top management tends to divide its small population of women managers among many projects in the interests of introducing diversity to them all. But several studies have found that, so outnumbered, the women tend to be ignored by the men. A female vice president of a manufacturing company described how, when she or another woman ventures an idea in a meeting, it tends to be overlooked: "It immediately gets lost in the conversation. Then two minutes later, a man makes the same suggestion, and it's 'Wow! What a great idea!' And you sit there and think, 'What just happened?'" As women reach positions of higher power and authority, they increasingly find themselves in gender-imbalanced groups—and some find themselves, for the first time, seriously marginalized. This is part of the reason that the glass ceiling metaphor resonates with so many. But in fact, the problem can be present at any level.

Help shore up social capital. As we've discussed, the call of family responsibilities is mainly to blame for women's underinvestment in networking. When time is scarce, this social activity is the first thing to go by the wayside. Organizations can help women appreciate why it deserves more attention. In particular, women gain from strong and supportive mentoring relationships and connections with powerful networks. When a well-placed individual who possesses greater legitimacy (often a man) takes an interest in a woman's career, her efforts to build social capital can proceed far more efficiently.

Prepare women for line management with appropriately demanding assignments. Women, like men, must have the benefit of developmental job experiences if they are to qualify for promotions. But, as one woman executive wrote, "Women have been shunted off into support areas for the last 30 years, rather than being in the business of doing business, so the pool of women trained to assume leadership positions in any large company is very small." Her point was that women should be taught in business school to insist on line jobs when they enter the workforce. One company that has taken up the challenge has been Procter & Gamble. According to a report by Claudia Deutsch in the *New York Times,* the company was experiencing an executive attrition rate that was twice as high for women as for men. Some of the women reported having to change companies to land jobs that provided challenging work. P&G's subsequent efforts to bring more women into line management both improved its overall retention of women and increased the number of women in senior management.

Establish family-friendly human resources practices. These may include flextime, job sharing, telecommuting, elder care provisions, adoption benefits, dependent child care options, and employee-sponsored on-site child care. Such support can allow women to stay in their jobs during the most demanding years of child rearing, build social capital, keep up to date in their fields, and eventually compete for higher positions. A study of 72 large U.S. firms showed (controlling for other variables) that family-friendly HR practices in place in 1994 increased the proportion of women in senior management over the subsequent five years.

Allow employees who have significant parental responsibility more time to prove themselves worthy of promotion. This recommendation is particularly directed to organizations, many of them professional services firms, that have established "up or out" career progressions. People not ready for promotion at the same time as the top performers in their cohort aren't simply left in place—they're asked to leave. But many parents (most often mothers), while fully capable of reaching that level of achievement, need extra time—perhaps a year or two—to get there. Forcing them off the promotion path not only reduces the number of women reaching top management positions, but also constitutes a failure by the firm to capitalize on its early investment in them.

Welcome women back. It makes sense to give high-performing women who step away from the workforce an opportunity to return to responsible positions when their circumstances change. Some companies have established "alumni" programs, often because they see former employees as potential sources of new business. A few companies have gone further to activate these networks for other purposes, as well. (Procter & Gamble taps alumni for innovation purposes; Booz Allen sees its alumni ranks as a source of subcontractors.) Keeping lines of communication open can convey the message that a return may be possible.

Encourage male participation in family-friendly benefits. Dangers lurk in family-friendly benefits that are used only by women. Exercising options such as generous parental leave and part-time work slows down women's careers. More profoundly, having many more women than men take such benefits can harm the careers of women in general because of the expectation that they may well exercise those options. Any effort toward greater family friendliness should actively recruit male participation to avoid inadvertently making it harder for women to gain access to essential managerial roles.

Managers can be forgiven if they find the foregoing list a tall order. It's a wide-ranging set of interventions and still far from exhaustive. The point, however, is just that: Organizations will succeed in filling half their top management slots with women—and women who are the true performance equals of their male counterparts—only by attacking all the reasons they are absent today. Glass ceiling-inspired programs and projects can do just so much if the leakage of talented women is happening on every lower floor of the building. Individually, each of these interventions has been shown to make a difference. Collectively, we believe, they can make all the difference.

The View from Above

Imagine visiting a formal garden and finding within it a high hedgerow. At a point along its vertical face, you spot a rectangle—a neatly pruned and inviting doorway. Are you aware as you step through that you are entering a labyrinth? And, three doorways later, as the reality of the puzzle settles in, do you have any idea how to proceed? This is the situation in which many women find themselves in their career endeavors. Ground-level perplexity and frustration make every move uncertain.

When the eye can take in the whole of the puzzle—the starting position, the goal, and the maze of walls—solutions begin to suggest themselves.

Labyrinths become infinitely more tractable when seen from above. When the eye can take in the whole of the puzzle—the starting position, the goal, and the maze of walls—solutions begin to suggest themselves. This has been the goal of our research. Our hope is that women, equipped with a map of the barriers they will confront on their path to professional achievement, will make more informed choices. We hope that managers, too, will understand where their efforts can facilitate the progress of women. If women are to achieve equality, women and men will have to share leadership equally. With a greater understanding of what stands in the way of gender-balanced leadership, we draw nearer to attaining it in our time.

ALICE H. EAGLY (eagly@northwestern.edu) is a professor of psychology and holds the James Padilla Chair of Arts and Sciences at Northwestern University, in Evanston, Illinois; she is also a faculty fellow at Northwestern's Institute for Policy Research. LINDA L. CARLI (lcarli@wellesley.edu) is an associate professor of psychology at Wellesley College, in Massachusetts; her current research focus is on gender discrimination and other challenges faced by professional women. The two are coauthors of *Through the Labyrinth: The Truth about How Women Become Leaders* (Harvard Business School Press, forthcoming in October), from which this article is adapted.

Getting Real about Fakes

If companies want to cut into sales of counterfeit products, they need to understand why consumers buy them in the first place.

PEGGY E. CHAUDHRY AND STEPHEN A. STUMPF

As the counterfeit trade booms, companies are rolling out massive campaigns to get people to stop buying fakes. But the messages they use are often off the mark. Companies have tried everything from threatening prosecution to linking phony products with organized crime. But marketers often don't pay attention to what actually drives people in particular markets to buy counterfeits and what messages will actually work to curb demand of fake goods.

Companies, for instance, might roll out ads in a country stressing that fake products are of poor quality. But those ads might ignore the fact that local consumers have little disposable income and consider knockoffs a bargain—so they are willing to accept a price-quality trade-off. A better approach might be to stress that the phony goods, such as fake cigarettes, are funding terrorism or, in the case of counterfeit pharmaceuticals, are actually killing people.

To figure out how companies can improve their antipiracy marketing, we surveyed consumers in five large markets—Brazil, Russia, India, China and the U.S.—to see what would make them opt for knockoffs. Then we used that information to figure out what messages might get people to stop buying the illegitimate goods.

Reality Check

- **Ineffective Messages:** The global trade in counterfeits is booming, but most attempts to get people to stop buying have not worked.
- **Listening to Consumers:** Companies need to pay attention to the factors that drive people in a particular market to seek out fakes—not simply decide on a standardized message and spread it across the globe.
- **The Real Story:** Our survey of consumers in five large country markets found a range of reasons why people opt for counterfeits. It also suggested a range of messages companies could use to get people to stop buying.

Why Consumers Buy

We presented consumers in each market with five possible motivations for buying counterfeits in two categories—movies and drugs—and asked them to rank the factors on a seven-point scale of importance. Here's what they said about each.

1. Quality and Performance

Consumers would buy a fake if they thought it was just as good as a legitimate product.

Only U.S. consumers ranked this as an important factor that would influence them. Elsewhere, this attribute was just "somewhat" important—and Russian consumers ranked it not important at all. Astonishingly, consumers in these country markets valued the quality of the fake medicine less than they did factors such as reduced price and availability.

On the other hand, the quality of bootleg movies was ranked as very important for Russian, Brazilian and Chinese consumers, and less so for people in the U.S. and India.

2. Cost

Consumers would buy a fake because they cannot afford a genuine product.

Not surprisingly, almost all consumers ranked this as a very important motivation for pursuing fake drugs and bootleg movies alike. The two exceptions: Chinese consumers said this factor was only somewhat important when it came to drugs; U.S. consumers said the same about movies.

3. Sentiment

Consumers would buy a fake because they do not like the big businesses that make the authentic products.

We expected some resentment here, since drugs and movies are usually produced by large corporations, and the people who buy counterfeits may believe that the industry is price-gouging consumers. But only in China did consumers express disapproval of the large movie studios as a significant motivator for buying bootlegs. And only U.S. consumers showed an anti-big-business sentiment for both the movie and drug industries.

Their Brazilian, Russian and Indian counterparts did not concur, and rated this as an unimportant justification.

4. Ethics

Consumers would buy a fake because they do not think it is illegal or immoral to do so.

In this area, consumers had very different attitudes about movies and drugs.

In Brazil, India and the U.S., consumers said that consumption of fake pharmaceuticals was an unethical behavior. In Russia and China, it was not important at all—in effect, consumers would buy the fake pharmaceuticals even if they realized it was an immoral or illegal act.

With movies, on the other hand, consumers in all markets but Brazil said that ethical behavior was unimportant when it came to obtaining counterfeit movies. (In Brazil, it was just somewhat unimportant.) These consumers simply do not see bootlegged movies as illegal or morally wrong, perhaps because of the ease and anonymity of Internet downloads and the widespread consumer acceptance of obtaining fake movies. In our survey, 50% of 1,910 consumers readily admitted to obtaining a bootleg movie.

5. Ease

Consumers would buy a fake because it is easy to obtain.

As with ethics, this factor brought up a big divide between movies and drugs. The ease of obtaining fake movies was a very important motivation in each market. However, with drugs, ease was an important factor only in the U.S., just somewhat significant in Brazil and India, and not significant at all in China and Russia.

Consumers, in other words, face different degrees of easy market access to counterfeit drugs and may pursue counterfeit drugs even if they are tougher to obtain.

What Companies Can Do

So, how can companies craft their marketing to answer these attitudes? Here are some messages they might want to push.

1. Fakes Are Poor Substitutes

In countries where people don't place a high priority on the quality of phony drugs, companies should inform the public about the dangers the drugs pose, especially when treating critical conditions. Companies should hammer home the idea that fake drugs are not generics—a common misperception—but dangerous lookalikes that can kill. For instance, one recent report says that pirates in countries such as China and India have used chalk, dust and contaminated water to make counterfeit drugs.

Drug makers should also highlight the fact that phony drugs could pose serious health risks not only to individuals but to nations. In some African countries, for instance, there are large counterfeit markets for treatments of malaria, among other serious conditions. If the antimalarial counterfeit contains a low dose of the active ingredient, it is actually helping the parasite to develop a resistance to the genuine medicine.

Movie makers have taken a similar strategy, and used trailers that reinforce the idea that quality is much worse for bootlegs. For instance, movies shot with camcorders in a theater usually have a herky-jerky picture and intrusive audience noises.

2. Pirates Are Not Robin Hoods

Companies should emphasize that pirates are not philanthropists and are lured by the high profits of selling fakes. Even if, say, pirated movies are offered free on the Internet, suppliers at the top of the piracy supply chain often provide the digital fakes more as a challenge to the companies that own the intellectual property.

What's more, many consumers think that counterfeit drugs help poor people by offering them a bargain. So, drug companies should stress that fakes end up hurting people by giving them potentially ineffective or dangerous treatments and many consumers unknowingly obtain counterfeit drugs.

Movie studios, meanwhile, should look to China's successful antipiracy efforts for ideas. One antipiracy campaign plays up nationalism to get the Chinese consumers to buy legitimate movies. The effort links counterfeiting to organized crime and shows how the revenue lost to piracy hurts the nation's film industry, robbing it of funds that could be used to produce smaller, independent movies.

Some Western film companies, meanwhile, have come up with their own successful measures for the Chinese market, such as offering prizes and contests for people who buy legitimate movies.

3. We're Not Faceless Corporations

Dislike of big business is a factor only in China and the U.S. China's antipiracy campaign addresses this attitude, once again, with nationalism: If you steal movies, the message goes, you're robbing resources from the country's culture—not just big, impersonal companies.

In the U.S., one possible solution is for big businesses to carefully publicize their good works—and give solid reasons why their prices are so high. Pharmaceutical companies, for instance, should emphasize that they rely on a few blockbuster drugs to fund future research. So, seemingly high drug prices are actually underwriting potential advances that might help countless people.

4. Push Ethical Concerns

In Brazil, India and the U.S., a clear conscience is a somewhat important motivation for buying counterfeit drugs; consumers think the practice is morally and legally sound. In these markets, drug makers should emphasize that the sale of fakes is not only against the law but also unethical, since counterfeits can end up harming consumers.

It might also help to stress the connection between counterfeits and organized crime. The pirates are not philanthropists helping the underprivileged, but profit-seeking criminals who provide useless or harmful medications with very few legal repercussions.

> **Behind the Study**
>
> We investigated how consumers viewed two booming categories of pirated goods: movies and pharmaceuticals. We chose these two, in part, for contrast. They elicit very different responses from consumers, so it takes very different strategies to battle these counterfeits.
>
> For instance, movies are bought purely for entertainment. They can be widely obtained and shared at little or no cost, without health or safety risks. Drugs, on the other hand, are often bought out of need, whether "lifestyle" products such as erectile-dysfunction medicine or treatments for serious conditions such as cancer, HIV/AIDS and heart disease. These products are often easy to obtain online, but using them carries considerable health risks. And, needless to say, if you buy the drugs for your own use, you can't share them.
>
> For all their differences, both categories have one thing in common: popularity. The World Health Organization has estimated that counterfeit drug sales will reach $75 billion world-wide in 2010, up more than 90% from 2005. (The WHO defines counterfeit medicines in a number of ways: products with the correct ingredients but fake packaging; products with incorrect ingredients; products lacking sufficient active ingredients, or having no active ingredients at all.)
>
> Pinning down the spread of counterfeit movies is tougher, since many bootlegs are widely copied and distributed online, often free of charge. For one snapshot, the Motion Picture Association of America estimates that $6.1 billion was lost to bootlegging, illegal copying and Internet piracy in 2005.
>
> As for the markets we looked at, we wanted areas with large numbers of consumers but big differences in gross domestic product per capita, intellectual-property protection and culture (which includes factors such as governance, personal values and religion). Each market also has a substantial estimated traffic in counterfeits. India comes in at $7 billion, with Brazil at $15 billion and Russia at $21 billion. Towering over the rest are China, at $80 billion, and the U.S., at $290 billion.
>
> —Peggy E. Chaudhry and Stephen A. Stumpf

With movies—where an overwhelming majority of consumers in all markets studied had a clear conscience about buying fakes—getting people to change their ways is potentially tougher. Bootleg movies are not a matter of life and death, and they can be obtained even more easily and anonymously than drugs. The best approach may be to appeal to people's basic sense of right and wrong, civic responsibility, and their personal risk of both civil and criminal penalties levied for engaging in this illicit consumption. Clearly, many people want to believe that counterfeits are ethically and legally sound. Remind them that the opposite is true.

5. We're Making Things Tougher

Unfortunately, the final motivation—counterfeits are easy to obtain—will be tough to battle with marketing alone.

As long as people know they can go online and get fake products with a few clicks, they will laugh off advertisements warning them about, say, digital copyright protection. (Some say that digital piracy actually provides a distancing effect for consumers, since they feel their illicit behavior is anonymous.) Likewise, as long as policing of counterfeits is spotty, people will not respond to ads warning them about the legal risks of buying fakes.

For these messages to have teeth, companies must push for tougher, more effective policing of both the legitimate and illicit supply chain, and sharper penalties. They must also come up with speed bumps that make it harder for crooks to copy their goods. For example, the Food and Drug Administration advocates the E-Pedigree system for prescription drugs, which documents each prior sale, purchase or trade of the drug to protect U.S. consumers from counterfeit pharmaceuticals.

Dr. Chaudhry is an associate professor of international business at the Villanova School of Business, Villanova, Pa. **Dr. Stumpf** is a professor of management and the Fred J. Springer chair of leadership at the school. They can be reached at reports@wsj.com.

The New E-spionage Threat

A *BusinessWeek* probe of rising attacks on America's most sensitive computer networks uncovers startling security gaps.

BRIAN GROW, KEITH EPSTEIN, AND CHI-CHU TSCHANG

The e-mail message addressed to a Booz Allen Hamilton executive was mundane—a shopping list sent over by the Pentagon of weaponry India wanted to buy. But the missive turned out to be a brilliant fake. Lurking beneath the description of aircraft, engines, and radar equipment was an insidious piece of computer code known as "Poison Ivy" designed to suck sensitive data out of the $4 billion consulting firm's computer network.

The Pentagon hadn't sent the e-mail at all. Its origin is unknown, but the message traveled through Korea on its way to Booz Allen. Its authors knew enough about the "sender" and "recipient" to craft a message unlikely to arouse suspicion. Had the Booz Allen executive clicked on the attachment, his every keystroke would have been reported back to a mysterious master at the Internet address cybersyndrome.3322.org, which is registered through an obscure company headquartered on the banks of China's Yangtze River.

The U.S. government, and its sprawl of defense contractors, have been the victims of an unprecedented rash of similar cyber attacks over the last two years, say current and former U.S. government officials. "It's espionage on a massive scale," says Paul B. Kurtz, a former high-ranking national security official. Government agencies reported 12,986 cyber security incidents to the U.S. Homeland Security Dept. last fiscal year, triple the number from two years earlier. Incursions on the military's networks were up 55% last year, says Lieutenant General Charles E. Croom, head of the Pentagon's Joint Task Force for Global Network Operations. Private targets like Booz Allen are just as vulnerable and pose just as much potential security risk. "They have our information on their networks. They're building our weapon systems. You wouldn't want that in enemy hands," Croom says. Cyber attackers "are not denying, disrupting, or destroying operations—yet. But that doesn't mean they don't have the capability."

A Monster

When the deluge began in 2006, officials scurried to come up with software "patches," "wraps," and other bits of triage. The effort got serious last summer when top military brass discreetly summoned the chief executives or their representatives from the 20 largest U.S. defense contractors to the Pentagon for a "threat briefing." *BusinessWeek* has learned the U.S. government has launched a classified operation called Byzantine Foothold to detect, track, and disarm intrusions on the government's most critical networks. And President George W. Bush on Jan. 8 quietly signed an order known as the Cyber Initiative to overhaul U.S. cyber defenses, at an eventual cost in the tens of billions of dollars, and establishing 12 distinct goals, according to people briefed on its contents. One goal in particular illustrates the urgency and scope of the problem: By June all government agencies must cut the number of communication channels, or ports, through which their networks connect to the Internet from more than 4,000 to fewer than 100. On Apr. 8, Homeland Security Dept. Secretary Michael Chertoff called the President's order a cyber security "Manhattan Project."

But many security experts worry the Internet has become too unwieldy to be tamed. New exploits appear every day, each seemingly more sophisticated than the previous one. The Defense Dept., whose Advanced Research Projects Agency (DARPA) developed the Internet in the 1960s, is beginning to think it created a monster. "You don't need an Army, a Navy, an Air Force to beat the U.S.," says General William T. Lord, commander of the Air Force Cyber Command, a unit formed in November, 2006, to upgrade Air Force computer defenses. "You can be a peer force for the price of the PC on my desk." Military officials have long believed that "it's cheaper, and we kill stuff faster, when we use the Internet to enable high-tech warfare," says a top adviser to the U.S. military on the overhaul of its computer security strategy. "Now they're saying, Oh, shit."

Adding to Washington's anxiety, current and former U.S. government officials say many of the new attackers are trained professionals backed by foreign governments. "The new breed of threat that has evolved is nation-state-sponsored stuff," says Amit Yoran, a former director of Homeland Security's National Cyber Security Div. Adds one of the nation's most senior military officers: "We've got to figure out how to get at it before our regrets exceed our ability to react."

The military and intelligence communities have alleged that the People's Republic of China is the U.S.'s biggest cyber menace. "In the past year, numerous computer networks around the world,

An Evolving Crisis

Major attacks on the U.S. government and defense industry—and their code names.

Solar Sunrise
February, 1998. Air Force and Navy computers are hit by malicious code that sniffed out a hole in a popular enterprise software operating system, patched its own entry point—then did nothing. Some attacks are routed through the United Arab Emirates while the U.S. is preparing for military action in Iraq. Turns out the attacks were launched by two teenagers in Cloverdale, Calif., and an Israeli accomplice who called himself the "Analyzer."

Moonlight Maze
March, 1998, through 1999. Attackers use special code to gain access to websites at the Defense Dept., NASA, the Energy Dept., and weapons labs across the country. Large packets of unclassified data are stolen. "At times, the end point [for the data] was inside Russia," says a source familiar with the investigation. The sponsor of the attack has never been identified. The Russian government denied any involvement.

Titan Rain
2004. Hackers believed to be in China access classified data stored on computer networks of defense contractor Lockheed Martin, Sandia National Labs, and NASA. The intrusions are identified by Shawn Carpenter, a cyber security analyst at Sandia Labs. After he reports the breaches to the U.S. Army and FBI, Sandia fires him. Carpenter later sues Sandia for wrongful termination. In February, 2007, a jury awards him $4.7 million.

Byzantine Foothold
2007. A new form of attack, using sophisticated technology, deluges outfits from the State Dept. to Boeing. Military cyber security specialists find the "resources of a nation-state behind it" and call the type of attack an "advanced persistent threat." The breaches are detailed in a classified document known as an Intelligence Community Assessment. The source of many of the attacks, allege U.S. officials, is China. China denies the charge.

including those owned by the U.S. government, were subject to intrusions that appear to have originated within the PRC," reads the Pentagon's annual report to Congress on Chinese military power, released on Mar. 3. The preamble of Bush's Cyber Initiative focuses attention on China as well.

Wang Baodong, a spokesman for the Chinese government at its embassy in Washington, says "anti-China forces" are behind the allegations. Assertions by U.S. officials and others of cyber intrusions sponsored or encouraged by China are unwarranted, he wrote in an Apr. 9 e-mail response to questions from *BusinessWeek*. "The Chinese government always opposes and forbids any cyber crimes including 'hacking' that undermine the security of computer networks," says Wang. China itself, he adds, is a victim, "frequently intruded and attacked by hackers from certain countries."

Because the Web allows digital spies and thieves to mask their identities, conceal their physical locations, and bounce malicious code to and fro, it's frequently impossible to pinpoint specific attackers. Network security professionals call this digital masquerade ball "the attribution problem."

A Credible Message

In written responses to questions from *BusinessWeek*, officials in the office of National Intelligence Director J. Michael McConnell, a leading proponent of boosting government cyber security, would not comment "on specific code-word programs" such as Byzantine Foothold, nor on "specific intrusions or possible victims." But the department says that "computer intrusions have been successful against a wide range of government and corporate networks across the critical infrastructure and defense industrial base." The White House declined to address the contents of the Cyber Initiative, citing its classified nature.

The e-mail aimed at Booz Allen, obtained by *BusinessWeek* and traced back to an Internet address in China, paints a vivid picture of the alarming new capabilities of America's cyber enemies. On Sept. 5, 2007, at 08:22:21 Eastern time, an e-mail message appeared to be sent to John F. "Jack" Mulhern, vice-president for international military assistance programs at Booz Allen. In the high-tech world of weapons sales, Mulhern's specialty, the e-mail looked authentic enough. "Integrate U.S., Russian, and Indian weapons and avionics," the e-mail noted, describing the Indian government's expectations for its fighter jets. "Source code given to India for indigenous computer upgrade capability." Such lingo could easily be understood by Mulhern. The 62-year-old former U.S. Naval officer and 33-year veteran of Booz Allen's military consulting business is an expert in helping to sell U.S. weapons to foreign governments.

The e-mail was more convincing because of its apparent sender: Stephen J. Moree, a civilian who works for a group that reports to the office of Air Force Secretary Michael W. Wynne. Among its duties, Moree's unit evaluates the security of selling U.S. military aircraft to other countries. There would be little reason to suspect anything seriously amiss in Moree's passing along the highly technical document with "India MRCA Request for Proposal" in the subject line. The Indian government had just released the request a week earlier, on Aug. 28, and the language in the e-mail closely tracked the request. Making the message appear more credible still: It referred to upcoming Air Force communiqués and a "Teaming Meeting" to discuss the deal.

But the missive from Moree to Jack Mulhern was a fake. An analysis of the e-mail's path and attachment, conducted for *BusinessWeek* by three cyber security specialists, shows it was sent by an unknown attacker, bounced through an Internet address in South Korea, was relayed through a Yahoo! server in New York, and finally made its way toward Mulhern's Booz Allen in-box. The analysis also shows the code—known as "malware," for malicious software—tracks keystrokes on the computers of people who open it. A separate program disables security measures such as password protection on Microsoft Access database files, a program often used by large organizations such as the U.S. defense industry to manage big batches of data.

An E-mail's Journey

While hardly the most sophisticated technique used by electronic thieves these days, "if you have any kind of sensitive documents on Access databases, this [code] is getting in there and getting them out," says a senior executive at a leading cyber security firm that analyzed the e-mail. (The person requested anonymity because his firm provides security consulting to U.S. military departments, defense contractors, and financial institutions.) Commercial computer security firms have dubbed the malicious code "Poison Ivy."

But the malware attached to the fake Air Force e-mail has a more devious—and worrisome—capability. Known as a remote administration tool, or RAT, it gives the attacker control over the "host" PC, capturing screen shots and perusing files. It lurks in the background of Microsoft Internet Explorer browsers while users surf the Web. Then it phones home to its "master" at an Internet address currently registered under the name cybersyndrome.3322.org.

The digital trail to cybersyndrome.3322.org, followed by analysts at *BusinessWeek*'s request, leads to one of China's largest free domain-name-registration and e-mail services. Called 3322.org, it is registered to a company called Bentium in the city of Changzhou, an industry hub outside Shanghai. A range of security experts say that 3322.org provides names for computers and servers that act as the command and control centers for more than 10,000 pieces of malicious code launched at government and corporate networks in recent years. Many of those PCs are in China; the rest could be anywhere.

The founder of 3322.org, a 37-year-old technology entrepreneur named Peng Yong, says his company merely allows users to register domain names. "As for what our users do, we cannot completely control it," says Peng. The bottom line: If Poison Ivy infected Jack Mulhern's computer at Booz Allen, any secrets inside could be seen in China. And if it spread to other computers, as malware often does, the infection opens windows on potentially sensitive information there, too.

It's not clear whether Mulhern received the e-mail, but the address was accurate. Informed by *BusinessWeek* on Mar. 20 of the fake message, Booz Allen spokesman George Farrar says the company launched a search to find it. As of Apr. 9, says Farrar, the company had not discovered the e-mail or Poison Ivy in Booz Allen's networks. Farrar says Booz Allen computer security executives examined the PCs of Mulhern and an assistant who received his e-mail. "We take this very seriously," says Farrar. (Mulhern, who retired in March, did not respond to e-mailed requests for comment and declined a request, through Booz Allen, for an interview.)

Air Force officials referred requests for comment to U.S. Defense Secretary Robert M. Gates' office. In an e-mailed response to *BusinessWeek*, Gates' office acknowledges being the target of cyber attacks from "a variety of state and non-state-sponsored organizations to gain unauthorized access to, or otherwise degrade, [Defense Dept.] information systems." But the Pentagon declined to discuss the attempted Booz Allen break-in. The Air Force, meanwhile, would not make Stephen Moree available for comment.

The bogus e-mail, however, seemed to cause a stir inside the Air Force, correspondence reviewed by *BusinessWeek* shows.

On Sept. 4, defense analyst James Mulvenon also received the message with Moree and Mulhern's names on it. Security experts believe Mulvenon's e-mail address was secretly included in the "blind copy" line of a version of the message. Mulvenon is director of the Center for Intelligence Research & Analysis and a leading consultant to U.S. defense and intelligence agencies on China's military and cyber strategy. He maintains an Excel spreadsheet of suspect e-mails, malicious code, and hacker groups and passes them along to the authorities. Suspicious of the note when he received it, Mulvenon replied to Moree the next day. Was the e-mail "India spam?" Mulvenon asked.

"I apologize—this e-mail was sent in error—please delete," Moree responded a few hours later.

"No worries," typed Mulvenon. "I have been getting a lot of trojaned Access databases from China lately and just wanted to make sure."

"Interesting—our network folks are looking into some kind of malicious intent behind this e-mail snafu," wrote Moree. Neither the Air Force nor the Defense Dept. would confirm to *BusinessWeek* whether an investigation was conducted. A Pentagon spokesman says that its procedure is to refer attacks to law enforcement or counterintelligence agencies. He would not disclose which, if any, is investigating the Air Force e-mail.

Digital Intruders

By itself, the bid to steal digital secrets from Booz Allen might not be deeply troubling. But Poison Ivy is part of a new type of digital intruder rendering traditional defenses—firewalls and updated antivirus software—virtually useless. Sophisticated hackers, say Pentagon officials, are developing new ways to creep into computer networks sometimes before those vulnerabilities are known. "The offense has a big advantage over the defense right now," says Colonel Ward E. Heinke, director of the Air Force Network Operations Center at Barksdale Air Force Base. Only 11 of the top 34 antivirus software programs identified Poison Ivy when it was first tested on behalf of *BusinessWeek* in February. Malware-sniffing software from several top security firms found "no virus" in the India fighter-jet e-mail, the analysis showed.

> **"Poison ivy" is part of a new type of digital intruder rendering traditional perimeter defenses like firewalls virtually useless.**

Over the past two years thousands of highly customized e-mails akin to Stephen Moree's have landed in the laptops and PCs of U.S. government workers and defense contracting executives. According to sources familiar with the matter, the attacks targeted sensitive information on the networks of at least seven agencies—the Defense, State, Energy, Commerce, Health & Human Services, Agriculture, and Treasury departments—and also defense contractors Boeing, Lockheed Martin, General Electric, Raytheon, and General Dynamics, say current and former government network security experts. Laura Keehner, a spokeswoman for the Homeland Security Dept., which coordinates protection of government computers, declined to comment on specific intrusions. In written responses to questions from

A BRILLIANT FAKE
The bogus e-mail aimed at Booz Allen Hamilton

From: "Stephen J. Moree"
Reply-To: "Stephen J. Moree"
Date: Wed, 5 Sep 2007 08:22:21 +0800
To:
Subject: India MRCA Request For Proposal

Sir,

This morning (28 Aug) we received the 211 page India Multi-Role Combat Aircraft (MRCA) Request for Proposal (RFP). The major RFP points are:

- 126 aircraft (86 single seat/40 dual); 18 built by OEM, 108 co-produced in India
- 1 or 2 engines; 14k–30k kg (30.9k–66.1k lb) max weight
- Active AESA radar capable of targeting 5 m2 at 130km (80.8 miles)
- 24 month fixed price validity of offer; option for 63 aircraft good for 3 years (fixed price)
- 50% Offset requirement
- Aircraft delivery to begin 36 months from contract, co-production begins 48 months from contract
- Tech transfer is broken into 5 categories, 60% is the highest percentage
- Performance Based Logistics (Life Cycle costs) are addressed, but India may/may not use as a final determiner
- Integrate US, Russian, and Indian weapons and avionics
- Source code given to India for indigenous computer upgrade capability

IAW the Teaming Directive I've attached a copy of the complete RFP; however, we will provide a more detailed summary after our Teaming Meeting. We'll include this development in the SAF/IA Update and Friday's CSAF Update slide.

vr
Steve

Stephen J. Moree
Northeast Asia Branch Chief
SAF/IA Pacific Division

CONFIDENTIALITY NOTICE: This electronic transmission is "For Official Use Only" and may contain information protected from disclosure under the Freedom of Information Act, 5 USC 552. Do not release outside of DoD channels without prior authorization from the sender.

BusinessWeek, Keehner says: "We are aware of and have defended against malicious cyber activity directed at the U.S. Government over the past few years. We take these threats seriously and continue to remain concerned that this activity is growing more sophisticated, more targeted, and more prevalent." Spokesmen for Lockheed Martin, Boeing, Raytheon, General Dynamics, and General Electric declined to comment. Several cited policies of not discussing security-related matters.

The rash of computer infections is the subject of Byzantine Foothold, the classified operation designed to root out the perpetrators and protect systems in the future, according to three people familiar with the matter. In some cases, the government's own cyber security experts are engaged in "hack-backs"—following the malicious code to peer into the hackers' own computer systems. *BusinessWeek* has learned that a classified document called an intelligence community assessment, or ICA, details the Byzantine intrusions and assigns each a unique Byzantine-related name. The ICA has circulated in recent months among selected officials at U.S. intelligence agencies, the Pentagon, and cyber security consultants acting as outside reviewers. Until December, details of the ICA's contents had not even been shared with congressional intelligence committees.

Now, Senate Intelligence Committee Chairman John D. Rockefeller (D-W. Va.) is said to be discreetly informing fellow senators of the Byzantine operation, in part to win their support for needed appropriations, many of which are part of classified "black" budgets kept off official government books. Rockefeller declined to comment. In January a Senate Intelligence Committee staffer urged his boss, Missouri Republican Christopher "Kit"

Anatomy of a Spear-Phish

The three stages of a successful spear-phishing attack.

Net Reconnaissance
Online cunning need not start with insiders or illegally obtained information. Attackers can scour the Web—studying public documents, chat rooms, and blogs—to build digital dossiers about the jobs, responsibilities, and personal networks of targets.

Constructing the "Spear-Phish"
Attackers build an e-mail with a Web link or attachment on a subject likely to trick the victim into clicking on it. Common spear-phish topics include news events, earnings results, and Word and PowerPoint documents containing real info. The e-mail address is made to look like it comes from a logical sender.

Harvesting the Data
When the victim opens the attachment or clicks on the Web link, malicious code hidden inside combs document files, steals passwords, and sends the data to a "command and control" server, often in a foreign country, which collects the data for study.

Bond, the committee's vice-chairman, to supplement closed-door testimony and classified documents with a viewing of the movie *Die Hard 4* on a flight the senator made to New Zealand. In the film, cyber terrorists breach FBI networks, purloin financial data, and bring car traffic to a halt in Washington. Hollywood, says Bond, doesn't exaggerate as much as people might think. "I can't discuss classified matters," he cautions. "But the movie illustrates the potential impact of a cyber conflict. Except for a few things, let me just tell you: It's credible."

"Phishing," one technique used in many attacks, allows cyber spies to steal information by posing as a trustworthy entity in an online communication. The term was coined in the mid-1990s when hackers began "fishing" for information (and tweaked the spelling). The e-mail attacks on government agencies and defense contractors, called "spear-phish" because they target specific individuals, are the Web version of laser-guided missiles. Spear-phish creators gather information about people's jobs and social networks, often from publicly available information and data stolen from other infected computers, and then trick them into opening an e-mail.

Devious Script

Spear-phish tap into a cyber espionage tactic that security experts call "Net reconnaissance." In the attempted attack on Booz Allen, attackers had plenty of information about Moree: his full name, title (Northeast Asia Branch Chief), job responsibilities, and e-mail address. Net reconnaissance can be surprisingly simple, often starting with a Google search. (A lookup of the Air Force's Pentagon e-mail address on Apr. 9, for instance, retrieved 8,680 e-mail addresses for current or former Air Force personnel and departments.) The information is woven into a fake e-mail with a link to an infected website or containing an attached document. All attackers have to do is hit their send button. Once the e-mail is opened, intruders are automatically ushered inside the walled perimeter of computer networks—and malicious code such as Poison Ivy can take over.

By mid-2007 analysts at the National Security Agency began to discern a pattern: personalized e-mails with corrupted attachments such as PowerPoint presentations, Word documents, and Access database files had been turning up on computers connected to the networks of numerous agencies and defense contractors.

A previously undisclosed breach in the autumn of 2005 at the American Enterprise Institute—a conservative think tank whose former officials and corporate executive board members are closely connected to the Bush Administration—proved so nettlesome that the White House shut off aides' access to the website for more than six months, says a cyber security specialist familiar with the incident. The Defense Dept. shut the door for even longer. Computer security investigators, one of whom spoke with *BusinessWeek*, identified the culprit: a few lines of Java script buried in AEI's home page, www.aei.org, that activated as soon as someone visited the site. The script secretly redirected the user's computer to another server that attempted to load malware. The malware, in turn, sent information from the visitor's hard drive to a server in China. But the security specialist says cyber sleuths couldn't get rid of the intruder. After each deletion, the furtive code would reappear. AEI says otherwise—except for a brief accidental recurrence caused by its own network personnel in August, 2007, the devious Java script did not return and was not difficult to eradicate.

The breach of a highly sensitive State Dept. Bureau posed a risk to CIA operatives in embassies around the globe.

The government has yet to disclose the breaches related to Byzantine Foothold. *BusinessWeek* has learned that intruders managed to worm into the State Dept.'s highly sensitive Bureau of Intelligence & Research, a key channel between the work of intelligence agencies and the rest of the government. The breach posed a risk to CIA operatives in embassies around the globe, say several network security specialists familiar with the effort to cope with what became seen as an internal crisis. Teams worked around-the-clock in search of malware, they say, calling the White House regularly with updates.

The attack began in May, 2006, when an unwitting employee in the State Dept.'s East Asia Pacific region clicked on an attachment in a seemingly authentic e-mail. Malicious code was embedded in the Word document, a congressional speech, and opened a Trojan "back door" for the code's creators to peer inside the State Dept.'s innermost networks. Soon, cyber security engineers began spotting more intrusions in State Dept. computers across the globe. The malware took advantage of previously unknown vulnerabilities in the Microsoft operating system. Unable to develop a patch quickly enough, engineers watched helplessly as streams of State Dept. data slipped through the back door and into the Internet ether. Although they were unable to fix the vulnerability, specialists came up with a temporary scheme to block further infections. They also yanked connections to the Internet.

One member of the emergency team summoned to the scene recalls that each time cyber security professionals thought they had eliminated the source of a "beacon" reporting back to its master, another popped up. He compared the effort to the arcade game Whack-A-Mole. The State Dept. says it eradicated the infection, but only after sanitizing scores of infected computers and servers and changing passwords. Microsoft's own patch, meanwhile, was not deployed until August, 2006, three months after the infection. A Microsoft spokeswoman declined to comment on the episode, but said: "Microsoft has, for several years, taken a comprehensive approach to help protect people online."

There is little doubt among senior U.S. officials about where the trail of the recent wave of attacks leads. "The Byzantine series tracks back to China," says Air Force Colonel Heinke. More than a dozen current and former U.S. military, cyber security, and intelligence officials interviewed by *BusinessWeek* say China is the biggest emerging adversary—and not just clubs of rogue or enterprising hackers who happen to be Chinese. O. Sami Saydjari, a former National Security Agency executive and now president of computer security firm Cyber Defense Agency, says the Chinese People's Liberation Army, one of the world's largest military forces, with an annual budget of $57 billion, has "tens of thousands" of trainees launching attacks on U.S. computer networks. Those figures could not be independently confirmed by *BusinessWeek*. Other experts provide lower estimates and note that even one hacker can do a lot of damage. Says Saydjari: "We have to look at this as equivalent to the launch of a Chinese Sputnik." China vigorously disputes the spying allegation and says its military posture is purely defensive.

Hints of the perils perceived within America's corridors of power have been slipping out in recent months. In Feb. 27 testimony before the U.S. Senate Armed Services Committee, National Intelligence Director McConnell echoed the view that the threat comes from China. He told Congress he worries less about people capturing information than altering it. "If someone has the ability to enter information in systems, they can destroy data. And the destroyed data could be something like money supply, electric-power distribution, transportation sequencing, and that sort of thing." His conclusion: "The federal government is not well-protected and the private sector is not well-protected."

Worries about China-sponsored Internet attacks spread last year to Germany, France, and Britain. British domestic intelligence agency MI5 had seen enough evidence of intrusion and theft of corporate secrets by allegedly state-sponsored Chinese hackers by November, 2007, that the agency's director general, Jonathan Evans, sent an unusual letter of warning to 300 corporations, accounting firms, and law firms—and a list of network security specialists to help block computer intrusions. Some recipients of the MI5 letter hired Peter Yapp, a leading security consultant with London-based Control Risks. "People treat this like it's just another hacker story, and it is almost unbelievable," says Yapp. "There's a James Bond element to it. Too many people think, 'It's not going to happen to me.' But it has."

Identifying the thieves slipping their malware through the digital gates can be tricky. Some computer security specialists doubt China's government is involved in cyber attacks on U.S. defense targets. Peter Sommer, an information systems security specialist at the London School of Economics who helps companies secure networks, says: "I suspect if it's an official part of the Chinese government, you wouldn't be spotting it."

The Government's Response

Key elements of the U.S. "Cyber Initiative," signed on Jan. 8.

Cut Connections
Aims to cut the number of portals between government networks and the Internet from more than 4,000 to fewer than 100.

Passive Intrusion Prevention
Requires a plan to identify when unauthorized entities have gained access to computer networks.

Active Intrusion Prevention
Requires a program to trace cyber intrusions back to their source, both countries and people.

Counterintelligence Strategy
Requires a plan to deter and prevent future computer network breaches.

Counterintelligence Tools
Launches a program to develop the technology for cyber forensic analysis.

Education
Creates training programs to develop technical skills to improve cyber security.

Fusing Operations
Combines the computer command posts known as "network operations centers" of an unknown number of agencies.

Cyber R&D
Launches a plan to develop offensive and defensive cyber capabilities, including those developed by contractors.

Leap-Ahead Technologies
Aims to invent "killer apps" to win the cyber arms race.

Critical Infrastructure Protection
Calls for a plan to work with the private sector, which owns and operates most of the Internet.

Revisit Project Solarium
Like the Eisenhower project to deter nuclear war, aims to prevent a cyber war.

Improve Federal Acquisitions
Starts program to ensure government IT products and services are secure.

A range of attacks in the past two years on U.S. and foreign government entities, defense contractors, and corporate networks have been traced to Internet addresses registered through Chinese domain name services such as 3322.org, run by Peng Yong. In late March, *BusinessWeek* interviewed Peng in an apartment on the 14th floor of the gray-tiled residential building that houses the five-person office for 3322.org in Changzhou. Peng says he started 3322.org in 2001 with $14,000 of his own money so the growing ranks of China's Net surfers could register websites and distribute data. "We felt that this business would be very popular, especially as broadband, fiber-optic cables, [data transmission technology] ADSL, these ways of getting on the Internet took off," says Peng (translated by *BusinessWeek* from Mandarin), who drives a black Lexus IS300 bought last year.

His 3322.org has indeed become a hit. Peng says the service has registered more than 1 million domain names, charging $14 per year for "top-level" names ending in .com, .org, or .net. But cyber security experts and the Homeland Security Dept.'s U.S. Computer Emergency Readiness Team (CERT) say that 3322.org is a hit with another group: hackers. That's because 3322.org and five sister sites controlled by Peng are dynamic DNS providers. Like an Internet phone book, dynamic DNS assigns names for the digits that mark a computer's location on the Web. For example, 3322.org is the registrar for the name cybersyndrome.3322.org at Internet address 61.234.4.28, the China-based computer that was contacted by the malicious code in the attempted Booz Allen attack, according to analyses reviewed by *BusinessWeek*. "Hackers started using sites like 3322.org so that the malware phones home to the specific name. The reason? It is relatively difficult to have [Internet addresses] taken down in China," says Maarten van Horenbeeck, a Belgium-based intrusion analyst for the SANS Internet Storm Center, a cyber threat monitoring group.

Target: Private Sector

Peng's 3322.org and sister sites have become a source of concern to the U.S. government and private firms. Cyber security firm Team Cymru sent a confidential report, reviewed by *BusinessWeek,* to clients on Mar. 7 that illustrates how 3322.org has enabled many recent attacks. In early March, the report says, Team Cymru received "a spoofed e-mail message from a U.S. military entity, and the PowerPoint attachment had a malware widget embedded in it." The e-mail was a spear-phish. The computer that controlled the malicious code in the PowerPoint? Cybersyndrome.3322.org—the same China-registered computer in the attempted attack on Booz Allen. Although the cybersyndrome Internet address may not be located in China, the top five computers communicating directly with it were—and four were registered with a large state-owned Internet service provider, according to the report.

A person familiar with Team Cymru's research says the company has 10,710 distinct malware samples that communicate to masters registered through 3322.org. Other groups reporting attacks from computers hosted by 3322.org include activist group Students for a Free Tibet, the European Parliament, and U.S. Bancorp according to security reports. Team Cymru declined to comment. The U.S. government has pinpointed Peng's services as a problem, too. In a Nov. 28, 2007, confidential report from Homeland Security's U.S. CERT obtained by *BusinessWeek*, "Cyber Incidents Suspected of Impacting Private Sector Networks," the federal cyber watchdog warned U.S. corporate information technology staff to update security software to block Internet traffic from a dozen Web addresses after spear-phishing attacks. "The level of sophistication and scope of these cyber security incidents indicates they are coordinated and targeted at private-sector systems," says the report. Among the sites named: Peng's 3322.org, as well as his 8800.org, 9966.org, and 8866.org. Homeland Security and U.S. CERT declined to discuss the report.

Peng says he has no idea hackers are using his service to send and control malicious code. "Are there a lot?" he says when asked why so many hackers use 3322.org. He says his business is not responsible for cyber attacks on U.S. computers. "It's like we have paved a road and what sort of car [users] drive on it is their own business," says Peng, who adds that he spends most of his time these days developing Internet telephony for his new software firm, Bitcomm Software Tech Co. Peng says he was not aware that several of his websites and Internet addresses registered through them were named in the U.S. CERT report. On Apr. 7, he said he planned to shut the sites down and contact the U.S. agency. Asked by *BusinessWeek* to check his database for the person who registered the computer at the domain name cybersyndrome.3322.org, Peng says it is registered to Gansu Railway Communications, a regional telecom subsidiary of China's Railways Ministry. Peng declined to provide the name of the registrant, citing a confidentiality agreement. "You can go through the police to find out the user information," says Peng.

U.S. cyber security experts say it's doubtful that the Chinese government would allow the high volume of attacks on U.S. entities from China-based computers if it didn't want them to happen. "China has one of the best-controlled Internets in the world. Anything that happens on their Internet requires permission," says Cyber Defense Group's Saydjari. The Chinese government spokesman declined to answer specific questions from *BusinessWeek* about 3322.org.

Britain's MI5 intelligence agency sent a warning in 2007 to 300 companies about thefts of corporate secrets by Chinese hackers.

But Peng says he can do little if hackers exploit his goodwill—and there hasn't been much incentive from the Chinese government for him to get tough. "Normally, we take care of these problems by shutting them down," says Peng. "Because our laws do not have an extremely clear method to handle this problem, sometimes we are helpless to stop their services." And so, it seems thus far, is the U.S. government.

Sustainable Success

For companies operating in developing countries, it pays to commit to improving social and environmental conditions.

LUTZ KAUFMANN ET AL.

A series of scandals over the years have taught Western companies an important lesson about operating in developing countries: Any indication that a company or one of its suppliers is exploiting workers or damaging the environment in these regions can have devastating effects on a company's reputation—world-wide. The result is fleeing customers and investors.

But here's a lesson many executives have yet to learn: A commitment to *improving* social and environmental conditions in the developing countries where a company operates is the key to maximizing the profits and growth of those operations.

That's the conclusion we drew after studying more than 200 companies. As a group, the companies most engaged in social and environmental sustainability are also the most profitable.

What does sustainable management entail?

On the production side, companies that are able to maximize their use of recycled or renewable raw materials and environmentally friendly energy supplies are also the most successful ones. They design their production lines to use water and energy efficiently, promptly replace obsolete machinery and continuously look for opportunities to reduce waste. And they minimize harmful emissions into the air and water.

Companies that excel in providing health insurance, retirement benefits and professional development for their employees also show above-average profitability.

The most successful companies not only enforce safety standards strictly but also improve them over time. And they support local communities with initiatives in education, health care, environmental protection and agricultural development.

Finally, the most successful companies set high social and environmental standards in the selection of their suppliers, monitor the suppliers to ensure compliance, and work with them to continually improve their performance in these areas.

How exactly do such efforts affect profits? We found that sustainable management yields six major competitive advantages:

A Sterling Reputation

A growing number of consumers consider competing companies' social and environmental records when deciding which products to buy. A reputation for concern about these issues sets a company apart from its competitors. Consider the popularity of fair-trade groceries, whose distributors promise to promote the welfare of the providers and the environment.

It's important to remember that a company's reputation in this regard depends not only on its own actions but also to a large degree on those of its suppliers.

Better Employees

In emerging countries, where living conditions are most in need of improvement, employees are especially proud of working for companies that are recognized as leaders in sustainability. That gives these companies a big advantage in all three areas of human-resources management: hiring, retaining and motivating the most talented workers.

And of course, more directly, employees greatly value supportive, fair and safe working conditions.

More-Efficient Production

In order to achieve environmental sustainability, companies need to consume as few resources as possible and also to produce as little waste as possible. That can be accomplished only by constantly striving to make production more efficient, which also reduces costs and eliminates glitches that affect product quality.

A Smoother Relationship with Authorities

Western companies operating in emerging countries face unfamiliar legal and regulatory systems that often are less formal than those in their home markets. These companies depend on cooperative relationships with local authorities to ensure the smooth development of their businesses, and those relationships are enhanced by companies' contributions to the welfare of local communities and the environment.

Better Coordination—Internally and with Suppliers

Sustainable management involves extraordinary cooperation among a company's various departments, including purchasing, research and development, and human resources. That's useful experience for other projects—say, product development.

Similarly, working together on sustainability allows a company and its suppliers to get to know each other better. That makes collaboration on other issues easier. And it gives companies a better understanding of how business is done in general in their suppliers' regions.

Suppliers That Are More Reliable and Flexible

Suppliers that work with companies to improve sustainability become more efficient and reliable, because they exert greater control over their production processes.

These efforts also sharpen suppliers' management skills. For instance, these suppliers often demonstrate greater flexibility, allowing them to respond more quickly and smoothly to changes in the purchasing company's needs.

DR. KAUFMANN is a professor of international business and supply management at WHU-Otto Beisheim School of Management, in Vallendar, Germany. **DR. REIMANN**, **DR. EHRGOTT**, and **MR. RAUER** are researchers in WHU's department of international business and supply management. They can be reached at reports@wsj.com.

From *The Wall Street Journal,* June 22, 2009, p. R6. Copyright © 2009 by Dow Jones & Company, Inc. Reprinted by permission via the Copyright Clearance Center.

Global Diversity: The Next Frontier

PETER ORTIZ

Corporate America faces a challenging enough task understanding the increasingly diverse United States, but to remain competitive, companies must address what happens on a larger playing field.

Embracing diversity globally requires an appreciation of distinctive societal, governmental and cultural values, including a lack of metrics that U.S. diversity leaders rely upon as benchmarking tools.

For example, while racial and ethnic demographics serve Rohini Anand as valuable measures for evaluating work-force diversity at Sodexho in the United States, the senior vice president and chief diversity officer doesn't always have that type of ready information in other countries.

"In France . . . you can't identity people by ethnicity or race," says Anand, whose company, Sodexho, is No. 14 on The 2006 DiversityInc Top 50 Companies for Diversity list. "All you can do is collect gender information, so it becomes extremely challenging if you don't know what the numbers and percentages are in your work force to establish any target."

So how does Sodexho handle this challenge? Inclusively. Anand relies on the viewpoints of a 12-person global task force from South America, Australia, Asia and Europe. The group meets virtually once a month to discuss the company's action plan and to share and report on best practices as well as understand the cultural nuances that define diversity in their respective societies.

Sodexho, which has operations in more than 70 countries, started its diversity initiative in North America four years ago when Anand came on board and found a champion in then-Sodexho CEO of North America, Michel Landel. Now as CEO of Sodexho Alliance, Landel advocates for diversity on a global scale. About 10 percent to 15 percent of managers' total bonuses are linked to diversity objectives for recruiting, retention and promotion of women and people of color in the United States, she says.

"That's his commitment, his passion, his realization of the need for cultural competence, and the success of our business is what really took it to [another] level," she says. "He has taken the same tenor and tone to the global arena as well where he is making it very much a part of his legacy and his strategy." With the global initiative 1.5 years old, Sodexho is beginning to address the diversity challenges in France. "One of the first things we're doing is to develop some training programs for our managers, particularly around recruiting to make sure that there is unbiased recruiting as well as to allow managers the opportunity to recognize talent," Anand says.

The Greater Global Challenge

Deeply embedded customs and values in countries can make it difficult for U.S. corporations to carry out even the most basic equality measures. In South Korea, for example, there still is a cultural expectation that women stay home and take care of their children, leading many companies, both South Korean and foreign, to ignore investment in training women, says Michalle E. Mor Barak, a professor at the University of Southern California's School of Social Work and Marshall School of Business.

"It's not just that you are not utilizing half of the potential work force to its fullest, but you're also not addressing the expectations of your potential [women] customers," Mor Barak says. "To some extent you need diversity to address the varying expectations of your potential customers. Different viewpoints can greatly enrich the company's vision."

Mor Barak, who has published articles on global work force diversity and inclusion, including a book, *Managing Diversity: Toward a Globally Inclusive Workplace,* says many U.S. companies don't know how to address diversity issues in other countries. This results in a disparity between diversity initiatives at home and abroad. A good first step is working with people who are familiar with the foreign and U.S. culture.

"You create a bridge between the two and come up with initiatives that will promote diversity while being respectful of the local culture," Mor Barak says.

In France, the principle behind not identifying residents by race and ethnicity is meant to promote equality by identifying every French citizen, regardless of skin color or ethnicity, as French. A potential drawback is a lack of data companies can use to learn about diversity in French society, but this shouldn't limit a proactive company from learning about its own workforce diversity. Mor Barak suggests distributing surveys that ask employees how they identify themselves and how included they feel in the organization.

"On the advantage side, any accommodation for diversity in the long run benefits the organizational mission because it introduces a variety of ideas and thinking that can help the company be more creative and cater to different groups of customers," she says.

American Express' global team is divided into a U.S. and international council and was created in 2003. The international council consists of four regions: Europe-Middle East-Africa; Latin America and Caribbean; Japan, Asia-Pacific, Australia; and Canada. American Express is No. 30 on The 2006 DiversityInc Top 50 Companies for Diversity list.

Henry Hernandez, vice president and chief diversity officer, says the company has "to be sensitive to the fact that we may have to differentiate between what might be able to be done or approached from a U.S. perspective versus international." Where American Express may be similar to other corporations that are proactive on diversity initiatives in the United States, the financial-services giant must be cognizant on a global scale as well. Nearly half of the company's more than 66,000 employees live outside the United States.

"It really does have to span across the globe," Hernandez says.

The company must remain sensitive to the knowledge, awareness, skill sets and competencies that will differ from region to region.

Different Historic Perspectives

The United States has had a head start in corporate diversity that can be traced back to the Civil Rights Movement and the fight for equality and rights.

"It wasn't even referred to then as diversity, but when you think of the evolution, it's been a long one, whereas outside the United States, it may not have even been addressed that way," Hernandez says.

Bernard Anderson, an assistant secretary in the U.S. Department of Labor under former President Clinton, points out that progressive diversity initiatives by U.S. corporations are rooted in the Civil Rights Movement. Only when the U.S. government made employment discrimination illegal and created opportunities through the Civil Rights Act of 1964 and Affirmative Action did opportunities start to really filter down through corporate America.

"Before 1964, it was perfectly legal to deny employment to minority groups and women without explaining why," Anderson says.

Anderson, who today is a professor of management at the Wharton School of Business at the University of Pennsylvania, says that during Clinton's term, critics unfairly linked affirmative action with taking away opportunities for white men. This led many corporations to instead adapt the term "diversity," which gave broader meaning.

"Affirmative action for the most part is limited to employment, and diversity goes beyond employment... Diversity deals with work and family life and a lot of things that affirmative action never touched," Anderson says. "Diversity is now the mechanism that, in addition to broadening opportunities to groups previously excluded, also helps the firms be more financially successful."

Anderson notes—and DiversityInc Top 50 research supports—that more than 80 percent of U.S. corporations don't have diversity initiatives, but most of those that do are Fortune 500 companies. At the same time, Anderson, a self-described "voracious" critic of U.S. corporations, says "there is not a country in this world" that offers the same opportunities for people of color and women as the United States. But Anderson is doubtful that many large corporations that also operate globally can ensure their proactive diversity practices are followed outside the United States.

"What they do overseas will depend entirely upon national policies of countries they are operating in regarding equal-employment opportunities," he says.

With the exception of a few countries, including South Africa and some Scandinavian countries, most foreign governments have not mandated laws that create a solid foundation for diversity initiatives to thrive. U.S. corporations with strong diversity programs that give them a competitive advantage at home may not see the same results overseas.

Anderson also advised the Rev. Leon Sullivan on the Sullivan Principles he developed in 1977. These principles pushed for companies operating in South Africa under apartheid to honor human rights and equal opportunity in their businesses. While a number of U.S. companies signed on during apartheid, Sullivan could not find any Western European company that would do the same, Anderson says.

That lack of comprehension of the value of diversity remains. In France today, he notes it is difficult for women to gain employment in certain occupations, such as construction and manufacturing.

"Unless the cultural and moralistic values of that country support equal employment... an American company attempting to operate diversity programs overseas might operate at a competitive disadvantage in that market," Anderson says.

The Global Success Stories

Global diversity at HSBC is embodied in its description as the "The World's Local Bank," encompassing 284,000 employees in 76 countries and territories. These employees also serve more than 125 million customers. HSBC's U.S. operation is No. 13 on The 2006 DiversityInc Top 50 Companies for Diversity list.

In 2005, the London-based financial-services organization counted one-third of its pretax profits from North America, another third from Europe and one-third from the Asia Pacific region, according to Michael Shearer, senior manager, global diversity. On a global level, diversity is not just about "visible difference such as gender, ethnicity, disability or age," Shearer says. "It is also about different perspectives on working and leadership style, problem solving, managing relationships, creativity and business growth. Put simply, we see this as [an] important and growing focus because, by drawing on local knowledge and different perspectives of colleagues around the world, [it] enables us [to] serve our customers better."

In Australia, Sodexho partners with organizations in developing strategies to better recruit and retain employees from the indigenous aboriginal population. But learning best practices goes both ways and any leading role the United States plays should not be interpreted as a "here we are to show you how it's done" attitude, Anand says.

"In Scandinavian countries, as far as gender was concerned, there were some big surprises around policies for me," she says. "Women get 12 months of maternity leave and men have to use one month of that leave."

Failure of fathers to use that one month results in forfeiture of the entire 12-months' leave, Anand says. In Norway, a law requires that at least one woman sit on corporate boards, she says.

"Many countries are much better than the United States in terms of work/life balance issues, and that has been a big learning [experience] for me," Anand says.

Companies in countries that fail to address shortcomings in best practices could hurt their operations as they increasingly find themselves competing for talent globally. As its global task force continues to exchange diversity practices, Sodexho hopes to draw talent worldwide.

"It's going to be another differentiator for us," Anand says. "It will position us to manage our work force better and position us to take advantage of emerging markets."

American Express utilizes a training module for managers, Valuing Diversity and Practicing Inclusion, to maintain a consistency with its world operations. But inherent in that consistency is the understanding that adjustments may be made to adapt to local cultures. The company piloted the training module in Latin America in 2004.

"We actually identify facilitators who are sensitive to and knowledgeable about those particular markets," Hernandez says. "We always allow them a period of time to be able to adapt, modify and customize some materials so that it resonates well with employees."

While many of the managers worldwide speak English, the company also finds that managers from outside the United States are more engaged during the training when it is done in their native languages. One training example, titled Alejandro's Dilemma, educates managers about missed opportunities during a virtual telephone conference call. An employee may come from a culture where it is impolite to interrupt and be reluctant to offer ideas during the conference call.

"You have to be cognizant of the fact that someone who is at a meeting might be sitting quietly and has an incredible amount to contribute but isn't given the opportunity, or when the call is over, might not know the way to express themselves," Hernandez says.

The company has diversity goals linked to compensation for vice presidents and higher.

The objective is "to equip our leaders with being able to address cultural differences and being able to manage across borders," Hernandez says. Another program, Cultures at Work, combines classroom learning and an online tool, "cultural navigator," for managers.

Through its Group Diversity Management Committee, HSBC shares best-practice approaches from different regions by using an employee-diversity intranet system. The company also offers in-depth cultural training that includes intensive language training for employees sent to other countries and 400 permanently expatriated, globally mobile international managers.

"We can see two benefits to cross-cultural competence," Shearer says. "It helps us understand the diversity—and needs—of customer markets . . . [and] it helps employees to think differently and openly, to see beyond established parameters."

Article 35

Cracks in a Particularly Thick Glass Ceiling

Women in South Korea are slowly changing a corporate culture that lags behind the rest of the country.

MOON IHLWAN

South Koreans are a bit conflicted about career women. Gender wasn't much of an issue in the selection of a female astronaut to fly this month on the country's first space mission. But when women are seeking workaday corporate jobs, some South Korean men still resist change. Outer space is one thing, but a woman in the next cubicle is something else.

For years, most educated women in South Korea who wanted to work could follow but one career path, which began and ended with teaching. The situation started to change after the 1998 Asian financial crisis. Thousands of men lost their jobs or took salary cuts, and their wives had to pick up the slack by starting businesses in their homes or seeking part-time work. A couple of years later, the government banned gender discrimination in the workplace and required businesses with more than 500 employees to set up child-care facilities. It also created a Gender Equality Ministry.

These days the government hires thousands of women (42% of its new employees last year), many for senior positions in the judiciary, international trade administration, and foreign service. Startups and foreign companies also employ (and promote) increasing numbers of Korean women.

One of the Guys

But at the top 400 companies, many of which are family-run conglomerates, it's hard for women to reach the upper ranks. In all, about 8% of working women hold managerial positions. (In the U.S. nearly 51% do.) "We have a long way to go," says Cho Jin Woo, director of the Gender Equality Ministry.

South Koreans are grappling with traditional attitudes about women, a hierarchical business culture, and the need to open up the workplace to compete globally. A senior manager at SK Holdings, which controls the giant mobile phone carrier SK Telecom (SKM), says he avoids hiring women because he believes they lack tenacity. When deadlines are tight, he says, "you need people prepared to put in long hours at the office." Park Myung Soon, a 39-year-old woman who is in charge of business development at the carrier, says, "Many men are preoccupied with the notion that women are a different species." To get ahead, Park says she had to achieve 120% of what her male colleagues did—as well as play basketball and drink with them after work. "Luckily, I like sports, and I like to drink," she says.

When Choi Dong Hee joined SK's research arm in 2005, she was the only woman there and had no major assignment until she created one. After conducting a yearlong study, Choi, 30, proposed changing the company's policy to allow subscribers to use any wireless portal. Her managers ignored her. She persisted. Finally, they agreed to let her brief the division head, who agreed to let her make her case to the company chairman. Choi worked on the presentation for three weeks straight, sometimes alone in the office overnight (to her boss's horror). In the end, the company did adopt the open policy she advocated. Now her managers are quick to say that women's perspectives can help SK better serve its customers.

Sonia Kim, who is in charge of TV marketing at Samsung Electronics, says her male colleagues rarely argue with the boss, even if they think he's wrong. Kim, though, persuaded her manager to let her develop a promotional campaign rather than rely on an ad agency she thought had lost its creative edge. Kim also says some of the men used to overturn decisions made during the day while out drinking after hours. Since she and other women at Samsung complained, Kim says, the practice has mostly stopped.

From *BusinessWeek*, April 21, 2008, p. 58. Copyright © 2008 by BusinessWeek. Reprinted by permission of the McGraw-Hill Companies.

UNIT 4
Ethics and Social Responsibility in the Marketplace

Unit Selections

36. **Is Marketing Ethics an Oxymoron?**, Philip Kotler
37. **The Rise of Trust and Authenticity,** Don Peppers and Martha Rogers
38. **Serving Unfair Customers,** Leonard L. Berry and Kathleen Seiders
39. **Dirty Deeds,** Michael Orey
40. **Searching for the Top,** Stephenie Overman

Key Points to Consider

- What responsibility does an organization have to reveal product defects to consumers?

- Given the competitiveness of the business arena, is it possible for marketing personnel to behave ethically and both survive and prosper? Explain. Give suggestions that could be incorporated into the marketing strategy for firms that want to be both ethical and successful.

- Name some organizations that make you feel genuinely valued as a customer. What are the characteristics of these organizations that distinguish them from their competitors? Explain.

- Which area of marketing strategy is most subject to public scrutiny in regard to ethics—product, pricing, place, or promotion? Why? Give some examples of unethical techniques or strategies involving each of these four areas.

Student Website
www.mhhe.com/cls

Internet References

Business for Social Responsibility (BSR)
http://www.bsr.org/

Total Quality Management Sites
http://www.nku.edu/~lindsay/qualhttp.html

U.S. Navy
http://www.navy.mil

From a consumer viewpoint, the marketplace is the "proof of the pudding" or the place where the "rubber meets the road" for business ethics. In other words, what the company has promulgated about the virtues of its product or service has little meaning if the company's actual marketing practices and its treatment of the consumer contradict its claims.

At its core, marketing has a very noble and moral purpose: to satisfy human needs and wants and to help people through the exchange process. Marketing involves the coordination of the variables of product, price, place, and promotion to effectively and efficiently address the needs of consumers. Unfortunately, at times, the unethical marketing practices of some firms have cast a shadow of suspicion over marketing in general. Since marketing is the aspect of business that is most visible to the public, it has perhaps taken a disproportionate share of the criticism directed toward the free-enterprise system.

This unit takes a careful look at the strategic process and practice of incorporating ethics into the marketplace. The first subsection, **Marketing Strategy and Ethics,** contains articles describing how marketing strategy and ethics can be integrated in the marketplace. The first article wrestles with the question: "Is Marketing Ethics an Oxymoron?" The last four articles in this subsection reveal the importance of trust and authenticity as being significant concomitants of ethical leadership, the use of DTC advertising of prescription drugs, how rude and blatantly

© Ryan McVay/Getty Images

unjust customers should be treated, and the culpability of the participants in the mortgage market meltdown. The last subsection, **Ethical Practices in the Marketplace,** takes a critical look at unscrupulous "headhunters."

Article 36

Is Marketing Ethics an Oxymoron?

PHILIP KOTLER

Every profession and business has to wrestle with ethical questions. The recent wave of business scandals over inaccurate reporting of sales and profits and excessive pay and privileges for top executives has brought questions of business ethics to the fore. And lawyers have been continuously accused of "ambulance chasing," jury manipulation, and inflated fees, leaving the plaintiffs with much less than called for in the judgment. Physicians have been known to recommend certain drugs as more effective while receiving support from pharmaceutical companies.

Marketers are not immune from facing a whole set of ethical issues. For evidence, look to Howard Bowen's classic questions from his 1953 book, *Social Responsibilities of the Businessman:*

"Should he conduct selling in ways that intrude on the privacy of people, for example, by door-to-door selling? Should he use methods involving ballyhoo, chances, prizes, hawking, and other tactics which are at least of doubtful good taste? Should he employ 'high pressure' tactics in persuading people to buy? Should he try to hasten the obsolescence of goods by bringing out an endless succession of new models and new styles? Should he appeal to and attempt to strengthen the motives of materialism, invidious consumption, and keeping up with the Joneses?" (Also see Smith, N. Craig and Elizabeth Cooper-Martin [1997], "Ethics and Target Marketing: The Role of Product Harm and Consumer Vulnerability," *Journal of Marketing,* July, 1–20.)

The issues raised are complicated. Drawing a clear line between normal marketing practice and unethical behavior isn't easy. Yet it's important for marketing scholars and those interested in public policy to raise questions about practices that they may normally endorse but which may not coincide with the public interest.

We will examine the central axiom of marketing: Companies that satisfy their target customers will perform better than those that don't. Companies that satisfy customers can expect repeat business; those that don't will get only one-time sales. Steady profits come from holding onto customers, satisfying them, and selling them more goods and services.

This axiom is the essence of the well-known marketing concept. It reduces to the formula "Give the customer what he wants." This sounds reasonable on the surface. But notice that it carries an implied corollary: "Don't judge what the customer wants."

Marketers have been, or should be, a little uneasy about this corollary. It raises two public interest concerns: (1) What if the customer wants something that isn't good for him or her? (2) What if the product or service, while good for the customer, isn't good for society or other groups?

When it comes to the first question, what are some products that some customers desire that might not be good for them? These would be products that can potentially harm their health, safety, or well-being. Tobacco and hard drugs such as cocaine, LSD, or ecstasy immediately come to mind.

As for the second question, examples of products or services that some customers desire that may not be in the public's best interest include using asbestos as a building material or using lead paint indiscriminately. Other products and services where debates continue to rage as to whether they are in the public's interest include the right to own guns and other weapons, the right to have an abortion, the right to distribute hate literature, and the right to buy large gas guzzling and polluting automobiles.

EXECUTIVE briefing

Marketers should be proud of their field. They have encouraged and promoted the development of many products and services that have benefited people worldwide. But this is all the more reason that they should carefully and thoughtfully consider where they stand on the ethical issues confronting them today and into the future. Marketers are able to take a stand and must make the effort to do so in order to help resolve these issues.

We now turn to three questions of interest to marketers, businesses, and the public:

1. Given that expanding consumption is at the core of most businesses, what are the interests and behaviors of companies that make these products?
2. To what extent do these companies care about reducing the negative side effects of these products?
3. What steps can be taken to reduce the consumption of products that have questionable effects and is limited intervention warranted?

Expanding Consumption

Most companies will strive to enlarge their market as much as possible. A tobacco company, if unchecked, will try to get everyone who comes of age to start smoking cigarettes. Given that cigarettes are addictive, this promises the cigarette company "customers for life." Each new customer will create a 50-year profit stream for the cigarette company if the consumer continues to favor the same brand—and live long enough. Suppose a new smoker starts at the age of 13, smokes for 50 years, and dies at 63 from lung cancer. If he spends $500 a year on cigarettes, he will spend $25,000 over his lifetime. If the company's profit rate is 20%, that new customer is worth $5,000 to the company (undiscounted). It is hard to imagine a company that doesn't want to attract a customer who contributes $5,000 to its profits.

The same story describes the hard drug industry, whose products are addictive and even more expensive. The difference is that cigarette companies can operate legally but hard drug companies must operate illegally.

Other products, such as hamburgers, candy, soft drinks, and beer, are less harmful when consumed in moderation, but are addictive for some people. We hear a person saying she has a "sweet tooth." One person drinks three Coca-Colas a day, and another drinks five beers a day. Still another consumer is found who eats most of his meals at McDonald's. These are the "heavy users." Each company treasures the heavy users who account for a high proportion of the company's profits.

All said, every company has a natural drive to expand consumption of its products, leaving any negative consequences to be the result of the "free choice" of consumers. A high-level official working for Coca-Cola in Sweden said that her aim is to get people to start drinking Coca-Cola for breakfast (instead of orange juice). And McDonald's encourages customers to choose a larger hamburger, a larger order of French fries, and a larger cola drink. And these companies have some of the best marketers in the world working for them.

Reducing Side Effects

It would not be a natural act on the part of these companies to try to reduce or restrain consumption of their products. What company wants to reduce its profits? Usually some form of public pressure must bear on these companies before they will act.

The government has passed laws banning tobacco companies from advertising and glamorizing smoking on TV. But Philip Morris' Marlboro brand still will put out posters showing its mythical cowboy. And Marlboro will make sure that its name is mentioned in sports stadiums, art exhibits, and in labels for other products.

Tobacco companies today are treading carefully not to openly try to create smokers out of young people. They have stopped distributing free cigarettes to young people in the United States as they move their operations increasingly into China.

Beer companies have adopted a socially responsible attitude by telling people not to over-drink or drive during or after drinking. They cooperate with efforts to prevent underage people from buying beer. They are trying to behave in a socially responsible manner. They also know that, at the margin, the sales loss resulting from their "cooperation" is very slight.

McDonald's has struggled to find a way to reduce the ill effects (obesity, heart disease) of too much consumption of their products. It tried to offer a reduced-fat hamburger only to find consumers rejecting it. It has offered salads, but they weren't of good quality when originally introduced and they failed. Now it's making a second and better attempt.

Limited Intervention

Do public interest groups or the government have the right to intervene in the free choices of individuals? This question has been endlessly debated. On one side are people who resent any intervention in their choices of products and services. In the extreme, they go by such names as libertarians, vigilantes, and "freedom lovers." They have a legitimate concern about government power and its potential abuse. Some of their views include:

- The marketer's job is to "sell more stuff." It isn't the marketer's job to save the world or make society a better place.
- The marketer's job is to produce profits for the shareholders in any legally sanctioned way.
- A high-minded socially conscious person should not be in marketing. A company shouldn't hire such a person.

On the other side are people concerned with the personal and societal costs of "unregulated consumption." They are considered do-gooders and will document that Coca-Cola delivers six teaspoons of sugar in every bottle or can. They will cite statistics on the heavy health costs of obesity, heart disease, and liver damage that are caused by failing to reduce the consumption of some of these products. These costs fall on everyone through higher medical costs and taxes. Thus, those who don't consume questionable products are still harmed through the unenlightened behavior of others.

Ultimately, the problem is one of conflict among different ethical systems. Consider the following five:

Ethical egoism. Your only obligation is to take care of yourself (Protagoras and Ayn Rand).

Government requirements. The law represents the minimal moral standards of a society (Thomas Hobbes and John Locke).

Personal virtues. Be honest, good, and caring (Plato and Aristotle).

Utilitarianism. Create the greatest good for the greatest number (Jeremy Bentham and John Stuart Mill).

Universal rules. "Act only on that maxim through which you can at the same time will that it should become a universal law" (Immanuel Kant's categorical imperative).

Clearly, people embrace different ethical viewpoints, making marketing ethics and other business issues more complex to resolve.

Let's consider the last two ethical systems insofar as they imply that some interventions are warranted. Aside from the weak gestures of companies toward self-regulation and appearing concerned, there are a range of measures that can be taken by those wishing to push their view of the public interest. They include the following six approaches:

1. Encouraging these companies to make products safer. Many companies have responded to public concern or social pressure to make their products safer. Tobacco companies developed filters that would reduce the chance of contracting emphysema or lung cancer. If a leaf without nicotine could give smokers the same satisfaction, they would be happy to replace the tobacco leaf. Some tobacco companies have even offered information or aids to help smokers limit their appetite for tobacco or curb it entirely.

> **Every company has a natural drive to expand consumption of its products, leaving any negative consequences to be the result of the "free choice" of consumers.**

Food and soft drink companies have reformulated many of their products to be "light," "nonfat," or "low in calories." Some beer companies have introduced non-alcoholic beer. These companies still offer their standard products but provide concerned consumers with alternatives that present less risk to their weight or health.

Auto companies have reluctantly incorporated devices designed to reduce pollution output into their automobiles. Some are even producing cars with hybrid fuel systems to further reduce harmful emissions to the air. But the auto companies still insist on putting out larger automobiles (such as Hummers) because the "public demands them."

What can we suggest to Coca-Cola and other soft drink competitors that are already offering "light" versions of their drinks? First, they should focus more on developing the bottled water side of their businesses because bottled water is healthier than sugared soft drinks. Further, they should be encouraged to add nutrients and vitamins in standard drinks so these drinks can at least deliver more health benefits, especially to those in undeveloped countries who are deprived of these nutrients and vitamins. (Coca-Cola has some brands doing this now.)

What can we suggest to McDonald's and its fast food competitors? The basic suggestion is to offer more variety in its menu. McDonald's seems to forget that, while parents bring their children to McDonald's, they themselves usually prefer to eat healthier food, not to mention want their children eating healthier foods. How about a first-class salad bar? How about moving more into the healthy sandwich business? Today more Americans are buying their meals at Subway and other sandwich shops where they feel they are getting healthier and tastier food for their dollar.

There seems to be a correlation between the amount of charity given by companies in some categories and the category's degree of "sin." Thus, McDonald's knows that over-consumption of its products can be harmful, but the company is very charitable. A cynic would say that McDonald's wants to build a bank of public goodwill to diffuse potential public criticism.

2. Banning or restricting the sale or use of the product or service. A community or nation will ban certain products where there is strong public support. Hard drugs are banned, although there is some debate about whether the ban should include marijuana and lighter hard drugs. There are even advocates who oppose banning hard drugs, believing that the cost of policing and criminality far exceed the cost of a moderate increase that might take place in hard drug usage. Many people today believe that the "war on drugs" can never be won and is creating more serious consequences than simply dropping the ban or helping drug addicts, as Holland and Switzerland have done.

Some products carry restrictions on their purchase or use. This is particularly true of drugs that require a doctor's prescription and certain poisons that can't be purchased without authorization. Persons buying guns must be free of a criminal record and register their gun ownership. And certain types of guns, such as machine guns, are banned or restricted.

3. Banning or limiting advertising or promotion of the product. Even when a product isn't banned or its purchase restricted, laws may be passed to prevent producers from advertising or promoting the product. Gun, alcohol, and tobacco manufacturers can't advertise on TV, although they can advertise in print media such as magazines and newspapers. They can also inform and possibly promote their products online.

Manufacturers get around this by mentioning their brand name in every possible venue: sports stadiums, music concerts, and feature articles. They don't want to be forgotten in the face of a ban on promoting their products overtly.

4. Increasing "sin" taxes to discourage consumption. One reasonable alternative to banning a product or its promotion is to place a "sin" tax on its consumption. Thus, smokers pay hefty government taxes for cigarettes. This is supposed to have three effects when done right. First, the higher price should discourage consumption. Second, the tax revenue could be used to finance the social costs to health and safety caused by the consumption of the product. Third, some of the tax revenue could be used to counter-advertise the use of the product or support public education against its use. The last effect was enacted by California when it taxed tobacco companies and used the money to "unsell" tobacco smoking.

5. Public education campaigns. In the 1960s, Sweden developed a social policy to use public education to raise a nation of non-smokers and non-drinkers. Children from the first grade up were educated to understand the ill effects of tobacco and alcohol. Other countries are doing this on a less systematic and intensive basis. U.S. public schools devote parts of occasional courses to educate students against certain temptations with mixed success. Girls, not boys, in the United States seem to be more prone to taking up smoking. The reason often given by girls is that smoking curbs their appetite for food and consequently helps them avoid becoming overweight, a problem they consider more serious than lung cancer taking place 40 years later.

Sex education has become a controversial issue, when it comes to public education campaigns. The ultra-conservative camp wants to encourage total abstinence until marriage. The more liberal camp believes that students should be taught the risks of early sex and have the necessary knowledge to protect themselves. The effectiveness of both types of sex education is under debate.

6. Social marketing campaigns. These campaigns describe a wide variety of efforts to communicate the ill effects of certain behaviors that can harm the person, other persons, or society as a whole. These campaigns use techniques of public education, advertising and promotion, incentives, and channel development to make it as easy and attractive as possible for people to change their behavior for the better. (See Kotler, Philip, Eduardo Roberto, and Nancy Lee (2002), *Social Marketing: Improving the Quality of Life,* 2nd ed. London: Sage Publications.) Social marketing uses the tools of commercial marketing—segmentation, targeting, and positioning, and the four Ps (product, price, place, and promotion)—to achieve voluntary compliance with publicly endorsed goals. Some social marketing campaigns, such as family planning and anti-littering, have achieved moderate to high success. Other campaigns including anti-smoking, anti-drugs ("say no to drugs"), and seat belt promotion have worked well when supplemented with legal action.

Social Responsibility and Profits

Each year *Business Ethics* magazine publishes the 100 best American companies out of 1,000 evaluated. The publication examines the degree to which the companies serve seven stakeholder groups: shareholders, communities, minorities and women, employees, environment, non-U.S. stakeholders, and customers. Information is gathered on lawsuits, regulatory problems, pollution emissions, charitable contributions, staff diversity counts, union relations, employee benefits, and awards. Companies are removed from the list if there are significant scandals or improprieties. The research is done by Kinder, Lydenberg, Domini (KLD), an independent rating service. (For more details see the Spring 2003 issue of *Business Ethics.*)

The 20 best-rated companies in 2003 were (in order): General Mills, Cummins Engine, Intel, Procter & Gamble, IBM, Hewlett-Packard, Avon Products, Green Mountain Coffee, John Nuveen Co., St. Paul Companies, AT&T, Fannie Mae, Bank of America, Motorola, Herman Miller, Expedia, Autodesk, Cisco Systems, Wild Oats Markets, and Deluxe.

The earmarks of a socially responsible company include:

- Living out a deep set of company values that drive company purpose, goals, strategies, and tactics
- Treating customers with fairness, openness, and quick response to inquiries and complaints
- Treating employees, suppliers, and distributors fairly
- Caring about the environmental impact of its activities and supply chain
- Behaving in a consistently ethical fashion

The intriguing question is whether socially responsible companies are more profitable. Unfortunately, different research studies have come up with different results. The correlations between financial performance (FP) and social performance (SP) are sometimes positive, sometimes negative, and sometimes neutral, depending on the study. Even when FP and SP are positively related, which causes which? The most probable finding is that high FP firms invest slack resources in SP and then discover the SP leads to better FP, in a viscious circle. (See Waddock, Sandra A. and Samuel B. Graves [1997], "The Corporate Social Performance-Financial Performance Link," *Strategic Management Journal, 18* (4), 303–319.)

Marketers' Responsibilities

As professional marketers, we are hired by some of the aforementioned companies to use our marketing toolkit to help them sell more of their products and services. Through our research, we can discover which consumer groups are the most susceptible to increasing their consumption. We can use the research to assemble the best 30-second TV commercials, print ads, and sales incentives to persuade them that these products will deliver great satisfaction. And we can create price discounts to tempt them to consume even more of the product than would normally be healthy or safe to consume.

But, as professional marketers, we should have the same ambivalence as nuclear scientists who help build nuclear bombs or pilots who spray DDT over crops from the airplane. Some of us, in fact, are independent enough to tell these clients that we will not work for them to find ways to sell more of what hurts people. We can tell them that we're willing to use our marketing toolkit to help them build new businesses around substitute products that are much healthier and safer.

But, even if these companies moved toward these healthier and safer products, they'll probably continue to push their current "cash cows." At that point, marketers will have to decide whether to work for these companies, help them reshape their offerings, avoid these companies altogether, or even work to oppose these company offerings.

Remember Marketing's Contributions

Nothing said here should detract from the major contributions that marketing has made to raise the material standards of living around the world. One doesn't want to go back to the kitchen where the housewife cooked five hours a day, washed dishes by hand, put fresh ice in the ice box, and washed and dried clothes in the open air. We value refrigerators, electric stoves, dishwashers, washing machines, and dryers. We value the invention and diffusion of the radio, the television set, the computer, the Internet, the cellular phone, the automobile, the movies, and even frozen food. Marketing has played a major role in their instigation and diffusion. Granted, any of these are capable of abuse (bad movies or TV shows), but they promise and deliver much that is good and valued in modern life.

ANNUAL EDITIONS

Marketers have a right to be proud of their field. They search for unmet needs, encourage the development of products and services addressing these needs, manage communications to inform people of these products and services, arrange for easy accessibility and availability, and price the goods in a way that represents superior value delivered vis-à-vis competitors' offerings. This is the true work of marketing.

Philip Kotler is S.C. Johnson and Son Distinguished Professor of International Marketing, Kellogg School of Management, Northwestern University. He may be reached at pkotler@nwu.edu.

Author's Note—The author wishes to thank Professor Evert Gummesson of the School of Business, Stockholm University, for earlier discussion of these issues.

From *Marketing Management*, November/December 2004, pp. 30–35. Copyright © 2004 by American Marketing Association. Reprinted by permission.

The Rise of Trust and Authenticity

By the year 2020, corporate sincerity will trump marketing's "four Ps".

DON PEPPERS AND MARTHA ROGERS

It's an exciting, perhaps even scary, time to be a marketer. Times are changing, media is changing and even customers are changing. If the present is so unpredictable, what will the future look like? We just completed a new study with our [to] Xchange panel that may provide some interesting answers.

We asked our panel of sales and marketing executives, "What will one-to-one marketing look like in 2020?" The results show promise for a more connected and informed customer-company relationship. The future looks bright, as 84% of respondents agree that there will be moderate to high levels of positive change occurring within one-to-one marketing by 2020. This means significant improvement in the ability of organizations to capture and share information, understand customer needs, calculate customer lifetime value, improve the customer experience and provide customers with relevant messaging in their preferred channel.

Similarly, 78% agree that the future of marketing will be based on building authentic relationships moreso than the development of new products. And customers will continue to gain control of the relationship. Online chats, blogs and Internet-based social communities increasingly put control of the brand image into the hands of customers. On the customer service side, one bad experience can have an exponential impact on a company's reputation as customers share their horror stories electronically.

Companies that will break through to customers are the ones that will focus on fairness, transparency and building trust across the board. By 2020, marketers will focus less on gaining short-term advantage and more on working to win and maintain customer trust—in fact, 84% of respondents agree that building customer trust will become marketing's primary objective.

To build customer trust an organization needs to build it into the culture. But that isn't easy. The habits and patterns that build up over time into a "culture" will have far more impact on a company's overall actions than will even the most detailed written procedures. Culture is hard to define, harder to manage and even harder to change. Nonetheless, here are a few pointers:

- You get what you pay for. People do what they are rewarded to do, so give employees incentives for practicing trust-based activities.
- Actions speak louder than words. If you're a senior person at your firm, your employees will imitate what you do, not what you say. The chief privacy officer cannot build customer trust alone. Don't hire a CPO as your privacy strategy. Hire one because of your strategy.
- Find the influencers in your organization. Networks of employees form spontaneously, and the key influencers of other employees' behaviors and attitudes are probably not the most senior people in your organization. Identify those employees that other employees turn to most when asking questions or solving problems.
- Focus on a single, simple, unifying mission. You can rally people around an idea if the idea is universally appealing but specific and tangible enough to offer guidance.
- Celebrate small victories. Find examples of the right cultural values being put into practice, and socialize them within your firm.

So how do you do prepare for the future? The first step is putting one-to-one principles into the day-to-day operation of the organization to improve the customer experience and build trust.

Organizations that plan accordingly will have the early mover advantage. Those that fall behind now by not acting in customers' best interests will fall even further behind their competitors. Keeping up won't be easy, but the effort will be well worth it.

From *Sales & Marketing Management*, May/June 2008, p. 10. Copyright © 2008 by Sales & Marketing Management/Billboard. Reprinted by permission.

Serving Unfair Customers

LEONARD L. BERRY AND KATHLEEN SEIDERS

1. Changing Focus: From Unfair Companies to Unfair Customers

Ten years ago, we published an article titled "Service Fairness: What It Is and Why It Matters" (Seiders & Berry, 1998). Therein, we argued that poor service is not always linked to unfair company practices, but that unfair company practices are always linked to customer perceptions of poor service. We also argued that companies can pay a heavy price when customers believe they have been treated unfairly because customers' responses to perceived injustice often are pronounced, emotional, and retaliatory. We concluded by providing guidelines for managers on preventing unfairness perceptions and effectively managing those that do arise.

Fairness remains a critically important topic today, for it is essential to a mutually satisfactory exchange between two parties. Perceived unfairness undermines trust and diminished trust undermines the strength of relationships. Perceived unfairness is always a negative development. The focus of our original article was company unfairness to customers. Fairness, however, is a two-way street; thus, our present focus is customer unfairness to companies. This time, we examine how customers can be unfair, why it is important, and what companies can do about it.

We are ardent champions of the customer, but we do *not* believe in the maxim that "the customer is always right." Sometimes, the customer is wrong and unfairness often results. That the customer is sometimes wrong is a dirty little secret of marketing, known to many but rarely discussed in public—or in print. What better occasion to broach this unmentionable topic than *Business Horizons'* 50th anniversary?

2. What Is Customer Unfairness and Why Does it Matter?

Customer unfairness occurs when a customer behaves in a manner that is devoid of common decency, reasonableness, and respect for the rights of others, creating inequity and causing harm for a company and, in some cases, its employees and other customers. Customer unfairness should be viewed independent of illegality because unfair customer behavior frequently is legal; repugnant, perhaps, but not necessarily illegal. Our focus in this article is legal customer behavior that is unfair, falling in the so-called "gray area" of company response.

When does a customer's bad judgment (or, when do bad manners) cross the line to "unfairness?" Three concepts are particularly useful in considering this question. The first is the severity of the harm the customer causes. The second is the frequency of the customer's problematic behavior. Figure 1 shows increasing levels of these two factors: "minor," "moderate," and "extreme" for severity of harm and "uncommon," "intermittent," and "recurrent" for frequency of occurrence. Customer behavior that reaches either the "moderate" or "intermittent" level would usually earn the unfairness label. At these levels, the customer crosses a threshold.

The third concept is intentionality. The customer who seeks to take advantage and inflict harm, who willfully disrespects the rights of other parties, will almost always deserve the unfairness label. In some cases, customers may seek to harm a company that they believe has harmed them. The customers' behavior in this case is an act of retaliation. When customers blame a company for unfair treatment, there are fair and unfair ways of responding. Intentionally unfair behavior is usually indefensible.

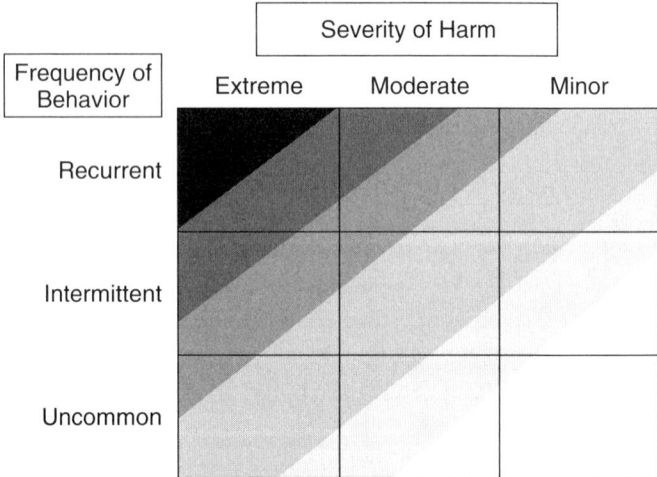

Figure 1 The threshold of customer unfairness. Adapted from Seiders and Berry (1998).

How do companies deal with unfair customers? We contacted executives from a variety of service organizations to solicit their opinions on the topic and to document examples drawn from their experiences. (We restricted our inquiries to consumer services executives based on the assumption that business-to-business services merit a separate exploration.) Our preliminary research reveals that some executives struggle with how to respond to customer unfairness. They don't want to respond in a way that confounds the company's commitment to quality service, which they and others worked hard to instill. Nor do they want to risk offending a still-profitable, albeit problematic, customer. The following comments from four executives illustrate:

- "I think there is a subservient or servant mentality to all service, and to stray from that causes confusion in taking clear and concise action that should be positive for the customer."
- "The lifetime cost of losing a guest exceeds $500, so we go to great lengths to avoid losing them, even when they're wrong. Rather than risk offending guests, we tend to let 'little things' go."
- "My philosophy is that the customer is always right to some degree. It is that matter of degree that determines the action of the company. I believe that if we ever think that the customer is 100% wrong, then we have a high risk of becoming arrogant and not being customer-focused. I know that this may sound crazy, but if we crack open the door to this idea, then I think we can very quickly go down the slippery slope."
- "We are just not used to thinking of guests 'crossing the line.' I don't know that I have ever set up boundaries. I always feel that guests have the right to say what they want and to do what they want, short of inconveniencing another guest or physically harming another guest or employee."

Our position is that companies cannot afford to ignore customer unfairness and should devise a plan to deal with it. Unfair customer behavior can exact a significant toll on employees' job satisfaction and weaken a company's overall service quality. We are not just speculating about this. Recent research by Rupp and Spencer (2006) found that customer injustice increased the degree of effort required for employees to manage their emotions in inter-personal transactions. This increased effort in what is termed *emotional labor* produces added stress, and contributes to employee turnover and overall unwillingness to perform (Grandey, Dickter, & Sin, 2004). Moreover, the injustice of one customer can negatively affect employee behavior toward other customers.

The effects of customer unfairness are often magnified because employees find it difficult to deal with customers who have treated their coworkers disrespectfully, even if the same customers treated them fairly (Rupp, Holub, & Grandey, 2007). Unfair acts are more memorable than typical encounters (Lind & Tyler, 1988), and employees may respond to customer unfairness by discussing incidents with other sympathetic employees, fostering negative word of mouth about customers.

When some customers systematically abuse company policies, such as retail return policies, companies are inclined to either clamp down with tougher rules or increase prices to cover losses. In effect, fair customers are penalized by the actions of unfair customers. Employees are put on the defensive and can become more sensitive to customer manipulation, and more inclined to question the sincerity of customers' communications and the motives that lie behind their actions (Tyler & Bies, 1990). The dynamic can turn adversarial. In short, both employees and customers pay for other customers' misdeeds.

3. Types of Unfair Customers

Over the last 30 years, justice research has focused on three types of justice. *Distributive justice* relates to the outcomes of decisions or allocations; *procedural justice* relates to the procedures used to arrive at those outcomes; and *interactional justice* relates to interpersonal treatment and communication. Interactional justice is demonstrated by interpersonal fairness (i.e., when individuals are treated with dignity and respect) and informational fairness (i.e., when communications are truthful and important decisions are explained) (Rupp & Spencer, 2006). Many studies have found that interactional injustice produces particularly strong responses.

Our exploration of customer unfairness led us to identify distinct types of problem customers. The categories we discuss are neither mutually exclusive nor comprehensive, but describe the most common and problematic types of unfair customers. Each category highlights a different facet of customer unfairness, although some behaviors may logically fit into more than one category. We exclude customers who use stolen credit cards, manipulate price tags, steal merchandise, and stage 'accidents' in service facilities (see, for example, Fullerton & Punj, 2004). The scenarios we consider involve more ambiguity than clear-cut illegality.

3.1. Verbal Abusers

Verbal abusers lash out at employees in a blatantly offensive and disrespectful manner whether in face-to-face transactions, over the telephone, or via the Internet. The verbal abuser capitalizes on the power imbalance commonly present in service encounters: the customer who is 'always right' has the upper hand by default and an opportunity to push the boundaries of fair behavior. One healthcare executive profiled this customer type as "patients and family members who belittle, demean, intimidate, and abuse staff members, and threaten litigation at the slightest lapse in service." Verbal abusers bully front-line employees who typically lack the freedom to defend themselves and, in fact, are expected not to react visibly to unfair treatment by customers. Given the importance of interactional injustice, it is no surprise that the verbal abuser's behavior can have such negative effects on employees.

Customers' verbal abuse of employees is probably more pervasive than most service industry executives would want to admit. There is no accepted protocol for managing a verbal abuse episode, and we suspect that most often this type of incident is not managed. Our favorite story involves the owner of a bicycle store well known for its dedication to customer service. A father was picking up a repaired bicycle for his daughter, who, without telling him, had approved the recommended replacement of both tires (a $40 service). Although the employee patiently and repeatedly explained that the purchase was approved and offered to further verify it, the customer made accusatory remarks and yelled at her angrily, saying at one point, "Either you think I'm stupid or you're stupid. You're trying to rip me off." At that point, Chris Zane, the store's owner, walked up to the customer and said, "I'm Chris Zane; get out of my store and tell all your friends!" After the customer wordlessly slapped $40 on the counter and stormed out, the besieged employee looked at Zane and asked "'... and tell all your friends'?"

Zane explained to her, and other employees who had gravitated to the front of the store, that he wanted it to be clear that he valued his employee infinitely more than a rude, belligerent customer. "I also explained that this was the first time I had ever thrown a customer out of the store and that I would not tolerate my employees being mistreated by anyone.... I believe that my employees need to know that I respect them and expect them to respect our customers. Simply, if I am willing to fire an employee for mistreating a customer (and I have), then I must also be willing to fire a customer for mistreating an employee."

Verbal abusers can also have a profound effect on other customers. This is illustrated by a customer who, during a lunch rush at a very busy restaurant location, insisted that his steak be prepared rare. Although a manager apologized and explained that each steak is prepared uniformly in order to maintain the best quality (and said there would be no charge for the lunch), the customer continued to voice his disapproval to the staff, creating a disturbance that distracted them and degraded the overall experience of the surrounding customers.

In another incident, two customers in a bar loudly criticized the bartender for assisting other patrons before them and then rebuked the restaurant manager who intervened to try to calm them down. The manager then went to the kitchen to check on the progress of their food; when he returned, the two customers were leaving and shouting obscenities as they walked out. A common device of the verbal abuser is the threat to report employees and/or their facility 'to corporate,' a way to prolong employee unease after the offensive incident is over.

3.2. Blamers

Whereas verbal abusers bring misery primarily to customer contact employees, blamers will indict a company's products, policies, and people at all levels for any perceived shortfall. With blamers, 'the company is always wrong.'

Because customers play a co-producer role in many services, they affect the service quality and final outcome. Blamers, however, never see themselves in any way responsible for the outcome, regardless of the scenario. Causal inferences or attributions individuals use to assess the failure of a product or service performance are based on the locus of blame and whether or not the incident could have been controlled (Sheppard, Lewicki, & Minton, 1992). From the blamer's perspective, not only is the company always at fault, but the perceived problem is always controllable.

Blamers are not discriminate about where they voice discord, and every service provider is familiar with this type of customer. A tennis coach had been working with an adult student for about six months when the student learned that an opponent in an upcoming match had worked briefly with the same coach in the past. The student asked for and received specific advice from the coach on how to win the match by attacking the opponent's greatest weaknesses. However, the opponent had corrected these weaknesses and much to the student's chagrin, she could find no way to beat her. In the clubhouse immediately after the match, she raged at her coach for not preparing her well, giving her poor information and lousy lessons, and causing her to lose the match.

In another example, a customer called the headquarters of a national casual dining chain to complain about the price of its cocktails. It seems the gentleman had spent $86 in the bar of this restaurant having drinks and appetizers after work the previous evening. He wanted to talk to someone about what he considered the excessive price of the drinks and how unfair he thought the cost. The switchboard operator noted the caller's angry tone and put him through to the president of the company.

The man re-explained to the president and said he could not believe the restaurant had charged him $7.50 for each of the beverages that he ordered. When asked how many he had consumed, the man said that was beside the point. The president asked the number in the man's party, and the man said only two. The president asked the man when he learned that the drinks were $7.50, which he said was after he paid the bill. The president then asked what the company might do to make it right. The customer replied that he wanted all of his money back; the president responded that this was unfair, as the customer and his guest had consumed enough appetizers and drinks to total $86. A full refund would not be equitable.

The customer became extremely angry, threatening to go online and destroy the company, report it to the Better Business Bureau, and picket in front of its restaurants for the next month. He raised his voice and asserted, "You will feel the effects of my negative PR efforts for a long time to come." Frustrated at the angry customer's threats, the president asked the customer how he could resolve this negative situation without giving the customer his money back for the food and drinks he consumed. The customer calmed down, thought about it, and told the president that if the company donated double the amount of the bill to the customer's favorite charity, he would consider the situation resolved. The president agreed to do so in order to move past the situation and end the disagreement.

The blamer is a particularly difficult type of customer for the healthcare industry. Patients who fail to take responsibility for their own health status often are blamers. Many such patients believe that a treatment cure exists for every condition and thus see no need to take measures to improve their own health. In one case, a patient was referred to a hospital's patient relations department after lodging serious complaints with the president's office. The patient claimed that his wound from surgery failed to heal because the staff ignored his complaints. In reality, the patient was non-compliant with recommended diet and wound care, refused to follow his doctor's recommendations for exercise and physical therapy, and failed to return for a follow-up appointment. At each point of contact, the patient threatened to hire a malpractice attorney.

This example may sound extreme, but in fact we heard a number of such stories. One healthcare professional noted, "I have been in patient relations for more than ten years now, and I can attest to the fact that these patients are a huge burden on the healthcare system. They tie up resources that could be used to improve services for all of our patients." An executive from a different healthcare institution expressed a similar view: "I hear from the same patients over and over again, and once a resolution is offered, many times it's a prolonged argument because it's their way or no way. Unfortunately, these cases are no longer rare."

3.3. Rule Breakers

Rule breakers readily ignore policies and procedures when they find them to be inconvenient or at odds with their own goals. Rule breakers generally ignore the honor code by which other customers abide. In chronic cases, a rule breaker may be a mild version of a con artist. Rule breakers are not concerned with equity, which is the first principle of distributive justice. Equity exists in an exchange when participants' rewards equal their contributions; rule breakers seek to optimize their rewards at the expense of the company. This not only harms the company, but also puts company employees in a tenuous and uncomfortable situation as they attempt to protect their employer from customer wrongdoing.

The damage done by rule breakers varies, of course, based on the nature of the rules and polices that are being broken. A restaurant that offers "all you can eat" shrimp entrees encounters some patrons who share with their tablemates, even though the menu clearly states that the price is per person. Managers are not quick to put servers in the awkward position of having to remind guests they are breaking the rule, but will do so if the 'sharing' gets out of hand.

A retailer with a catalog operation is subject to 'customers who bend the facts' (in the words of one executive) when post-delivery complainers assert that a telephone sales associate told them that shipping was free. When this happens, a company representative will listen to a tape of the original call and will usually hear the shipping charges discussed. For smaller transactions with first-time customers, the retailer apologizes, deducts the shipping charge, and restates the shipping fee policy for future transactions. For larger transactions, the customer is told that the call was reviewed and the company is not sure why there was confusion. Once customers realize that a company representative has reviewed the call and knows what actually was said, they rarely demand a shipping refund. "It's a nice way of saying we know what happened without becoming confrontational," explains a company manager.

One type of rule breaker can be termed a *rule maker*. Rule makers expect to be exempted from the rules and demand special treatment because of perceived superior status. Both rule breakers and rule makers demonstrate unfairness to other customers who are behaving according to norms and convention. When certain customers are allowed to break the rules because of their social or financial status, the equality principle of distributive justice is defied (Grover, 1991). A hospital executive describes the rule maker in this way:

"We have had patients who believe that there is some special level of care that we are constantly holding back, and if we knew how special they were that they would get this special executive level care. This is common in the family of trustees and board members. These are families that expect to be cared for only by departmental chairmen. We have coined the concept *chairman syndrome*."

Often, it is the family-member-turned-advocate who demands to make the rules. For example, a patient's daughter insisted, "I want all of the labs printed out each day and handed to me when I walk in in the morning." A patient's son threatened, "I am an attorney and I demand to know what is going on with my mother!" A corporate chairman transferred his child by private jet to a hospital in another city when his company's physicians (non-pediatric, without privileges to practice in the hospital) were not allowed to direct the team of hospital physicians who were treating the child. These scenarios seem almost amusing until one considers the extent to which medical staff members and other hospital patients may be adversely affected by this disregard for the rules.

3.4. Opportunists

Opportunists have their antennae up for easy paths to personal financial gain. This customer's modus operandi can be demanding compensation by fabricating or exaggerating problems or flaws in a product or service. While this type of opportunist stiffs the company, there is a second type that stiffs 'the little guy.' These penny-ante opportunists, for example, don't tip (or don't adequately tip) service employees because they don't have to; that is, they can get away with it. This behavior is distasteful because, like many cases of verbal abuse, it hurts front-line employees whose tips often represent a significant percentage of their pay.

Opportunists frequently use gamesmanship to optimize their gain. A customer observed a plumbing problem in a restaurant restroom and complained to the manager, who called a plumbing service for the repair, and sent an employee to clean up. The customer contacted the company's customer relations office, complained about the state of the restroom, and requested a refund for his party's $80 meal. In response, the company sent $30 in gift certificates, in addition to an $80 check and an apology. The customer called the company again, stating that $30 was not enough to cause him to return to the restaurant because it would not cover the cost of his dining companions' meals. He was persistent, calling several times to express his displeasure in the amount of the gift certificates. In turn, the company sent an additional $50 in gift certificates, bringing the total compensation to $160, a nice return for encountering a plumbing problem.

The opportunist may not be a chronic gold digger, but rather just someone who recognizes an opportunity to take financial advantage of a company's service failure and recovery efforts. For example, when an ambulatory surgery patient complained to her hospital that her lingerie had been lost, she was offered reimbursement. She claimed that the cost was $400 and, because this was an unusually high amount, the hospital inquired about the value of the items. The patient said she had not kept the receipts. To maintain good will, the hospital paid the $400 and apologized.

The opportunist doesn't require a service failure to take action. Some users of professional services, for example, maneuver to gain pro bono consultation from a prior provider. A communications coach periodically receives 'pick your brain' phone calls from former clients. Because these customers don't intend to pay for this 'informal' advice, the consultant is forced into an awkward position by clients attempting to exploit the relationship.

3.5. Returnaholics

This customer is a hybrid, with traits common to rule breakers and opportunists but engaged in a specific type of activity: returning products to stores. Returnaholics are rule breakers in that they don't adhere to the spirit of the company's return policies, whereby returns are accepted for defective products, a post-purchase change of mind, and gift exchange. In many cases, the returnaholic never intends to keep the product to begin with. Returnaholics are opportunists because they exploit retailer return policies for their own benefit. There are two types of returnaholics: situational and chronic.

Situational returnaholics become active under certain conditions. For example, one retailer's sales of equipment such as snow blowers, generators, and chainsaws would spike just before a major weather event but then fall precipitously shortly thereafter when many customers returned new *and* used equipment, and even products such as ice melt and flashlights, demanding refunds. It was not unusual for a store to see more than half the generators sold the week before a storm returned within two weeks after the storm. This phenomenon was a painful and expensive exercise for the retailer and its vendors. Reluctantly, the company adopted a stricter return policy covering specific items to better manage after-the-storm return rates.

Some situational returners use an item until it is damaged or worn out and then return it for a full refund or new item, claiming it is defective because it 'should have held up better.' They expect the refund to be 100% of purchase price because they believe that retailers carry a manufacturer's warranty for all items indefinitely.

Chronic, or serial, returnaholics are referred to by some store operators as "rental" customers. One customer of a men's shoe and accessories chain started shopping at two of the company's stores in 2001. The customer would often buy a product in store A and return it (after wearing it) to store B, using a different name for the return transaction. He also would complain to upper management about quality or the service he received in hopes of getting discounts on future purchases. The company realized this pattern of behavior spanned six years, once it figured out that all of this activity involved one customer rather than two. In that period, the customer had purchased 23 pairs of shoes and returned 17 for net sales of $381 (which obviously did not come close to covering the cost of 17 pairs of worn and returned shoes). When the customer was contacted about his serial returning behavior, he became angry; he was told it was obvious the company could not please him and that it could no longer afford to do business with him.

Chronic returnaholics can be very crafty. Some purchase expensive items with credit cards to earn rewards or airline points and then return the merchandise during certain periods of the billing cycle when the points will not be removed from their account. Some purchase large quantities of items, try to sell them on the Internet or in private shops, and then return them for a refund if they don't sell. Some interior designers will purchase items for a specific event, such as an open house or a staged model home, and then return the items for a refund. These are but a few examples of how chronic returnaholics operate.

4. What Managers Can Do

Unfair customers need to be dealt with effectively. They can be a big problem for poorly managed companies with customer unfriendly policies and practices that provoke retaliatory customer behavior. Unfair customers also can bedevil well-managed companies that devote considerable energy and investment to serving customers superbly. After all, these companies build their culture on delivering an excellent experience and value to customers. As a long-time operations executive of one of America's most admired supermarket chains told us:

"I think companies that are truly committed to customer service have a difficult time dealing with unfair customers. We always [tell] our store managers that we will give the unfair customer the benefit of the doubt one or two times. The third time, we [will] fire them as a customer."

So, what should managers do about unfair customers?

4.1. Manage Customers to a Standard of Behavior

Companies cannot build a reputation for service excellence unless, in addition to serving customers competently, they treat them with respect and commitment. Treating customers with respect and commitment requires an organizational culture in which employees, themselves, are treated with respect and commitment. Managers that allow customers to behave badly (e.g., to verbally abuse employees, to create a disturbance, to rip off the company) in the name of "customer service" undermine the organizational culture upon which excellent service depends. Appeasing a customer who doesn't deserve appeasement does not go unnoticed within the organization. The bicycle shop owner who ordered an abusive customer out of the store strengthened his culture that day, rather than weakened it.

Just as managers need to manage employees, they should also "manage" customers when the situation warrants. A good manager certainly would intervene if made aware of an employee who treated customers rudely or broke important company policies. Likewise, a manager should be ready to intervene when made aware of customer misbehavior. Effective "customer management," as illustrated by the manager's intervention in the bar ruckus, demonstrated to employees and nearby customers that the disruptive party's behavior was unacceptable and would not be allowed to continue. If the customers did quiet down, the bartender could more easily interact with them because the manager, and not he, addressed their misbehavior.

4.2. Don't Penalize Fair Customers

Companies should design their business operations for the vast majority of their customers who are fair and responsible, rather than for the unfair minority. Firms should not allow unfair customer behavior to instigate needlessly restrictive policies that disrespect the good intentions of most customers. The better approach, for the business culture and reputation, is to deal fairly but firmly with unfair customers specifically.

The retailer experiencing heavy returns of outdoor power equipment following a major storm illustrates this guideline. The retailer could have done nothing, in effect enabling unreasonable customer behavior. Alternatively, the company could have installed a more restrictive return policy for all merchandise, which would have affected all customers, not just returnaholics, and likely hurt the company's reputation for customer service. The company's implementation of a more restrictive return policy for specific products with high afterstorm return rates made returns more difficult for situational returnaholics. The new policy was designed specifically to deal with opportunistic customers.

The goodwill created by *not* treating all customers as untrustworthy is an investment worth making. A supermarket operations executive illustrates this lesson with the following story:

"When I was at [Company X], we had a policy that if customers forgot their checkbook, we would let them leave with their groceries after filling out a simple IOU. The great majority of customers would immediately return to pay the amount. This policy created a great deal of positive goodwill. However, every year we had to write off a significant amount of loss because some customers would not come back to pay off the IOU. I remember one year it was in excess of $30,000. We would make attempts to recover the money, but I don't recall trying to prosecute anyone for it. Our CFO wanted to stop giving the IOUs, but I would not let him. I treated it as a marketing expense because it created so much goodwill. Interestingly, when we started accepting credit, I thought that the loss number would plunge, assuming customers would carry their credit card and use that instead of a check. However, the loss number remained the same. I believe there will always be customers who will take advantage of you. They are very intentional about their unfairness. The loss incurred by them has to be built into your financial model because you should not penalize the great customers for the deeds of a few bad customers."

4.3. Prepare for Customer Unfairness

Companies should strive to both reduce the frequency of unfair customer episodes and effectively manage specific incidents. This requires advance planning. Managers need to determine the kinds of situations that are most likely to produce unfair customer behavior, given the nature of the company's business. Managers can determine at-risk situations for unfairness by: (1) using past experiences to identify conditions in which customer and company goals might conflict; (2) soliciting employee input on causes of customer unfairness; and (3) surveying customers previously involved in unfairness incidents to gain their perspective on what happened and why. Once at-risk exchanges are identified, managers can evaluate the firm's existing practices to consider needed changes. Employee and customer input can again be helpful at this stage (Seiders & Berry, 1998).

Preparing for customer unfairness also involves investing in education and training of front-line employees and managers on how to prevent and manage the most likely types of incidents. Particular emphasis should be placed on the rationale for company policies that respond to customer misbehavior, or that may encourage it. Employees who intervene need to be able to explain the company's position effectively, which makes communications training for dealing with problem customers a priority. Contact personnel (and their managers) would benefit from focused training on the best ways to interact with verbal abusers, rule breakers, returnaholics, and other problem customers. Organizational justice researchers recommend the use of explanation as an impression management strategy (Sitkin & Bies, 1993). Explanations have been found to diffuse negative reactions and convey respect, among other positive outcomes (Seiders & Berry, 1998), although they will not always be effective with unfair customers.

Collecting pertinent information is another way to prepare for customer unfairness. Information can clarify the appropriate company response to a customer incident. The catalog retailer which captures information on every shipping transaction is better prepared to assess post-transaction claims. Has the customer complained about this issue before? If so, did the company explain its policy? What is the customer's purchase history? "Research is a great way to keep things on the up and up," explains a company executive. "It's on a case-by-case basis."

4.4. Don't Reward Misbehavior

As mentioned, companies that take pride in the quality of their service often struggle to satisfactorily resolve acts of customer opportunism. Such companies are so culturally focused on serving customers well and giving them the benefit of the doubt when problems arise that they may offer more than they should to reach resolution. Doing more than should be done for an unfair customer rewards misbehavior and encourages future incidents.

Companies need to respond to customer unfairness with fairness—and firmness. They should respond to unreasonableness with reason. It isn't easy. The case of the restaurant bathroom plumbing problem is instructive. The customer had a legitimate complaint about the state of the restroom, but then used the incident opportunistically to extract as much as possible from the restaurant. The company's first response of a full refund for the party's meal, a small gift certificate, and an apology was fair. The additional gift certificates went beyond fair. The second helping of gift certificates was excessive, reinforcing customer opportunism. Companies need to be willing to cut the cord with unfair customers.

Sometimes unfair customers recant when dealt with appropriately, as shown by a postscript to the bicycle story. The abusive customer phoned the owner to apologize three hours after being told to leave the store, explaining that he had argued with his wife prior to visiting the store. Once he returned home and verified the accuracy of the store employee's explanation, he realized he had been unreasonable. He asked that the store not blame the daughter for his actions and that he be allowed to shop in the store again. He also commented that he respected the owner for supporting his employee, even if it might mean losing a customer. The owner thanked him for the call, welcomed him back to the store, and indicated that the apology would be conveyed to the employee.

5. Rethinking Old Wisdom

Following the old wisdom—the customer is always right—has operated as the basic rule in business for so long that it has become entrenched as an "absolute truth." The practical reality, however, is that sometimes the customer is wrong by behaving unfairly.

Customer unfairness can exact a heavy cost. Company goodwill, employee relations, financial position, and service to responsible customers can deteriorate when customers engage in unfair tactics such as verbal abuse, blaming, rule breaking, opportunism, and "returnaholism."

Companies must acknowledge the unfair behavior of certain customers and manage them effectively. Some customers may need to be fired. Denying the existence and impact of unfair customers erodes the ethics of fairness upon which great service companies thrive.

References

Fullerton, R. A., & Punj, G. (2004). Repercussions of promoting an ideology of consumption: Consumer misbehavior. *Journal of Business Research, 57*(11), 1239–1249.

Grandey, A. A., Dickter, D. N., & Sin, H. P. (2004). The customer is not always right: Customer aggression and emotion regulation of service employees. *Journal of Organizational Behavior, 25*(3), 397–418.

Grover, S. L. (1991). Predicting the perceived fairness of parental leave policies. *Journal of Applied Psychology, 76*(2), 247–255.

Lind, E. A., & Tyler, T. R. (1988). *The social psychology of procedural justice.* New York: Plenum Press.

Rupp, D. E., & Spencer, S. (2006). When customers lash out: The effects of customers' interactional injustice on emotional labor and the mediating role of discrete emotions. *Journal of Applied Psychology, 91*(4), 971–978.

Rupp, D. E., Holub, A. S., & Grandey, A. A. (2007). A cognitive–emotional theory of customer injustice and emotional labor. In D. De Cremer (Ed.), *Advances in the psychology of justice and affect* (pp. 199–226). Charlotte, NC: Information Age Publishing.

Seiders, K., & Berry, L. L. (1998). Service fairness: What it is and why it matters. *Academy of Management Executive, 12*(2), 8–21.

Sheppard, B. H., Lewicki, R. J., & Minton, J. W. (1992). *Organizational justice: The search for fairness in the workplace.* New York: Lexington Books.

Sitkin, S. B., & Bies, R. J. (1993). Social accounts in conflict situations: Using explanations to manage conflict. *Human Relations, 46*(3), 349–370.

Tyler, T. R., & Bies, R. J. (1990). Beyond formal procedures: The interpersonal context of procedural justice. In J. Carroll (Ed.), *Advances in applied social psychology: Business settings* (pp. 77–98). Hillsdale, NJ: Lawrence Erlbaum Associates.

From *Business Horizons*, 2008. Copyright © 2008 by Kelley School of Business. Reprinted by permission of Elsevier Inc. via Rightslink.

Article 39

Dirty Deeds

The mortgage crisis has blighted the landscape with boarded-up houses. Now a few cities are holding giant lenders accountable for what foreclosure leaves behind.

MICHAEL OREY

On Dec. 17 in a windowless Buffalo courtroom, Cindy T. Cooper, a prosecutor for the city, buzzes among a dozen men in suits, cutting deals. "You've got to unboard [the house], go in, and clean it out," she tells one. "If all the repairs are done quickly, I wouldn't ask for any fines." To another, she says, "the gutters weren't done right," and asks to see receipts for the work. It's "Bank Day" in Judge Henry J. Nowak's housing courtroom, more typically a venue where landlords and tenants duke it out over evictions and back rent. Instead, Cooper is asking lawyers for CitiFinancial, JPMorgan Chase, and Countrywide Financial to fix problems like peeling paint, broken masonry, and overgrown or trash-filled yards at houses the city says the banks are responsible for maintaining. It may be surprising to find these financial-services giants hauled before this obscure local tribunal. In fact, Cooper and Nowak are at the forefront of a pioneering effort to deal with a vexing problem: the surging number of vacant and abandoned homes resulting from the mortgage market meltdown. The vacancies occur when lenders bring foreclosure suits against delinquent borrowers. Mere notice that such an action might be filed often sends residents packing. In Buffalo and other Rust Belt cities, the problem has been particularly acute, because in many cases banks are abandoning the houses, too, after determining that their value is so low that it's not worth laying claim to them. When city officials try to hold someone responsible for dilapidated properties, they often find the homeowner and bank pointing fingers at each other. Indeed, the houses fall into a kind of legal limbo that Cleveland housing attorney Kermit J. Lind calls "toxic title". While formal ownership remains with a borrower who has fled, the bank retains its lien on the property. That opens up a dispute over who is responsible for taxes and maintenance. Even when lenders do complete the foreclosure, they may walk away from the property, leaving it to be taken by a city for unpaid taxes, a process that can take years. Orphaned properties quickly fall into disrepair, the deterioration sometimes hastened by vandals who trash the interiors, lighting fires and ripping out wiring and pipes to sell for scrap. Squatters or drug dealers may move in.

The impact goes far beyond the defaulting homeowner, as neighbors and entire communities confront a spreading blight. Vacant residences deprive cities of tax revenue and can cost them thousands to maintain. A 2001 Temple University study in Philadelphia found that simply being within 150 feet of an abandoned property knocked $7,600 off a home's value.

> **"The days are gone when you can do a foreclosure and walk away without taking care of the property."**
> —Cooper

In Buffalo, prosecutor Cooper is bringing lenders before Judge Nowak to hold them accountable. Wielding the threat of liens, which can hold up the lenders' other real estate transactions, she aims to make banks keep foreclosed homes in good condition until a buyer can be found. As an alternative, Cooper or Nowak may try to get lenders to donate properties to community groups or to pay for demolition when houses are beyond repair. "At least in Buffalo," says Cooper, "the days are gone when you can do a foreclosure and walk away without taking care of the property."

Those charged with violations by Cooper include participants all along the complex mortgage-industry food chain, from loan originators to servicers to the Wall Street trusts that buy up the vast majority of home loans and then securitize them. A similar initiative is under way in Cleveland, where Judge Raymond L. Pianka puts lenders on trial in absentia when they fail to respond to charges.

Even places with high property values, like Chula Vista, Calif., a San Diego suburb, are taking steps to avoid the neglect that can occur during lengthy foreclosures. "It seems like a number of the lenders aren't even doing things that are in their own best interest to preserve the asset," says Pianka—a problem he attributes to the fragmented nature of the business. "It's not an address.

It's not a property. It's just a loan number," he says. "So they'll push a button in San Francisco, and it will set things in motion to do things with [a] property that don't even make sense."

Spreading the Pain

The proceedings in Pianka's and Nowak's courtrooms offer a sobering reminder that underlying the attenuated ownership and esoteric products spun out of mortgages are actual buildings, some with leaky roofs or broken porch railings. The industry denies responsibility for properties to which it has not taken title. "The notion that a mortgage company has an obligation to make repairs on a property that it doesn't even own is very hard to comprehend," says Marco Cercone, a Buffalo attorney who represents a range of lenders before Nowak in the courtroom. Cooper says that banks and other financial firms once extolled houses as the best possible collateral for a loan. Now they're stuck with that collateral, and they don't like it.

If there ever is a national response to the messy legacy left by foreclosures, it might include something like the Buffalo system, which seeks to take action before the presence of abandoned houses hurts entire neighborhoods and which spreads the pain among many players. "We're kind of a crystal ball into what might happen" elsewhere, Cooper says.

Lenders may rue the day the State University of New York at Buffalo admitted Cooper to pursue a PhD in sociology and a law degree. The subject of her doctoral thesis, submitted in December, 2006: the role of banks in residential abandonment and why they should be accountable for property-code violations. The fourth-generation Californian says she quickly became attached to Buffalo for its history and architecture. Now 33, Cooper and her husband are rehabilitating a house that she bought after getting an IRS tax lien removed from the property. "My passion for this work is because I love this town," she says.

While researching her thesis, Cooper interned for Judge Nowak. Tall, soft-spoken, and unfailingly courteous, the judge, 39, began holding Bank Day earlier this year and schedules it once a month. The civility of the proceedings and the large number of bank lawyers in attendance belie a noteworthy fact: They are there under coercion. A few years ago, Nowak says, "the city became increasingly frustrated with the banks' role" in contributing to Buffalo's abandoned-property problem. (Estimates put the number of abandoned homes in the city at between 5,000 and 10,000.) In 2004, New York State amended the definition of "owner" in its property maintenance code to include not just titleholders but others who had "control" over a premises.

While the statute makes no reference to lenders, Nowak contends that the letters banks send to defaulting homeowners threatening to boot them from their houses show that they have begun to "assert some measure of control." On this premise, Nowak says, Buffalo began contacting banks "en masse" about foreclosed properties, but "a lot of times we'd just be rebuffed and ignored."

Cooper, as an intern, suggested a tactic that the judge adopted. When banks ignored summonses for code violations, Nowak began entering default judgments against them and imposing the maximum fine, which can reach $10,000 to $15,000. For a big bank, that's not much. The real pain comes because the fines give the city a lien that impedes the banks' ability to buy or sell other properties in the area. In addition, when lenders come to his court to get residents evicted from a particular property, Nowak refuses to grant the request until the bank addresses violations outstanding on other properties. Judge Pianka employs similar tactics in Cleveland. On Dec. 10, for example, he assessed a $50,000 fine against an absentee defendant, Mortgage Lenders Network USA, for 21 code violations at a home.

Even far from the Rust Belt, in places where empty houses retain significant value, the lending industry seems to have trouble preserving its collateral when homes are abandoned during foreclosure. In Chula Vista, a number of houses have been trashed by college students who have held parties in the vacant properties. In other cases, pillagers pull up in rental trucks to cart away cabinets, wood flooring, and fixtures stripped from the homes. But in October, an ordinance went into effect requiring lenders to register and maintain houses that have been abandoned during foreclosure.

The Story of an Orphaned Home

How properties descend into legal limbo—and how communities are trying to deal with the problem.

1. Abandonment

The borrower leaves the house. Sometimes this happens as soon as the lender sends a letter announcing that a mortgage has gone into default; sometimes it happens after the lender begins to foreclose.

2. Neglect

The foreclosure process, which gives the bank the legal right to seize the house as collateral, can take 12 months or more. If the property is left unprotected, it can become a magnet for vandalism and decay.

3. Ownership Limbo

The lender decides that the value of the loan, plus legal costs of foreclosure, back taxes, and repairs, exceeds the potential sale price. So the lender stops foreclosure efforts. The title remains in the name of the borrower.

4. Public Nuisance

Housing inspectors finally crack down. Consulting property records, they cite the borrower for violations, which can lead to fines and even jail. But the borrower appears in court and says he thought the bank took the house.

5. Resolution

Officials are expanding the definition of who owns a house. In Buffalo, prosecutors are hauling banks that abandon foreclosure proceedings into court and seeking stiff fines. If the house is unsalable, lenders may have to pay for demolition.

Compliance, says Chula Vista code enforcement manager Doug Leeper, has been spotty. "What I need them to do is keep the water on and keep the lawn green," he says, noting that the first sign of abandonment is often a yard that has turned brown and a pool that has gone murky green.

That slide into decrepitude is exactly what Cooper is trying to head off in Buffalo. In February, she joined the city's law department, where one of her duties is prosecuting banks. She and Nowak each say their main objective is not collecting fines but bringing banks to the table to try to find constructive solutions for dealing with abandoned property. That doesn't mean borrowers are off the hook. Cooper typically charges both borrowers and lenders, and Nowak may fine homeowners or sentence them to community service. "Can both be responsible?" asks Cooper. "Absolutely."

The approach in Buffalo is paying dividends. In a case on Dec. 17, attorney Cercone addressed the status of a house that had gone into foreclosure in 2006. Cercone was representing JPMorgan Chase and Ocwen Loan Servicing (which in turn were representatives of a securitized trust that had purchased the mortgage). Cercone submitted an affidavit showing that Ocwen, which had been cited for violations in December, 2006, had spent $30,000 to repair the property, including scraping lead paint from the entire house. In September, the affidavit notes, JP Morgan Chase sold the property at a loss of $19,500, not including the cost of repairs. "The bank in this case dealt with the property as well as could be done under the circumstances," Nowak said from the bench, and he agreed not to impose any fines.

Tortuous Trails

Still, even with novel and aggressive tactics, the path to resolution for many properties in Buffalo can be tortuous and protracted. A house at 1941 Niagara St.—one of dozens of properties that Cooper examined as a graduate student—has yet to see its final chapter, though it may be close.

In 1998, Elizabeth M. Manuel obtained a $34,500 mortgage on the property from IMC Mortgage (since acquired by Citibank). By 2002, the loan had been sold into a securitization trust administered by Chase Manhattan (now JPMorgan Chase) as trustee. It also went into default, and Chase began foreclosure proceedings. In a court filing, Manuel (who could not be located for comment) said she left the home while the foreclosure action was pending. More than five years later, though, the title remains in her name. The house, although still standing, has become a fire-gutted wreck.

In May 2007, Nowak issued a default judgment against Chase for $9,000. But these cases can be notoriously difficult to untangle. Thomas A. Kelly, a spokesman for the bank, notes that Chase sold its trustee business to the Bank of New York Mellon in October, 2006, and couldn't locate anyone at Chase able to comment. But he reiterates the industry view that Chase can't be held responsible for maintaining a property it never owned. He acknowledges that if a home didn't seem worth taking as collateral, the bank may have made a decision to "just walk away."

The value of 1941 Niagara, estimate city assessors, is $4,500, of which $4,300 represents the value of the land. The home, Cooper says, is slated for "imminent" demolition.

From *BusinessWeek*, January 2008. Copyright © 2008 by BusinessWeek. Reprinted by permission of the McGraw-Hill Companies.

Searching for the Top

HR professionals need to know how to tell if an executive search firm is walking the straight and narrow or crossing the line.

STEPHENIE OVERMAN

Executive search consultants, often called headhunters, wrestle with various ethical issues, but the question of whether it's OK to raid a company for candidates isn't one of them.

Executive search "by definition moves people from one firm to another. We should not feel ashamed about it," says Christopher J. Clarke, president and chief executive officer of Boyden World Corp., a global executive search firm headquartered in Hawthorne, N.Y. "We are helping market forces to operate efficiently. By providing the best leaders for clients, we are helping these firms to create growth, wealth and employment."

Industry spokesman Peter M. Felix makes a similar economic case. "You want a mobile labor market," he says, because mobility "is part of the reason you have a dynamic economy."

Felix is president of the New York-based Association of Executive Search Consultants (AESC), representing retained executive search consulting firms. It would be "ludicrous," he says, to think that "an individual can't consider an offer from an alternative employer." Besides, he continues, "you don't 'raid' a company for senior executives. You carefully and sensibly recruit them. . . . You approach a candidate in a sensitive way to find out if [the position] is appropriate for them."

The aboveboard purposes notwithstanding, executive search practitioners regularly encounter ethical issues as they gain access to clients' internal staffing matters and potential candidates' personal and professional information. In fact, for an executive search firm, an ethical concern can center on what it does with what it knows about companies or executives.

So when HR decides to enlist an executive search firm's help in filling a top slot, it becomes important to determine how a given firm does business in sensitive circumstances and how it handles inside information. In effect, HR professionals need to know whether an executive search firm's practices and assurances are ethical and not dubious.

The Ground Rules

Keep in mind that the profession is not regulated, says David Lord, founder of Executive Search Information Services, a consulting firm in Harrisville, N.H. The firm helps boards of directors, line executives and executive staffing directors evaluate, select and contract with well-qualified search consultants. It also measures search firms' performances.

"There's nothing [a firm] can get certified in," Lord says. "It is very much 'buyer beware' for companies."

Nonetheless, the AESC has developed a code of ethics for the profession, and there are executive search principles to which a firm should adhere if it is committed to behaving ethically and acting first and foremost in its clients' interests. Two major principles: confidentiality and loyalty.

The AESC's ethics code says executive search consultants should display professionalism, integrity and competence; they also should be objective and accurate, maintain confidentiality and "serve their clients loyally."

Confidentiality, in particular, "is the hallmark of our profession," says Peri Z. Hansen, a client partner in the Los Angeles office of Korn/Ferry International, a major executive search company.

The AESC's professional guidelines call on members to "use confidential information received from clients only for purposes of conducting the assignment. Disclose such confidential information only to those individuals within the firm or to those appropriately qualified or interested candidates who have a need to know the information. [Do] not use such confidential information for personal gain, nor provide inside information to any other parties for their personal gain."

To most executive search consultants, loyalty to the client means there should be no "parallel processing"—no offering of a candidate to more than one client at a time. "We see that as putting two clients in conflict over the same person," Clarke says. The practice amounts to "representing the candidate rather than the client," he says.

What's Off-Limits

Loyalty can also mean keeping the newly placed candidate and the client off-limits for future recruiting. Lord explains the rationale: "If I'm a search firm doing work for your company, I had better not be taking people out of your company."

Recruiters on Recruiting

Richard E. Barnes
The president and co-owner of Barnes Development Group in Mequon, Wis., a boutique firm specializing in manufacturing, has seen much change during two decades. "I used to jump on a plane and interview all over the country. Today, we get far more regional searches because companies don't want to relocate candidates." Candidates in manufacturing are less receptive to being contacted and considered for jobs, he says, because they receive commissions and bonuses and they're worried about "last in, first out." In other words, "people are fearful of changing from a good job where they have security to the unknown."

Peri Z. Hansen
The client partner in the Los Angeles office of Korn/Ferry International, and a member of its Legal Specialist Group, previously practiced law in Southern California. She also was associated with a national legal search firm, where she specialized in the placement of attorneys. Having been a practicing attorney "certainly helps in terms of due diligence, in understanding the work of the client and in vetting candidates" she says. "It's a matter of trust and credibility."

Linda Bialecki
The founder of Bialecki Inc., a New York boutique firm that recruits senior Wall Street talent for investment banks, hedge funds and private equity firms, says having an MBA helps establish her credibility. "You really have to understand what's going on" in the industry, she says, and her graduate degree makes clear "that my interest is finance. . . . You have to be involved in an industry that you have personal interest in."

Wendy Murphy
A leader in the Chief Human Resources Officer functional practice at Heidrick & Struggles, and managing partner in the firm's Stamford, Conn., office, has extensive HR experience, including 10 years with Organizational Dynamics Inc., a global consulting and training company, where she worked in the Asia Pacific region. Other executive positions include partner in TMP Worldwide Executive Search and managing director of the Human Resources Center of Excellence at Korn/Ferry International. "It's easier to work with HR people [as candidates] because they do understand" the process. "Their ability to answer some of the tough questions . . . tells you how effective they are."

Dr. Gilbert J. Carrara Jr.
The partner in charge of New York-based Battalia Winston International's Life Science practice conducts senior-level searches for pharmaceutical, biotechnology, health-care and health-information companies, managed-care organizations and academic medical centers. Venture capital firms have retained him to find leaders for small and medium-sized biotechnology and biopharmaceutical companies. Previously, he worked at Nicholson International and Korn/Ferry International, founded the Total Pediatric Extended Care Center and was associate medical director for a small pharmaceutical company. Being a physician helps him stay current with the technology of the life sciences, he says. Plus, "people feel more comfortable with like-thinking folks."

Tim Ward
A principal with the McCormick Group's Government Contracting Services practice in Washington, D.C., specializes in placing senior executives with providers of government information technology services. With "an even tighter IT market today," he says, he relies on the latest technology and a strong network "to keep in touch with the best and brightest." His background includes five years in mortgage sales, including two years as owner of a mortgage brokerage firm.

> "Any client that we've done work for is off-limits for at least five years' as a recruiting target."
>
> —Richard E. Barnes, president and co-owner, Barnes Development Group

For smaller search firms, such as Barnes Development Group in Mequon, Wis., and Bialecki Inc. in New York, establishing what is off-limits can be straightforward. "Any client that we've done work for is off-limits for at least five years" as a recruiting target itself, says Richard E. Barnes, president and co-owner of the Barnes firm. "We're small enough that we don't have a lot of problems," he says, and "we will never recruit the person we put in the company as long as he or she is with the company. That's a lifetime hands-off policy. We have search engagement details that specifically spell that out."

Linda Bialecki, founder of the Bialecki firm, agrees that "it's very simple for a small firm" to keep its clients off-limits because it deals with only a few companies. Yet other types of questions still arise: "What if the client cancels the search? Is it still off-limits? What if they paid you a retainer?" Does the search firm then keep the retainer?

A large executive search company or one that does a great deal of work in one industry finds it harder to impose areas that are off-limits because doing so would severely restrict its business opportunities, Lord says. The trend is to narrow the scope, for example, to exclude the just-placed person and immediate co-workers instead of the entire company. "But some companies really care about this. They do not want to work with a search firm that would be taking people out."

Indeed, many clients "lay a great deal of emphasis that you're not going to take their people away," Clarke says. "It's unethical to place somebody in a firm and, knowing all we do, then go back and take their people away."

> ### Approaching a Possible Candidate
>
> A good executive search consultant is trained to find out exactly why a candidate really wants to leave his or her current employer, says Leslie Sorg Ramsay, a principal with the McCormick Group in the executive search firm's Washington, D.C., office. "We ask, 'Can you get what you need by staying where you are?'"
>
> If a candidate is considering changing jobs primarily for more money, the client may lose out to a counter offer from the current employer, Ramsay says, meaning that the candidate was a risky prospect from the beginning. "Part of ethics" in the executive search profession, she says, "is making sure we are not wasting people's time."
>
> Executives who are happy where they are probably are not good recruitment candidates, says Dale Winston, chair and chief executive officer of Battalia Winston International in New York. "We recruit people who are blocked from moving to the next step, who have a problem with a new boss. There's nothing unethical about helping a frustrated person move. There's no more cradle to grave, no hidden contract on either side," to keep an employee at one company.
>
> Winston finds that when executives make a move, there are three reasons for the decision:
>
> First, the new post is a better opportunity, a promotion.
>
> Second, the executive likes the people making the offer. "They don't move unless they're comfortable," Winston says.
>
> Third is the money—but "it's third," she emphasizes, "and if the first two aren't there, you can throw in all the money in the world and the person won't take the job."
> —Stephenie Overman

Large search companies are taking a closer look at who's off-limits because it's increasingly challenging to recruit great talent.

Large search companies are taking a closer look at who's off-limits because it's increasingly challenging to recruit great talent. "We want to provide diverse options," Hansen says. "We want balance, to do what's reasonable for both sides. Gone are the days of clear-cut rules [on who is off-limits]. It's more finely tailored to take into consideration the length and volume of the relationship."

No Fudging, No Shortcuts

Ethical headhunters take care not to misrepresent themselves, their clients or the candidates during the search process. They treat candidates fairly and "avoid being used as a tool to discriminate against qualified candidates" by agreeing to restrict the pool of candidates in some unfair way, Lord says. They are honest about the purpose of initial calls to potential candidates.

Barnes notes that it may be difficult to get into organizations to find names of good candidates, but "lying to get access to them" is not acceptable practice.

When a headhunter discovers that a candidate has lied—about a degree or a job title, for example—or has tried to conceal a material fact, the headhunter's responsibility is to "have the candidate help you understand how that error or omission occurred," says John Rothschild, managing director of the Chicago office of Edward W Kelley & Partners.

Sometimes, cutting corners results in what seems to be misrepresentation of a candidate. "When searches get long in the tooth, some recruiters try to get them filled. They don't care, so long as they get filled," even by a candidate who really isn't quite right, Rothschild says. "They try to force a square peg into a round hole. We can subtly direct a candidate's thinking. When we know the candidate is not best served, it's a mistake. It will end in failure at some point."

Clarke says he has heard of "lazy searchers" who "push the usual suspects. Often, these are their favorite candidates, their golf partners and, in some countries, even family or friends. They do not search the market and find the best candidates. There are, of course, cases where the client has underestimated the market rate for the position. An honest search firm will make them aware of this, rather than shoo in a weak candidate to close the case."

Many searchers try to maximize the number of searches under way, Clarke continues. "The client sees the impressive business developer, but [then] the action is handed off to a second-rate team. The biggest client complaint is of nondelivery, or the assignment taking too long because such searchers work on too many cases and give them a low priority."

Clarke adds that unethical headhunters may go so far as to attempt to advance the highest-priced candidates or push a client to increase the salary for a position to increase their own shares because headhunters' fees are a percentage of a placed candidate's annual salary.

Reasonable Expectations

HR professionals have the right to expect a search consultant to take the time and effort necessary to conduct a good search for top-level candidates, and that includes gathering a lot of information about the client.

"Studies show the more prospective candidates learn about the clients, the greater their success," says Dale Winston, chair and CEO of Battalia Winston International in New York. Before taking an assignment, her representatives meet with "the client [and] the hiring manager so we can flesh things out," she continues. "That way, when we meet with the candidate, we can give a lot of data" to help candidates and clients determine if they share the same values.

"A bad hire is worse than no hire," Winston adds, but that rarely occurs when there is plenty of upfront due diligence.

Overall, HR professionals and their companies "have a right to expect a rigorous and effective process of research, candidate appraisal and support during negotiations, by a trained and experienced search team including professional researchers and searchers," Clarke says. "This team should put the client's interests before their own and offer unbiased advice as to remuneration, candidate fit and any other important matters."

Setting Standards

Although there is no organization certifying executive search firms on the basis of performance standards (the AESC does offer certification for researchers and associates), some companies in the field have established their own standards. The Boyden firm, for example, has an internal certification program, and CEO Clarke says all firms "should go toward more certification and training. Anybody can start a search firm. You can say you're an executive search consultant" without any type of standards or quality assurance. "We need to be more professional, to have no tolerance for slack performance."

If a client suspects that a headhunter has acted unethically, Lord notes, there may be little recourse. Few search firms have ethics officers. The AESC does have an ethics and professional practices committee to investigate complaints, he adds, but "it's limited. [The AESC] does care about professionalism. [It has] worked hard to publish the code of ethics. Other than that, there is no real way to bring people to justice, if you will."

While there may be few formal mechanisms for righting perceived wrongs in the executive search industry, there's still the power of the marketplace. "What drives search firms to follow rules is the fact that their reputations are extremely important," Lord says. If a search firm does something such as violate an off-limits agreement, he says, "it's a serious problem. People get fired. It can end relationships."

STEPHENIE OVERMAN is editor of *Staffing Management Magazine*.

UNIT 5
Developing the Future Ethos and Social Responsibility of Business

Unit Selections
41. **Creating an Ethical Culture,** David Gebler
42. **Hiring Character,** Dana Telford and Adrian Gostick
43. **Outside-the-Box Ethics,** Luis Ramos
44. **The Business Case for Diversity,** Adrienne Selko
45. **The True Measure of a CEO,** James O'Toole

Key Points to Consider
- In what areas should organizations become more ethically sensitive and socially responsible in the next five years? Be specific and explain your choices.
- Obtain codes of ethics or conduct from several different professional associations (for example, doctors, lawyers, CPAs). What are the similarities and differences between them?
- How useful do you feel codes of ethics are to organizations? Defend your answer.

Student Website
www.mhhe.com/cls

Internet References
International Business Ethics Institute (IBEI)
   http://www.business-ethics.org/index.asp
UNU/IAS Project on Global Ethos
   http://www.ias.unu.edu/research/globalethos.cfm

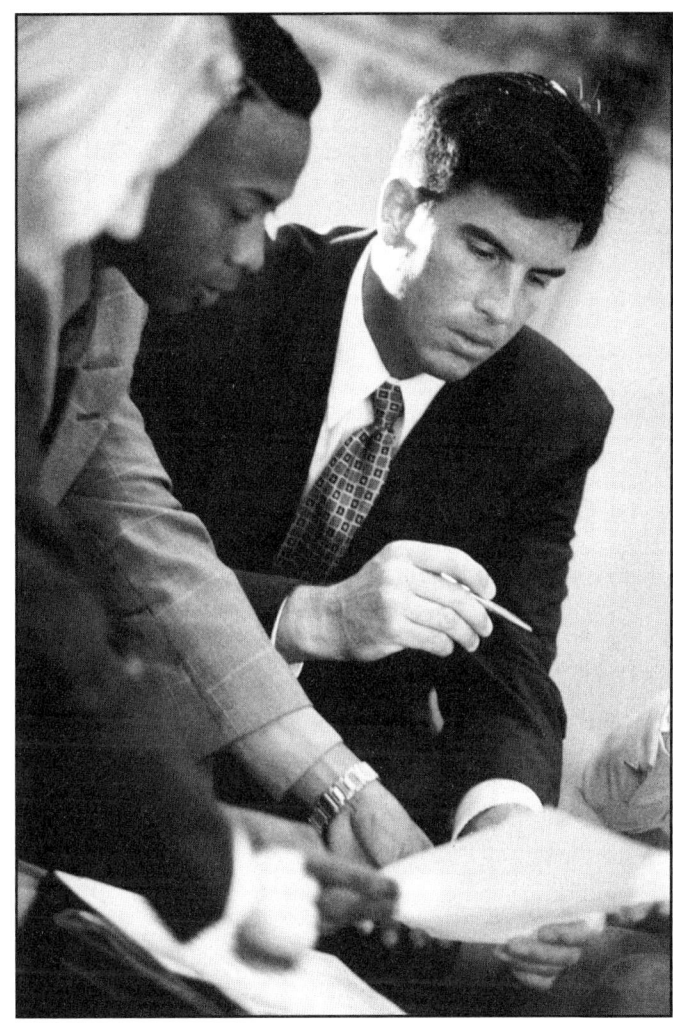
© Photodisc/Getty Images

Business ethics should not be viewed as a short-term, "knee-jerk reaction" to recently revealed scandals and corruption. Instead, it should be viewed as a thread woven through the fabric of the entire business culture—one that ought to be integral to its design. Businesses are built on the foundation of trust in our free-enterprise system. When there are violations of this trust between competitors, between employer and employees, or between businesses and consumers, the system ceases to run smoothly.

From a pragmatic viewpoint, the alternative to self-regulated and voluntary ethical behavior and social responsibility on the part of business may be governmental and legislative intervention. From a moral viewpoint, ethical behavior should not exist because of economic pragmatism, governmental edict, or contemporary fashionability—it should exist because it is morally appropriate and right.

This last unit is composed of articles that provide some ideas, guidelines, and principles for developing the future ethos and social responsibility of business. The first article, "Creating an Ethical Culture," discloses how values-based programs can help employees judge right from wrong. "Hiring Character" presents a look at business leader Warren Buffett's practice of hiring people based on their integrity. The next article, "Outside-the-Box Ethics," discusses five characteristics of an ethical culture. "The Business Case for Diversity," covers how diversity in the workplace has become a competitive advantage for manufacturers. The last article, "The True Measure of a CEO," discusses Aristotle's ethical questions and applies them to today's business environment.

Article 41

Creating an Ethical Culture

Values-based ethics programs can help employees judge right from wrong.

DAVID GEBLER, J. D.

While the fate of former Enron leaders Kenneth Lay and Jeffrey Skilling is being determined in what has been labeled the "Trial of the Century," former WorldCom managers are in jail for pulling off one of the largest frauds in history.

Yes, criminal activity definitely took place in these companies and in dozens more that have been in the news in recent years, but what's really important is to take stock of the nature of many of the perpetrators.

Some quotes from former WorldCom executives paint a different picture of corporate criminals than we came to know in other eras:

> "I'm sorry for the hurt that has been caused by my cowardly behavior." —*Scott Sullivan, CFO*

> "Faced with a decision that required strong moral courage, I took the easy way out.... There are no words to describe my shame."
> —*Buford Yates, director of general accounting*

> "At the time I consider the single most critical character-defining moment of my life, I failed. It's something I'll take with me the rest of my life."
> —*David Myers, controller*

These are the statements of good people gone bad. But probably most disturbing was the conviction of Betty Vinson, the senior manager in the accounting department who booked billions of dollars in false expenses. At her sentencing, U.S. District Judge Barbara Jones noted that Vinson was among the lowest-ranking members of the conspiracy that led to the $11 billion fraud that sank the telecommunications company in 2002. Still, she said, "Had Ms. Vinson refused to do what she was asked, it's possible this conspiracy might have been nipped in the bud."

Judge Jones added that although Ms. Vinson "was among the least culpable members of the conspiracy" and acted under extreme pressure, "that does not excuse what she did."

Vinson said she improperly covered up expenses by drawing down reserve accounts—some completely unrelated to the expenses—and by moving expenses off income statements and listing them as assets on the balance sheet.

Also the company's former director of corporate reporting, Vinson testified at Bernie Ebbers's trial that, in choosing which accounts to alter, "I just really pulled some out of the air. I used some spreadsheets." She said she repeatedly brought her concerns to colleagues and supervisors, once describing the entries to a coworker as "just crazy." In spring 2002, she noted, she told one boss she would no longer make the entries. "I said that I thought the entries were just being made to make the income statement look like Scott wanted it to look."

Standing before the judge at her sentencing, Vinson said: "I never expected to be here, and I certainly won't do anything like this again." She was sentenced to five months in prison and five months of house arrest.

Pressure Reigns

While the judge correctly said that her lack of culpability didn't excuse her actions, we must carefully note that Betty Vinson, as well as many of her codefendants, didn't start out as criminals seeking to defraud the organization. Under typical antifraud screening tools, she and others like her wouldn't have raised any red flags as being potential committers of corporate fraud.

Scott Sullivan was a powerful leader with a well-known reputation for integrity. If any of us were in Betty Vinson's shoes, could we say with 100% confidence that we would say "no" to the CFO if he asked us to do something and promised that he would take full responsibility for any fallout from the actions we were going to take?

Today's white-collar criminals are more likely to be those among us who are unable to withstand the blistering pressures placed on managers to meet higher and tougher goals. In this environment, companies looking to protect themselves from corporate fraud must take a hard look at their own culture. Does it promote ethical behavior, or does it emphasize something else?

In most companies, "ethics" programs are really no more than compliance programs with a veneer of "do the right thing" messaging to create an apparent link to the company's values. To be effective, they have to go deeper than outlining steps to take to report misconduct. Organizations must understand what causes misconduct in the first place.

We can't forget that Enron had a Code of Ethics. And it wasn't as if WorldCom lacked extensive internal controls. But both had cultures where engaging in unethical conduct was tacitly condoned, if not encouraged.

Building the Right Culture

Now the focus has shifted toward looking at what is going on inside organizations that's either keeping people from doing the right thing or, just as importantly, keeping people from doing something about misconduct they observe. If an organization wants to reduce the risk of unethical conduct, it must focus more effort on building the right culture than on building a compliance infrastructure.

The Ethics Resource Center's 2005 National Business Ethics Survey (NBES) clearly confirms this trend toward recognizing the role of corporate culture. Based on interviews with more than 3,000 employees and managers in the U.S., the survey disclosed that, despite the increase in the number of ethics and compliance program elements being implemented, desired outcomes, such as reduced levels of observed misconduct, haven't changed since 1994. Even more striking is the revelation that, although formal ethics and compliance programs have some impact, organizational culture has the greatest influence in determining program outcomes.

> **Leadership must know how the myriad human behaviors and interactions fit together like puzzle pieces to create a whole picture. An organization moves toward an ethical culture only if it understands the full range of values and behaviors needed to meet its ethical goals.**

The Securities & Exchange Commission (SEC) and the Department of Justice have also been watching these trends. Stephen Cutler, the recently retired SEC director of the Division of Enforcement, was matter of fact about the importance of looking at culture when it came to decisions of whether or not to bring an action. "We're trying to induce companies to address matters of tone and culture.... What we're asking of that CEO, CFO, or General Counsel goes beyond what a perp walk or an enforcement action against another company executive might impel her to do. We're hoping that if she sees that a failure of corporate culture can result in a fine that significantly exceeds the proverbial 'cost of doing business,' and reflects a failure on her watch—and a failure on terms that everyone can understand: the company's bottom line—she may have a little more incentive to pay attention to the environment in which her company's employees do their jobs."

Measuring Success

Only lagging companies still measure the success of their ethics and compliance programs just by tallying the percentage of employees who have certified that they read the Code of Conduct and attended ethics and compliance training. The true indicator of success is whether the company has made significant progress in achieving key program outcomes. The National Business Ethics Survey listed four key outcomes that help determine the success of a program:

- Reduced misconduct observed by employees,
- Reduced pressure to engage in unethical conduct,
- Increased willingness of employees to report misconduct, and
- Greater satisfaction with organizational response to reports of misconduct.

What's going to move these outcomes in the right direction? Establishing the right culture.

Most compliance programs are generated from "corporate" and disseminated down through the organization. As such, measurement of the success of the program is often based on criteria important to the corporate office: how many employees certified the Code of Conduct, how many employees went through the training, or how many calls the hotline received.

Culture is different—and is measured differently. An organization's culture isn't something that's created by senior leadership and then rolled out. A culture is an objective picture of the organization, for better or worse. It's the sum total of all the collective values and behaviors of all employees, managers, and leaders. By definition, it can only be measured by criteria that reflect the individual values of all employees, so understanding cultural vulnerabilities that can lead to ethics issues requires knowledge of what motivates employees in the organization. Leadership must know how the myriad human behaviors and interactions fit together like puzzle pieces to create a whole picture. An organization moves toward an ethical culture only if it understands the full range of values and behaviors needed to meet its ethical goals. The "full-spectrum" organization is one that creates a positive sense of engagement and purpose that drives ethical behavior.

Why is understanding the culture so important in determining the success of a compliance program? Here's an example: Most organizations have a policy that prohibits retaliation against those who bring forward concerns or claims. But creating a culture where employees feel safe enough to admit mistakes and to raise uncomfortable issues requires more than a policy and "Code training." To truly develop an ethical culture, the organization must be aware of how its managers deal with these issues up and down the line and how the values they demonstrate impact desired behaviors. The organization must understand the pressures its people are under and how they react to those pressures. And it must know how its managers communicate and whether employees have a sense of accountability and purpose.

Categorizing Values

Determining whether an organization has the capabilities to put such a culture in place requires careful examination. Do employees and managers demonstrate values such as respect? Do employees feel accountable for their actions and feel that they have a stake in the success of the organization?

How does an organization make such a determination? One approach is to categorize different types of values in a way that lends itself to determining specific strengths and weaknesses that can be assessed and then corrected or enhanced.

The Culture Risk Assessment model presented in Figure 1 has been adapted from the Cultural Transformation Tools® developed by Richard Barrett & Associates. Such tools provide a comprehensive framework for measuring cultures by mapping values. More than 1,000 organizations in 24 countries have used this technique in the past six years. In fact, the international management

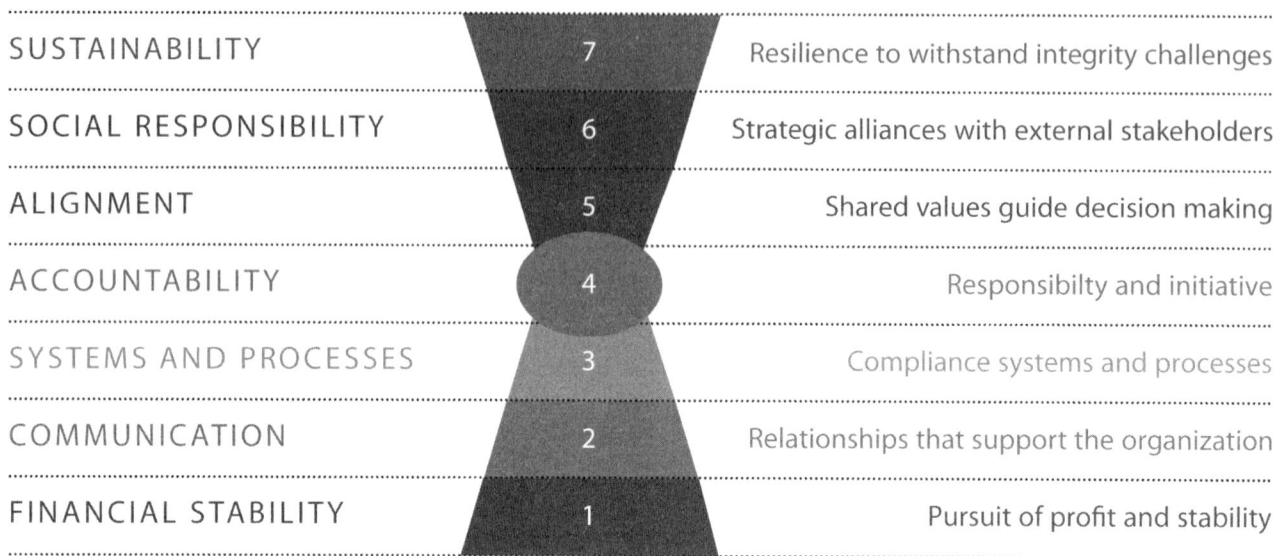

Figure 1 Seven levels of an ethical organization.

consulting firm McKinsey & Co. has adopted it as its method of choice for mapping corporate cultures and measuring progress toward achieving culture change.

The model is based on the principle, substantiated through practice, that all values can be assigned to one of seven categories:

Levels 1, 2, and 3—The Organization's Basic Needs

Does the organization support values that enable it to run smoothly and effectively? From an ethics perspective, is the environment one in which employees feel physically and emotionally safe to report unethical behavior and to do the right thing?

Level 1—Financial Stability. Every organization needs to make financial stability a primary concern. Companies that are consumed with just surviving struggle to focus enough attention on how they conduct themselves. This may, in fact, create a negative cycle that makes survival much more difficult. Managers may exercise excessive control, so employees may be working in an environment of fear.

In these circumstances, unethical or even illegal conduct can be rationalized. When asked to conform to regulations, organizations do the minimum with an attitude of begrudging compliance.

Organizations with challenges at this level need to be confident that managers know and stand within clear ethical boundaries.

Level 2—Communication. Without good relationships with employees, customers, and suppliers, integrity is compromised. The critical issue at this level is to create a sense of loyalty and belonging among employees and a sense of caring and connection between the organization and its customers.

The most critical link in the chain is between employees and their direct supervisors. If direct supervisors can't effectively reinforce messages coming from senior leadership, those messages might be diluted and confused by the time they reach line employees. When faced with conflicting messages, employees will usually choose to follow the lead of their direct supervisor over the words of the CEO that have been conveyed through an impersonal communication channel. Disconnects in how local managers "manage" these messages often mean that employees can face tremendous pressure in following the lead established by leadership.

Fears about belonging and lack of respect lead to fragmentation, dissension, and disloyalty. When leaders meet behind closed doors or fail to communicate openly, employees suspect the worst. Cliques form, and gossip becomes rife. When leaders are more focused on their own success, rather than the success of the organization, they begin to compete with each other.

Level 3—Systems and Processes. At this level, the organization is focused on becoming the best it can be through the adoption of best practices and a focus on quality, productivity, and efficiency.

Level 3 organizations have succeeded in implementing strong internal controls and have enacted clear standards of conduct. Those that succeed at this level are the ones that see internal controls as an opportunity to create better, more efficient processes. But even those that have successfully deployed business processes and practices need to be alert to potentially limiting aspects of being too focused on processes. All organizations need to be alert to resorting to a "check-the-box" attitude that assumes compliance comes naturally from just implementing standards and procedures. Being efficient all too often leads to bureaucracy and inconsistent application of the rules. When this goes badly, employees lose respect for the system and resort to self-help to get things done. This can lead to shortcuts and, in the worst case, engaging in unethical conduct under the guise of doing what it takes to succeed.

Level 4—Accountability

The focus of the fourth level is on creating an environment in which employees and managers begin to take responsibility for their own actions. They want to be held accountable, not micromanaged and supervised every moment of every day. For an ethics and compliance program to be successful, all employees must feel that they have a personal responsibility for the integrity of the organization. Everyone must feel that his or her voice is being heard. This requires managers and leaders to admit that they don't have all the answers and invite employee participation.

Levels 5, 6, and 7—Common Good

Does the organization support values that create a collective sense of belonging where employees feel that they have a stake in the success of the ethics program?

Level 5—Alignment. The critical issue at this level is developing a shared vision of the future and a shared set of values. The shared vision clarifies the intentions of the organization and gives employees a unifying purpose and direction. The shared values provide guidance for making decisions.

The organization develops the ability to align decision making around a set of shared values. The values and behaviors must be reflected in all of the organization's processes and systems, with appropriate consequences for those who aren't willing to walk the talk. A precondition for success at this level is building a climate of trust.

Level 6—Social Responsibility. At this level, the organization is able to use its relationships with stakeholders to sustain itself through crises and change. Employees and customers see that the organization is making a difference in the world through its products and services, its involvement in the local community, or its willingness to fight for causes that improve humanity. They must feel that the company cares about them and their future. Companies operating at this level go the extra mile to make sure they are being responsible citizens. They support and encourage employees' activities in the community by providing time off for volunteer work and/or making a financial contribution to the charities that employees are involved in.

Level 7—Sustainability. To be successful at Level 7, organizations must embrace the highest ethical standards in all their interactions with employees, suppliers, customers, shareholders, and the community. They must always consider the long-term impact of their decisions and actions.

Employee values are distributed across all seven levels. Through surveys, organizations learn which values employees bring to the workplace and which values are missing. Organizations don't operate from any one level of values: They tend to be clustered around three or four levels. Most are focused on the first three: profit and growth (Level 1), customer satisfaction (Level 2), and productivity, efficiency, and quality (Level 3). The most successful organizations operate across the full spectrum with particular focus in the upper levels of consciousness—the common good—accountability, leading to learning and innovation (Level 4), alignment (Level 5), social responsibility (Level 6), and sustainability (Level 7).

Some organizations have fully developed values around Levels 1, 2, and 3 but are lacking in Levels 5, 6, and 7. They may have a complete infrastructure of controls and procedures but may lack the accountability and commitment of employees and leaders to go further than what is required.

Similarly, some organizations have fully developed values around Levels 5, 6, and 7 but are deficient in Levels 1, 2, and 3. These organizations may have visionary leaders and externally focused social responsibility programs, but they may be lacking in core systems that will ensure that the higher-level commitments are embedded into day-to-day processes.

Once an organization understands its values' strengths and weaknesses, it can take specific steps to correct deficient behavior.

Starting the Process

Could a deeper understanding of values have saved WorldCom? We will never know, but if the culture had encouraged open communication and fostered trust, people like Betty Vinson might have been more willing to confront orders that they knew were wrong. Moreover, if the culture had embodied values that encouraged transparency, mid-level managers wouldn't have been asked to engage in such activity in the first place.

The significance of culture issues such as these is also being reflected in major employee surveys that highlight what causes unethical behavior. According to the NBES, "Where top management displays certain ethics-related actions, employees are 50 percentage points less likely to observe misconduct." No other factor in any ethics survey can demonstrate such a drastic influence.

So how do compliance leaders move their organizations to these new directions?

1. **The criteria for success of an ethics program must be outcomes based.** Merely checking off program elements isn't enough to change behavior.

2. **Each organization must identify the key indicators of its culture.** Only by assessing its own ethical culture can a company know what behaviors are the most influential in effecting change.

3. **The organization must gauge how all levels of employees perceive adherence to values by others within the company.** One of the surprising findings of the NBES was that managers, especially senior managers, were out of touch with how nonmanagement employees perceived their adherence to ethical behaviors. Nonmanagers are 27 percentage points less likely than senior managers to indicate that executives engage in all of the ethics-related actions outlined in the survey.

4. **Formal programs are guides to shape the culture, not vice versa.** People who are inclined to follow the rules appreciate the rules as a guide to behavior. Formal program elements need to reflect the culture in which they are deployed if they are going to be most effective in driving the company to the desired outcomes.

Culture may be new on the radar screen, but it isn't outside the scope or skills of forward-thinking finance managers and compliance professionals. Culture can be measured, and finance managers can play a leadership role in developing systematic approaches to move companies in the right direction.

DAVID GEBLER, J. D., is president of Working Values, Ltd., a business ethics training and consulting firm specializing in developing behavior-based change to support compliance objectives. You can reach him at dgebler@workingvalues.com.

Hiring Character

In their new book, ***Integrity Works,*** authors Dana Telford and Adrian Gostick outline the strategies necessary for becoming a respected and admired leader. In the edited excerpt that follows, the authors present a look at business leader Warren Buffett's practice of hiring people based on their integrity. For sales and marketing executives, it's a practice worth considering, especially when your company's reputation with customers—built through your salespeople—is so critical.

DANA TELFORD AND ADRIAN GOSTICK

This chapter was the hardest for us to write. The problem was, we couldn't agree on whom to write about. We had a number of great options we were mulling over. Herb Brooks of the Miracle on Ice 1980 U.S. hockey team certainly put together a collection of players whose character outshined their talent. And the results were extraordinary. We decided to leave him out because we had enough sports figures in the book already. No, we wanted a business leader. So we asked, "Who hires integrity over ability?"

The person suggested to us over and over as we bandied this idea among our colleagues was Warren Buffett, chairman of Berkshire Hathaway Inc.

Sure enough, as we began our research we found we had not even begun to tell Buffett's story. But we were reluctant to repeat his story. Buffett had played an important part in our first book. And yet, his name kept coming up. So often, in fact, that we finally decided to not ignore the obvious.

Perhaps more than anyone in business today, Warren Buffett hires people based on their integrity. Buffett commented, "Berkshire's collection of managers is unusual in several ways. As one example, a very high percentage of these men and women are independently wealthy, having made fortunes in the businesses that they run. They work neither because they need the money nor because they are contractually obligated to—we have no contracts at Berkshire. Rather, they work long and hard because they love their businesses."

The unusual thing about Warren Buffett is that he and his longtime partner, Charlie Munger, hire people they trust—and then treat them as they would wish to be treated if their positions were reversed. Buffett says the one reason he has kept working so long is that he loves the opportunity to interact with people he likes and, most importantly, trusts.

Buffett loves the opportunity to interact daily with people he likes and, most importantly, trusts.

Consider the following remarkable story from a few years ago at Berkshire Hathaway. It's about R.C. Willey, the dominant home furnishings business in Utah. Berkshire purchased the company from Bill Child and his family in 1995. Child and most of his managers are members of the Church of Jesus Christ of Latter-day Saints, also called Mormons, and for this reason R.C. Willey's stores have never been open on Sunday.

Now, anyone who has worked in retail realizes the seeming folly of this notion: Sunday is the favorite shopping day for many customers—even in Utah. Over the years, though, Child had stuck to his principle—and wasn't ready to rejigger the formula just because Warren Buffett came along. And the formula was working. R.C.'s sales were $250,000 in 1954 when Child took over. By 1999, they had grown to $342 million. Child's determination to stick to his convictions was what attracted Buffett to him and his management team. This was a group with values and a successful brand.

Arnie Ferrin, longtime friend of Child, said, "I believe that [Child] is a man of extreme integrity, and I believe that Warren Buffett was looking to buy his business because he likes to do business with people like that, that don't have any shadows in their lives, and they're straightforward and deal above-board."

This isn't to say Child and Buffett have always agreed on the direction of the furniture store.

"I was highly skeptical about taking a no-Sunday policy into a new territory, where we would be up against entrenched rivals open seven days a week," Buffett said. "Nevertheless, this was Bill's business to run. So, despite my reservations, I told him to follow both his business judgment and his religious convictions."

Proving once again that he believed in his convictions, Child insisted on a truly extraordinary proposition: He would personally buy the land and build the store in Boise, Idaho—for about $11 million as it turned out—and would sell it to Berkshire at his cost if—and only if—the store proved to be successful. On the other hand, if sales fell short of his expectations, Berkshire could exit the business without paying Child a cent. This, of course, would leave him with a huge investment in an empty building.

You're probably guessing there's a happy ending to the story. And there is. The store opened in August of 1998 and immediately became a huge success, making Berkshire a considerable margin. Today, the store is the largest home furnishings store in Idaho.

Child, good to his word, turned the property over to Berkshire—including some extra land that had appreciated significantly. And he wanted nothing more than the original cost of his investment. In response, Buffett said, "And get this: Bill refused to take a dime of interest on the capital he had tied up over the two years."

And there's more. Shortly after the Boise opening, Child went back to Buffett, suggesting they try Las Vegas next. This time, Buffett was even more skeptical. How could they do business in a metropolis of that size and remain closed on Sundays, a day that all of their competitors would be exploiting?

But Buffett trusts his managers because he knows their character. So he gave it a shot. The store was built in Henderson, a mushrooming city adjacent to Las Vegas. The result? This store outsells all others in the R.C. Willey chain, doing a volume of business that far exceeds any competitor in the area. The revenue is twice what Buffett had anticipated.

As this book went to print, R.C. Willey was preparing to open its third store in the Las Vegas area, as well as stores in Reno, Nevada, and Sacramento, California. Sales have grown to more than $600 million, and the target is $1 billion in coming years. "You can understand why the opportunity to partner with people like Bill Child causes me to tap dance to work every morning," Buffett said.

Here's another example of Buffett's adeptness at hiring character. He agreed to purchase Ben Bridge Jeweler over the phone, prior to any face-to-face meeting with the management.

Ed Bridge manages this 65-store West Coast retailer with his cousin, Jon. Both are fourth-generation owner-managers of a business started 89 years ago in Seattle. And over the years, the business and the family have enjoyed extraordinary character reputations.

Buffett knows that he must give complete autonomy to his managers. "I told Ed and Jon that they would be in charge, and they knew I could be believed: After all, it's obvious that [I] would be a disaster at actually running a store or selling jewelry, though there are members of [my] family who have earned black brits as purchasers."

Talk about hiring integrity! Without any provocation from Buffett, the Bridges allocated a substantial portion of the proceeds from their sale to the hundreds of coworkers who had helped the company achieve its success.

Overall, Berkshire has made many such acquisitions—hiring for character first, and talent second—and then asking these CEOs to manage for maximum long-term value, rather than for next quarter's earnings. While they certainly don't ignore the current profitability of their business, Buffett never wants profits to be achieved at the expense of developing ever-greater competitive strengths, including integrity.

It's an approach he learned early in his career.

Warren Edward Buffett was born on August 30, 1930. His father, Howard, was a stockbroker-turned-congressman. The only boy, Warren was the second of three children. He displayed an amazing aptitude for both money and business at a very early age. Acquaintances recount his uncanny ability to calculate columns of numbers off the top of his head—a feat Buffett still amazes business colleagues with today.

At only six years old, Buffett purchased six-packs of Coca-Cola from his grandfather's grocery store for twenty-five cents and resold each of the bottles for a nickel—making a nice five-cent profit. While other children his age were playing hopscotch and jacks, Buffett was already generating cash flow.

Buffett stayed just two years in the undergraduate program at Wharton Business School at the University of Pennsylvania. He left disappointed, complaining that he knew more than his professors. Eventually, he transferred to the University of Nebraska–Lincoln. He managed to graduate in only three years despite working full time.

Then he finally applied to Harvard Business School. In what was undoubtedly one of the worst admission decisions in history, the school rejected him as "too young." Slighted, Buffett applied to Columbia where famed investment professor Ben Graham taught.

Professor Graham shaped young Buffett's opinions on investing. And the student influenced his mentor as well. Graham bestowed on Buffett the only A+ he ever awarded in decades of teaching.

While Buffett tried working for Graham for a while, he finally struck out on his own with a revolutionary philosophy: He would research the internal workings of extraordinary companies. He could discover what really made them tick and why they held a competitive edge in their markets. And then he would invest in great companies that were trading at substantially less than their market values.

Ten years after its founding, the Buffett Partnership assets were up more than 1,156 percent [compared to the Dow's 122.9 percent], and Buffett was firmly on his way to becoming an investing legend.

In 2004, Warren Buffett was listed by Forbes as the world's second-richest person (right behind Bill Gates), with $42.9 billion in personal wealth. Despite starting with just $300,000 in holdings, Berkshire's holdings now exceed $116 billion. And Buffett and his employees can confidently say they have made thousands of people wealthy.

We often ask business leaders one simple question: Which is more dangerous to your firm—the incompetent new hire or the dishonest new hire? It's the part of our presentation where attendees sit up straight and start thinking.

We always follow the question with an exercise on identifying and hiring integrity. Though it becomes obvious that many of the executives and managers haven't given employee integrity much thought, most of the CEOs in the audiences are increasingly concerned about hiring employees with character.

So, how do you hire workers with integrity? It's possible, but not easy. It is important to spend more time choosing a new employee than you do picking out a new coffee machine. Here are a few simple areas to focus on:

First, ensure educational credentials match the resume. Education is the most misrepresented area on a resume. Notre Dame football coach George O'Leary was fired because the master's degree he said he had earned did not exist, the CEO of software giant Lotus exaggerated his education and military service, and the CEO of Bausch & Lomb forfeited a bonus of more than $1 million because he claimed a fictional MBA.

It is important to spend more time choosing a new employee than you do picking out a new coffee machine.

Job candidates also often claim credit for responsibilities that they never had. Here's a typical scenario:

Job candidate: "I led that project. Saved the company $10 million." Through diligent fact checking, you find an employee at a previous employer who can give you information about the candidate:

Coworker: "Hmm. Actually, Steve was a member of the team, but not the lead. And while it was a great project, we still haven't taken a tally of the cost savings. But $10 million seems really high."

How do you find those things out? Confer with companies where the applicant has worked—especially those firms the person isn't listing as a reference. Talk to people inside the organization, going at least two levels deep (which means you ask each reference for a couple more references). Talk to the nonprofit organizations where the person volunteers. Tap into alumni networks and professional associations. Get on the phone with others in the industry to learn about the person's reputation. Check public records for bankruptcy, civil, and criminal litigation (with the candidate's knowledge). In other words, check candidates' backgrounds carefully (but legally, of course).

We find that most hiring managers spend 90 percent of their time on capability-related questions, and next to no time on character-based questions. In your rush to get someone in the chair, don't forget to check backgrounds and be rigorous in your interviewing for character. Hiring the wrong person can destroy two careers: your employee's—and your own.

Ask ethics-based questions to get to the character issue. We asked a group of executives at a storage company to brainstorm a list of questions they might ask candidates to learn more about their character. Their list included the following questions:

- Who has had the greatest influence on you and why?
- Who is the best CEO you've worked for and why?
- Tell me about your worst boss.
- Who are your role models and why?
- How do you feel about your last manager?
- Tell me about a time you had to explain bad news to your manager.
- What would you do if your best friend did something illegal?
- What would your past manager say about you?
- What does integrity mean to you?
- If you were the CEO of your previous company, what would you change?
- What values did your parents teach you?
- Tell me a few of your faults.
- Why should I trust you?
- How have you dealt with adversity in the past?
- What are your three core values?
- Tell me about a time when you let someone down.
- What is your greatest accomplishment, personal or professional?
- What are your goals and why?
- Tell me about a mistake you made in business and what you learned from it.
- Tell me about a time when you were asked to compromise your integrity.

It's relatively easy to teach a candidate your business. The harder task is trying to instill integrity in someone who doesn't already have it.

Of course, we don't want to imply that it's impossible. Sometimes people will adapt to a positive environment and shine. Men's Wearhouse has certainly had tremendous success hiring former prison inmates, demonstrating everyone should have a second chance.

But integrity is a journey that is very personal, very individual. An outside force, such as an employer, typically can't prescribe it. It's certainly not something that happens overnight. That's one reason many of the CEOs we have talked with prefer promoting people from inside their organizations when possible.

Don Graham, chairman and CEO of the Washington Post Company, said, "There's a very good reason for concentrating your hires and promotions on people who already work in your organization. The best way to predict what someone's going to do in the future is to know what they've done in the past—watch how people address difficult business issues, how they deal with the people who work for them, how they deal with the people for whom they work. You may be able to put on a certain face for a day or even a week, but you're not going to be able to hide the person you are for five or ten years."

Graham tells a story about Frank Batten, who for years ran Landmark Communications and founded The Weather Channel. "Frank is a person of total integrity," Graham says. "Frank once said, 'When you go outside for hire you always get a surprise. Sometimes it's a good surprise. But you never hire quite the person you thought you were hiring.'"

What do you look for in a job applicant? Years of experience? College degree? Specific skill sets? Or do you look for character? If so, you're in good company.

Years ago, Warren Buffett was asked to help choose the next CEO for Salomon Brothers. "What do you think [Warren] was looking for?" Graham asks. "Character and integrity—more than even a particular background. When the reputation of the firm is on the line every day, character counts."

Don't like surprises? Then hire people who have integrity. Want to ensure a good fit with the people you hire? Then hire people who have integrity. Want to ensure your reputation with customers? Then hire people who have integrity.

Are we saying that nothing else matters? No. But we are saying that nothing matters more.

From *Integrity Works: Strategies for Becoming a Trusted, Respected and Admired Leader* by **DANA TELFORD** and **ADRIAN GOSTICK**.

From chapter 9 of *Integrity Works* (Gibbs Smith, 2005). Copyright © 2005 by Dana Telford and Adrian Gostick. Reprinted by permission of the authors.

Outside-the-Box Ethics

Take "boring" out of ethics training.

LUIS RAMOS

In the quest for an ethical culture, leaders are finding that one-size-fits-all ethics training doesn't work. *Rightsizing* behavior starts with messaging that speaks directly to employees about specific ethical issues they are likely to encounter on the job. And it delivers the resources and tools they need to do the right thing when it comes to their own actions and to speak out against unethical activity by others when they see it.

Companies that consistently rank high on the lists of *best corporate citizens* tend to make ethics training part of a company-wide initiative to promote integrity. They look for ways to tackle tough subjects and benchmark results to ensure that people don't just get the message, but understand and apply it. These companies see that an investment in an ethical workplace delivers dividends—including a more unified workforce and stock growth.

Cisco does ethics right. With more than 65,000 employees worldwide, building and sustaining an ethical culture is complicated, but the commitment the company has made to an ethical workplace has earned it the status of "repeat performer" on the *Corporate Responsibility Officer's* (CRO's) 100 Best Corporate Citizens.

Five Key Characteristics

Five key characteristics set apart companies with an ethical culture:

1. Leaders Encourage a Two-Way Dialogue about Business Conduct

The message about ethics starts at the top with support from executives and top management who show their commitment to an ethical workplace by modeling behaviors they want to instill in employees. Words like *trust, honesty, values* are part of the vernacular in an ethical company. Internal and external communications reflect the behavioral expectations for every stakeholder.

2. The Company's Code of Ethics Is a Living Document

A code that's built to satisfy curious investors or to fill newhire packets underserves the company. A code should represent the centerpiece of an ethical culture and serve as a ready resource. It should also reflect the look, tone, and voice of the company. Although crafters should work with the legal department to review and approve policies, the code should reflect an easy-to-read style that reinforces the company's core values, and guides ethical decision-making.

When Cisco rewrote its *Code of Conduct,* active voice and user-friendly language drove the process. Once topics were defined, each section began with an affirmative statement written in an employee voice—"I Respect Others," "I Protect What Is Ours," "I Follow the Law." The language was conversational in tone, suggestive of one Cisco employee speaking to another. The design was crafted to complement the user-friendly style, with quick-read call-out boxes that helped employees to "Connect with the Code," "Learn More" links that provided more detailed policy and "What If" scenarios that customized the Code to address Cisco-specific issues.

Although Cisco's Code won awards, the real winners were Cisco employees: 95 percent of them agreed that the new Code was easy to read and comprehend. And a code that's easy to read is also likely to be easy to follow.

3. Ethics Isn't a "Program" but a Way of Doing Business

The word *program* suggests a starting and stopping point—not a defining feature of an ethical culture. In its Code, Cisco emphasizes "doing the right thing is part of our DNA." An ethical culture is the result of a continuous, dynamic process that engages every employee; keeping the ethics *message* visible through media keeps ethical *behavior* at the forefront.

Branding enhances visibility—a name makes an ethics initiative recognizable. Then promote it using media that "fit" your workplace and employee demographics. Monthly manager meetings provide great forums for discussing conflicts of interest, proprietary information, or corporate gift policy. A mix of traditional communication vehicles and customized interactive components—translated into every language that employees speak—helps to disperse and reinforce the message about ethics.

4. Training about Ethics Is Relevant, Maybe Even Fun

If the people depicted in an ethics training don't look or sound like its employees or face ethical situations that employees face, the message won't resonate with them. If the messaging is one-way, they will tune out. If the training is long and boring, they will multitask until it's over.

Cisco knew that ethics initiatives needed to appeal to a global workforce that was highly technical. They wanted something dynamic and interactive, easily accessible from desktops and relevant to the Cisco experience.

The result was "Ethics Idol" a series of four, fun modules, each of which introduced an animated "contestant" who told the story of his or her ethical dilemma using action-packed visuals and witty song parody. Once each episode played out, three quirky judges offered their opinion and employees voted on which judge provided the most ethical answer.

The parody of *American Idol* created a buzz about ethics, winning awards and showing that learning about ethics didn't have to be rote, boring, or easy. Scenarios were designed so that the proper course of action wasn't obvious.

5. Employees Are Actively Engaged as Corporate Citizens, Aligned with the Company's Values

A poster on the wall tells employees that ethical behavior is important. A certification program tells employees that ethical behavior is mandatory. Thanks to an effective launch and a multilingual format, Cisco's annual *Code of Business Conduct* certification process was seamless; within the four-week period of the certification campaign, 98 percent of employees certified that they had received and read the *Code* and, within 10 weeks, 99.6 percent of employees certified.

Companies with an ethical culture ensure employees have the resources they need to promote ethics. Leaders have the power to shape and sustain an ethical culture and inspire people to do the right thing.

LUIS RAMOS is CEO of The Network, providing ethics and compliance services. Visit www.towinc.com.

Article 44

The Business Case for Diversity

Far from being just another feel-good initiative, diversity in the workforce has become a competitive advantage for manufacturers.

ADRIENNE SELKO

Having a diverse workforce is a competitive advantage and not merely a human resources initiative, according to Cate Roberts, director of diversity and community affairs at Textron Inc. The conglomerate, which is staffed with 44,000 employees and is comprised of Bell Helicopter, Cessna Aircraft Co. and many other companies, approaches diversity with a strategic objective.

"The three tenets of our business case are: Race for Talent, Need to Globalize and Innovation," explains Roberts. "We believe that diverse work teams create more innovative products and make us more competitive."

How does Textron embrace diversity? One way is through employee network groups, which include African-American, Asian-American, Generation Y, Native American, Hispanic, women and gay groups.

At W.R. Grace & Co., a producer of chemicals and materials with 6,500 employees located in more than 40 countries, diversity takes on a different meaning as the company prefers to move away from the traditional definition of race and gender. Grace's goal is to set up a structure that creates an inclusive environment in which diversity can flourish.

"We established a global diversity council that includes 20 people from 10 countries and 14 functions," explains Alfonso Gonzales, chairman of Grace's Diversity and Inclusion Council and director of Leadership Organizational Effectiveness. "Our goal is to provide a place where everyone feels their voices can be heard. The results of inclusion are increased production and innovation."

The company has developed a Diversity Toolkit as a point of reference to help employees discuss the attributes of diversity and discover inroads to tap into the expansive knowledge that comes with each culture. And these efforts add to the bottom line. Gonzales cites a study in which diverse teams outperformed non-diverse teams by 12% with respect to productivity.

To attract a diverse workforce, companies turn to mentoring and educational programs. At Textron, its year-long TXTConnect program pairs managers with employees—many of whom come from diverse backgrounds—to provide a well-rounded view of the company.

Recruiting efforts have paid off as well for Textron's Engineering Boot Camp Program, which boasts of a 90% hiring rate for its 75% diverse class. The first Boot Camp program took place in January 2008 at Bell Helicopter. Aerospace and mechanical engineering students from the local university, who were assisted by Bell engineers who had graduated less than three years ago, participated in designing a specific project. They toured five facilities and were flown to visit an assembly facility. The company feels this kind of hands-on learning experience appeals to students at the right time in their college experience.

Continually building on this effort, next year the company's Textron University will include in its curriculum a class entitled, "Doing Business Cross-Culturally." The program will address the issue of varying work traditions across different cultures.

Wider Definition of Culture

Although most companies wouldn't categorize military personnel as a separate culture, Advanced Technology Services Inc. (ATS) does. Over 30% of its 2,200-person workforce is comprised of former military members or current reservists. ATS manages services of production equipment maintenance, information technology and spare parts repair for manufacturers.

> **"Military personnel are a perfect fit for manufacturing. Their technical skills are excellent and their familiarity with a process-oriented system fits right in."**
>
> —Jeff Owens

"Military personnel are a perfect fit for manufacturing. Their technical skills are excellent and their familiarity with a process-oriented system fits right in," says Jeff Owens, president of ATS. The company has hired a dedicated military recruiter, Holly Mosack, who previously served as a company commander for the 82nd Airborne Division in Fallujah, Iraq.

ATS is also looking to recruit the next generation of workers and has created a program called Technical Leadership in Manufacturing. Working with Southern Illinois University's College of Engineering, the company offers 30–40 college students tuition-free scholarships for their junior and senior years. A summer internship, which could be onsite for clients such as Caterpillar, is part of the program. Students receive training in courses as varied as Six Sigma and etiquette.

Convincing today's students that manufacturing is an exciting and fulfilling career is a challenge to many companies. "We demonstrate to students the fast-paced field of automation and show them how its dynamic applications impact factories," Owens says. "We also offer students a career path that includes working at various client sites so they gain different experiences."

Since locating students is yet another challenge, manufacturers need to be tapped into social networks, notes John Hauger, vice president of client services for Global Lead Management Consulting, an international diversity management consulting firm. Job seekers are very sophisticated today, he points out, and companies should be tapped into Facebook and other social networking sites.

Recruiting employees who can connect with the customers and the community is essential, Hauger notes, adding that leadership must have a clear understanding of inclusion. "Cultural dexterity is essential. Leaders and managers must have the ability to move between various cultures and tailor their communication and problem-solving skills in a way that is comfortable for each culture."

For example, when working with a U.S.-based auto parts supplier that was setting up shop in Japan, employees were immersed in cultural activities as a way to learn the norms of the society. "It worked out well and other clients are using this method of cultural dexterity as well," says Hauger.

Widening the Talent Pool

Companies that actively pursue diversity find that the talent pool widens significantly. Non-traditional employees are how Sandra Westlund-Deenihan, president of Quality Float Works, views her workforce. Of her 26 employees, 11 are minorities, four are women and four are veterans. "We bring in non-traditional workers, such as low income people and women from shelters. We provide whatever skills people need to be successful," says Westlund-Deenihan, whose company produces metal float balls for a number of industries.

Quality Floats will hire people who might have disabilities in some areas but are great with their hands and are an asset to her operations. The company provides training for basic skills in math, English and communication and offers on-the-job training as well.

As the company grows and its product line expands, including a product that helps purify water in third-world countries, the workforce must remain constant and strong. For this reason Westlund-Deenihan will assist with the childcare needs of her employees by paying for their children to go to summer camp.

Addressing the needs of employees and providing a supportive environment is one reason that Air Products, a producer of gases and equipment, created a program called Two in a Box. "We look at this program as a personal tutor for our new employees. We find that it helps employees get up to speed very quickly," explains Norma Curby, vice president, strategic planning for the company, which employs 22,000 in 40 countries.

It is the exchange of ideas from a diverse workforce that fuels the future growth opportunities of the company, Curby points out, and to that end effective talent management is key to Air Products' growth.

> "By bringing together people with diverse back-grounds, who have a variety of experiences, there are more actionable ideas."
>
> —Norma Curby

"You never know where the next idea will come from," she says. "By bringing together people with diverse backgrounds, who have a variety of experiences, there are more actionable ideas. We find new ways to approach markets, our processes and our business model."

From *Industry Week*, September 2008, pp. 46–50. Copyright © 2008 by Penton Media Inc. Reprinted by permission.

The True Measure of a CEO

Aristotle has something to say about that.

JAMES O'TOOLE

In 400 B.C., Aristotle argued that a leader's task is to create conditions under which all followers can realize their full human potential. In this view, leadership is not about the leader's needs for wealth, power, and prestige—rather, it is about the leader's responsibility to create an environment in which followers can develop the capabilities with which they were born.

Today, given the nature of 24/7 work conditions, and the commitment to long hours that American corporations demand of employees, the only place where most people have the opportunity to develop their capacities is at work. Hence, if corporations and their CEOs do not provide the opportunity for their employees to grow, they effectually deny them their basic humanity. That is why creating a culture in which the true and basic needs of employees are addressed is the core ethical issue in corporate leadership today.

Aristotle provides us with a set of ethical questions to determine the extent to which an organization provides an environment conducive to human growth and fulfillment. And, he would say, not only does an ethical leader create that environment—he does so consciously, and not coincidentally. Motivation is important in ethics. Miami hoteliers cannot claim credit for sunny days, and leaders in Silicon Valley get no ethical credit for providing jobs that are accidentally developmental. Just because working with computers may be inherently a developmental task, one is not necessarily a marvelous employer for providing people with that opportunity.

Aristotle also asks the extent to which we as leaders observe decent limits on our own power in order to allow others to lead and develop. He says that too many leaders turn their people into passive recipients of their moral feats. In practice, celebrity CEOs such as Citigroup's Sandy Weill and Sun's Scott McNealy have behaved as if there were only one leader in each of their respective organizations—themselves—and not only have garnered credit for all good decisions made in their companies but have amassed for themselves the best opportunities to learn through leading. Worse, they have dismissed and discouraged executives who have challenged their authority, particularly upcoming stars who shined too brightly and thus threatened the CEO's status as the sole source of organizational enlightenment.

In essence, here are the questions that Aristotle asks CEOs and other leaders to ask themselves:

- To what extent do I consciously make an effort to provide learning opportunities to everyone who works for me?
- To what extent do I encourage full participation by all my people in the decisions affecting their own work?
- To what extent do I allow them to lead in order to grow?
- To what extent do I measure my own performance as a manager or leader both in terms of realizing economic goals and, equally, creating conditions in which my people can fulfill their own potential in the workplace?

I do not pretend that it is easy for leaders to create ethical cultures. Tough sacrifices and trade-offs are demanded. For starters, leaders must behave courageously and consistently to meet their ethical responsibilities to employees. For example, during the extended 2001–04 recession, when hundreds of thousands of American workers were losing their jobs, most corporate leaders assumed they had no other choice but to lay off workers. But out in Silicon Valley, the CEO of Xilinx Inc., Wim Roelandts, believed that there had to be other alternatives, even when his company's profits plummeted by 50 percent in 2001. His own board and some of his top executives argued that the only way he could stem the flow of red ink was to lay off workers. But driven by his stated communitarian values of respect for employees and commitment to their development, he charged a task force of managers with finding alternatives to layoffs. They came up with a dozen programs that were put into place, including funding educational sabbaticals for workers and paying them modest stipends for volunteering in nonprofit organizations.

I do not pretend that it is easy for leaders to create ethical cultures.

A year later, Xilinx came roaring back, with its workforce intact and committed to making their company a financial success. Significantly, Roelandts is a self-described "geek"

Aristotle on CEO Pay

No matter how one cuts the figures, even moderately well-paid CEOs of large corporations make about as much in a day as their workers make in a year. Even if the point of reference is the more modest salaries of CEOs of midsized American companies, the average for them is some 34 times that of industrial workers (the comparable ratios are 13-to-1 in Germany and 11-to-1 in Japan). Keep in mind, too, that the $35,864 earned by the average American worker is exactly that, *an average*, one that includes the astronomical salaries of CEOs, sports figures, and Hollywood celebs on the high end and the minimum-wage earners on the low end, who, if employed full time, make about $9,888 per year before taxes.

Averages also conceal extreme behavior, such as Kmart CEO Charles Conway drawing down some $23 million during his two-year reign, during which time he terminated some 22,000 employees with zero severance. In 2001, while Wal-Mart CEO H. Lee Scott was receiving something like $17 million in total compensation, many of his lowest-paid hourly employees were suing the company because they claimed they were forced to punch out at the end of their eight-hour day, then made to continue working overtime without additional compensation.

Few American executives appear to apply the same standards of justice they demand and expect for themselves to compensation issues relating to their subordinates. In 2002, employees of Hershey Foods went on strike after the company raised their share of health-insurance premiums at a time when the company's sales and profits were up. The workers thought this hefty increase was particularly unfair because it occurred the year after the company's new CEO earned $4.6 million in salary, bonuses, and stock options—in just nine months on the job. Assuming Hershey's CEO was entitled to what he earned, the Aristotelian question is, *Was he virtuous in reducing the benefits of those who earned far less?*

Admittedly, it is hard to reckon what is just and fair. But it is not impossible. For example, Disney's board compensated its CEO, Michael Eisner, with $285 million between 1996 and 2004. We can't pretend to have all the data required to decide how much Eisner deserves, but, thanks to Aristotle, we have a question that a virtuous member of the Disney board's compensation committee might ask in making that decision: Is the CEO's proportionate contribution to the organization really ten—or a hundred, or a thousand—times greater than that of a cartoon animator at the company's Burbank studios or the operator of Disneyland's Space Mountain ride? Alas, I sincerely doubt the Disney board has ever examined the ethics of its pay policies in this way.

Although asking such a question is practically unheard of in the boardrooms of giant companies, a few small- and medium-sized companies have done so and established ratios as low as 20-to-1 between the compensation of their highest-paid executive and average worker. That may sound unrealistic, but when you run the numbers it makes some sense. If the average worker makes $20 an hour, the CEO of even a "low-paying" company can make a million dollars a year. This ratio is "unrealistic" only because the current ratio in Fortune 500 companies approaches 500-to-1.

Creating an ethical corporate culture turns out to be a far more difficult task than the authors of Sarbanes-Oxley anticipated. As smart as Aristotle was, even he couldn't provide a clear moral principle for the just distribution of enterprise-created wealth. He admits that it's harder to distribute wealth fairly than it is to make it. Nonetheless, here are some Aristotelian questions that virtuous leaders might ask themselves, particularly before awarding themselves large bonuses at the same time they are outsourcing jobs to contractors who don't pay health benefits:

- Am I taking more in my share of rewards than my contributions warrant?
- Does the distribution of goods in the organization have a negative effect on morale?
- Would everyone in the organization enter into the employment contract under the current terms if they truly had other choices?
- Would we come to a different principle of allocation if all of the parties concerned were represented at the table?

We will all answer such questions differently, and that is to be expected, but if we want businesses that are perceived as fair in their dealings with employees, then CEOs must start asking them.

—James O'Toole

---

engineer who, in discovering the importance of ethical analysis, learned that leadership requires moral imagination, which begins with spotting ethical issues, asking oneself tough questions about the consequences of one's actions, and finding better alternatives when all those available have unacceptable consequences.

Of course, this runs against prevalent assumptions not only about corporate finance but also about leadership. In the dominant philosophy, there is only one dimension: A leader is simply measured in terms of her effectiveness at achieving a goal, whether that goal be profits or personal power. Jack Welch proudly proclaimed that he should be judged solely by the criterion of how much wealth he created for shareholders. The leadership philosophy of Roelandts and others like him stands in stark contrast. While they are as concerned as Welch with their effectiveness at producing financial results, they believe they must also be judged by the extent to which they create a corporate culture in which the ethical principle of respect for people is never violated.

Very few CEOs today set such high standards for themselves. Indeed, many successful and admired corporate leaders consciously reject such ethical measures of performance as inappropriate, impractical, and irrelevant to the task their boards have hired them to do, which is to create wealth. They say their responsibility is to their shareholders, not their employees, and if the social responsibility of employee development interferes with profit-making, then workers' needs must be sacrificed. Aristotle would answer that virtuous leaders have responsibilities to both their owners and their workers and, if there's a conflict between the two, it is the leader's duty to create conditions in which those interests can be made the same.

This two-dimensional standard of leadership is doubly hard to meet because it entails practicing what one preaches—that is, consistency between word and act. That consistency is known as integrity, and it leads to the most important element in creating an ethical corporate culture: trust. Unfortunately, it is in the realm of integrity that too many corporate executives are failing today. For example, at one of the nation's fastest-growing financial-services companies, the CEO speaks enthusiastically and proudly about his "values-based leadership," the value of his people being at the top of his list of things he says the company holds dear. The company is a success. It has basically doubled its sales and its profits over the last couple of years. While doing so, it has halved its workforce through domestic outsourcing and by selling off divisions and then contracting for the services of its former employees—naturally, at lower rates.

In essence, the policy of the company is to find ways to pay people less for doing the same work and, now, with fewer benefits. Significantly, it has not been driven to do so by foreign competitors paying lower wages. What is interesting is that no one in top management, as far as I can discern, sees this as an ethical issue. It is simply considered what a company must do in order to succeed in business. But what is the effect on employee trust, morale, and the senses of community and commitment?

I don't know, and a precise answer is impossible, but I do know that the consequences may be indirect and unexpected. For example, in January, near Los Angeles, a suicidal motorist drove his Jeep Cherokee onto railroad tracks. At the last moment, he thought the better of it and abandoned the SUV, and seconds later, a full commuter train crashed into the vehicle, killing eleven people and injuring 120. The accident occurred directly behind a Costco store. Almost immediately, the blue-collar Costco employees organized themselves into an emergency brigade and, armed with forklift trucks and fire extinguishers, set out to rescue trapped passengers and to deliver first aid to the wounded.

It is not coincidental, I believe, that Costco's culture stresses the importance of each worker, rewards individual initiative, and trusts frontline employees to solve problems in the absence of supervision and detailed rules. Costco is among the retail industry's leaders in terms of investing heavily in the training and development of its workforce. Hence, if the train accident had to occur, I believe the passengers were at least fortunate that they ended up near a group of people whose skills and instincts had been well primed to spring to their aid. Of course, we cannot know what might have happened had the accident occurred outside a store owned by one of those retail chains that has adopted the currently more-prevalent HR strategy: viewing employees as simply factors of production, the cost of which needs to be minimized—if their jobs cannot be eliminated altogether.

Here I will go out on a limb: I cannot help but suspect that people who are treated as fungible, told simply to obey their supervisors, and whose development is not seen as a corporate responsibility would be far less prepared than the Costco people to respond to an emergency as quickly, effectively, and appropriately.

In the 1990s, many corporations abandoned the Costco approach of paying living wages, providing decent health care, and treating employees with dignity and respect by rewarding them for participating in self-management. Numerous companies—to cite the most obvious example, Wal-Mart—went in the opposite direction, believing that investing in workers is too costly and leaves the company vulnerable to low-price competitors. Sometimes that is true, but in many cases, executives have had room for choice. For example, while FedEx has moved to a low-cost model for its drivers (even contracting out), its competitor UPS has stayed with its commitment to long-term employment, high pay, and individual development. And UPS believes that its drivers are key to corporate success, and that having informed and committed workers is the best way to serve customers. It is also true that the leaders of UPS are former drivers themselves and so have moral empathy with their workers. They understand that the lowliest worker in the organization is as human as they are, with much the same basic needs.

This kind of understanding lies at the root of Aristotelian leadership. But many large corporations today have become depersonalized; not only do the executives not know their workers personally—they come from different educational backgrounds and live in different neighborhoods. That makes moral empathy increasingly rare. For example, a few months ago I witnessed a two-hour discussion among corporate board members in which they debated what portion of their expected record-high profits should go to top management, and what portion should go to shareholders, profits that could lead to a windfall of as much as a million dollars to each of the company's top people. At the end of the discussion, they reviewed the prime risks facing the company, one of which was a possible increase in the minimum wage in China to $71 per month. Since all the company's manufacturing was in China, that event would greatly increase labor costs. The CFO proposed a solution: The company could reduce this increase's bottom-line impact by charging employees more for their room and board. That settled, the board and the executives present went on to other matters.

It happened so quickly that it was easy to miss what had occurred. In effect, the board decided to reduce the net take-home pay of their poorest workers so that the top people's bonuses would not be reduced by a few percentage points. If that isn't an ethical issue, I don't know what is. But the CEO and members of the board not only failed to address it—they didn't even recognize it.

Unfortunately, this is probably not that extreme an example. In my frequent interactions with executives from large U.S. corporations, it is clear from what they say—and do—that the prevalent assumption is that the only part of the workforce that is indispensable, and therefore the part in which an investment in development is justified, is the few highly trained and skilled people at the top of the hierarchy. Moreover, in too few of those large corporations do managers believe they have a moral responsibility to address the needs of workers; instead, the assumption is that if workers do not like the conditions being offered, they are free to quit and look for employment elsewhere.

Certainly, Aristotle would have something to say about that.

JAMES O'TOOLE is research professor at the Center for Effective Organizations at the University of Southern California's Marshall School of Business, Mortimer J. Adler Senior Fellow at the Aspen Institute, and author of, most recently, *Creating the Good Life: Aristotle's Guide to Getting It Right,* from which this article is adapted.

Test-Your-Knowledge Form

We encourage you to photocopy and use this page as a tool to assess how the articles in *Annual Editions* expand on the information in your textbook. By reflecting on the articles you will gain enhanced text information. You can also access this useful form on a product's book support website at *http://www.mhhe.com/cls*.

NAME:

DATE:

TITLE AND NUMBER OF ARTICLE:

BRIEFLY STATE THE MAIN IDEA OF THIS ARTICLE:

LIST THREE IMPORTANT FACTS THAT THE AUTHOR USES TO SUPPORT THE MAIN IDEA:

WHAT INFORMATION OR IDEAS DISCUSSED IN THIS ARTICLE ARE ALSO DISCUSSED IN YOUR TEXTBOOK OR OTHER READINGS THAT YOU HAVE DONE? LIST THE TEXTBOOK CHAPTERS AND PAGE NUMBERS:

LIST ANY EXAMPLES OF BIAS OR FAULTY REASONING THAT YOU FOUND IN THE ARTICLE:

LIST ANY NEW TERMS/CONCEPTS THAT WERE DISCUSSED IN THE ARTICLE, AND WRITE A SHORT DEFINITION:

We Want Your Advice

ANNUAL EDITIONS revisions depend on two major opinion sources: one is our Advisory Board, listed in the front of this volume, which works with us in scanning the thousands of articles published in the public press each year; the other is you—the person actually using the book. Please help us and the users of the next edition by completing the prepaid article rating form on this page and returning it to us. Thank you for your help!

ANNUAL EDITIONS: Business Ethics 10/11

ARTICLE RATING FORM

Here is an opportunity for you to have direct input into the next revision of this volume.
We would like you to rate each of the articles listed below, using the following scale:

1. **Excellent: should definitely be retained**
2. **Above average: should probably be retained**
3. **Below average: should probably be deleted**
4. **Poor: should definitely be deleted**

Your ratings will play a vital part in the next revision.
Please mail this prepaid form to us as soon as possible.
Thanks for your help!

RATING	ARTICLE	RATING	ARTICLE
	1. Thinking Ethically: A Framework for Moral Decision Making		21. The Factory That Refused to Die
	2. Business Ethics: Back to Basics		22. Fear of Firing
	3. Ethics: The Framework for Success		23. Protecting the Whistleblower
	4. Authentic Leaders Add Value		24. On Witnessing a Fraud
	5. The Ethical Employee		25. His Most Trusted Employee Was a Thief
	6. Truth or Consequences: The Organizational Importance of Honesty		26. The Parable of the Sadhu
	7. How to Make Unethical Decisions		27. An Ethical Dilemma: How to Build Integrity into Your Sales Environment
	8. Create a Culture of Trust		28. Trust in the Marketplace
	9. Building an Ethical Framework		29. Businesses Grow More Socially Conscious
	10. Ethical Leadership: Maintain an Ethical Culture		30. Women and the Labyrinth *of* Leadership
	11. Your Privacy for Sale		31. Getting Real about Fakes
	12. Employers Are Stung with a Hefty Price When Employees Suffer an Identity Theft		32. The New E-spionage Threat
	13. Are You Too Family Friendly?		33. Sustainable Success
	14. Employee Theft: Who, How, Why, and What Can Be Done		34. Global Diversity: The Next Frontier
	15. Businesses Say Theft by Their Workers Is Up		35. Cracks in a Particularly Thick Glass Ceiling
	16. Gender Issues: Sex Discrimination Lawsuits Are on the Rise. Is Your Company at Risk?		36. Is Marketing Ethics an Oxymoron?
	17. Hiring Older Workers		37. The Rise of Trust and Authenticity
	18. Keeping Your Senior Staffers		38. Serving Unfair Customers
	19. The War over Unconscious Bias		39. Dirty Deeds
	20. Reflecting on Downsizing: What Have Managers Learned?		40. Searching for the Top
			41. Creating an Ethical Culture
			42. Hiring Character
			43. Outside-the-Box Ethics
			44. The Business Case for Diversity
			45. The True Measure of a CEO

ANNUAL EDITIONS: BUSINESS ETHICS 10/11

BUSINESS REPLY MAIL
FIRST CLASS MAIL PERMIT NO. 551 DUBUQUE IA

POSTAGE WILL BE PAID BY ADDRESSEE

McGraw-Hill Contemporary Learning Series
501 BELL STREET
DUBUQUE, IA 52001

NO POSTAGE
NECESSARY
IF MAILED
IN THE
UNITED STATES

ABOUT YOU

Name   Date

Are you a teacher? ☐ A student? ☐
Your school's name

Department

Address   City   State   Zip

School telephone #

YOUR COMMENTS ARE IMPORTANT TO US!

Please fill in the following information:
For which course did you use this book?

Did you use a text with this ANNUAL EDITION? ☐ yes ☐ no
What was the title of the text?

What are your general reactions to the Annual Editions concept?

Have you read any pertinent articles recently that you think should be included in the next edition? Explain.

Are there any articles that you feel should be replaced in the next edition? Why?

Are there any World Wide Websites that you feel should be included in the next edition? Please annotate.

May we contact you for editorial input? ☐ yes ☐ no
May we quote your comments? ☐ yes ☐ no